Trucking Mergers

Trucking Mergers

A Regulatory Viewpoint

James C. Johnson
The University of Tulsa

Lexington Books
D.C. Heath and Company
Lexington, Massachusetts
Toronto   London

Library of Congress Cataloging in Publication Data

Johnson, James C.   1944-
  Trucking mergers.

    Bibliography: p.
    1. Transportation, Automotive-United States—Laws and regulations.
    2. Transportation, Automotive—United States—Consolidation. I. Title.
KF2265.J6   353.008'78'324   73-11481
ISBN 0-669-89466-4

Published simultaneously in Canada.

Printed in the United States of America.

International Standard Book Number: 0-669-89466-4

Library of Congress Catalog Card Number: 73-11481

To My Four Perfect Girls:
    Cammy
    Amy
    Lori
    Sebby

Contents

List of Figures and Tables

Preface

TRUCKING MERGERS: A REGULATORY VIEWPOINT has been designed to present a comprehensive discussion of the basic regulatory issues involved in the current "urge-to-merge" in the trucking industry. Its purpose is to enable anyone interested in trucking mergers to become acquainted with the basic issues and questions involved in unification cases before the ICC. To achieve this objective, the book is broken down into eight chapters.

The initial chapter presents an introduction to the subject. The next chapter provides the layman with an overview of the basic characteristics of the motor trucking industry. The third chapter briefly traces the development of the economic regulation found in the trucking industry and sets forth the regulatory framework within which the ICC determines Section 5 merger proceedings. Chapter 4 is an introduction to the subject of trucking unifications. Chapter 5 is a discussion of the criteria for ICC approval of trucking consolidations.

The sixth chapter, the longest in the book, examines the competitive issues involved in trucking merger proceedings. Both intermodal and intramodal considerations are considered. Chapter 7 discusses additional significant factors considered by the ICC in unification proceedings.

The eighth and final chapter addresses itself to a general discussion of the ICC's administration of Section 5 trucking merger cases.

Acknowledgments

The author wishes to extend his gratitude to the following people who have both kindled and sustained his interest in the field of transportation and logistics. Dr. Donald V. Harper, Professor of Transportation and Logistics at The University of Minnesota, has been a constant source of inspiration and encouragement to the author during his graduate school education. His thought-provoking comments and suggestions in regard to this study have improved it considerably. Professors Nicholas A. Glaskowsky, Jr. (currently, President of National Distribution Services, Inc.) and Rodney C. Loehr, also from The University of Minnesota, read the first draft of the manuscript and provided the author with numerous penetrating observations. Their time and thoughtfulness are greatly appreciated.

In addition, thanks are also due to Professor Edmund A. Nightingale and Associate Professor Frederick J. Beier of The University of Minnesota, and to Professors Gilbert L. Gifford and Helmut J. Frank of The University of Arizona. All of these men have helped to instill in the author an overall appreciation and understanding of both transportation and business logistics.

The author also wishes to express his appreciation to Mr. Lester H. Mehling and Mrs. Margaret Carpenter, who have been extremely helpful in preparing this manuscript for publication.

Finally, a very special thank-you is due my patient and long-suffering wife, Cammy. She has consistently performed "above and beyond the call of duty," especially in her typing and editing of this study.

1 Introduction

Origin and Importance of the Subject

American industry is presently experiencing the greatest merger movement in the history of our country. A recent Federal Trade Commission study has declared that, "The American economy is experiencing a major change in industrial organization as the result of a merger movement of unprecedented dimensions. For nearly two decades mergers have been increasing. During the years 1967 and 1968 and early in 1969 they have reached all-time peaks."[1] The trucking industry is also very actively involved in the unification movement. In fact, one observer has noted, "Unless Congress halts or reverses the current trend, interstate motor transportation will be dominated, if not monopolized, by a limited number of relatively large corporate entities."[2]

The purpose of this study will be to carefully examine the trucking merger movement from the regulatory point of view. It is interesting to note that the subject of trucking unifications and mergers has received very little formal analysis, especially when compared to the railroad industry. For example, the Walter Adams and James B. Hendry study contained this note in its foreword, which was true in 1957 when it was written and is just as valid today, "The paucity of data and literature on the subject [trucking unifications] is indicative of the lack of attention that has been given to this aspect of the motor-carrier industry in the past."[3] The present study, which will limit itself strictly to intramodal motor truck mergers, should fill a need for that reason.

To date, there have been only three significant studies of the merger movement in the trucking business. The first was a June 1941 *Yale Law Journal* article by Professors John F. Meck, Jr., and Robert W. Bogue entitled "Federal Regulation of Motor Carrier Unification." The second was written by Professor John E. Altazan. His 39-page monograph was entitled *I.C.C. Policy Concerning Consolidations and Acquisitions of Control in the Motor Carrier Industry*, and it was published in June 1956. The third, the most extensive study to date, was done in 1957 by Professors Walter Adams and James B. Hendry for the Senate Select Committee on Small Business. This study was entitled *Trucking Mergers, Concentration, and Small Business: An Analysis of Interstate Commerce Commission Policy, 1950-56.*

The objective of this study is to fill a void by providing an overall and up-to-date analysis of trucking mergers covering the period from 1935 to 1973. Specifically, it is hoped that this paper and its appropriate evaluations and

1

conclusions will be of considerable aid to the trucking industry itself, so that practitioners in this area can better understand and appreciate the current trend of mergers in their industry. Also, this thesis should prove to be worthwhile reading for the ICC and Congress, because the latter two organizations have a vested interest in achieving an efficient and highly workable transportation system, of which the trucking industry is a major segment. Finally, shippers should profit by reading this book, because it identifies trends and other significant developments in the trucking industry that will directly affect the rates and service levels that shippers will receive in the future.

The overall significance of this subject is highlighted by the fact that the ICC has extremely broad authority (under Section 5 of the Interstate Commerce Act) over trucking mergers. For example, a Federal court has declared, "It would be difficult to conceive of a statute which confers broader authority and greater administrative discretion than Section 5 of the Interstate Commerce Act. Under that section, the Commission may approve any merger, purchase, consolidation, lease, or contractual arrangement affecting motor carriers which it finds will be 'consistent with the public interest.' "[4] Therefore, because of the Commission's broad authority over trucking unifications, it is important to study, analyze, and evaluate their conduct and stewardship under Section 5. As an example of the issues that will be examined herein, witness this comment by Professor Donald S. Watson, remarking on why the trucking merger trend should not continue. "Remember that the industry seems to have no economies of scale. If this is so, there can be no good economic reason for mergers, however beneficial they may be to their promoters. If gigantism comes to the trucking industry, ICC permissive policy and not natural forces would be the cause."[5] As will be seen, the author generally takes exception to this comment.

2 Characteristics of the Motor Trucking Industry

Operating Characteristics of Motor Truckers

Average Size of the Firm

The motor trucking industry is composed of many relatively small operating companies. This is in direct contrast with the railroad industry. As the Interstate Commerce Commission stated in 1938:

> The very limited number of railroads jointly operate a homogeneous system of transportation. The motor carriers constitute no such system, but are instead hardly more than a mere aggregation of hundreds of individual carriers whose operations, many of which are very small, are disconnected to a greater extent than they are connected.[1]

Specifically, in 1940, there were more than 26,000 regulated intercity Class I, II, and III motor carriers of property.[2] By 1955, this number was approximately 18,000,[3] and in 1972 there were 15,138 regulated intercity motor truckers.[4] While the number of motor carrier companies is decreasing, their total number is still striking compared to the 342 Class I and II line haul railroads regulated in 1972.[5]

Another indication of the relatively small size of most motor carriers can be seen by these statistics. In 1965, only 137 general commodity motor carriers had gross revenues of over $10 million. Furthermore, only 7.31 percent, or 407 carriers of general commodities, had gross revenues of greater than $2.5 million.[6] Since the Small Business Administration defines a "small" trucking business as one with gross revenues of $3 million or less,[7] it can be seen that somewhat less than 7 percent of all general commodity carriers are "big" businesses; therefore, greater than 93 percent of these carriers are defined as "small" businesses.

A final indication of the relatively small size of motor truckers can be appreciated by the testimony of Edward M. Welliver before the House of Representatives Small Business Committee in 1948. Mr. Welliver stated that about 26 percent of all interstate regulated carriers had only one truck and that 92 percent operated ten or fewer trucks.[8] By contrast, in 1966, the average Class I and II motor carrier operated 60 power units and 91 trailers.[9] Furthermore, our hypothetical "average" trucker had 144 employees, a gross investment of $632,906 and total operating revenues of $2,934,489, for a capital turnover

3

ratio of 464.[10] As can be seen, while the average size of motor carriers is increasing over the years, they still remain relatively small companies. In addition, it should be pointed out that the above figures for Class I and II motor carriers tend to overstate the size of a typical trucking firm. This results from the fact that the Class I and II truckers (see footnote 2, *supra* for the definitions of Class I, II, and III intercity truckers) are the "giants" of the industry, while the Class III truckers are the numerical majority of the 15,138 regulated intercity truckers. Specifically, Class III carriers account for 11,165 of this total.[11]

It is interesting to note that the small relative size of trucking companies is not unique to the United States. Erick Schenker reports the same situation in England,[12] as does H. Kolsen in Australia.[13]

As noted above, the capital costs needed to enter the trucking industry are rather small. Although they are increasing, entry costs are still far from insurmountable. As Professor John R. Meyer, et al. have observed, "In the 1930s an over-the-road truck could be bought for less than $2,000; today's trailer-truck costs $25,000, and the efficient use of such equipment requires several units."[14]

In a later section we will discuss the pricing problems arising from the ease of entry into the trucking industry. Here an interesting sidepoint can be mentioned. Richard N. Farmer summed up the situation well when he stated, "Trucking has created a group of independent, dedicated managers who operate largely among themselves, and the management revolution of the 1950s and 1960s has passed them by."[15] Or as another observer declared, "Trucking management is medieval. . . ."[16] Of course, this situation is improving, partly as a result of consolidated companies, as will be shown when motor truck mergers are discussed in more detail.

Capacity to Produce

Types of Goods Carried

The motor truck is capable of carrying, and generally does carry, almost any type of product imaginable, and this capability is one reason why the trucking industry has expanded as rapidly as it has.[17] For example, in 1963, Class I motor carriers transported mainly manufactured goods, which accounted for 86.31 percent of all their truck-load tonnage.[18] Furthermore, trucks (both for-hire and private) hauled 42.1 percent of all intercity tonnage of manufactured products.[19] Specifically, truckers hauled greater than 75 percent of total intercity tonnage in these product categories: textile mill and leather products; instruments, photographic equipment, watches, and clocks; and furniture and fixtures.[20] Finally, it should not be inferred that truckers haul only relatively high value goods. In 1970, truckers carried 90 percent of all sand and gravel shipments, 73 percent of all crushed stone shipments, and 79.7 percent of all Portland cement shipments.[21]

Size of Shipments

The motor carrier industry specializes in carrying relatively lightweight shipments. For example, a continuing traffic study by the ICC in the Middle Atlantic Conference showed that 91.4 percent of all shipments tendered to these for-hire regulated truckers were under 2,000 pounds.[22] The *1968 ICC Annual Report* stated:

Class I and II motor carriers of general freight now dominate small shipment tonnage and revenue. For example, in 1964, these carriers handled 73 million tons of less-than-truckload shipments or approximately four times the small shipment tonnage generated by all other regulated carriers combined.[23]

As a final indicator of the relatively small size of most truck shipments, a recent statement by Earle N. Hoekenga, President of Ryder Truck Lines, can be mentioned. Mr. Hoekenga pointed out that 60 percent of his firm's shipments were less than 300 pounds, with an average weight of 128 pounds.[24]

Right-Of-Way and Its Costs to the
Motor Carrier

The United States highway system is composed of about 3.6 million miles of road, of which approximately 490,000 miles are urban roads, the remainder being rural. In addition, of the 3.6 million miles, about 77 percent are hard surfaced.[25]

The Federal Government's Role. The Federal Government did not play a dominant role in highway construction until 1916, when the Federal-Aid Road Act passed into law. The act appropriated $75 million over a period of five years for the purpose of constructing rural post roads. A precedent was set in that the national government would contribute 50 percent, and the states the remainder of the construction costs.[26] The Federal Government has since continuously supplied aid to highways on a 50-50 basis, with its most ambitious supplemental project taking effect in 1956. It was then that the Federal-Aid Highway Act provided funds for the National System of Interstate and Defense Highways. This system was originally planned to include 40,000 miles of limited access, basically divided superhighways. A companion act created a trust fund and user-fees, which will be discussed shortly. The original cost of the project, to be completed in 1972, was estimated to be about $27 billion.[27] The system is now scheduled to be 42,500 miles long and was 70 percent complete in April 1970. Federal Highway Administrator Francis C. Turner estimated in 1970 that the total cost of the Interstate system will be $73.4 billion.[28] It is interesting to note that one authority believes the final total cost will be greater than $120 billion.[29]

The Theory and Practice of "User-Charges." Expenditures for the use of the highway are generally called "user-charges," defined as:

A user charge is defined as any charge made to beneficiaries or users of services and facilities directly related to transportation and furnished in whole or in part by the Federal Government. Such charges must be paid for use of such service or facility to recover part or all of the capital, operating and maintenance cost of such service or facility. The services shall not include cash subsidies, mortgage aid, or tax-aid, or certain other activities not confined to transportation or involving transportation only incidentally.[30]

Before 1956, there was no direct relationship between Federal excise taxes collected on gasoline and other associated products and the disbursements for Federal highway aid. In other words, excise taxes collected on gasoline were treated in the same manner as those on whiskey, i.e., they reverted to the general fund of the United States Treasury. On the disbursement side, the funds allocated to highway aid were in no way connected to the funds collected in this area. While *The Doyle Report* refers to a *de facto* linkage of expenditures to revenues,[31] the *de jure* direct relationship was specifically stipulated in the 1956 Highway Revenue Act, which placed the proposed Interstate system and other Federal-aid highways on a strictly pay-as-you-build basis. This was accomplished by requiring all Federal-aid highways (basically the ABC program)[32] to take precedence over the expenditures for the Interstate system, and by requiring that allocations to both programs must be strictly limited to anticipated revenues to be collected in the current period. The act also provided that the ABC program would continue on a 50-50 Federal-state allocation of costs, while the Interstate system would operate on a 90-10 basis.[33]

The 1956 Highway Revenue Act has contributed significantly to putting our highway system on a "user-charge" basis. In 1940 the ratio of user contributions to the total was 44 percent. In 1950 this ratio was 59.8 percent; passage of the Highway Revenue Act helped it to rise to 79.9 percent by 1963.[34]

Table 2-1 on pages 8 and 9 presents an excellent summary of the user-charges as they were drawn up in the 1956 Highway Revenue Act and its subsequent amendments. Notice that all the taxes generally decline from 1970 to 1973.

In addition to these Federal user-charges, each state assesses similar taxes. In general, the states use three types of user-charges:

(1) The first is the registration and license fee. This tax usually is calculated on a progressive basis, with the newer and heavier vehicles paying the largest tax.

(2) The second tax is on gasoline and diesel fuel. This tax is often greater per gallon of diesel fuel than on gasoline, because diesel fuel is more efficient in vehicles of greater than 40,000 pounds, and such vehicles derive the greatest user-benefits from highways.[35]

(3) The final typical state tax is a weight-distance type. This tax was implemented by a few states because it was believed that the other two taxes did

not adequately tax the heavier weight truck combinations. In general, the weight-distance tax has not been successful because of its difficult administrative features. In fact, *The Doyle Report* mentions that eleven states have had this type of tax and have subsequently repealed them.[36]

Average Length of Haul

The motor truck has always specialized in flexible, short distance hauling. In 1945, the average haul of a Class I intercity common carrier truck was 177 miles, and from 1960 to 1970 the length has stabilized between 255 and 270 miles.[37] Specifically, in 1962, the motor common carrier average haul for petroleum and coal was 114 miles; for meat and dairy products it was 487 miles; and for photo equipment, instruments, and watches it was 590 miles. In addition, it should be pointed out that for distances of less than 100 miles, private and for-hire motor carriers command about 65 percent of all tonnage. However, for hauls of greater than 2,000 miles, their share drops to 8 percent.[38]

Service Standards

As early as 1931, the ICC well summarized the inherent service advantages of trucks in the famous *Fifteen Per Cent Rate Case:*

In addition to rates, the advantages which it offers to the shipper are in rapid and flexible service, store-door receipt and delivery, the transportation at carload rates of much smaller lots than are possible by railroad and elimination of costly railroad packing requirements. The carriers (railroads) introduced evidence to show that it would be feasible for the trucks to divert only a comparatively small amount of additional tonnage, even if rates were increased. But without exaggerating the menace of this form of competition, we are convinced that the carriers have underrated it, and that its possibilities are materially greater than they are prepared to concede.[39]

Specifically, the service advantage of trucks can be surveyed under four basic topics: speed, economy, reliability, and convenience. In regard to speed, the truck is generally superior to railroad service, especially if the total distance is less than 500 miles. The reasons for this outcome are well summarized by Professor Taff,

Operating with a unit of less capacity than the average freight car, the trucker does not have to wait too long to accumulate sufficient freight and usually is in a position to depart immediately after the vehicle is loaded. With the larger share of operations consisting of direct single-line service, the trucker is not delayed by the necessity of making connections in the same degree as a railway. Freight can be collected at its source and delivered to its final destination with a minimum of rehandling.[40]

Table 2-1
Federal Highway-Related Excise Taxes and the Highway Trust Fund

Tax	Rate Basis	Tax Rate[1]										
		Before 7/1 1956	From 7/1 1956	From 10/1 1959	From 7/1 1961	From 1/1 1966	From 3/15 1966	From 1/1 1970	From 1/1 1971	From 1/1 1972	From 10/1 1972	From 1/1 1973
Dedicated to Highway Trust Fund:												
Motor fuel	cents per gallon	2¢	3¢	4¢	4¢	4¢	4¢	4¢	4¢	4¢	1½¢	1½¢
Rubber:												
Tires[2]	cents per pound	5¢	8¢	8¢	10¢	10¢	10¢	10¢	10¢	10¢	5¢	5¢
Tubes	cents per pound	9¢	9¢	9¢	10¢	10¢	10¢	10¢	10¢	10¢	9¢	9¢
Retread	cents per pound	none	3¢	3¢	5¢	5¢	5¢	5¢	5¢	5¢	none	none
New trucks, buses, and trailers[3]	percent of mfgr's sales price	8%	10%	10%	10%	10%	10%	10%	10%	10%	5%	5%
Annual heavy vehicle use tax[4]	per 1,000 pounds per year	none	$1.50	$1.50	$3.00	$3.00	$3.00	$3.00	$3.00	$3.00	none	none
Lubricating oil[5]	cents per gallon	(5)	(5)	(5)	(5)	6¢	6¢	6¢	6¢	6¢	6¢	6¢
Truck and bus parts and accessories[6]	percent of mfgr's sales price	(6)	(6)	(6)	(6)	8%	8%	8%	8%	8%	5%	5%
Other Highway-Related Excise Taxes:												
Lubricating oil[5]	cents per gallon	6¢	6¢	6¢	6¢	(5)	(5)	(5)	(5)	(5)	(5)	(5)
New automobiles[7]	percent of mfgr's sales price	10%	10%	10%	10%	6%	7%	5%	3%	1%	1%	(5)
Motor-vehicle parts and accessories[6]	percent of mfgr's sales price	8%	8%	8%	8%	(6)	(6)	(6)	(6)	(6)	(6)	(6)

1 "Before 7/1/56" rates are those in effect just prior to passage of the 1956 legislation. "From 10/1/72" rates are those to which the taxes revert under existing (July 1965) law. Some changes in the "From 1/1/66" column became effective on different dates, as indicated in footnotes 3 and 7. (Legislation in 1959 called for portions of the taxes on new automobiles and parts to go to the Trust Fund during fiscal years 1962-64, and the fuel tax to revert to 3¢ during the same period, but legislation of 1961 nullified these provisions.)
2 The tax rate on tires other than for highway use has remained at 5¢ per pound.

[3]From 7/1/56 to 7/1/62 only half the tax on new trucks, buses, and trailers was dedicated to the Trust Fund Beginning 6/21/65 the following are tax-exempt: bodies for camper coaches and self-propelled mobile homes; house trailers; bodies designed for seed, feed, and fertilizer; small 3-wheeled trucks; and school buses.

[4]Annual use tax on vehicles over 26,000 pounds gross weight (vehicle plus load); levied on total weight, not just on excess over 26,000 pounds.

[5]Prior to 1/1/66, the lubricating oil tax went to the General Fund. Beginning 1/1/66, this tax (excluding cutting oil) was dedicated to the Trust Fund, and refunds can be claimed for nonhighway use (applicable to motor fuel also).

[6]The 8% tax on motor-vehicle parts and accessories, in effect prior to 7/1/56, continued thereafter with revenue going to the General Fund. Effective 1/1/66, the tax on automobile parts and accessories was repealed; the tax on truck and bus parts and accessories remains in effect, with revenue dedicated to the Trust Fund.

[7]The tax rate on new automobiles, 10% until 5/14/65, was scheduled to gradually decrease over a period of years under a provision of the Excise Tax Reduction Act of 1965. Under later amendments, however, the tax rate schedule will be 7% until 1/1/70, 5% until 1/1/71, 8% until 1/1/72, and 1% until 1/1/73 when it falls to zero.

Source: Bureau of Public Roads, U.S. Department of Transportation.

"The Highway Trust Fund," *Transportation and Distribution Mangement* (July, 1969), p. 16. Used with permission.

Of course, truck speed also depends on the size of the cargo, with L.T.L. (less than truckload) receiving slower service than T.L. (truckload), because the former requires more handling at intermediate terminals.

Today, most modern intercity trucks and tractor-trailer combinations are designed to operate safely at 60 miles per hour (m.p.h.). Their effective rate is 35 m.p.h., however, because of fuel stops, maintenance checks, meals, et cetera. This effective rate of 35 m.p.h. can be feasibly and legally maintained on a continual 24 hours a day basis. This can be done by using sleeper cabs (with two or three drivers) and/or the use of drivers located at designated stages along the route traversed.[41] While the above driver schedules are feasible, continuous 24 hour operations are seldom found in practice. Typically, on hauls of 300 miles or less, general freight carriers will give T.L. freight overnight service. On a transcontinental T.L. trip, most truckers furnish seventh morning service from New York to Los Angeles and fifth morning from Chicago.[42]

The second advantage of truck service is that of economy. Truck rates can be less than rail rates for distances of less than 100 to 200 miles, because unlike railroads they do not have such large fixed costs to allocate to each movement. However, on hauls of greater than 200 miles, the truck rate will often be greater than the railroad rate. That being the case, how can economy be called a positive feature of motor carriers? The answer lies in the fact that trucks may have a higher rate per hundred pounds, but the total cost of the shipment for both the shipper and receiver can be less with a truck because of the following factors. First, because trucks offer faster service, less inventory and its associated costs are incurred. In addition, motor carriers generally have fewer damage claims than the railroads, because the cargo rides on pneumatic tires rather than steel wheels, and because the truck trailer is not subject to the cargo shock that is experienced when rail cars couple. These factors in turn mean that less protective packaging is needed when truck service is used. Finally, while the rail rate per hundred pounds may be less, it does not include pickup and delivery on some shipments (pickup and delivery service are included on carload traffic when shipper and receiver both have rail sidings); almost all truck rates do include this service.

A third service advantage of the trucker is his generally very reliable service standard. Heskett, Ivie, and Glaskowsky make the following observation on a major factor that brings about this reliability.

One of the elements which makes motor carriers more dependable than the modes discussed below is that they depend upon relatively few people (principally drivers) in order to accomplish effective performance. On a truckload movement from Cleveland, Ohio, to Houston, Texas, where a sleeper cab operation is used, the dependability of the motor carrier service will depend upon the two drivers and their ability to perform over a period of time. By comparison, a rail carload shipment between these points must depend upon adequate performance by literally hundreds of people in the organizations of several rail carriers in order to accomplish the same movement.[43]

The final basic service advantage of truckers is the convenience of their offering. Specifically, service is available almost anywhere, to everyone, whereas to use rail if no siding is accessible, the freight must be physically transported to the public team track at a cost that would not be incurred if truck service were used. Another way of visualizing the ubiquity of truck service is to remember that there are about 3.6 million miles of road available, but only 205,000 miles of railroad line.[44] In other words, as Professor Heskett et al. have so clearly pointed out:

It has been suggested that the primary attribute of the motor carrier, and the chief reason for the spectacular growth of this mode, is its ability to render door-to-door service. With the exception of remote locations, inaccessible by any other means other than light aircraft or boats, highway service is available to practically every shipper. There is a wide gap between the extent of the availability of motor carrier service and the availability of any other mode of transportation.[45]

The Cost Structure and Pricing Methods in Trucking

Joint and Common Costs

A joint cost arises when the production of one product necessarily creates another. A classic example of this is hides, which are a byproduct of beef marketing. Common costs, on the other hand, are those costs that are simultaneously incurred in the production of two or more products. The difference between these two terms is succinctly noted by Germane et al. as follows:

"Technically, common costs are expenses associated with two or more products, services, or activities, the proportions of which can be varied at the discretion of management. Joint costs are distinguished as a case in which the proportions of the output are not subject to management decision. . . . "[46]

There are many examples of joint and common costs in the trucking industry, especially of common costs. An example of a joint cost would be the return or backhaul movement; that is, for every truck movement there is a return haul (a joint cost) that is not subject to any management discretion. As opposed to the relatively few examples of joint costs, "Almost all costs of providing highway transportation service are common costs, considered at one time or another."[47] For example, if a truck is traveling from A to B, carrying shipments of many customers, there are a large number of common costs present. Examples would be the driver's wages, fuel and oil consumed, tire wear, wear and tear on the vehicle, et cetera. Of course, the common costs are minimized when shipments are sent out in truck load lots from single customers, but even then there is the allocation problem of constant common costs to the shipment.

The allocation of joint and common costs to a particular shipment has always been a vexing problem. Referring to joint cost allocation, Professor Taff clearly states: " ... there is no justification from a cost-of-service standpoint for distributing any more of these joint costs to any one unit of output resulting from the joint operation than to any other unit."[48] Nor is common cost allocation any more precise. As John J. Coyle observed, " ... some arbitrary allocation of common cost is required. This arbitrary allocation has no logical foundation in economic theory.[49]

Fixed and Variable Cost

Before fixed and variable costs can be defined, it is necessary to understand the difference between what Alfred Marshall originally referred to as the "short run" and the "long run" time periods. Referring to the "short run", Marshall declared:

The supply of specialized skill and ability of suitable machinery and other material capital, and of appropriate industrial organization has not time to be fully adapted to demand; but the producers have to adjust their supply to the demand as best they can with the appliances already at their disposal. On the one hand there is not time materially to increase those appliances if the supply of them is deficient; and on the other, if the supply is excessive, some of them must remain imperfectly employed, since there is not time for the supply to be much reduced by gradual decay, and by conversion to other uses.[50]

Describing the "long run," the eminent English economist of the late Victorian Age said:

In long periods on the other hand all investments of capital and effort in providing the material plant and the organization of a business, and in acquiring trade knowledge and specialized ability, have time to be adjusted to the incomes which are expected to be earned by them: and the estimates of those incomes therefore directly govern supply and are the true long-period normal supply price of the commodities produced.[51]

This dichotomy is important, because it is in the "short run" that both fixed and variable costs are encountered. Fixed or constant costs are those expenses of the firm that do not vary with a firm's quantity of production or volume of business. They can be thought of as expenses that are needed to establish the business as a whole, but that cannot be directly allocated to any specific unit of output. In addition, they can only be avoided by discontinuing the operation (in the "long run" time period), or a major part thereof.

Variable costs, on the other hand, are those that, " . . . vary directly with the volume of traffic moved, rising in total amount as traffic increases and declining as traffic falls off."[52] Variable costs are often referred to as "out-of-pocket costs" in transportation jargon, but theoretically at least "out-of-pocket costs" is a more restricted term.[53]

Finally, it is important to note that this distinction between fixed and variable costs applies only to the "short run" time period, because, "Over a long-run period, since all factors are adjustable, all costs are variable; factor units which are fixed in the short run (and so are responsible for some costs being fixed in this period) are adjustable over a longer period."[54]

This discussion suggests a basic question: approximately how long is the "short run" period for a trucking company? While this question can't be answered in absolute terms, Professor D. Philip Locklin points out that the "long run" period can be a relatively short calendar period.[55]

Finally, it should be noted that variable costs are at the same time almost always joint and/or common costs. This fact, as noted before, makes specific cost allocations to product units or customers very difficult, because it involves arbitrary assignments of these expenses.

Specifically, in the "short run," what costs can be considered fixed or constant in the trucking industry? Professor G. Lloyd Wilson has supplied the most comprehensive list of motor trucking constant costs:

1. Interest on the fair value of all property used for transportation service at a reasonable rate of interest.
2. License and registration fees assessed by local, state and federal governments.
3. Taxes upon the property, business, assets and other bases by municipalities, states or the federal government.
4. Insurance on property used for transportation service. This does not include insurance premiums paid on the property carried, but only those paid on the vehicles and property owned by the operator.
5. Superintendence and general overhead expenses.
6. Rentals on property leased for transportation service by the carrier.
7. Depreciation of property owned where depreciation does not vary with use.[56]

In regard to this list, perhaps the factor that has changed the most dramatically over the recent years is the increased cost in motor carrier terminals. Mr. W.D. Baker, President of Cooper-Jarrett, Inc., has commented that:

Over the years, motor carrier operations have significantly changed in order to handle greater quantities of small shipments. Carriers have invested heavily in large freight handling facilities equipped with modern mechanical devices. Today's capital investment in terminal facilities has dramatically increased the motor carrier's cost of doing business. Motor carriers are no longer able to operate a volume business out of a telephone booth, because the warehouse type of volume movements which existed years ago, today constitute only a very small portion of a carrier's business.[57]

Furthermore, Professor Wilson also supplies a comprehensive list of fluctuating or variable costs:

1. Wages of employees engaged in actual operation where wages fluctuate with amount of traffic carried. Fixed salaries are, of course, properly charged to overhead or superintendence.
2. Depreciation of tires and other equipment where depreciation varies with use.
3. Repairs and maintenance expenses.
4. Fuel, gasoline, kerosene or electric current used for motive power.
5. Lubricants, waste, and other supplies.
6. Insurance of cargo carried.
7. Expenses of obtaining cargo.[58]

Now that the specific fixed and variable costs have been surveyed, an interesting and provocative question is: what percent of the total costs of a trucking company tend to be constant and what percent are variable? This query has been studied by the ICC's Bureau of Accounts, Cost Finding, and Valuation and others. The Bureau, in a substantial 1954 study,[59] declared that the constant costs in trucking *approximated* 10 percent of the total costs.

One recent article in regard to the relative sizes of trucking fixed and variable costs was done by Professor Robert E. Shirley of Oregon State University. He reasoned that:

The fixed costs which result from increase in capacity reflect, in a sense, management's ability to sustain a planned level of activity. Once the increase in capacity is effected, management is under great pressure to obtain new business, possibly with traffic moving below present average rates, in order to utilize the added service potential. The unit cost of handling the new business acquired is related to the extent the new capacity is utilized, i.e., with greater utilization of equipment, unit fixed costs will decline. . . . However, it seems that the ICC cost formulae as presently compiled do not give enough weight to the effect of capacity utilized on unit costs.[60]

Therefore, it appeared to Shirley that perhaps the ICC's formula understated the fixed costs of a trucking company. To test this hypothesis, he compared what the ICC cost formula for the Pacific Region would yield compared to what the actual costs were for two real motor trucking firms. The results are shown on Table 2-2. What is interesting is that in both cases the ICC cost formula grossly underestimated the actual fixed expenses. While the ICC assumed the constant costs would be 10 percent, for Carrier X, they were about 31 percent and about 25 percent for Carrier Y. It should be pointed out that these significant

Table 2-2
Application of ICC Cost Formulae, Year 1966

Costs Grouped by Function	Carrier X (000's)		Carrier Y (000's)	
	Actual	ICC Formula	Actual	ICC Formula
Line haul	$ 785	$ 555	$ 818	$ 644
Pickup and delivery	422	856	701	1,240
Dock transfer	300	673	299	986
Billing and collecting	230	103	222	150
Sub total	1,737	2,187	2,040	3,020
Overhead (constant costs)	768	243	696	335
Total costs	$2,505	$2,430	$2,736	$3,355

Source: Robert E. Shirley, "Analysis of Motor Carrier Cost Formulae Developed by the Interstate Commerce Commission," *Transportation Journal* (Spring, 1969), p. 23. Used with permission from the *Transportation Journal*, a quarterly publication of the American Society of Traffic and Transportation, Inc.

differences are not based upon different accounting methods, because standard ICC methods were used in both cases. Finally, it should be noted that the revenues generated by Carriers X and Y were smaller than those of the major carriers that report their operating data to the ICC for the Pacific Region.

This writer would not presume to be able to state dogmatically that the average regulated for-hire trucker has X percent fixed costs and Y percent variable costs. However, it can be concluded that truckers do have a low percentage of fixed costs (for reasons to be discussed shortly), especially when compared to the railroad industry. In addition, it is felt that while the percentage of fixed costs is relatively small, it is undoubtedly increasing slowly over the years. This results basically from the increase in the fixed costs associated with trucking terminals, as previously noted by W.D. Baker. As terminals become more sophisticated and specialized, it often becomes more difficult for truckers to lease these facilities, and hence they must be purchased, which means that their fixed costs of operation are increased. Furthermore, even if leasing arrangements are available, the lessor will usually demand a long term contract, because the specialized terminal would be difficult to rent to anyone but another trucking company. Here again, the long term lease arrangement takes on the characteristics of a fixed expense. It is for this reason that the author believes that trucking fixed expenses are probably higher than the standard calculation of 10 percent of total costs (based on the 1954 ICC study, which is undoubtedly somewhat obsolete by 1973), and that they will probably be steadily increasing as a percentage of total costs in the future.

This discussion can be summarized by noting that compared to the rail, air, pipeline, and water carriers, trucking is generally considered to have the lowest fixed costs of any mode of transportation. A logical sequel to the last statement would be—why? The basic reason why the trucking industry has such relatively low fixed costs today is that they do not have to construct and maintain their right-of-way. While they do pay user-charges for the highways, the costs are basically incurred only as they are used, and hence they are a variable cost to the trucking industry. In addition, total labor costs (wages and fringe benefits), which amounted to 59.8 percent of Class I regulated intercity truckers' total revenues in 1970,[61] are also a variable cost as previously noted. Another major expense of trucking operations, the associated costs of running the vehicle (fuel, oil, repairs, cargo insurance, et cetera) are direct costs.

The Question of Ruinous Competition

Ruinous competition can be defined as forcing rates below the cost of production for an indefinite time period. Of course, in the long run, under such circumstances the carriers involved will go out of business, because if there is not an adequate return on invested capital, there will be no inducement to replace the committed capital as it wears out. In regard to the trucking industry, Professor Dudley F. Pegrum has flatly stated, "Competition among motor carriers *cannot* be ruinous. Ruinous competition, it should be emphasized, can arise only when fixed costs are a large part of the total costs of a firm. . . . " (Emphasis added)[62] Apparently, this statement is slightly too dogmatic, for it does not sit well with "real world" experience in this area. If it is true that truckers have a relatively small percentage of fixed costs, how can ruinous competition materialize in this industry? The answer lies in the ease of entry into the industry and the subsequent constant and perpetual overcapacity that therefore results. From an individual trucker's point of view, once he has obtained his "rig," he is operating in the "short run" time period. In this case (the "short run" time period), he finds that a substantial portion of his costs can be considered fixed. Professor Locklin gives a lucid description of the consequences:

If he finds it difficult to obtain business, he is tempted to take any business that he can get at a cut-rate price, which may be a price that will give him some revenue above gasoline and oil costs and any other immediate outlay. Under these circumstances he recognizes that interest on investment in vehicles, property taxes on the vehicles, motor-vehicle registration fees, and at least part of the depreciation on the vehicle are fixed costs and are incurred whether he moves any traffic or not. Short-run variable costs, rather than long-run variable costs, will determine what rate he charges.[63]

This situation has in fact become so prevalent in the industry, that it has been a constant problem area for the ICC in the past.[64] In addition, an English authority speaking on the same problem in his country has remarked that small truckers operating in the "short run" generally " . . . make no allowance for depreciation and renewal. The rates charged may not cover even the less obviously direct costs of repairs and tyres."[65]

Full Cost v. Value-of-Service

Full cost pricing generally refers to setting a price that covers both fixed and variable costs plus a profit margin. Value-of-service pricing, on the other hand, uses variable costs only to establish a floor below which prices should normally not go. Specifically, the objective here is to set prices that will maximize the contribution received over and above the variable costs incurred in each situation in order to achieve profit maximization. This methodology is subject to three specific conditions. First, as already indicated, the price must be at least equal to, and preferably greater than, the variable costs involved, so that some contribution to the constant costs can be made. Secondly, the product will not be sold unless the low price is used. Lastly, the firm has no better use of the facilities in question, that is, it has excess capacity. Finally, in regard to setting specific prices on commodities, "The proportion in which the rate on each commodity contributes to the constant costs depends on the intensity of the demand . . . "[66] That is to say, the ceiling price that can be charged is limited by the value-of-service, which is the highest charge that can be extracted without preventing the shipment from moving.

Referring to the trucking industry, Professor Locklin has noted, " . . . there is less scope for the play of value-of-service factors in motor-carrier rate making."[67] Why is this? Basically, because two of the three provisions previously discussed as advantageous for value-of-service pricing are not adequately found in the trucking industry. First, as has been previously indicated, the trucking industry possesses a very high ratio of variable costs to total costs. Therefore, they have very little leeway to go below full costs before the variable cost floor is encountered. Secondly, truckers generally have relatively little excess capacity, because the main operating unit, the truck, can be—and usually is—only acquired as it is needed.

The reason that truckers fear value-of-service pricing on the less than full cost side is that it is becoming more and more difficult to offset these prices with charges greater than the fully allocated costs. Why? Because as Professor G. Lloyd Wilson points out, any rates greater than full costs will merely encourage the growth of private or contract carriage on the high-rated commodities.[68]

Finally, it should be noted that value-of-service considerations will always be of prime importance in the distribution of constant and/or joint costs.

The Use of Class v. Commodity Rates

Classification rates can be thought of as standard rates that can be determined for almost all commodities transported. They are determined with the help of a classification tariff. This tariff gives each commodity a *rating* ranging from 500 to 35, with 23 separate ratings in total for the widely used National Motor Freight Classification. The higher the rating number, the greater is the charge for transporting the product. Many factors may be encountered in determining a specific rating. Because of the complexity involved, only a comprehensive list of the basic considerations will now be enumerated.

1. Shipping weight per cubic foot.
2. Liability to damage.
3. Liability to damage other commodities with which it is transported.
4. Perishability.
5. Liability to spontaneous combustion or explosion.
6. Susceptibility to theft.
7. Value per pound in comparison with other articles.
8. Ease or difficulty in loading or unloading.
9. Stowability.
10. Excessive weight.
11. Excessive length.
12. Care or attention necessary in loading and transporting.
13. Trade conditions.
14. Value of service.
15. Competition with other commodities transported.[69]

Once the commodity *rating* is determined, it is necessary to get the rate basis number from an applicable tariff. This number is the approximate distance between any two city pairs between which the commodity is being transported. With the commodity rating and the rate basis number, a specific *rate* per hundred pounds can be determined from another tariff. Finally, to get the specific cost of moving commodity X from city Y to city Z, the formula—*weight x rate = charge*—must be applied.

Commodity rates, on the other hand, can be thought of as custom-made economy rates that are available as the result of a commodity's being generally moved in large quantities and/or at frequent intervals. They are extremely important in the railroad industry and are also used by truckers. In fact, one authority has asserted, "The economy of this country has been built around the commodity rate."[70] The railroads use commodity rates on an average of 80 percent of all their freight, and on about 95 percent in the Mountain-Pacific territory.[71] Truckers, on the other hand, have a much smaller percentage of commodity rated goods. This is to be expected, when it is remembered that commodity rates basically only apply to large volume movements. The ICC recently reported that for the Middle Atlantic Conference of truckers, 91.4 percent of their shipments were under 2,000 pounds;[72] hence, they were generally unable to take advantage of commodity rates. Another reason that truckers use fewer commodity rates is that they are in a precarious cost position to cut rates because, as has been previously noted, their high variable cost structure allows them little leeway to cut their rates below the full cost of producing the service. Professor Taff reports that a 1966 study of the U.S. truckers determined that 25 percent of their tonnage moved on commodity rates, and the rest on class or class-related rates.[73]

The Question of Economies of Scale

Economies of scale generally refers to a situation where as production increases, the cost per unit of production decreases. Or as Professor George J. Stigler has remarked, "Increasing returns to scale arise when a doubling of output does not require a doubling of every input."[74]

The question has often been asked, are there any substantial economies of scale in the trucking industry? Professor James C. Nelson has recently presented a stimulating summary of the majority opinion in this quandary, which will serve as an excellent introduction to the following discussion.

All past studies of the economies of scale in size of trucking firms have resulted in pessimistic conclusions. And the logic of the economic characteristics of trucking, considering public ownership of the highways and variable cost payments for highway services, points clearly to the conclusion that economies of scale, if any, are not significant and provide no basis for organizing the industry into a few large firms or one firm on each route and in each class of service in the interest of lowering the costs of essential truck transport.[75]

Most transport economists acknowledge a 1956 study[76] by Professor Merrill J. Roberts as the most authoritative analysis of scale economies in the trucking industry. Roberts studied 114 Class I regular commodity truckers in the Central Territory. Every attempt was made to achieve a homogeneous sample, so that no spurious relationships would occur. The basic unit of efficiency used in the study was the average cost of producing a unit of capacity—in this case a vehicle-mile. Companies were arranged according to assets, with "small" companies having up to $350,000 in tangible assets, "medium" companies having from $350,000 to $1 million, and "large" companies having greater than $1 million. The average cost per vehicle-mile, in cents, was 67, 56, and 51 respectively for the small, medium, and large carriers. Significantly, however, about half of the small carriers, when grouped separately, achieved an average vehicle cost per mile of 51 cents. Therefore, Roberts concluded, "According to this evidence, small firms are commonly as efficient as large ones."[77] Specifically, he found that small firms generally had comparable cost patterns with the larger carriers, when they had similar route characteristics. That is, all the smaller firms achieved an average higher cost per vehicle-mile because they generally operated over inferior routes compared to the larger carriers. This resulted in the smaller carriers achieving a lower rate of utilization, as measured by vehicle-miles per route mile, and significantly shorter average length of hauls. In summary, Professor Roberts found that there are no significant economies of scale in the trucking industry, once a very modest minimum size has been achieved.

A second important study of the economies of scale in the trucking industry was done by Professor Robert A. Nelson.[78] This study surveyed the cost per vehicle-mile of 102 Class I carriers of general commodities in the New England area. Nelson's conclusion, like Roberts', was that there are no significant economies of scale in trucking. Specifically, his report declared, "It is clear for carriers domiciled in and out of New England and operating in New England that size of firm bears little relation to operating cost. Consequently, it can hardly be maintained that there are economies of large size available in the industry . . ."[79] Professor Edward W. Smykay took issue[80] with the statistical approach of Nelson to which the latter confidently replied, "Smykay has not made a dent in the *a priori* case against the presence of economies of scale in trucking. . . ."[81]

A third basic study in this area was done in the Harvard Economics Studies by Meyer, Peck, Stenason, and Zwick. They concluded the following:

The observable economies of scale in the trucking industry are, therefore, probably a function of the intensity to which a given geographical route pattern is utilized and not of the total volume of the firm. (In ICC terminology, utilization is defined as the traffic density, the ratio of ton miles to route miles.) These economies of scale in a high traffic density are equally available to the absolutely large and small firm. For example, a small firm with a short route and a high traffic density on that route would realize more economies of scale and lower costs than would a larger firm, in terms of revenue or assets, with longer routes and a lower density of traffic.[82]

Now, if the above statement is valid, a pertinent question becomes: does a typical trucking merger increase the traffic density over the firm's routes; or in other words, does the typical load factor[83] of their vehicles increase? A related and extremely significant question then becomes, what are the current load factor levels of motor common carriers? This must be known, for if they are currently near 100 percent, then it is impossible to raise them significantly under any type of trucking merger. Meyer et al. estimate that about a 50 percent load factor is encountered for all Class I and II intercity motor common carriers.[84] Professor Nelson, in another study of the New England area, reports that the regulated carriers had an average load factor of 60.5 percent.[85] Another indication of load factors is a 1961 study by the Highway Research Board. On a sample of 23,610 line-haul loadings of 611 common motor carriers, they found 52.4 percent of all trips fully loaded in both directions. In addition, only 13.9 percent of the truckers had fully loaded trips in one direction, and empty on the backhaul.[86]

The implication of the above load factor statistics is that there is substantial excess capacity available to motor common carriers. In other words, the potential is there for scale economies, *if* larger firms do in fact achieve increased load factors. To date, the evidence on this question appears to support both sides of the issue. First, it should be noted that most trucking mergers are of an end-to-end variety.[87] In this type of merger, load factors apparently do not increase significantly. "Although volume increments are often associated with density increases, this is clearly a special case. . . . If a firm extends its routes to serve new points, the new traffic would not contribute to a density increase on the old routes."[88] On the other hand, Professors Walter Adams and James B. Hendry conclude, "Extension of average mileage seems to bring with it an increase in average loads and is, therefore, one way to achieve higher load factors."[89]

Another significant study[90] in this area was done by Paul W. Emery, II, in 1965. He surveyed 233 Class I and II Middle Atlantic common carriers of general commodities. The carriers were grouped into seven categories, graded basically on operating revenues. Emery discovered very interesting results, compared to other studies in this area. He found that the operating expenses per ton-mile (not vehicle-mile) for these carriers varied as follows, from the smallest to the largest carriers in terms of operating revenues: 21.7 cents, 20.2 cents, 15.9 cents, 13.3 cents, 11.3 cents, 9.7 cents, and 8.9 cents. He attributed these spectacular cost savings to administrative and general expenditures; that is, a more efficient spreading of overhead costs and increased load factors. Specifically, he found that load factors for the largest carrier size group to be about three times greater than the smallest carrier size group. Based on these findings, Emery concluded, "This empirical evidence in addition to the commonly accepted advantages of large scale operations . . . present a rather strong case for the existence of relative scale economies within this industry."[91]

In conclusion, the author believes that due to the high variable cost structure of the trucking industry, the dramatic scale economies of the railroad industry would never be possible. However, the issue of load factors was raised by a number of authors, and their point certainly seems valid to this writer. Apparently, common-carrier trucks consistently have load factors far below 100 percent. However, extreme care must be used so that two closely related aspects of scale economies do not become confused. One refers to the cost of producing a unit of *capacity*, generally a *vehicle-mile*. This type of analysis was done by Merrill J. Roberts and most of the other authors surveyed. In this case, because of the truckers' high variable cost structure, very limited economies of scale were found. The second concept refers to the cost of hauling a unit of *service*, generally a *ton-mile*. In other words, as the trucker increases his load factor per truck, the cost per unit in each vehicle declines, even though the cost of running the truck from A to B generally does not. That is, as load factors increase, the cost per ton-mile of goods decreases, while the cost of producing the unit of capacity, the vehicle-mile, is not affected by the changes in the load factor involved. It is the second aspect of scale economies that Emery refers to in his article. This second aspect apparently is the key to trucking scale economies. That is, if service and other advantages of large scale truckers allow them to increase their load factors, then a valid argument in favor of large size truckers exists. In closing, it would certainly appear that blanket denials of scale economies in trucking is too dogmatic a position.

Now that the basic characteristics of the motor trucking industry have been surveyed, the next chapter will introduce the regulatory framework within which the common carrier trucker operates.

3

The Development of Economic Regulation in the Trucking Industry

Early Trucking Regulation by the States

The number of motor carriers increased rapidly after World War I. However, motor trucks were subjected to state regulation as early as 1914; and by 1925, forty states had some type of regulatory power over the operations of motor carriers.[1]

The Legal Basis for State Regulation of Motor Carriers

The Tenth Amendment to the U.S. Constitution specifically provides that those powers not delegated to the Federal government and not explicitly prohibited to the states, may then be in the jurisdiction of the latter body. The wording of the Constitution prompted Professor Donald S. Watson validly to observe that, "The constitutional restrictions on the conduct of economic policies by the state governments are therefore far fewer than those applying to the Federal government."[2]

Specifically, when the states exercise their broad authority to legislate for the protection of the health, safety, morals, and general welfare of its constituents, the state is using its "police powers." An excellent, concise definition of the latter phrase is the following: "The power vested in the legislature to make, ordain, and establish all manner of wholesome and reasonable laws, statutes, and ordinances, either with penalties or without, not repugnant to the constitution, as they shall judge to be for the good and welfare of the commonwealth, and of the subjects of the same."[3]

The landmark case that set the precedent for future regulation of motor carriers was *Munn v. Illinois*,[4] decided by the U.S. Supreme Court in 1877. In this case Munn operated a grain elevator in Chicago. In 1872 the State of Illinois passed a law that regulated the maximum rates that Munn could charge. Munn and his partner Scott ignored this state law and were tried, found guilty, and fined $100. They appealed their case all the way to the U.S. Supreme Court. The latter court decided against Munn and Scott and set forth the following extremely consequential precedent.

"Property does become clothed with a public interest when used in a manner to make it of public consequence, and affect the community at large. When,

23

therefore, one devotes his property to a use in which the public has an interest, he, in effect, grants to the public an interest in that use, and must submit to be controlled by the public for the common good. . . ."[5]

To recapitulate, it was the police power of the state that allowed Illinois to regulate Munn and Scott in their grain elevator business.[6] Similarly, it was the public nature of motor carriers that allowed the states to regulate trucking activities. However, the Supreme Court apparently ceased trying to decide if a business was basically of a public or private nature in the famous 1934 case of *Nebbia v. New York*.[7] Justice Owen J. Roberts concisely stated the core of this decision when he noted, ". . . there can be no doubt that upon proper occasion and by appropriate measures the state may regulate a business in any of its aspects, including the prices to be charged for the products or commodities it sells."[8] The net result of the *Nebbia* case yields further basis for motor carrier regulation, if the public so desires. Wilcox well sums up the current situation: "As the law now stands, an industry can be regulated whenever the legislature decides to act. If some rates are controlled, it is because the people have demanded action. If others are uncontrolled, it is because they have not."[9]

The second broad source of state regulatory authority over motor carriers is referred to by Professor Harper as the states' "proprietary power." Thus, Harper concluded, "The operations of motor carriers are conducted on highways constructed at public expense primarily for the use of the general public. Hence, the states have an indisputable right to regulate the conditions of highway use in the interests of conservation and to protect the rights of all users."[10]

*The Reasons for State Regulation
of Motor Truckers*

The previous section indicated that after the *Nebbia* case practically any industry could be subjected to state regulation if the states deemed it desirable. This subsection will briefly survey the main points that were significant in bringing state regulation to the trucking industry.

It is interesting to note that there was little, if any general public demand for state regulation of motor carriers. This is in direct contrast to the forceful state regulation of the railroads, beginning with the Granger Laws in 1871.[11]

Professor Harper, in his text on state regulation of trucking, suggested that there were four primary reasons why states subjected the trucking industry to regulations:[12]

The first was a desire to protect the highways from undue physical abuse and to provide safety regulations in order to safeguard private motorists and pedestrians.

Secondly, regulation was instituted to prevent excess competition and the consequences of this situation. However, as previously mentioned, it was not the general public, but the competitors themselves, that demanded this control. Hudson and Constantin remarked that, "In a number of states, the existing motor carriers joined forces with other organizations seeking regulation, not only that they might be present to defend their interests when the regulatory legislation was being considered, but also that they might seek the enactment of measures designed to impede the establishment of other competitors in motor transportation."[13] In addition, the railroads were very much in favor of regulation of trucking activities. ". . . it is interesting that railroads were very active both in proposing economic regulation of motor carriers on the state level and often in opposing the issuance of specific certificates of public convenience and necessity on the basis that they (the railroads) already adequately served the public. Without doubt one of the primary motives for regulation of motor carriage was the control of intermodal competition."[14] Finally, it should not be inferred that the general public received no benefits from this regulating of excess competition. On the contrary, some shippers benefited greatly from the increased service and financial stability of the truckers that regulation made feasible.

The third basic goal was to guarantee to the public adequate motor transportation service. One author believes this point to be of fundamental significance and of the greatest importance to the public.[15] Harper notes that this point is often explicitly expressed in state statutes regulating motor carriers. Thus, the Wisconsin Supreme Court has remarked that: "The paramount goal . . . is that of providing adequate motor-transportation service to meet the public needs, and any other objective is secondary."[16]

The fourth and final fundamental objective of trucking regulation was to achieve overall coordination of transportation facilities. Regulation was believed necessary to obtain this goal because it was very difficult to coordinate two modes of transport when one was completely regulated (the railroads) and the other was comparatively free (the truckers). For example, the regulatory laws of Oregon and New Hampshire stated that motor carriers are regulated so that the various transport modes can be effectively coordinated in order to best serve the needs of the public.[17]

Three Basic Types of Trucking Regulation

There are three basic types of regulation that the states can apply to trucking. The first type of regulation is to protect the highway system from unnecessary physical abuse. This type of regulation basically deals with the maximum number of pounds a vehicle and its cargo can weigh. The states have built their highway system at great expense, and it is therefore completely proper for them to impose appropriate restrictions to protect their investment from destruction.

A second type of control is safety regulation, designed to protect the general users of the highways. Professor Locklin well sketches the basic factors under this form of regulation.

These measures specify limitations on the width of trucks and buses; maximum heights; maximum lengths of vehicles and of combinations of vehicles; speed limits; requirements to insure the equipment of vehicles with safety appliances such as speedometers, adequate brakes, horns, lights, windshield wipers, mirrors, and bumpers. Under this type of regulation also is included the requirement that motor-vehicle operators carry liability insurance against personal injuries and property damage caused in the operation of vehicles.[18]

The last basic type of regulation is directed at the for-hire sector of motor truckers. This type of control is commonly called economic regulation, because it involves such factors as the regulation of rates and services, and the issuance of certificates of public convenience and necessity. This aspect of regulation is the subject of the next section.

A Survey of State Economic Regulation to 1935

This subsection will survey the three primary aspects of state economic regulation over motor common carriers.[19] The following section will delve into the unique regulatory problems involved with contract carriers. The three areas of economic regulation to be discussed are: control over common carrier entry, rates, and service.

Entry Control. The phrase "public convenience and necessity" appears to have been first used in early highway construction, when the state laws often imposed the obligation to build highways to certain places if "public convenience and necessity" so necessitated. The final duty of determining the precise meaning of the phrase usually fell upon the courts. "Having decided that 'public convenience and necessity' warranted the construction, the finding and opinion of the court were reported in a certificate which has become to be known as a certificate of public convenience and necessity."[20] (Hereafter abbreviated as a "certificate".) The use of certificates increased rapidly after 1900 in all public utility fields.

Perhaps at this point a definition of public convenience and necessity is in order. This phrase is extremely difficult to define precisely, and it is certainly susceptible to many interpretations. However, the following definition is useable and concise. "A public convenience and necessity exists when the proposed facility will meet a reasonable want of the public and supply a need, if existing facilities, while in a sense sufficient, do not adequately supply that need."[21]

Dr. Shan Szto, writing in 1934, well summarized the primary aim of a certificate as a state regulatory device:

That the object of a certificate is not to create a legal monopoly is seen in court and commission decisions. If there is need for additional service, the commission is in duty bound to grant additional certificates to qualified applicants. The number of certificates along certain routes is limited only by the demand of public convenience and necessity. Truly, the commission regulates and restricts competition among carriers by deciding which one or ones shall be allowed to operate, and protects them against the destructive competition of the un-authorized operators. While this benefits the certificated carriers, it is only incidental to the purpose of securing reliable, continuous and efficient service at reasonable rates to the public. In a sense, that a certificate gives its holder legal protection is undeniable. However, protection to the authorized carriers is of secondary importance; protection to the public interest is the primary consideration.[22]

The basic criteria used to issue certificates were (and still are) several in number. Professors John J. George and Szto suggested that there were four basic factors that the states considered.[23]

The first was the absence of existing adequate transportation facilities. "Other things being considered, if the existing service is reasonably adequate to meet the public needs, the (state) commission is expected to refuse an application; otherwise, the certificate will be granted."[24] In other words, most states appeared to have a policy of protecting existing carriers if the carriers were ready and able to offer the public reasonable service. The first factor must be tempered somewhat by the second, that of popular preference for motor carrier service. When there was no existing truck service, even though rail service was adequate, numerous states have allowed the former a certificate.[25] A third relevant factor was the probable volume of business that the proposed service would generate. If it did not appear adequate, the certificate usually was denied. This point, of course, is very similar to the first. It is just another way of protecting the existing carriers. The final factor was the financial strength and the ability of the applicant carrier to serve. This point is self-explanatory.

Two of the four factors, those relating to the protection of existing carriers, yield illuminating insight into why the truckers were so anxious to have their industry subjected to state economic regulation.

Rate Regulation. The foregoing discussion may possibly have given the impression that economic regulation of truckers was strictly a "one-way street"—strictly in the direction of helping and benefiting the existing motor carriers. This, however, was not the case. While it is true that the truckers under regulation were somewhat shielded from the full forces of competition, the following legal maxim also applied: *Qui sentit commodum sentire debet et onus.*[26]

The "burden" was rate and service regulation. Generally, the state laws required that all rates of motor common carriers be just and reasonable. In addition, rates were to be filed in tariffs and strictly complied with in most states. Furthermore, as an indication of the general all-inclusive nature of state rate regulation, witness the following statement by Szto:

"The regulatory body is often vested with authority not only to suspend rates proposed or in effect, but also to fix or approve the maximum or minimum rates, fares, charges, classification and rules and regulations pertaining thereto, of each motor carrier, and to prescribe even exact or precise rates and fares to be charged in lieu of those found to be unreasonable or unjustly discriminatory."[27]

Finally, in regard to the reasonableness of rates, many states followed the precedent in *Smyth v. Ames*[28] of a "fair return on fair value," which refers to allowing a carrier's owner a reasonable rate of return on the fair value of his invested capital.

Service Regulation. As we have seen, the regulation of service standards was one of the paramount reasons for states to initiate motor common carrier regulation. Because of the complexity and vast quantity of service requirements, only the most important will be briefly enumerated here.[29]

Most states were empowered to change the truckers' schedules if for some reason they were found to be unsatisfactory. In addition, carriers usually had to have permission from the regulatory body before they were allowed to change their service schedules.

Unification of existing truck routes and the establishment of through routes and joint rates[30] also had to have prior commission approval in most cases. In addition, in order to insure satisfactory service for the public, the states generally had control over the following factors: the type, adequacy, amount, safety-features, and cleanliness of equipment used in performing the trucking service; the minimum qualifications of the truck driver; and the minimum amount of cargo and collision insurance the carrier had to possess. Finally, most state regulatory bodies had complete control over the prevention of discriminatory service practices.

State Regulation of Contract Carriers:
A Special Problem

A contract carrier is a for-hire trucker that operates strictly on predetermined contracts and does *not* hold itself out to perform transportation services for the general public. One eminent student of transport economics suggested that there were two primary reasons that states had to regulate contract carriers along with common carriers.[31] The first reason was that if the contract carriers were not regulated and the common carriers were, there would exist a strong temptation for common carriers to resort to contract carrier status as a subterfuge to avoid economic regulation. Secondly, contract carriers were regulated in order to protect the profitability of common carriers. This point was premised on the valid assumption that common carrier service was of greater overall benefit to the public than contract carrier service, because common carriers were prepared to serve the general public in a nondiscriminatory manner. The problem was that contract carriers could often take the best customers away from the common carriers, whose remaining business might then become unprofitable or at best marginal.

With these considerations in mind, the states attempted to regulate contract carriers from an early date. The best method of analyzing the difficulties and results of these regulatory efforts is to briefly trace three landmark cases that well illustrate the issues and problems involved.

Michigan Public Utilities Commission v. Duke

The first significant test of the state power to regulate contract carriers was the *Duke* case.[32] The state of Michigan in 1923 passed a law stating that from that day forward all for-hire motor carriers were to be considered common carriers for regulatory purposes. Specifically, the law declared:

"Any and all persons engaged in transportation of persons or property by motor vehicle for-hire, upon or over the public highways of this state shall be common carriers, and so far as applicable, all laws of this state now in force or hereafter enacted, regulating transportation by other common carriers, including regulation of rates, shall apply with equal force and effect to such common carriers by motor vehicle."[33]

At the time when this law was passed, C.W. Duke had three contracts to haul automobile bodies from Detroit to Toledo, Ohio. He had no other business, and he definitely did not propose to serve the general public. Duke did not believe that he should be subjected to the stringent common carrier regulatory features and therefore failed to comply with the instant legal decree. The case finally was appealed to the U.S. Supreme Court, which decided in favor of Duke. Justice Butler remarked that:

"Moreover, it is beyond the power of the state by legislative fiat to convert property used exclusively in the business of a private carrier into a public utility, or to make the owner a public carrier, for that would be taking private property for public use without just compensation, which no state can do consistently with the due process of law clause of the Fourteenth Amendment."[34]

Frost v. Railroad Commission of California

The second important step in the states' attempt to regulate contract carriers was the *Frost* case,[35] which was very similar to the *Duke* case. The California Auto Stage and Truck Act of 1919 declared that all for-hire carriers on California highways must secure a certificate and be regulated as a common carrier. Frost was then transporting citrus fruits under specific contracts. He refused to be regulated as a common carrier and took his case to court. The litigation reached the U.S. Supreme Court in 1926. Again the Court held that a private contract carrier could not be converted against his will to common carrier status by mere legislative fiat. This meant that state economic regulation of contract carriers was not possible.

The *Duke* and *Frost* decisions generally became the leading interpretations for lower courts to follow when applying the legal procedure of *res judicata*[36] and *stare decisis*.[37] It was not until 1932 that the situation materially changed.

Stephenson v. Binford

In 1932, the state of Texas enacted a law that had the effect of regulating contract carriers by requiring them to possess a "permit" and not the usual certificate of common carriers. The required permits were to be granted only after a hearing and were specifically to be denied if the state commission found, "... that the proposed operation of any such contract carrier will impair the efficient public service of any authorized common carrier or common carriers then adequately serving the territory."[38]

Stephenson and other contract carriers brought suit against Binford, a state official. Again the case[39] was ultimately decided by the U.S. Supreme Court. This court was sympathetic with the state law and subsequently upheld it. The high court could have based its decision on two possible theories: (1) the state's power to regulate the use of its highways, or (2) the designation of contract carriers as a business that is "affected with the public interest" and therefore subject to state control. Surprisingly, the court rested its case on the state's power to regulate. It appeared that during the interim six-year period after the *Frost* case, the high court had observed the inherent problems of having two sets of for-hire motor carriers, of which only one was subjected to economic regulation. Why, however, did not the Supreme Court admit the latter situation and regulate contract carriers under the second theory above? Instead, the high court chose the timid and less controversial rationale to support its changed position. In any case, one must agree with Elwood Murphey when he concluded:

The result of the *Stephenson* case is undoubtedly beneficial, but it is submitted that the court has permitted the state in an indirect manner to accomplish that which was invalidated in the *Michigan* and *Frost* cases. The fault, however, does not seem to lie in the rationalization of the present case but rather in the earlier cases, which did not recognize that the business of motor transportation as a whole, or at least so far as carriage for-hire is concerned, is a business affected with a public interest and that the state should be able to impose such regulations as a condition of the use of the highways for gain.[40]

The precedent established in the *Stephenson* case of regulating contract carriers by the use of "permits" was followed by a number of states after this landmark decision. In fact, this dichotomy between "permits" and "certificates" established the pattern that was eventually adopted in the Motor Carrier Act of 1935. It should also be pointed out that the regulation applied to contract carriers was less strict than that in force for common carriers. This will also be seen when the Federal regulation of contract and common carriers is discussed.

To recapitulate, the real importance of the *Stephenson* case was that it established the precedent for state regulation of contract carriers, which was later followed by other states.

A Knotty Question: State Regulation
of Interstate Transportation

Anyone familiar with the early history of state regulation of the railroads would be able to predict that the motor carrier industry would some day have to face the perplexing problem of overzealous states attempting to regulate interstate commerce. For the railroads, this situation was clarified in the famous *Wabash*[41] case.

With the rise of the trucking industry and its accompanying regulation, the state governments were not unaware of the precedent that had been established in the *Wabash* case. However, the state governments reasoned that, in the absence of Federal interstate regulation, the states were empowered to provide nondiscriminatory regulation of *interstate* carriers in order to guarantee public safety and convenience. It was mandatory, however, that such regulation should not burden interstate commerce and thus become contrary to the commerce clause of the Federal Constitution.[42]

Buck v. Kuykendall

The first basic case that upset the feeling of "security" that the states previously felt concerning their regulation of interstate motor carriers was the famous *Buck*[43] case, decided by the U.S. Supreme Court on March 2, 1925. In this landmark case, Buck wanted to establish an auto stage line between Seattle, Washington, and Portland, Oregon. He had obtained all the necessary documents from Oregon and then applied to the state of Washington for the required certificate. The state of Washington studied the situation and decided that since the Seattle area was already adequately served by four existing carriers, and hence Buck was denied his certificate. Buck immediately brought suit against Washington's director of public works, claiming the state had violated the commerce clause of the Constitution and the Fourteenth Amendment. The case was finally decided in favor of Buck by the U.S. Supreme Court, which stated:

The primary purpose of the provision here in question is not regulation with a view to safety or to conservation of the highways, but the prohibition of competition. . . . Thus . . . the Washington statute is a regulation, not of the use of its own highways, but of interstate commerce. Its effect upon such commerce is not merely to burden but to obstruct it. Such state action is forbidden by the Commerce Clause. It also defeats the purpose of Congress expressed in the legislation giving federal aid for the construction of interstate highways.[44]

This telling judicial blow by the high court ". . . created serious doubt in the minds of state officials as to just how much power they retained over interstate commerce."[45]

Bush v. Maloy

Indeed, if doubt existed after the *Buck* case, the *Bush*[46] case reinforced it among state regulatory bodies. The Bush Company had applied to the state of Maryland for permission to perform strictly interstate common carrier service. The question was referred to the Maryland Public Service Commission, which was charged with the duty to investigate the situation and empowered to deny permits if it decided that granting them would be prejudicial to the overall welfare and convenience of the public.[47] Based on the latter criteria, Bush's application was denied.

Highlights of the testimony indicated the following: the Maryland highways were not unreasonably congested, the trucks of the Bush Company would damage the streets to no greater extent than the existing motor carriers, and that the Maryland Public Service Commission considered merely the need of the state for additional motor common carrier service.

The Supreme Court overruled the Maryland decision and the statute because they attempted to regulate interstate commerce. In other words, the court declared that states do not have the constitutional power to arbitrarily decide which interstate carriers will be allowed to transgress their respective states.

Finally, it should not be assumed that the above decisions of *Buck* and *Bush* were the unanimous conclusions of the highest court in land. Indeed, many students of transport problems were in accord with Mr. Justice McReynolds' dissenting opinion in the *Buck* case. "The federal government has not and cannot undertake precise regulations. Control by the states must continue, otherwise chaotic conditions will quickly develop. The problems are essentially local, and should be left with the local authorities unless and until something is done which really tends to obstruct the free flow of commercial intercourse."[48]

In closing, the *Buck* and *Bush* cases of 1925 together are analogous to the previous *Wabash* case. However, after the latter adjudication there was great public demand and clamor for Federal railroad regulation. This was not true for motor carriers. In fact, many people were in sympathy with the position expressed by Justice McReynolds. As will be seen in a later section, this general apathy of the public toward Federal motor carrier regulation (as reflected by the low priority given this measure by Congressional leaders) was one of the main reasons that ten years elapsed after the *Buck* and *Bush* cases before Federal control was effectuated.

The Pros and Cons of Federal Regulation

The momentous *Buck* and *Bush* cases clearly pointed out to many students of transport regulation the need to correct the "no man's land" of interstate motor common carriers. However, this point of view was by no means a unanimous one. This section will briefly discuss the main points for and against Federal regulation.

Affirmative Arguments

A survey of the contemporary literature of the 1930-35 period indicates that there were seven basic reasons advanced in favor of Federal motor carrier regulation. By far the most publicized argument for regulation was the stability of rates and the related decrease in discrimination that would result from Federal control. In addition, a corollary problem was that the uneconomically low rates generally necessitated a very low level of service quality. It must be remembered that the 1930-35 period was amidst the "Great Contraction" (Milton Friedman's term). This depressed condition of the general economy had pregnant consequences for the trucking industry. Discussing this point, Joseph B. Eastman stated:

It has drawn many thousands into the business, has made thousands of second-hand trucks available at low prices, and by low labor, fuel, and tire costs has invited their purchase. The abundance of labor to be had at low wages has stimulated cutthroat competition between operators who have wanted to maintain high or reasonable standards of employment and those who have been willing to exploit labor, either as a matter of deliberate policy or from necessity. In brief, the depression has lowered the standard of living of the industry.[49]

These abnormal conditions discussed by Eastman indicated that all the necessary conditions for extremely unstable rates, poor service quality, and discriminatory practices were present in the first half of the 1930s. Indeed, they did exist! The above problems were especially prevalent among the *interstate* carriers, who were under no economic regulation after the *Buck* and *Bush* cases. Perhaps one of the best summaries of this problem was given by the California Railroad Commission in 1932.

The chief cause of the disturbed condition of transportation is the operation of these trucks. ... Their rates vary from day to day and are not uniform as between shippers and communities... The things they do which regulated carriers can not do may be summarized in part as follows: (a) Discriminate between persons and places; (b) make rebates; (c) grant secret rates; (d) change rates at any time without notice.... The over-whelming majority of the witnesses for industry, agriculture, and business, and shippers and receivers of freight were emphatic in their desire to see transportation stabilized.... A system of unknown transportation charges and practices is being introduced by unregulated carriers into an economic structure which has been built upon a system of known charges and practices with demoralizing results. ... The public interest demands that regulation be extended over all or withdrawn from all.[50]

A second argument that was also highly publicized concerned the question of equality. That is, if interstate railroads were subjected to Federal control, then it is only fair to do the same to the motor carrier industry. Hudson and Constantin believe that this factor was the most important reason for the eventual Federal regulation of trucking.[51] Professor Szto also discussed this point and concluded that to be fair to the railroads, the trucking industry also had to be regulated.[52]

Another major point advanced in favor of Federal regulation of motor carriers was that it would facilitate effective transport coordination among the modes. This objective is difficult to achieve when some modes are highly regulated and others are not. It is for this reason that the ICC did not allow any through routes and joint rates between railroads and motor carriers prior to 1935.[53] Furthermore, the *Report of the Federal Coordinator of Transportation* stated unambiguously the gravity of this objective:

"Public advantage will also result from the opportunities which regulation will create for coordinating rail, water, and motor services. There is no other way to prevent unnecessary duplication and waste and to give each form of transportation a chance to develop in the field where it can function the best, without destructive competition from inferior forms. Such coordination is the foundation for financial stability and lower transportation costs and rates."[54]

A fourth influential factor leading to Federal regulation was the rising subterfuge that appeared after the *Buck* and *Bush* cases. The idea was to attempt to make the trucking activity interstate in nature, for then the operation was in the proverbial "no man's land" as far as economic regulation was concerned. Professor George enumerated some of the most ingenious chicaneries: driving a few feet into another state and then returning to the main route, fixing circuitous routes that encompassed a few hundred yards of another state, and placing a station just on the other side of the state border, which was designed to produce no traffic.[55]

Many other major points in favor of Federal trucking regulation were also suggested. They are only listed here and not expanded on. When the U.S. Senate was considering Federal control in this area, they held their usual hearing on the topic. The following factors developed from these hearings in 1935:

1. Federal regulation would improve financial stability of the carriers.[56]
2. Effective safety regulation of drivers and vehicles in interstate commerce could be achieved.[57]
3. The final goal was to achieve uniformity in regulatory laws. It was hoped that most states would pattern their regulatory laws after those of the Federal government.[58]

Negative Arguments

As is true in almost every significant controversy, there are telling arguments for each point of view. There were three basic arguments advanced against Federal regulation of motor carriers.

Perhaps the most prevalent position against Federal regulatory activity centered around the impracticability of the proposed legislation. Thus, Joseph B. Eastman, in his famous report of 1934 stated, "The most serious argument against federal regulation of motor carriers is that, to be effective, it would require a large, costly, and bureaucratic establishment with a small army of agents and investigators, the remedy being worse than the disease."[59]

A second point put forward by those opposed to Federal control was that the states can best regulate the for-hire motor carrier industry. This position was summarized previously in this chapter in the quote from Mr. Justice Mc-Reynolds.

A third and somewhat all-inclusive attack against Federal control of trucking stated that the public did not favor this regulation because it would prevent the relatively low level of truck rates that were available in interstate commerce. Furthermore, this argument stressed that it was the large motor trucking companies and the railroads who demanded this legislation—not the general populace. An excellent summary of this position was given by Mr. Fred Brenkman, representing the National Grange at the 1935 Senate hearings on Federal trucking regulation. Mr. Brenkman pointed out that before the trucking industry developed, farmers were at the mercy of the railroads, because the latter had no effective competition to force their rates down. However,

. . . the advent of the for-hire truck has given the farmer a chance to market his products at lower transportation costs and to retain something for himself from the proceeds of the sale of his commodities. There has been no complaint by shippers of any kind that prevailing trucking rates are too high. Hence, if there is any demand for regulation, it must be because those making the demand consider trucking rates too low. This fault, if fault it be, does not affect the public. It only affects the carriers thrown into competition with the trucks.[60]

Mr. Brenkman further contended that, in the past, the primary objective of regulating public utilities had been to protect the public against excessive rates. In the interstate trucking situation, however, the objective was to *raise* their level of rates. Mr. Brenkman concluded, "To us, such a proposal seems utterly preposterous. . . ."[61]

Finally, the Grange representative stressed that it had been the railroads that primarily favored this regulation. To substantiate this point of view, Mr. Brenkman quoted from the 1932 ICC Annual Report, which stated, "There is substantially no demand for public regulation of the charges of motor trucks to protect shippers against exorbitant or discriminatory charges. The demand has been chiefly from the railroads, and for the prescription of minimum rather than maximum charges."[62]

A Brief Legislative History of the Motor Carrier Act of 1935

The previous section indicated the primary arguments for and against Federal motor carrier regulation. Apparently enough people favored the affirmative position (especially after the *Buck* and *Bush* cases), so that from 1925 to 1935 many bills were introduced to bring this control to fruition. This section will present a succinct survey[63] of the legislative history of the Motor Carrier Act of 1935.

The Cable Bill of March, 1925 (proposed prior to the *Buck* and *Bush* Supreme Court decisions), introduced into the House of Representatives, would have authorized the ICC to have jurisdiction over the operations of both freight and passenger interstate motor carriers. This bill was never reported out of the Committee on Interstate and Foreign Commerce.[64]

In December of 1925, after the *Buck* and *Bush* cases, Senator Albert B. Cummins of Iowa introduced a bill that bore his name. This bill proposed approximately the same regulatory measures as the Cable Bill. The Cummins' proposal faltered because (a) the industry was in its infancy, (b) not enough information was available to establish a need for regulation, (c) the railroads favored the bill, and (d) the bill may have been unconstitutional.[65]

In 1929 and 1931, Representative James S. Parker introduced similar bills. The first bill never got out of committee. The second Parker Bill passed the House in 1931, but was left as unfinished business at the close of the 1931 Senate session.[66]

The Couzens Bill was introduced into the Senate in 1932 and provided for the regulation of interstate buses by joint boards and a permit system for interstate trucks. Hearings were held, and this bill also died in committee.[67]

After the Couzens Bill, Representative Sam Rayburn, Chairman of the House Committee on Interstate Commerce, introduced a bill requiring a certificate from the ICC and other comprehensive measures. Muller concluded, "The bill was offered, not for immediate passage, but for study looking toward legislation at a later session."[68]

Finally, in February of 1934, Senator Burton K. Wheeler, Chairman of the Senate Committee on Interstate Commerce, introduced S. 1629, a bill entitled "Motor Carrier Act, 1935." This bill contained comprehensive regulatory powers over passenger and freight interstate motor carriers and was to be administered by the ICC. This bill was based primarily on the recommendations of Joseph B. Eastman, Federal Coordinator of Transportation.

Extensive hearings on this bill were held by the Senate Committee on Interstate Commerce from February 25 to March 6, 1935. In addition, a House Subcommittee of the Committee on Interstate and Foreign Commerce also held lengthy hearings on their version of this bill from February 19 to March 1, 1935.

Because the Senate's hearings were more comprehensive, the discussion here will be limited to them. Many of the main points of these hearings have already been enumerated in the preceding section. One point that immediately came up when the Federal Coordinator of Transportation, Joseph B. Eastman, testified was the following:

" 'Chairman: Let me ask you right there, Mr. Eastman: are you taking this (the regulation of motor carriers) up today from the standpoint of help to the railroads or from the standpoint of the public interest?' "

" 'Mr. Eastman: I am taking the matter up from the standpoint of the public interest.' "[69]

Because this hearing has been discussed previously, suffice it to say that it was very lengthy (the report is 607 pages) and somewhat dull. The hearing contained an almost insufferable amount of duplication, because almost inevitably the speaker was in favor of the bill. Indeed, even Chairman Wheeler appeared to be getting irritated by the facsimile type testimony that was being presented. Witness his following instructions to Mr. George Whitehead: " 'The Chairman: If you have anything that has been covered by previous witnesses, try to eliminate that. You may put your full statement in the record if you desire to do so. What we are specifically interested in knowing is whether or not you favor the bill.' "[70]

Generally, the hearings indicated that the following groups were in favor of S. 1629: the railroads, the motor common carriers' associations, the state regulatory bodies, the ICC, labor organizations, and shippers to whom service dependability and financial stability were more important than low rates.

Conversely, opponents to the act were farmers[71] and other shippers to whom low line-haul truck rates were the primary consideration.

The Senate Committee on Interstate Commerce reported favorably on S. 1629 on April 12, 1935, and recommended to the Senate that it be passed. Chairman Wheeler, in the customary summary report from his committee, recapitulated the primary reason why his committee favored Federal regulation over interstate carriers. "This competition has been carried to an extreme which tends to undermine the financial stability of the carriers and jeopardizes the maintenance of transportation facilities and service appropriate to the needs of commerce and required in the public interest. The present chaotic transportation conditions are not satisfactory to investors, labor, shippers, or the carriers themselves."[72]

On April 16, 1935, the Senate passed S. 1629. On the following day, S. 1629 was referred to the House Committee on Interstate and Foreign Commerce for consideration. This House Committee issued its report on S. 1629 on July 24, 1935, and this was adopted by the House of Representatives on July 31, 1935. The Senate then approved the House version on August 5, 1935. Finally, President Franklin D. Roosevelt signed the "Motor Carrier Act, 1935" into law on August 9, of that year.[73]

The Main Provisions of the 1935 Motor Carrier Act and Its Subsequent Amendments

Motor Common Carriers of Freight and Their Federal Economic Regulation

The 1935 Act gave a statutory definition of a common carrier,[74] which was changed in 1940 to what is still on the statute books:

Section 203(a) (14) The term "common carrier by motor vehicle" means any person which holds itself out to the general public to engage in the transportation by motor vehicle in interstate or foreign commerce of passengers or property or any class or classes thereof for compensation, whether over regular or irregular routes, except transportation by motor vehicle by an express company to the extent that such transportation has heretofore been subject to part I, to which extent such transportation shall continue to be considered to be and shall be regulated as transportation subject to Part I.[75]

The ICC has defined common carriers on numerous occasions. In one case, the Commission declared that a common carrier is one that conducts his business "... in such a manner as to demonstrate that in a general way it was, subject to his equipment limitations, ... available to shippers generally or to all of a particular class of shippers."[76] Transport attorney, Warren H. Wagner, summed up the controlling factor in determining a common carrier when he observed that, "... whether or not a given operator is a common carrier depends in the most part upon his actions."[77]

In general, the 1935 Motor Carrier Act subjected common carrier truckers to nine basic regulatory provisions. A very basic provision designed to control the supply of common carrier truckers was the requirement that each carrier must have a certificate. Those carriers already in business on June 1, 1935, were eligible for "grandfather" certificates. Since the purposes of a certificate have already been discussed in some detail, suffice it to say that each certificate states the area, commodities, and routes each carrier is authorized to use. The objective here, of course, is to stabilize the industry by preventing the tremendous excess capacity and its attendant problems that plagued the trucking industry prior to Federal regulation. Finally, the determination of public convenience and necessity[78] in each case rests with the ICC. Professor Norton humorously points out that this task requires careful consideration because, "Few things are necessities in life, and motor transportation service is not one of them."[79]

A second basic type of regulation applies to rates. All rates must be properly published, strictly adhered to, and adequate notice given before rates are changed. In addition, each rate filed must be just and reasonable.[80] Finally, the ICC has the power to set the maximum, minimum, and the actual rate, if the existing rate was found to be unlawful.

Consolidations and mergers are also covered by the 1935 Act, and this provision will be discussed in some detail shortly. Also, common carrier truckers' securities are regulated. Specifically, ICC approval is required to issue securities, only if the total par value of the securities of the carrier, either outstanding or to be issued, exceeds $1 million. In addition, notes that mature within two years and do not total greater than $200,000, can be issued without ICC approval. These exemptions are provided to help relatively small carriers avoid unnecessary "red tape" and also so as not to burden the ICC with additional paperwork.[81] This regulation was believed necessary for the larger truckers, in order to make sure they were using the proceeds from the security issues for legitimate purposes such as providing working capital for replacement and rehabilitation of operating property. Permission to issue securities has been denied if the proceeds were found to be used primarily to get rid of competitors or to give special salaries and bonuses to employees.[82]

A fifth requirement is that common carrier truckers maintain reasonable levels of insurance, both for cargo and collision. The level of coverage is periodically reviewed by the ICC, but most authorities believe that the levels set are strictly minimums.[83] Another requirement is that uniform accounting procedures are followed. In addition, the 1935 Act prohibited "dual" operations in most cases, which refers to a trucking company operating as both a common and contract carrier in the same territory. This provision was designed to prevent a type of discrimination in which the carrier would be forced to give especially low contract rates to a shipper, or the latter would not patronize the trucker's common carrier service. In other words, the larger shipper could receive more beneficial contract rates compared to smaller shippers.[84] However, Professor Pegrum, referring to this type of situation, has declared, "It is difficult to see how this could be of any particular danger in view of the fact that the large shipper would have the advantage of being able to secure the services of a competing contract carrier in any case."[85]

An eighth requirement is that all unreasonable discrimination must be prevented. That is, no unreasonable advantage or preference can be given to any person, town, region, or type of traffic. The final basic provision refers to safety regulation, and this aspect has been outlined previously. Besides providing specific rules regarding the safety features of the vehicle, this form of regulation also prescribes the qualifications and maximum number of hours that an operator can drive his vehicle within certain time periods.

Contract Carriers and Their Federal Regulation

The statutory definition of contract carriers was enacted in 1935,[86] and revised in 1940[87] and 1957. The last revision was necessitated by a 1956 U.S. Supreme Court decision. As has been pointed out by many transport experts, "The line of demarcation between a common and contract motor carrier is very thin."[88] One test that at least had achieved *de facto* recognition in determining the difference between common and contract carriers was the number of contracts operated by the contract carrier. Obviously, the greater the number of contracts, the more the carrier tended toward common carrier status. In 1954, the ICC found that Contract Steel Carriers, Inc., had illegally converted its authorized contract carrier status to that of a common carrier. Specifically, Contract Steel in a few years prior to 1954 increased its number of contracts from 13 to 69.[89] This ICC decision was appealed to the Supreme Court, which decided against the ICC. The high court declared that, "A contract carrier is free to aggressively search for new business within the limits of his license."[90]

The Commission believed that this case had set a dangerous precedent because it allowed a contract carrier to seek an unlimited number of contracts and hence actually serve the general public. To rectify this situation, the ICC requested, and Congress enacted, a new definition of contract carriers in 1957.[91] The current statutory definition of a contract carrier is the following:

Section 203(a) (15); The term "contract carrier by motor vehicle" means any person which engages in transportation by motor vehicle of passengers or property in interstate or foreign commerce, for compensation (other than transportation referred to in paragraph (14) and the exception therein), under continuing contracts with one person or a limited number of persons either (a) for the furnishing of transportation services through the assignment of motor vehicles for a continuing period of time to the exclusive use of each person served or (b) for the furnishing of transportation services designed to meet the distinct need of each individual customer.[92]

As can be seen, the new definition stresses that a contract carrier offers a specialized service to a restricted number of clients. Because of this definitional change, many contract carriers found that their operations now appeared to be more closely aligned to common carriers than previously. Congress had anticipated this problem, and had provided a procedure for converting contract carrier rights to those of a common carrier. In August, 1957, there were 2,620 Federally regulated contract carriers of which 1,801 were found to be still contract carriers under the new amended definition. The remainder had the option of filing for common carrier status or defaulting their contract carrier rights.[93] Finally, the question remains—how many are a "limited number" of contracts for a contract carrier? While this question was purposely left up to the discretion of the ICC by Congress, the Commission has stated emphatically that for unspecialized transport, greater than 6 to 8 contracts would be carefully scrutinized.[94]

Since the rationale for contract carrier regulation has been noted, the specific provisions of the 1935 Act as they affect contract carriers can be surveyed. Following the precedent of *Stephenson v. Binford*, the 1935 Act required "permits" for all interstate contract carriers. To be eligible for a permit, a contract carrier must be fit, willing, and able; and his application to the ICC must prove that the proposed service will be "consistent with the public interest and the national transportation policy." Most transport experts believe that this test is less stringent than that applied to common carrier applications, i.e., proving "public convenience and necessity."[95] As was true for common carriers, a "grandfather" clause was also included for contract carriers, using July 1, 1935, as the line of demarcation.

In regard to contract carrier rates, most administrative procedures are identical with those of common carriers. Originally contract carriers had only to file their minimum rates with the Commission, but this was changed in 1957, and now the actual rates must be filed and adhered to. One significant difference between contract and common carriers is that the ICC can only set minimum and not maximum rates for the former type of carrier.[96]

One important difference between contract and common carriers deals with discrimination. The former group, is under no legal obligation to render equal service to the public and only has to serve those customers with whom he has contracts.[97] Furthermore, the contract carrier is under no obligation to treat all his contract customers on an equal basis. Professor Westmeyer explains the rationale for this provision:

The amount a contract carrier charges any given shipper will vary with the volume of traffic the shipper can offer, the regularity of the traffic, the possibility of obtaining a back haul for trucks which would otherwise have to return to their point of origin without a pay load, the cost and practicability of a shipper providing his own motor transport facilities, and possibly other factors which vary from shipper to shipper. To attempt to establish a uniform schedule of rates under such conditions would destroy the peculiar advantages of this type of transportation.[98]

In regard to insurance, the 1935 Act does not require contract carriers to have cargo insurance, because this class of carriers does not have the strict cargo liability responsibilities of common carriers.[99] However, contract carriers must carry adequate collision insurance.

Finally, contract carriers are subject to the same provisions as common carriers in regard to dual operations, securities, accounts, safety regulations, and consolidations.

Private Carriers and Brokers and Their
Respective Regulation

The statutory definition of private carriers has not changed since the original 1935 Act. Specifically, Section 203 (a) (17) states:

The term "private carrier of property by motor vehicle" means any person not included in the terms "common carrier by motor vehicle" or "contract carrier by motor vehicle," who or which transports in interstate or foreign commerce by motor vehicle property of which such person is the owner, lessee, or bailee, when such transportation is for the purpose of sale, lease, rent, or bailment, or in the furtherance of any commercial enterprise.[100]

In regard to the definition of private carriers, a real controversy has arisen in regard to the question of what standard should be applied to determine whether a carrier is operating as a private carrier or as a contract carrier. The importance of this question is that if trucking involved is found to be a contract carrier, the trucker is legally bound to be regulated as such. More importantly, he must apply for a contract carrier permit and in the process must prove that his proposed service will be consistent with the public interest. The ICC eventually evolved the "primary business" test, which faced its first major challenge in the *Woitishek Common Carrier Application* case.[101] In this decision, the ICC found that Mr. Woitishek was primarily a wholesaler of construction equipment, and that the transportation of his sales, in his own vehicles, was incidental to his primary business; hence, he was a private carrier. This test was further strengthened by the *Lenoir* case,[102] in which the ICC declared, "We conclude that applicant is primarily engaged in the manufacture of furniture, that its motor carrier operations are a bona fide incident to and in furtherance of its primary business, and that the transportation performed by it is not performed with a purpose to profit from the transportation as such."[103]

The "primary business" test finally became codified in the Interstate Commerce Act in 1958, becoming a part of Section 203(c).[104] The ICC has used the "primary business" test to combat two aspects of the "gray area,"[105] each of which attempts to imitate the private trucker. The first type is the so-called "buy and sell" operation. In this case, the operator pretends to be shipping his own products from city A to city B, hence qualifying as a private carrier and evading all state or Federal economic regulation. In fact, the operator buys the goods at city A, drives to city B, where he then sells them. Often the selling price is only his cost of the goods plus the gas and oil consumed from driving from A to B. In other words, the purpose of the "buy and sell" operation is often designed merely to cover the out-of-pocket costs of running his vehicle from A to B. The primary business test is very effective in outlawing this type of activity because, obviously, in the above case, the primary business of the operator was supplying a transportation service for-hire and, hence, should be subjected to economic regulation.[106]

A second major ruse, designed to appear as private transportation, is the leasing of a vehicle and its driver. Professor Hilton has observed that, "The ICC has long held, as a corollary to the primary business test, that lease of a vehicle with driver was illicit for-hire transportation. Following the passage of the Act of 1958, this doctrine was implemented within the general scope of the primary business test."[107] The ICC generally has evolved the rule that the leased vehicle must be under the *complete* control of the shipper. In addition, the driver must be on the shipper's payroll, as witnessed by the shipper carrying workman's compensation on the driver, as well as collecting his income and social security taxes. Finally, unless the trucking operation can be proven to be merely incidental to the primary business of the firm, then the lessor (the owner of the vehicles) is engaged in for-hire transportation and should be regulated as such.[108]

The actual regulation of private truckers, is minimal.[109] This type of carrier needs no authority to operate (i.e., a certificate or a permit) and is subject only to the safety provisions on the 1935 Act.

Brokers were also subjected to regulation under the 1935 Act. The statutory definition of a broker is the following:

Section 203(a) (18): The term "broker" means any person not included in the term "motor carrier" and not a bona fide employee or agent of any such carrier, who or which, as principal or agent, sells or offers for sale any transportation subject to this part, or negotiates for, or holds himself as one who sells, provides, furnishes, contracts, or arranges for such transportation.[110]

Brokers originated in the early days of trucking, when many carriers were so small that they could not afford even a part-time salesman. Hence, the broker developed to help both the shipper and the carrier achieve efficient motor transportation service. Problems developed however, because often the carrier would become dependent on the broker for his tonnage, and hence the broker would be able to extract unreasonable fees from the carriers. In addition, other undesirable practices emerged.[111] It should be pointed out that the significance of brokers is considerably less in 1973 than in 1935. The reason being that, over the years, both shippers' and carriers' average size of operations have increased, and hence each group is better equipped to know the needs and abilities of each other without the need of a middleman, i.e., a broker.[112]

The 1935 Act required brokers to secure a license from the ICC before commencing business; and a "grandfather" provision was provided for existing brokers at the time of the Act's passage. In general, the criterion for securing a license is the same as applied to contract carriers. The service must be found to be consistent with both the public interest and national transportation policy. In addition, the applicant must be found to be fit, willing, and able to perform the functions of a broker. The Act of 1935 stated that the ICC *may* require accounts, reports, and other rules and regulations as necessary to protect the public. In fact, the ICC has issued a minimum of such requirements.[113]

The Exemptions in the 1935 Act

Section 203(b) of the Interstate Commerce Act enumerates a considerable number of exemptions from economic regulation (not safety specifications) in the motor carrier industry. The great majority of these exemptions have not caused any particular problems, and therefore they will only be listed and not discussed. There are exemptions for (a) school buses, (b) taxicabs, (c) hotel limousines, (d) vehicles operated by the Department of the Interior in and about national parks, (e) vehicles used to distribute newspapers, (f) vehicles used when incidental to air transportation, (g) vehicles within one municipality, even if it involves interstate or foreign territory, and (h) the casual, occasional, or incidental transportation of passengers or property for compensation when this service is not the regular occupation of the vehicle operator or firm.[114] These exemptions probably exist for any or all of these reasons: (a) the services involved were not considered to be of national transportation importance; (b) if they were regulated, the administrative burden would be greater than the benefits received, and (c) the exemptions were the result of special interest groups that did not want to be Federally regulated.[115]

The agricultural exemptions under Section 203(b), however, has raised the most difficult problems in regard to exemptions from economic regulation.[116] In general, the 1935 Act exempted the for-hire carriers of agricultural products from economic regulation. The rationale for this exemption was stated succinctly by a veteran observer as follows, "The debate on the exemption of agricultural products, fish, and shellfish clearly showed that the purpose was to assist the farmer or fisherman in getting his products to market."[117] Specifically, the 1935 Act recognized the need for extremely flexible trucking service at harvest and other times that would probably not be feasible under a regulated trucking system. In other words, because they are seasonable and perishable, these products need a trucking service that can swell up to gigantic portions at harvest time and then slide back to nothing at other times. These extreme fluctuations in demand, of course, are not conducive to a regulated type of motor carrier as this exclusive hauler. Therefore, Congress thought it best to exempt this category of products[118] in order to achieve the flexibility of transportation needed.[119]

Specifically, the agricultural exemption for truckers contained three sections, each of which will be briefly discussed. Section 203(b) (4a) exempts vehicles owned and operated by farmers when used in connection with their work. This section has caused little if any controversy, because as Professor Locklin points out, this section is redundant, in that it only reaffirms that the provision on private carriage also applies to farmers.[120]

Section 203(b) (5) allows agricultural cooperative associations to haul farm products for members and nonmembers, as long as the revenue collected from nonmembers does not exceed 50 percent of the cooperative's total revenue. Occasionally, a co-op would attempt to haul nonfarm related goods for nonmembers, but the ICC would void all such arrangements. The Commission would typically state, "We conclude that the backhaul transportation by the association of nonfarm-related commodities for nonmembers is a service, functionally unrelated to the association's farming activities and it is not an operation in which a cooperative association properly may engage within the partial exemption of Section 203(b) (5)."[121]

This interpretation of Section 203(b) (5) stood until an adjudication was reached in 1965 by the Ninth Circuit U.S. Court of Appeals (Judge James R. Browning). In this case, Northwest Agricultural Cooperative, Inc., was allowed to backhaul nonfarm related goods for nonmembers. Specifically, Judge Browning declared,

Its trucking operation, viewed as a whole, is a farm service performed jointly by Northwest's members for themselves. The return hauls enjoined are connected with farm operations, for they are *incidental* and *necessary* to the effective performance of Northwest's farm-related operations. This return haul transportation therefore did not deprive Northwest of its essential character as a 'cooperative association' under the Agricultural Marketing Act. Since it retained this character it retained its right to exemption under Section 203(b) (5) of the Interstate Commerce Act.[122] (Emphasis added).

The key words in this decision were "incidental and necessary." That is, as long as the "co-op's" hauling of nonfarm related commodities for nonmembers was incidental and necessary to their main business, that type of transport was legalized.

Mr. John W. Bush, then chairman of the ICC, immediately recognized the gravity of the court's decision and issued the following statement: "There goes business which regulated carriers have to be authorized to haul. If that isn't simply legalizing what the transportation industry, the Congress, and the Commission has long fought as a type of 'gray area' operation, I don't know what it is."[123]

The ICC requested Congress, in three consecutive *Annual Reports*,[124] to change Section 203(b) (5) so that agricultural co-ops could no longer haul general commodities. These requests became all the more pertinent because the Department of Defense started using co-op vehicles,[125] with the blessings of the newly formed Department of Transportation. In fact, John L. Sweeny, Assistant

Secretary for Public Affairs, declared that the D.O.T. was of the opinion that the present exemption was consistent with Congressional intent and that at present it had not been abused, nor had it caused any significant detriment to the regulated carriers.[126]

Finally, in light of the ICC's requests and subsequent events, Congress enacted Public Law 90-433, which significantly amended Section 203(b) (5) of the Interstate Commerce Act.[127] This amendment became effective on July 7, 1969. Specifically, it created the "15/50" rule in regard to agricultural co-ops. Basically, the law provides a 15 percent maximum amount of tonnage that a co-op can haul for nonfarmer nonmembers. In addition, a maximum of 50 percent of total co-op tonnage can be carried for farmer, nonmembers of the co-op. Furthermore, any co-op that plans to haul for a nonmember nonfarmer must so notify the ICC prior to commencing this service.[128]

The final section dealing with agricultural exemptions is 203(b) (6), which defines the agricultural products that are exempt from motor trucking economic regulation. Again, like Section 203(b) (5), this section has caused considerable discussion and controversy, which eventually led to a clarifying Congressional amendment. This section declared that agricultural commodities, including ordinary livestock and fish (not including manufactured products thereof), were exempt. The trouble began when an attempt was made to define the phrase in parentheses. The ICC preferred a broad definition of "manufactured" agricultural commodities. In fact, Senator John J. Sparkman has charged, "Yet, despite the clear intent of Congress and the plain language of the law, the Commission has waged an aggressive campaign to narrow the scope and neutralize the effectiveness of the exemption."[129] On the other hand, the courts, beginning in 1948 and continuing through to 1957, consistently overruled the ICC and narrowed the definition of "manufactured" commodities, and hence broadened the applicability of the exemption. In other words, more and more goods were able to qualify under the agricultural exemption because of the courts' decisions.[130] However, in 1956 a U.S. Supreme Court decision,[131] subsequently called the "Chicken Case," reached an apex in interpretations that broadened the applicability of the agricultural exemption. In the instant adjudication, the high court ruled that henceforth fresh and frozen dressed poultry were exempt commodities. The real significance of the case is that the Supreme Court outlined a rule to be used in similar situations, i.e., when deciding if a product should be exempt or not. The rule, known as the "continuing substantial identity" test, declared that as long as the original product can still be basically detected after its processing, it is not to be considered a "manufactured" commodity. This, of course, on reflection, is an extremely narrow interpretation of manufacturing. That is, the instant test had the effect of greatly enlarging the number of commodities that were now eligible to be exempt agricultural goods. The ICC subsequently asked Congress to specifically define what "manufactured" products are, because the Commission believed that the "continuing substantial identity" test was too liberal an interpretation of the 1935 Act.

Congress responded by amending Section 203(b) (6) in the Transportation Act, 1958. Specifically, this act returned a small number of commodities that previously were exempt to the regulated category. In addition, the 1958 Act froze the exempt status of commodities to those explicitly listed by the Bureau of Motor Carriers at that time.[132] Also, this act provided a "grandfather" clause for those truckers who were carrying previously exempt commodities that came under regulation via the 1958 Act.[133] Finally, it should be noted that the "continuing substantial identity" test did not become a dead rule after the 1958 Act. Instead, the ICC now uses it to determine if an agricultural product is eligible for exempt status, when the product is not specifically enumerated on the Bureau of Motor Carriers' list of exempt and nonexempt commodities.[134]

The Administrative "Headache" of the 1935 Act: "Grandfather" Applications

Section 206(a) of the Interstate Commerce Act, which was provided in the 1935 Motor Carrier Act, said that all existing carriers on June 1, 1935, that wished to continue as such could apply for a "grandfather" certificate. The theory of this provision was that, since hereafter a certificate would be mandatory to operate as an interstate common carrier, it was only fair that all existing common carriers (at the time this requirement became effective) should automatically receive a certificate.[135] In "grandfather" applications, and only in this situation, is a specific showing of public convenience and necessity not required.[136] However, the applicant trucker under the "grandfather" clause must meet these three conditions: (1) the carrier must prove that it was in bona fide operation, over the routes applied for, consistently prior to June 1, 1935; (2) and/or, if the carrier did seasonal work, it must have rendered its service during the prior season before June 1, 1935; (3) the carrier must request its certificate within 120 days past the start of the act, or by February 12, 1936.

The 1935 Act created a massive administrative headache for the ICC; in fact, some observers wondered if the ICC was the equal of the task ahead. To this charge, the venerable Interstate Commerce Commissioner Joseph B. Eastman replied:

You may think that the ICC is old, hidebound, and railroad oriented. Maybe it is, but not to the extent that it cannot undertake a new job. The Commission will be impartial, tolerant to a degree, and anxious to serve the industries and the public. We will make mistakes. If you will point them out, they will be corrected. We will have poor judgment at times. You can take us to court. We may be deceived. If so, it is your fault. But we will never quit trying to serve you and the public to the best of our human capacity.[137]

To tackle the "grandfather" clause, the Bureau of Motor Carriers was created, as was a new ICC division, number 5. John L. Rogers, first director of the former organization, reminiscing in 1965 about the early days of the 1935 Act, made this interesting statement:

One of the most important problems was to acquaint the thousands of operators subject to the act with its provisions and their rights and obligations. Many of these operators had only one vehicle and never heard of the Commission or the Motor Carrier Act. This is illustrated by reference to a lady operator from Pennsylvania who had made no effort to comply with the act. When this was brought to her attention she said that she had belonged to the NRA but never got anything out of it and she didn't think she wanted to join the ICC.[138]

The first basic job of Division 5 was to "drum up business" for itself. As the February 12, 1936, date approached (the deadline for common carriers to protect their "grandfather" rights) only a handful of applications had been received by the ICC. Therefore, Division 5 started a comprehensive educational campaign to make sure all interested truckers knew the provisions and mandatory requirements of the 1935 Act. Apparently, they did a first-rate job because over 81,000 "grandfather" applications were filed before the deadline.[139]

After February 12, 1936, each of the above applications had to be checked by the ICC to insure their validity. Of course, there was a tremendous temptation for a carrier to ask for more routes than he had previously serviced. As one author has observed:

With such a short period of time in which to amass data, the carriers were necessarily slipshod in their petitions and thus made doubly difficult the work of the Commission. Together with these difficulties stemming from the pressure of time, the Commission very quickly realized that thousands of claims were being submitted that were wholly or partially false. Again many carriers were "asking for the moon."[140]

Many of the "grandfather" applications were processed entirely by mail, under informal procedures.[141] The more complicated proceedings required a hearing with an ICC examiner presiding. While some examiners held hearings from 9:00 A.M. to 6:00 P.M. and then from 7:00 P.M. to 10:00 P.M.,[142] the gigantic number of applications made progress appear to be very slow. Of course, as long as a trucker had made a timely filing of his "grandfather" rights, he could continue operating until his case had been fully decided by the ICC, and the courts if necessary. Finally, however, by about 1941 the great majority of cases had been terminated.[143]

In concluding this section, it should be pointed out that apparently the ICC often unduly restricted the operating rights of trucking companies that applied under their "grandfather" rights.[144] Professor James C. Nelson, testifying before the Senate Select Committee on Small Business, stated this position:

It was perhaps inevitable that certificates and permits would describe the high degree of specialization that had developed in the trucking industry. But it is exceedingly doubtful if anyone imagined that the grandfather clauses would be so interpreted that many existing carriers, the smaller ones in particular, would have their lawful operations curtailed, or that the existing pattern of operations under free entry or the regulated pattern after the carriers had been blanketed under the law would be frozen despite inconsistencies, circuitous routes, empty mileage occasioned by insufficient commodity authority for return hauls, and the lesser availability of service to shippers in the case of perhaps a majority of the regulated carriers.[145]

This situation, that of fragmented motor trucking operating rights, will be discussed later, when it is shown as a pertinent reason for merged or consolidated trucking companies.

Two Other Significant Transport Acts That Affect Trucking

The 1948 Reed-Bulwinkle Act

The Reed-Bulwinkle Act of 1948 created Section 5a of the Interstate Commerce Act. Specifically, this act authorized the use of rate bureaus or conferences for all land common carriers. However, the conferences cannot be intermodal. Each conference, besides providing a place for carriers to coordinate through routes and joint rates, has the power to set and publish uniform rates and services for its member carriers. However, each carrier that wishes to establish independent rates from the other members is guaranteed this privilege, which is known as "flagging-out" a conference rate. Finally, the Reed-Bulwinkle Act specifically provides that conferences that fully conform to the ICC's rules and procedures for them shall be exempt from the antitrust laws.

The Reed-Bulwinkle Act finally legalized what had been in effect for railroads well before the start of the Twentieth Century. In fact, the U.S. Supreme Court, in 1897[146] and 1898,[147] had declared that formal railroad rate associations were illegal under the Sherman Anti-Trust Act. The railroads, therefore, changed their procedures, so as to make them somewhat more palatable to the Justice Department, and continued the use of rate associations. The ICC appeared to accept the latter organization, at least with *de facto* status.[148]

However, the state of Georgia[149] and the Department of Justice[150] accused the Pennsylvania Railroad and the Association of American Railroads, respectively, of using rate associations to circumvent the anti-trust laws. Before the Justice Department case became finally adjudicated, Congress stepped into the picture. Professor Locklin comments that:

"It was because of the questionable legality of the rate bureaus and the general belief among carriers, shippers, and regulatory bodies that the rate bureaus performed very necessary functions in rate making that Congress passed the Reed-Bulwinkle Act in 1948, which legalized rate bureaus but placed them under the control of the Interstate Commerce Commission."[151]

It should be pointed out that the Reed-Bulwinkle Act had overwhelming support from shipping associations,[152] even though the act was originally vetoed by President Truman and subsequently had to be passed over his veto by Congress.[153]

Today, the Reed-Bulwinkle Act is a fairly noncontroversial subject. "All the historical experience and current economic thinking would seem to support the continuation of the present system."[154] One notable exception to this point of view comes from Meyer, Peck, Stenason, and Zwick. They believe that the mores that exist in transport modes generally mitigates the probability that an individual carrier will "flag-out" a rate. Therefore, flexibility and dynamic changes to an evolving situation become much slower, because the carriers are burdened with bureaucratic machinery at the conference level. In addition, rate-making carrier executives can become complacent, because the mores of the industry apparently indicate that only a "chisler" would lower his firm's rates when the other carriers do not wish to change the official conference rates.[155] This writer is generally sympathetic with these views of Meyer et al.

The 1965 "Gray Area" Act

Congress passed what most observers believed was a rather inconsequential act in 1965,[156] because it dealt mainly with the "gray area" problem. However, those familiar with transport problems realized the importance of this act, because the "gray area" operations of illegal truckers was a constant source of revenue losses to the common carrier truckers. This act, which took two years to get through Congress,[157] closed some existing loopholes and has proved to be a needed and valuable addition to the ICC's enforcement programs. Basically, this act contained five provisions, the first four of which only need to be mentioned and the fifth will be discussed in some detail.

First, the act provided the use of civil forfeiture procedures along with substantial increases in fines for illegal operations. Secondly, the bill set up better working relationships between the states and the ICC in regard to better enforcement of both safety and economic regulation. A third provision allows the ICC to prosecute both shippers and carriers, regardless of their official residence. The fourth provision provides for a more efficient way of informing states which interstate common and contract carriers are authorized to serve their respective areas.

The fifth provision, by far the most important, did not deal with the "gray area" problem but was part of the act. It corrected a basic deficiency of the 1935 Motor Carrier Act. Specifically, the act did not give the ICC power to award reparations to shippers when they had incurred injuries as a result of being charged an unreasonable and hence an unlawful rate. Locklin points out that most shippers believed, however, that they could achieve redress through the courts in this case, based on the common law.[158] However, the U.S. Supreme Court ended this belief in 1959, when it decided in the *T.I.M.E. v. United States* case[159] that the common law recovery from carriers was voided with the enactment of the 1935 Act. Therefore, from 1959 to 1965, the shipper who believed he had been damaged by an unreasonable rate had absolutely no recourse or remedy available to him. The 1965 Act corrected this situation by authorizing shippers to recover alleged damages in the courts.

Now that the development of economic regulation in the trucking industry has been surveyed, the specific provisions of the 1935 Motor Carrier Act concerning mergers and consolidations will be examined in some detail.

Merger Provisions in the 1935 Motor Carrier Act

*Congressional Hearings and Debate in Regard
to Trucking Mergers*

The House of Representatives' Committee on Interstate and Foreign Commerce held extensive hearings on a proposed bill to regulate buses and trucks in early 1934. However, the dominant issue was whether the regulation in question should exist or not; and therefore the issue of the merger provision in the act did not come up.[160]

The following year, both the Senate and the House held lengthy hearings, at about the same time, on the regulation issue. Coordinator of Transportation Joseph B. Eastman was the principal author of the 1935 Act.[161] Explaining the provisions of his act, he stated, "Another objective is control over unifications, such as we are now exercising in the case of the railroads but did not exercise until 1920."[162] Again, the major tone of these hearings was the broader question: should there be Federal regulation of interstate trucks and buses? However, one spokesman at these hearings, Charles E. Blaine (a traffic manager from Phoenix, Arizona), believed that Section 313,[163] the clause dealing with unifications, was too loosely written, because it would allow railroads to operate trucking companies under some circumstances.[164]

The House's hearings on this subject were almost a carbon copy of the Senate's, with practically no mention of the section dealing with consolidations and mergers.[165]

The Senate first debated the 1935 Motor Carrier Act, changing Section 313 to Section 213, because the water carrier regulation bill was not to be considered at this time.[166] Specifically, Senator Burton K. Wheeler, explaining the reason for Section 213 declared,

At present most truck operations are small enterprises. However, there are many rumors of plans for the merging of existing operations into sizable systems. In view of past experience with railroad and public-utility unifications, it is regarded as necessary that the Commission have control over such developments, where the number of vehicles involved is sufficient to make the matter one of more than local importance. This section, therefore, confers on the Commission jurisdiction over all consolidations, mergers, purchases, leases, operating agreements, and acquisitions of control through stock ownership where two or more motor carriers are involved or where a person other than a motor carrier undertakes to acquire control through stock ownership of two or more motor carriers, and prohibits all other forms of unification. An amendment made by the committee makes this jurisdiction applicable, except in the case of rail, express, or water carrier affiliations, only where the total number of vehicles involved is more than 20.

Carriers by rail, express, or water are permitted to consolidate or merge with motor carriers or to obtain control in any of the ways indicated above, but only on a showing that "the transaction proposed will promote the public interest and enable such a carrier other than a motor carrier to use service by motor vehicle to public advantage in its operations and will not unduly restrain competition." With this limitation, it will be possible for the Commission to allow acquisitions which will make for coordinated or more economical service and at the same time to protect the public against the monopolization of highway carriage by rail, express, or other interests.[167]

A very interesting and informative aspect of the meaning of Section 213 came out when Congressman George G. Sadowski was explaining the parts of the 1935 Act to the House of Representatives. Referring to Section 213, he declared:

I will say in this respect that it is the intent, and it is important to the welfare and progress of the motor carrier industry, that the acquisition of control of the carriers be regulated by the Commission so that the control does not get into the hands of other competing forms of transportation, who might use the control as a means to strangle, curtail, or hinder progress in highway transportation for the benefit of the other competing transportation.[168]

No additional discussion or comments were made concerning Section 213 prior to the Motor Carrier Act's passage into law on August 9, 1935. Section 213 stayed in effect until passage of the Transportation Act, 1940. At that time, Section 213 was repealed, and its provisions were basically transferred into Section 5 of Part I of the Interstate Commerce Act. In addition, Section 212(b), which had read, "Except as provided in Section 213, any certificate or permit may be transferred, pursuant to such rules and regulations as the Commission may prescribe,"[169] was changed by the 1940 Act to strike out 213 and insert Section 5.[170]

A Synopsis of the Current Provisions of
Section 5, As They Relate to Intramodal
Motor Carrier Unifications

Section 5(2) of the Interstate Commerce Act authorizes motor carriers to consolidate or merge their operations if the proposed action is found to be "in the public interest." Section 5(2) (b) authorizes the ICC to modify the proposed merger plans as may be just and reasonable, so as to make the proposed unification consistent with the public interest. Specifically, in regard to truck mergers, Section 5(2) (c) provides three basic criteria that the ICC must consider in each unification proceedings. First, the effect of the proposed transaction upon adequate transportation service for the public should be considered. Secondly, the total fixed charges of the unified company must be checked. Finally, the interest of all involved employees in the transaction must be considered. In regard to the fixed costs, the ICC cannot authorize a unification if the combined fixed costs are greater than the sum of each firm before the merger, unless the Commission finds that the increase in overall total costs will not be contrary to the public interest.

Section 5(10) contains the exemption that states that if the combining carriers have a total number of less than twenty vehicles, then this transaction does not require Commission approval under Section 5 of the Interstate Commerce Act. This section was amended by P.L. 89-93 on July 27, 1965. The new rule for exemption under Section 5 is that if the combining firms have gross operating revenues of less than $300,000 for a twelve month period before the unification, the provisions of Section 5 are voided in this case. This change in the exemption rule had previously been requested by the ICC because of difficulties that had been encountered under the old 20 vehicle rule. Specifically, Commissioner Webb stated that the new dollar maximum rule was needed, because in applying the old rule,

... numerous questions have arisen as to whether certain vehicles should or should not be included, as, for example, (a) those used in intrastate commerce, exempt transportation, or private carriage, but which are available or suitable for regulated interstate service, (b) equipment of noncarrier affiliates, (c) vehicles leased for short periods, (d) disabled vehicles, and (e) combinations of vehicles. The amount of time and effort expended in establishing the number of vehicles on which jurisdiction depends, has, where the question is close, proved to be disproportionate to the benefits intended by the exemption.[171]

Furthermore, the ICC believed that the $300,000 maximum rule would be much easier to administer, because the information needed was, in most cases, readily available from previous reports that had been filed by the involved carriers.[172] Finally, it was felt that, " ... the proposed $300,000 restriction on the exemption corresponds roughly to the present scope of the exemption in paragraph (10)."[173]

Finally, Section 5(11) exempts the approved trucking merger from the operation of the federal and state antitrust laws.[174] In addition, it should not be assumed that because the merger is not covered by Section 5, that no regulatory requirements must be fulfilled in this type of a trucking unification. If Section 5 is a moot provision, then Section 212(b) becomes the ruling proviso. This section was designed to simplify, in terms of time and expenses, the unifications of smaller trucking concerns. However, the ICC has listed a number of rules and regulations that do apply to Section 212(b) consolidations and mergers. Most of these requirements are such that they have no effect upon preventing a legitimate merger or consolidation between relatively small motor truckers. For example, the vendee (purchaser) must be fit, willing, and able to perform the service authorized by the operating rights to be transferred. In addition, the vendor's (seller's) rights must not be dormant.[175]

4

Introduction to Trucking Unifications

Brief History of the Number and Magnitude of Motor Trucking Mergers

Prior to 1935, trucking companies were free to consolidate at will, with the only legal complications being the antitrust laws. The ICC, of course, had no jurisdiction over truck mergers until the 1935 Motor Carrier Act was signed into law on August 9, 1935. There is no way of knowing the number of mergers prior to 1935, but there were probably a substantial number. A search of the literature indicates that no trucking mergers were blocked prior to 1935 on the grounds of the antitrust laws. This, of course, is logical, because the trucking industry was certainly one of the classic examples of a purely atomistic industry prior to 1935.

From 1935 to 1973. Even before interstate truckers came under Federal regulation in 1935, it had been predicted that this regulation would necessitate a consolidation movement in trucking. Joseph B. Eastman, then Federal Coordinator of Transportation, made this interesting prognostication in a Senate hearing that was discussing Federal regulation of trucking. "It is also very likely that regulation of the kind proposed will considerably increase the average size of operations, both by discouraging the smaller scale operations and by introducing greater order into the industry, so essential to planning and operation on a broad scale."[1] While Eastman stated that regulation would certainly not directly put any small truckers out of business, it would be possible that regulation would " ... set up requirements which small or poorly financed operators will not be able to meet."[2]

Apparently, Coordinator Eastman's prediction in regard to the number of trucking companies has been validated by the test of time. In 1940, there were more than 26,000 Class I, II, and III regulated motor carriers operating in interstate commerce.[3] By 1955, this number was about 18,000[4] and in 1972, there were 15,138 regulated intercity truckers.[5] Therefore, from 1940 to 1969 the number of regulated intercity motor truckers decreased on the average of 375 per year. The great majority of this decrease was due to motor carrier unification proceedings.[6] In regard to the latter, about twice as many of these unifications, between 1950 and 1956, were filed under Section 212(b) as opposed to Section 5.[7]

The mid-1950s experienced the start of the current trend to trucking unifications. In November 1955, an official of Pacific Intermountain Express stated that the then current attitude of the ICC toward trucking mergers was much more favorable than it had been five years previously.[8] Also, in April 1956 a leading financial weekly magazine proclaimed that the current wave of trucking mergers was producing financially strong carriers that operated from coast-to-coast. In fact, the article likened the trucking unification trend to what happened in the railroad industry between 1880 to 1900.[9] This observation was substantiated eight years later when Mr. William G. White, president of Consolidated Freightways, Inc., declared: "We're just about where the railroad industry was in 1880, when the era of railroad mergers and consolidations began."[10]

In the period from 1957 to 1967, the ICC approved 467 unifications that involved the 100 largest regulated interstate motor carriers.[11] However, during this time period, there were only fourteen unifications that were between carriers in the top one hundred.[12] This trend toward consolidations has led Colin Barrett to observe, "Although, there still may be some room for the 'little fellow' on the fringes of the motor carrier industry, the industry's main stream, by shifting its focus to the dominating influence of huge multimillion-dollar corporations, is rapidly following the railroads over the 'strength-by-consolidation' course they have chosen."[13]

Another interesting question in this light is the extent that trucking mergers will continue in the future. One prognosticator sees the eventual stabilization point for regulated interstate motor truckers at about 1,000 carriers, compared to the approximately 15,000 in 1969.[14] The American Trucking Associations see the future number at 10,000 to 11,000 carriers.[15] Still others believe the stabilization point to be around 200 carriers.[16] Finally, James R. Hoffa, past president of the Teamsters Union, predicts that there will be 20 transcontinental and 200 regional trucking lines by 1980,[17] and one other group of experts visualizes eight to ten Penn-Central type motor carriers in the distant future.[18]

An interesting corollary question in regard to the recent trucking merger movement is the attitude that organized labor takes in this respect. Undoubtedly, it is a safe statement to say that organized labor in the rail industry generally takes a negative attitude toward rail unification proceedings.[19] However, this is not generally the case in the trucking industry. Why? Because this industry is still growing and mergers apparently do not adversely affect labor's position.[20] The flamboyant head of the Teamsters Union gave this rationale for encouraging trucking mergers, "Look, these little companies are dying. They're not worth organizing, because you can't milk a dead cow. I want healthy companies in this industry."[21] When Hoffa was queried about his reactions in regard to unifications that decrease the number of laborers, he replied, "It's only temporary. Our experience is this: You have a merger, about a third of the workers are fired. If the merger works out, six months later all the men and then some will be back at work. In the long run, mergers create jobs."[22]

Now that the merger movement in the trucking business has been surveyed, a typical merger proceeding can be briefly examined in order to indicate the regulatory problems (or lack of them) involved in such a situation.

A Case Study – The T.I.M.E.-D.C.
Merger Proposal

In July 1967, the president of T.I.M.E. Freight, L.M. Lanotte, announced that his company had tentatively agreed to merge with D.C. International and Los Angeles-Seattle Motor Express. The new system would have a 37,000 mile route structure, and revenues of almost $150 million annually. Both T.I.M.E. and D.C. are coast-to-coast carriers and L.A.S.M.E. operates from Los Angeles to Vancouver, British Columbia.[23]

In November 1967, the three firms formally applied to the ICC for permission to consummate their merger.[24] The merger application was heard by Examiner Kenneth A. Jennings, who ruled in favor of the unification in November 1968. Jennings found the proposed merging companies to be "largely complementary." Also, he noted that while there was some duplications of operating authority (this was a typical end-to-end merger), they would be eliminated at the time of the consummation. Referring to the competition issue, Jennings declared: "There is no contention here, nor any evidence, that the proposed transaction would result in a monopoly or restrain competition. While the merger would unit three carriers—two of them large trans-continental operators—neither that alone nor service by T.I.M.E. to a large portion of the United States permits such a conclusion. To the contrary, the record indicates that numerous competitive carriers remain."[25]

Finally, Examiner Jennings stated that unless exceptions were filed, the merger could be brought to fruition thirty days after his order was served, or by December 5, 1968.[26] One exception petition was filed by Navajo Freightlines and General Expressways in concert. However, Division 3 of the ICC acted on the petition and denied its motion on December 27, 1968, less than two months after the original Examiner's report. Division 3 based its denial on the grounds that Examiner Jennings' conclusions had not been disproved.[27] Finally, the proposed new company, T.I.M.E.-D.C., was officially merged on January 17, 1969, just fourteen months after its original merger application to the ICC in November 1967.[28]

For a discussion of another very current merger case involving the Pacific Intermountain Express Co. and the Ryder Truck Lines, please see the following references.[29]

The next section will briefly discuss a significant reason for the trend of smaller trucking firms to be absorbed into larger ones.

An Explanation of Why so Many Smaller
Trucking Companies Wish to be Absorbed
into Larger Trucking Firms

The most prevalent reason in recent years that many relatively small trucking lines have desired absorption into other trucking systems is that the former firms lack desire or ability to continue as separate entities. That is, in the early days of trucking, the "Mama-Papa" type of trucking firm was the dominant type of carrier. This type of trucking company was generally started and managed by the immediate members of the family. However, as years went by and the founder of the firm died or retired, a vacuum was often left in regard to continued management of the trucking firm. Generally, the heirs to the firm didn't wish to continue in this line of business, or the ones that tried to run it were incompetent; and hence, the result was that the firm's operating rights, property, and equipment were put up for sale.[30]

Commissioner Clarke made this interesting observation in regard to what happens to the operating rights and other assets that are put up for sale.

These small businesses frequently are desirable to round out operating authorities of larger carriers, thereby enabling the latter to serve the shipping public more efficiently. In many instances, if the larger carriers were not permitted to purchase these small businesses, those who desire to sell would have no market. At other times the sale is to another small carrier, thus permitting the purchaser to grow larger. This merely parallels the history of industrial progress in America.[31]

Finally, it should not be inferred that the only reason small truckers desire to consolidate is that their owners lack interest or managerial ability in the company; because, as the next section will indicate, there are a number of significant advantages that accrue to a larger consolidated trucking firm.

A Survey of the Proposed Advantages of
Larger Consolidated Trucking Firms

Reduction in Costs

Professor Norton has observed in his text on transport economics that the unification savings from trucking mergers are less substantial than those from railroad mergers, primarily because truckers do not provide their own right-of-way, and their fixed plant facilities are much less extensive than the railroads.[32] Another reason truckers' cost savings are less spectacular than railroads' is that there are no appreciable economies of scale to be had in the trucking industry. However, as was previously indicated, larger firms often achieve better load-factors; and hence, they are able to reduce the cost per unit sold. In concluding this point, while substantial economies of scale do not exist in producing a unit of capacity, a vehicle-mile; presumably in some cases significant economies do exist in producing a unit of service, a ton-mile, because of increased load-factors that probably are a result of improved service advantages.[33]

Besides the above cost reductions, another area that is often singled out as a significant advantage to consolidated motor carriers is the increased feasibility of specialized staff personnel. As Mr. James E. Pinkney, vice-president of Ryder Truck Lines, has pointed out, "We have been weak in staff functions of these kinds (research, finance, law, and safety) because of our small corporate structures in the motor carrier field, and, by acquiring sufficient resources, we have been able, many of us, to augment our specialized staffs and for the first time to get into worthwhile research. . . ."[34]

Additional areas of cost savings are the following: reduced insurance costs by self-insurance, consolidation of terminals (if there are any in common over the new route structure), and better access to the capital markets.[35] Referring to the latter point, Professor Wilson made this penetrating observation:

. . . in a general era of inflation with money tight and interest rates high, it does not take much prescience to decide which firms will have the easiest time obtaining funds for expansion. . . . Present and future capital needs in the motor carrier industry involve primary reliance upon external financing; and under present institutional arrangements the larger firms with long records of profitable, responsible operation will inevitably receive priority and preferred treatment. The small firm is in general a reminder to many financial institutions of the rough and tumble, slightly chaotic and largely unstable conditions which characterized motor transportation in the late 1920s and 1930s. It is the large firm with modern facilities, including data-processing equipment, which conjures up those visions of permanence and stability so essential to the credit-seeker.[36]

One final area of significant cost savings made feasible by larger size is the use of a computer system.[37] As one trucking executive declared, "Computers were invented for us. They make it possible to keep track of your trucks, of who's carrying what and where the guy is, of what terminal is overloaded and what terminal isn't. You can reroute trucks while they are still on the highways. You can figure out which truck is cheaper to reroute."[38]

Finally, it should be pointed out that the venerable Joseph B. Eastman probably foresaw many of the above techniques to reduce trucking costs, because he stated in 1935 that there would be " . . . a development of larger operations, because I believe that they will be more economical when well organized."[39]

Improvement in Service

The second and more important advantage in favor of trucking mergers is the accompanying increase in customer service standards.[40] Specifically, the prime advantage of trucking consolidation is that it enables a shipper to have one carrier service from city A to city B. Referring to this point, former ICC Commissioner Anthony F. Arpaia has observed that there " . . . is not a shipper in this country who would not prefer to have [a] single-line haul."[41] From the shippers' point-of-view, this is certainly preferable to a multi-carrier arrangement, for these reasons: the goods are less physically handled, so there is less chance for damage and pilferage; because interlining is eliminated, the goods should spend less time in transit; tracing is much easier; and loss and damage claims are usually paid faster.[42]

The second major reason that consolidated truckers can offer better service is that they tend to be stronger financially. For example, Meyer and his associates stated that the best argument for motor carrier mergers is that they have the probability of creating " . . . a stable, more dependable, financially stronger industry that would be better able to execute its duties and compete as a common carrier."[43] Along these same lines, Mr. Allan C. Flott of the American Trucking Association stated that a consolidated trucking firm, by means of an end-to-end merger, is better diversified on a geographical basis. Therefore, the firm would still be able to render adequate service to *all* its customers, even if one area of its system was in a locally depressed area.[44]

A Possible Drawback to Trucking Mergers

Professor Healy is concerned that the consolidated motor carriers may suffer from bureaucratic tendencies of stagnation. Specifically, he has challenged, "The risks are great that a general merger movement, by eliminating strong, medium and small-sized firms from, or weakening their participation in rate-making processes would remove an important protection for the economic community against failure of carriers to pass on to it the advantages of new technologies and to make reasonably rapid adjustment to changing locational factors."[45] This position is fully supported by Nelson's analysis of trucking mergers.[46]

The Methodology of the Forthcoming Case Study Analysis

To obtain the raw material for the next sections, it was necessary to read a large number of representative ICC cases dealing with intramodal trucking mergers. The methodological problem was, of course, to decide how many cases, and which specific ones, should be read and briefed in order to discuss accurately the topics of the following sections. It was initially decided that it would not be feasible or desirable to read *all* the cases contained in the 29 volumes of the *Interstate Commerce Commission Reports, Motor Carrier Cases, Finance Reports.* To substantiate this decision, even the ICC has declared, "The most time-consuming, expensive and burdensome method is a complete count or 'census' of all items within the group being studied. . . . In many instances, it is neither necessary nor practical to conduct a complete census-type study."[47]

The next question, then, was to decide upon a method of selecting "representative" cases that would illustrate the ICC's policies, attitudes, et cetera, toward motor carrier unifications. At first, it was decided to consult all known texts that discussed this subject and then read the cases that were referenced in these books. However, this plan was immediately abandoned for two basic reasons. First, it soon became obvious that a definite bias would be built into the study, because only cases that other authors believed were significant would be read. In other words, this writer would only read cases that had previously been "filtered" from the mass of pertinent cases by other authors. To remove this bias, it appeared that the present researcher would have to go directly to the cases, without any "middlemen" to prejudice the selection of his cases. In addition, a second difficulty also arose, which was that the dearth of recent texts in motor carrier economics would allow only a few references to relatively current (1965-1973) trucking merger cases.

To solve these problems, it was decided that an appropriate sampling procedure must be executed. As the ICC has observed, "Properly drawn, a study using sampling procedures permits logical inferences to be drawn about the characteristics of an entire body of information by examining and processing only a small portion."[48] Specifically, it was decided that a simple random sampling plan would be appropriate. The primary requirement of a simple random sample is that each and every element in the universe, as defined, has an equal chance of being selected.[49] As the latter statement implies, three basic conditions must be fulfilled before valid simple random sampling can be accomplished. First, the universe to be sampled from must be accurately defined. In the universe used in this paper, the following case report types were excluded from those found in the *Interstate Commerce Commission Reports, Motor Carrier Cases, Finance Reports:* (1) cases involving motor carriers of passengers, (2) cases dealing with the merging of a railroad controlled motor carrier,[50] (3) cases where water carriers attempt to unify with motor carriers, (4) cases that report the Commission's findings in regard to carrier applications for the issuance of stock or notes, (5) ICC investigation of control cases, and (6) carrier applications to pool freight. In other words, this study will only deal with intramodal trucking unifications.

A second basic condition for random sampling is that the universe, as defined, must be representative of the entire area that conclusions are to be drawn about.

In the instant analysis, the problem was the following: while an extremely large number of ICC merger cases involving trucking companies are printed, a substantial number of such cases are decided each year that are *not* printed in the official ICC report volumes. Therefore, the question became: are the cases that are printed fully representative, typical, and illustrative of those cases that are not printed? Because of the serious bias that this issue could inject into the study, a letter explaining the problem was written to the Chairman of the ICC, George M. Stafford, on March 28, 1970. Chairman Stafford answered the letter promptly on April 6, 1970. In regard to a query on what criterion or criteria are used when deciding if a trucking unification case will be printed or not, Stafford declared:

The determination of whether the Commission report should be printed usually depends on the precedent-making nature of the case or what seems to be its significance from a transportation standpoint rather than its importance to the immediate parties to the case. In view of the delegation by the Commission to Employee Boards, composed of experienced staff attorneys, of decision making in the more routine cases, those proceedings which are reserved to the entire Commission or its three decision-making Divisions for decision fall into the important or precedent-making class. Those decided by the Employee Boards are, for the most part, matters in which the precedents have been long established and where printing of the reports at this late date, where the law is well-established, would be cumulative as well as expensive.[51]

Finally, in reference to the question about a bias being injected because of the printed cases being unrepresentative, Chairman Stafford replied: "I do not believe that any problem is being presented by an absence of sampling of nonprinted cases for the reason that those which have been printed in the bound volumes of the Commission's reports discuss the same issues that are repetitive in the cases which today are not printed in full."[52]

The third requirement for simple random sampling is that each element in the universe, as defined, must be assigned a specific individual number. If the universe elements are not already numbered, all that is necessary is that each element can be *conceptually* numbered, which was the procedure used in this study.[53] To accomplish this specific numbering of each relevant case in the universe, the following procedure was used. The first case dealing with intra-modal trucking unifications was assigned number 0001, the second case number 0002, and so on through all the 29 volumes of *Interstate Commerce Commission Reports, Motor Carrier Reports, Finance Reports.*[54] The last case to be included in the universe was assigned number 2,340, appearing in volume 116 at page 1 of the motor carrier reports, having been served on March 8, 1972.

The next basic question was how many cases should be picked at random to be read from the population of about 2,300 relevant cases? This question was answered after considerable thought and consultation with experts in both transport economics and quantitative analysis. The figure of 450 cases was selected because it appeared to be a reasonable number to both groups of experts. Professor Herbert Arkin gives a lucid statement about the problem of selecting an appropriate sample size:

Statistical techniques provide the method by which the appropriate sample size can be selected by using the proper statistical formulas or even more simply by resorting to statistical tables such as those included in this book. *However, the process of determining sample size is not a mechanical operation. It requires considerable thought and judgment on the part of the auditor* [researcher]. (Emphasis added.)[55]

Therefore, the figure of 450 cases was first selected after careful thought and then it was confirmed by the use of a statistical table, as mentioned by Professor Arkin above. To be extremely conservative, the value of p (the expected rate of occurrence in the population) was set equal to 0.50. As Arkin has observed,

Thus, one possible solution would be to solve the above formula, using $p = .50$. This would always result in a conservative statement of sample reliability. Conversely, the solution of the formula to determine the sample size required to achieve a specified sample reliability would always give the largest sample necessary to achieve the objective. If p is actually some value other than .50 (or 50%), the sample size would then result in a better reliability than that specified.[56]

Using a p value of 0.50, a confidence level of 95 percent, a population size of 2,300, and a reliability of plus or minus 3 percent, the sample size required can be found directly in one of Arkin's tables, being equal to 729. If a reliability of plus or minus 4 percent was needed, a sample size of 476 would be required. With reliabilities of plus or minus 5 percent and 7 percent, the required sample sizes are 329 and 181, respectively.[57] Hence, it appeared that a reasonable compromise in this situation would be to select 450 cases at random.

To choose the specific 450 cases to read, a table of random numbers was used.[58] Four hundred and fifty numbers were found, using proper random table selection procedures, numbering less than or equal to 2,340. These cases were then read and briefed. It should be noted that occasionally a case selected would have to be disqualified, because it was not properly thrown out on the initial scanning designed to discard all cases not relevant to this study. In this situation, a new case number was drawn from the table of random numbers.

Finally, in regard to the case selection methodology, it was realized that some cases of extreme importance would undoubtedly not be chosen in the simple random sample. Therefore, a procedure was established to catch these "key" cases so that they could be read, briefed, and used in the analysis. Specifically, it was decided that in reading the 450 cases chosen at random, each case cited by the ICC in their decision would be noted. Any case referred to five more times would be known as a "key" case and included in the analysis, along with the 450 cases selected at random. A list of these "key" cases, as determined by the above criterion, is included in Appendix A of this study.

The following analysis of the ICC's attitudes and findings toward trucking unifications will be based exclusively on the 450 cases selected at random and the "key" cases that were also read. In other words, no attempt was made to secure additional references to other cases on each topic discussed. This was done because it was felt that enough cases had been read and briefed to be fully able to discuss the ICC's position on each issue and to be able to cite illustrative cases to support each generalization drawn by the author.

Finally, it should be specifically noted that only illustrative cases will be cited on each issue and that no attempt was made to cite each case that dealt with the topic under discussion.

5

The Reasons for ICC Approval of Trucking Mergers and Consolidations[1]

Improvement in Service

Improved service is the most widely acknowledged reason given by the ICC for authorizing trucking unifications. It can safely be said that this factor was mentioned by the Commission in well over 75 percent of all cases surveyed in which the transaction was authorized. Many types of improved service have been enumerated by the ICC, with the most important being: faster service, more and better timed schedules, decreased loss and damage, better available equipment; and faster tracing. These advantages and other less significant ones will be briefly discussed on the following pages.

Faster Service

One of the problems inherent in a national trucking system composed of thousands of separate firms is the interchange delay that takes place at points on their respective route structures. The respite takes place when trucker A transfers either his cargo or his loaded trailer to trucker B, who is authorized to haul the lading either towards its final destination or directly to it. Single-carrier service can avoid these delays between markets, and that is why single-carrier service is the most frequently mentioned advantage of unified trucking companies. Thus, in an early case, the ICC noted with approval that the single-line service to be made available between Dallas and Corpus Christi would save approximately eighteen hours over the former schedules.[2] In another proceeding, the Commission stated that the elimination of the present interchange at New York City would shorten transit time approximately twenty-four hours between Eastern city points.[3] In a November 1941 decision, the ICC observed that the proposed unification would allow over night service from Memphis to Nashville in lieu of the former second-morning delivery schedule.[4]

It should not be inferred that the time savings are always measured in mere hours, because in fact they are often of substantial magnitude. In a 1950 decision, the Commission stated that, "Under the unified rights, the interchange would be eliminated and a savings of from 1 to 4 day's time in transit on traffic moving between Milwaukee and Ohio points would be effected."[5] In another case, the unified trucking operation would be able to save approximately one week by eliminating the interchange delay at Toledo on shipments from the Chicago area to Cleveland.[6]

Another reason single-carrier service can offer expedited transit is that the delays often involved in dealing with irregular-route interchange partners can be eliminated. Thus, the ICC has noted, "In some instances traffic destined to the area has been held until sufficient tonnage to justify a trip has accumulated, which condition would be alleviated under the regular scheduled operations proposed by the vendee."[7] In a similar case decided in 1963, the Commission's decision was influenced by the fact that when the operations of the vendor were temporarily controlled and operated by the vendee under Section 210a (b)[8] of the Interstate Commerce Act, the average transit time from Kingsport, Tennessee, to Chicago and Indiana points was reduced from six days to a minimum of two days. This substantial time savings was due to the policy of the vendee of transporting all traffic tendered the same day it was received.[9]

In summary, the ICC has consistently found that expedited trucking service is a factor that deserves considerable weight in deciding if a transaction is consistent with the public interest.[10] Hence, the ICC has typically declared, "The shipping public is entitled to the improved and more expeditious service which would result from these transactions."[11] Finally, in a 1966 case involving the consolidation of four trucking firms, the Commission issued this lucid statement that well summed up their position, *ceteris paribus*, in regard to expedited single-carrier service. "Consummation of the transaction under section 5 and consolidation and merger of the various applicants into one entity . . . would result in the performance of Motor Lines of a single-line through service in lieu of the interline service now existing, resulting in more efficient and expeditious service to the shipping public. Such is the public interest."[12]

More and Better Timed Schedules

The service advantages that accrue from more frequent and better timed scheduling are very similar to the advantages of faster service. In a 1941 case the Commission noted with approval that the vendee proposed to add at least one round trip daily to the vendor's present schedule between Kansas City and Tulsa.[13] In another authorized case, the acquiring carrier doubled the number of schedules per week to northern Minnesota cities.[14]

A corollary of more schedules is better timing of departures and arrivals after the vendee acquires the vendor's operations. Specifically, the Commission has looked with favor on cases where the vendee would carefully plan arrivals and departures to coordinate through expedited movements over its authorized system.[15] Thus, the ICC has remarked in another case, "Schedules on applicants' north-south line would be closely coordinated with its east-west schedules to facilitate interchange."[16]

Reduced Loss and Damage

The possibility of freight being damaged is significantly increased as it is handled more often. Hence, when cargo must be interchanged with another trucker, particularly on small shipments that are unloaded at the interchange point and reloaded on to the connecting carrier's vehicle, the chance of it becoming damaged increases proportionately. For example, the ICC has noted favorably the need for a shipper to have single-carrier service, because his yarn products were easily damaged by transfer in transit.[17] The same reasoning was noted in an oilfield equipment hauling case, in which physical interchange at intermediate points was said to create a situation highly conducive to damaging the expensive and sophisticated equipment.[18]

Another way freight damage can be reduced is by more attention to this problem by the acquiring carrier. In a 1954 case the ICC noted that Pacific Intermountain Express would undoubtedly reduce the damage claim ratio of the vendor by initiating P.I.E.'s sound program of claim prevention.[19]

Less theft and pilferage is another service advantage that accrues to truckers who offer single-line service, because the occurrence of this problem greatly increases as interchanging of cargo between truckers takes place. The Commission has taken cognizance of this service advantage in a number of unification proceedings.[20]

Better Available Equipment

The availability of adequate equipment in reasonable quantities is a factor that is often mentioned by the Commission in regard to an improved transportation service. In a very early case, the ICC took notice that the vendee would provide more adequate and appropriate equipment and then stated that, "...the acquisition will further be advantageous to the public in that the service theretofore performed by vendor will be continued by a carrier equipped to furnish a better grade of service than can be provided by vendor."[21] In another case, the Commission looked with favor on a situation in which the vendor operated in the mountainous area between California and Nevada, and the acquiring carrier offered improved four-wheel drive equipment that was especially advantageous in the winter months.[22] The availability of more modern equipment and a larger variety of vehicles is often mentioned by the ICC as an important way that an improved service can be rendered to the public.[23]

Another factor in regard to equipment is its accessibility. Thus, the Commission took official notice of a situation in which shippers required specialized liquid bulk equipment and the vendee had the needed vehicles but more importantly had it physically located near the shippers, so that the equipment could be provided within a few hours after it was requested.[24]

Tracing Advantages

Tracing refers to a procedure to determine the location of goods that have been tendered to a carrier but have become lost or delayed in transit. Hence, one advantage of a unified trucking company offering one-carrier service from city A to city B is that it can offer the shipper the potential of needing less tracing. That is, the possibility of freight being lost and/or delayed generally increases significantly when freight must be interlined between two or more carriers because of the problems involved when there is divided responsibility for the delivery of shipments on time.[25]

A second advantage of unified trucking service that the ICC has taken official notice of is that if the shipment does become lost or delayed, the tracing service available is much faster. This again is possible because of the communication problems involved when two or more carriers are responsible for the timely arrival of a shipment.[26]

Miscellaneous Service Advantages

The following types of service advantages available to a consolidated trucking company have been mentioned by the Commission in unification proceedings, but less frequently than the above listed factors.

One advantage of a consolidation can be the acquiring of better management which will be able to offer the shipping public a better service. Thus in a 1939 decision, the ICC remarked that the "Vendor is inexperienced in the transportation business, and his principle interests are in other fields. Applicant's personnel is experienced in transportation of liquid petroleum products, and it would be able to render an improved service to the public."[27]

Faster payment of loss and damage claims is mentioned occasionally, because there is no argument over which interlining carrier was responsible for the situation.[28]

A final obvious, but little thought of advantage to consolidated trucking firms exists when both of the merger partners had previously served either the same shippers or consignees. Specifically, because only one vehicle must now report to consignees, it decongests their shipping or receiving docks, respectively.[29]

Revive Failing Trucking Firms

A very prevalent factor in many unification proceedings is that the vendor is in serious financial difficulty. In most cases, he is generally so low on working funds that he lacks enough capital to make needed improvements in his physical plant and equipment. In extreme cases, the vendor is in such financial straits that the continuation of his operation as a for-hire carrier is in doubt. In this section, the Commission's policy toward reviving these failing trucking firms will be surveyed. It should be noted that often the Commission's motive in its unification approvals is to assure that the shipping public will continue to receive the transport service they have come to depend on. Furthermore, when the vendor's service has deteriorated, the ICC wishes to see it built back to a consistently high level of service quality, such as the Commission has found to be definitely in the public interest.

Capital Shortage

The dominant situation here involves a vendor who lacks adequate capital to render a satisfactory service to the shipping public. Thus, in an early merger proceeding, the Commission noted that while the vendor, Seaboard Freight Lines, had been offering commendable service considering the facilities at its command, its overall service level had not been adequate to meet the needs of its shippers. This situation could be corrected because of the superior financial strength of the vendee, Keeshin Transcontinental Freight Lines.[30] Similarly, the vendor in another case had such a lack of equipment that he often had to reject traffic tendered to the firm. Again, as in all these types of cases, the vendors' superior financial strength would eradicate the problem.[31] In a consistent series of cases,[32] the ICC has affirmed its desire to help weak carriers unify with stronger ones when the net result will be an improved service to the public. A typical statement by the Commission is the following: "Operations of vendor and its predecessor have been handicapped by lack of capital, and vendor is financially unable to replace equipment necessary to render adequate and efficient service. Applicant, on the other hand, has sufficient equipment and working capital to provide an adequate, dependable, and efficient public service."[33]

Finally, it should not be assumed that the problem of financially weak vendors occurred only in the early years of economic regulation. Witness, for example, this ICC statement in a unification decision decided in May, 1969: "There seems to be no argument with the fact . . . that Dance's deteriorating financial condition warrants its transfer to another viable carrier. . . ."[34]

Cessation of Vendor's Operations

In extreme cases, the vendor's financial difficulties are so severe that if the proposed merger is not consummated, the vendor's operations will necessarily cease. The ICC generally takes the position, *ceteris paribus*, that this situation would not be in the public interest, because it would work an undue hardship on the shipping public that currently depends on the vendor's transportation service. An early example of this policy is illustrated by this Commission's statement and finding:

Vendor's operation provided the only regular daily truck service to the small communities south of Toledo and afforded delivery from 24 to 48 hours faster than available rail service. Being apprehensive of the additional responsibilities required of operators under Federal regulation, vendor contemplated abandonment of his line, but was prevailed upon by applicant to continue the service for a sufficient period to permit transfer of the intrastate rights. The unification would assure the shipping public of a continued common-carrier truck service with the added advantages of applicant's superior facilities and operating methods.[35]

In another case the ICC gave considerable weight to the fact that if the vendor failed, eighteen New Hampshire and Vermont communities would suffer disadvantages and inconveniences.[36] A case during World War II was influenced by the fact that the vendor was a significant hauler of iron and steel products necessary for the country's defense needs and that cessation of its operations would have a detrimental effect on the war effort.[37] In a more recent proceeding the vendor had incurred net negative profits for two consecutive years and bankruptcy appeared imminent without the financial aid of the vendee, Denver-Chicago Trucking Co., Inc. In this situation, the ICC remarked, "Approval herein would increase the possibility of its [the vendor] being able to preserve its property and facilities, and continue service to the public. The parties should be afforded the opportunity to preserve its operations."[38]

Finally, the Commission's overall attitude and predisposition towards unification proceedings that will enable the shipping public to continue to receive a service that they are dependent on is well summed up by this ICC declaration, "Consummation of the transaction would assure the public that a service which has been available for years will be continued."[39]

Operating Economies

The ICC has consistently noted with approval unification proceedings that result in more efficient trucking companies. The reason, of course, is that when a trucking company is able to achieve a lower cost per unit of operation through improved operating economies, it is possible for the firm to lower its charge to the shipping public, to increase its level of service, or at least stall off future rate increases that would have been needed in an inflationary economy.[40] Both of the latter alternatives have been found to be in the public interest according to the ICC. This section will discuss the following types of operating economies that have been enumerated in ICC unification proceedings: increased load-factors, less circuitous routes, less pick-up and delivery expenses, decreased loss and damage claims, reduced maintenance costs, consolidated terminals and other facilities, better management, and overall decreased labor costs.

Increased Load-Factors

A prime reason that trucking unifications are able to achieve increased load-factors is that their prior operating rights, granted under "grandfather" applications, were often overly restrictive in regard to the commodities and specific points that each trucker was authorized to serve.[41] In addition, changing business conditions and market locations can transform a once adequate operating authority into one that is badly out of balance, with very unfavorable load-factor ratios. This section will discuss the relationship between trucking unifications and increased load-factors in some detail, because as previously indicated[42] the key to trucking economies of scale rests on this relationship.

Better Balanced Traffic Patterns

The ICC has consistently been favorably impressed by unifications that will help to achieve a better traffic balance for the merged firm.[43] In a 1940 decision the Commission issued this typical statement: "Vendor's traffic has been preponderately south-bound into Boston, while applicant's traffic moves principally in the reverse direction. Unification of the operations would tend to equalize the movement of freight resulting in a reduction of many nonrevenue truck-miles."[44] In another case, the ICC noted that the vendee's traffic was predominately north-bound from the Illinois area to the Twin Cities of Minnesota, while the vendor's traffic pattern was the reverse. The increased load-factors that each carrier could achieve were key items in this merger being authorized.[45]

The Commission forcefully stated the following rationale for authorizing a 1951 unification: " . . . vendee and vendor are at present conducting wasteful and uneconomical transportation, with vendee operating empty equipment north-bound and vendor empty equipment south-bound. . . . Acquisition of vendor's rights . . . would afford vendee an opportunity to balance its lading north-bound and south-bound and thereby to render a more efficient service."[46] Finally, it should be noted that the ICC has generally been very impressed, *ceteris paribus*, with unifications that resulted in a better balanced traffic pattern, which in turn allowed less empty and hence wasteful truck mileage. This conclusion has been substantiated in a long series of ICC unification cases.[47]

Authority to Serve New Cities and
Commodities in the Same Area

A second very important way to achieve increased load-factors is to acquire the Commission's authority to serve new cities and to be able to transport additional commodities in the same area that the trucker already serves. Again, all other things being equal, the ICC has generally taken a favorable attitude on mergers that accomplish increased load-factors by this means. In a 1943 proceeding, the Commission authorized a merger in which the vendee received the rights to serve a large number of the intermediate points on his prior route structure that he formerly was not authorized to serve. The ICC noted that his load-factor would increase which meant that his equipment would be used more efficiently in the future.[48] Another proceeding was influenced by the fact that the vendee had authority to transport only a limited number of commodities between certain Eastern cities and Philadelphia. This situation could be corrected by purchasing vendor's general-commodity, regular-route operating rights. The Federal regulatory authority remarked that, " . . . the operating rights he proposes to purchase would substantially broaden the commodity scope of the present operations, and thereby enable him to increase the use [load] factor of the equipment he now operates."[49]

The Commission authorized a 1956 proceeding because the rights to be acquired by the vendee would fill a "gap" in its system route structure by allowing it to serve points between Tracy, Minnesota, and Mankato, Minnesota, in both interstate and intrastate commerce.[50]

In summary, the ICC has consistently recognized the importance of removing restrictions on operating rights that cause inefficient use of available equipment. Hence, in a case that was denied on other grounds, the Commission did take official notice that, "Unification of the two authorities would primarily result in vendee's rendering a direct service into an expanding area and would remove much of the burdensome restrictions now placed on its operations in that area."[51]

Authority to Serve New Points Near
the Present Route System

The third basic method for a trucking firm to increase its vehicle load-factor is to acquire authority to serve new cities that are near its previous route structure. Thus, the ICC approved a unification in which the vendee would be able to significantly broaden the destination territory that it could serve from ex barge traffic at Camden, Arkansas.[52] In another proceeding a merger was consummated in which the vendee would acquire additional territory to be served from the New York City area. The ICC noted that this additional authority would allow the vendor to increase his load-factor and in general permit more efficient use of the carriers' equipment and other facilities.[53]

A typical statement by the Commission on this subject is the following, "The proposed unification would permit elimination of such interchange and open to Holdcroft (Illinois) important sources of traffic, particularly in the Twin Cities and Kansas City areas, which is needed to balance its lading and to utilize its equipment more efficiently."[54] Finally, in a more recent case, the ICC noted with approval that the unification would allow the vendee to render service to many points contiguous to those already authorized to serve, which would result in higher vehicle load-factors.[55]

Decreased Circuitous Routes

An advantage of no small importance that often results from trucking unifications, especially of a side-by-side variety, is that the most direct route between two cities can be utilized by the new firm. In other words, assume that both vendee and vendor have authority to haul general commodities from city A to city B. However, the vendee's route is quite circuitous compared to the vendor's. In this case, the unified company would use the direct and more efficient route obtained by the merger with the vendor. Thus, in a 1938 case, the ICC approved a unification in which the acquired route of the vendor between Council Bluffs, Iowa, and Kansas City would involve a physically superior road that would reduce transit time between the two cities. In addition, the vendor's route between Kansas City and Sioux City was fifteen miles shorter. The Federal regulatory body observed that these advantages would decrease transit time and hence allow both a more efficient operation and a more satisfactory service to the shipping public.[56]

The ICC authorized a unification that allowed the vendee to acquire from the vendor a more direct route from St. Louis to Kansas City. Formerly, the vendee served these cities via Springfield, Illinois, which is about 156 miles longer than the direct route between these cities. The Commission noted with approval that the merger would reduce the operating costs per truck approximately $25 per round trip.[57]

In summary, the ICC has generally reacted favorably to unifications that can achieve less circuitous routes and hence allow a more efficient trucking service.[58]

Reduced Pick-Up and Delivery Expenses

An operating advantage that accrues to unified trucking companies that previously served the same cities is reduced pick-up and delivery expenses. This is possible because, after the unification, it is necessary for the combined firm to send only one vehicle to a particular customer or area of the town to perform pick-up or delivery service, where before *each* company would have had to send its own vehicle. The ICC commented on this operating advantage in one of its earliest trucking unification cases when it declared, "Existing separate pick-up and delivery service maintained by Seaboard and Keeshin companies in the important New York City area would be handled by one company. The tendency of this would be to avoid congestions in the streets and at the shippers' place of business. . . ."[59] In the *Associated Transport, Inc.—Control and Consolidation* case, the Commission again noted that, " . . . there would be a large reduction in the number of trucks required for peddler runs and for pick-up and delivery service at terminal points."[60]

To recapitulate, the ICC has consistently recognized the cost savings available to a unified firm by combining their pick-up and delivery services.[61]

Reduced Loss and Damage Costs

Reduced loss and damage costs are possible because the number of physical interchanges generally are reduced after the trucking unification. The ICC has always recognized that loss and damage claims are directly related to the number of interchanges needed to transport a commodity to its destination. Therefore, the Commission has constantly recognized the potential savings that a unified trucking firm would have in this area when the number of interchanges could be reduced or eliminated.[62]

The second basic method of reducing loss and damage costs is by upper management to stress the importance of keeping this expense item to a minimum. The ICC has taken official notice of this operating advantage in approving unification proceedings.[63]

Reduced Maintenance Costs

A cost reduction that is often mentioned in trucking unification cases involves reduced overall maintenance expenses. The obvious advantage of a unified company is that previously separate maintenance facilities in the same general locality can be consolidated into one organization. Once the operations are combined into a larger maintenance facility, a number of benefits accrue. First, better trained mechanics can be hired, because the increased volume of work will support them. As a corollary point, better supervisors are hired because of the increased number of mechanics that must be directed. Also, fewer spare parts are needed at the combined facility. Finally, because of the increased activity, scheduling into the various departments becomes more efficient by keeping all phases of the operation running at full capacity.[64]

To recapitulate, the ICC has typically reacted favorably to reduced maintenance costs by unified carriers. Thus, in a large consolidation case in 1942, the
Commission observed that the unified firm would allow,

Extension throughout the proposed system . . . of scientific maintenance and
safety programs, which the carriers involved have been unable to undertake to
the extent which would be possible to applicant with the combined facilities and
resources, would add to the average life of equipment and result in more
economical and safe operation and in fewer road failures. The experience, and
the garage and testing facilities of Consolidated and Horton, would be of
material assistance in carrying out such a program.[65]

Elimination of Duplicate Terminals

A cost saving that is consistently enumerated by the ICC as a substantial plus
factor in trucking unifications is the consolidation of terminals in cities where
each of the prior firms had maintained separate facilities.[66] This kind of
consolidation can often be accomplished because the terminal to be retained can
probably handle the added traffic of the phased out terminals by more efficient
scheduling of arrivals and departures. In other cases, the use of separate
terminals would be changed, such as having one facility for inbound shipments
and another for outbound shipments. The latter concept was suggested by
Associated Transport, Inc., in order to reduce congestion and confusion in the
handling of shipments.[67]

The Commission gave an excellent summary of other operating advantages to
the carrier and the shipping public in the *Associated Transport* case.

Consummation of the proposed transactions would result in substantial economies in terminal expense, and, through more efficient use of facilities, would
expedite the movement of traffic. Additional terminals would be established at
some points where there is at present insufficient traffic accruing to any one of
the carriers to justify its maintaining such facilities. This would be of convenience to shippers in those localities. Some of the carriers, particularly Transportation, have been using poor terminal facilities because they have not had
sufficient capital or credit to undertake construction of proper terminals, or to
interest private capital in such construction. This has materially increased the
cost of operation. With the resources available to applicant, it would be able to
remedy that situation.[68]

Reduced Interchanging Expenses

An operating advantage that has previously been implied is that as the need for
interchanging of traffic is decreased, so obviously is its attendant expenses.
Again, the Commission has often taken official notice of this merger advantage
in numerous proceedings.[69] In a 1939 case the ICC approved a unification in

which a savings of $5,000 per year was projected because the previous interchange costs at Akron, Ohio, could be eliminated.[70]

Managerial Advantages

There are two basic types of managerial advantages that are feasible from a trucking unification. The first involves the possibility of acquiring more sophisticated and competent upper management for the newly enlarged firm. Secondly, the number of upper management positions can be generally decreased, and this often represents substantial savings.

More Competent Managers. The ability of the unified firm to command a higher quality of upper managerial positions has often been recognized by the Commission as an advantage of consolidation. The ICC, especially in the earlier cases, often observed that the managers of the acquiring firm were of superior quality and had greater knowledge of the trucking industry; and hence, they were better able to run the unified firm more efficiently and to give the shipping public a better quality of service.[71] Thus, the Commission noted in one case that the vendee, N.D. McCue, had been in the trucking industry for twenty-nine years, and that for eleven of those years he had operated his own trucking business. The ICC then noted with approval that, "He [McCue] is of the opinion that vendor has not given his operation the attention it deserves, which the latter admits, and is 'positive' that vendee, through the purchase and under his supervision and control, will be able to develop and handle a substantially greater volume of freight at a lesser cost than vendor."[72]

Reduced Upper Managerial Costs. The second managerial advantage is that the number of upper managerial positions can often be consolidated after the trucking unification. For example, the combined firm will only need one president, where at least two existed prior to the unification. The same argument, of course, is true for other key positions in the organizational structure. Again, the ICC has consistently taken cognizance of this cost reducing situation.[73] It is interesting to note the range of the dollar magnitude that this cost saving factor can represent. In a 1954 case[74] this savings was estimated at only $4,500 per year, while in a 1961 proceeding,[75] about $100,000 per annum was the projected savings made possible by decreased top management salaries.

Reduced Labor Costs

The effect of a trucking unification on the carriers' employees is an area that the ICC is specifically charged with in considering trucking consolidation cases.[76] In general, after a unification the labor force is not greatly reduced. Specifically, routine assignments that are staffed by clerks are the most vulnerable to being phased out of the operation (the reasons for this will be enumerated in the following section), while the number of truck drivers is seldom affected by the merger consummation. This results from the basic autonomy of the individual truck or tractor-trailer unit, which always requires a driver. In other words, while at first a small percentage of drivers may be released as schedules are consolidated, this often will only be the short-term consequence. If the merger results in an increased quality of service to the shipping public, which it should, then the unified carrier will start to experience an increased volume of business. As this takes place, more truck schedules are added, and hence the number of drivers employed generally reaches its prior level rapidly and often surpasses the former level.

It should be pointed out that in the majority of cases that have been read and briefed by this researcher, it was found that the labor force had not significantly decreased.[77] However, in a few cases, the number of personnel has decreased, especially office and clerical workers.[78] In these cases, the ICC has typically stated, "Present employees of Michigan Motor would be retained, except where efficiency measures and the consolidation of functions reduce the need for certain types of personnel. The resulting improvement in service, in our opinion, would outweigh the possible loss by some employees of their positions."[79] In another, the Commission followed a similar line of reasoning when they declared, "It is proposed that all qualified personnel of the two carriers be retained. Realization of some of the estimated economies may result in some adverse effect on carrier employees. However, no employee or his representative has intervened in the proceedings or expressed any opposition, and the evidence showing that the transaction is in the public interest outweighs any potential adverse effect on carrier employees."[80]

Finally, it should not be assumed that the ICC always takes a passive position in regard to employees that are adversely affected by trucking unifications. In a 1961 proceeding the Commission ordered that the vendee pay three months severance pay to any employee of either the vendor or the vendee who lost his job as a result of the unification.[81] A 1963 merger proceeding involved a situation where a number of general and supervisory officers lost their positions, along with two over-the-road drivers. The latter two employees, however, asked the ICC to intervene in their favor. To this request, the ICC declared, "Helm [the vendee] is financially able to consummate the transaction, but its condition is not sufficiently affluent to warrant an undue financial drain upon its resources. On the evidence adduced we do not consider that the protesting employees were unfairly treated or have been adversely affected by the transaction to such an extent as to warrant the award of compensation."[82] The Commission also noted that in reaching the above decision, they had taken official notice of the fact that no employee or his representative had originally opposed the transaction or had requested that any sort of protective conditions be imposed upon the unified firm.[83] However, the ICC stated that it would follow a precedent used in other motor carrier Section 5 proceedings of retaining jurisdiction over the merged company for a period of 2 years past the consummation date, in order to make additional findings and impose such terms and conditions as may be required to protect the employees of the company.[84]

Finally, in a very recent case, the ICC restated emphatically that it does have jurisdiction over the question of employee treatment in trucking unifications.[85] Furthermore, the Commission remarked, " . . . the interest of carrier employees affected is one of the factors which we are expressly enjoined by the act to consider in passing upon the merits of each section 5 proceedings, and to this end our application form for approval of a transaction requires an affirmative statement by an acquiring applicant as to the effect of the transaction upon the interests of carrier employees affected."[86]

Now that the operating economies and advantages in favor of a consolidated trucking company have been discussed, the next section will enumerate the administrative benefits of a unified firm.

Administrative Advantages

There are four primary administrative advantages that the ICC has recognized in favor of unified trucking firms. These four plus factors are: purchasing discounts, decreased paper work, lower insurance costs, and decreased costs of financing. Each of these topics will now be examined.

Purchasing Discounts

The ICC has consistently recognized the administrative advantage of purchasing commodities in large quantities and hence receiving an appropriate purchase discount. A spectacular illustration of a quantity discount available prior to the 1936 Robinson-Patman Act[87] was given in the *Keeshin Transcon. Freight Lines, Inc.—Control—Seaboard* case.[88] In this proceeding, the ICC noted that the vendor was paying about $2,000 to $2,200 for semi-trailers. However, the Keeshin Company in 1935 was paying (because of its large quantity purchases) only $1,080 for trailers of a superior quality.[89] Quantity discounts after the Robinson-Patman Act are still of importance, although the magnitude of the price reduction for quantity purchases has been moderated in many cases. Nevertheless, the ICC has taken official cognizance of the price reductions possible because of quantity purchases in a long series of cases.[90] Thus, in a 1952 proceeding, the Commission noted that the vendor was so short of working capital that he was not able to take advantage of the discounts available from quantity purchases. However, when the merger was authorized on a temporary basis under Section 210 a (b), the new firm arranged to purchase their supplies at a savings of 15 to 20 percent less than the vendor had previously paid.[91]

Less Paper Work

A significant administrative advantage of unified firms is that the relative amount of paperwork for the combined firm is less than the total that each firm incurred separately before the consolidation. For example, the following costs are often pointed out as illustrative of this situation: tariff publishing costs, accounting costs, general administrative record expenses, billing costs, and regulatory reporting expenses. These savings are often referred to together by the ICC and are seldom singled out individually. In other words, when they are combined, they do represent a significant cost reduction for the unified firm. For example, in a 1939 merger proceeding involving the Consolidated Forwarding Company, the Commission noted that the proposed transaction would, " ... permit economies in operation through elimination of duplicate tariffs, personnel, accounting, and other separate functions, including corporate taxes and separate reports to regulatory authorities."[92] It should be noted that the ICC has consistently recognized this administrative advantage of unified trucking firms.[93]

Lower Insurance Costs

The third administrative savings often made possible by a trucking unification is decreased insurance costs. One reason these costs decrease is that as terminals and other facilities are consolidated, the insurance costs decrease because there are fewer buildings that need insurance protection. This factor has often been noted by the ICC.[94] A second basic reason is that if the vendee has previously had an exemplary safety record in regard to his trucking company, it is often possible for the combined firm to qualify for insurance rates lower than the vendor previously paid.[95]

Reduced Financing Costs

The final basic administrative advantage that can accrue to a unified firm is reduced financing costs. This is generally possible because the vendee is financially stronger and more stable than the vendor, and hence the combined firm can qualify for more favorable financing. Thus, in an early case, the ICC noted that the vendor, in 1936, was paying 4 percent interest on its loans, while the vendee, Keeshin Transcontinental Freight Lines, was paying only 2 per-cent.[96] The advantage of reduced financing costs has been recognized by the ICC as an advantage of larger, financially more stable firms in a number of merger proceedings.[97]

Corporate Simplification

The ICC has always sought to achieve simplified corporate structures in Section 5 trucking merger proceedings. The Commission believes that this policy is in the public interest because it simplifies regulation and eliminates the economic waste of maintaining separate companies that are commonly controlled. A typical ICC observation on this subject is the following, "In view of the present common control and management, the maintenance of separate corporations would be wasteful and serve only to increase operating costs without compensating advantages to the public."[98] In another case, where both trucking firms were owned by the same stockholders and operated in the same basic area, the Commission declared that, under these circumstances, the present maintenance of separate corporate structures served no useful purpose. In addition, because substantial savings would be available to the unified firm in regard to consolidated accounting, regulatory reports, and other duplicate functions, the transaction was authorized by the ICC.[99]

Occasionally, there are exceptions to the Commission's policy of encouraging corporate simplification. For example, a 1947 proceeding involved a situation where the corporate structure of the various carriers involved became more complex by means of additional holding companies being interjected into the chain of control. The ICC noted that this procedure was contrary to their policy of corporate simplification, but authorized the consolidation because of the extenuating circumstance that all the companies involved were Canadian corporations that were domiciled and operated primarily in Ontario, Canada.[100]

To summarize the ICC's basic position towards corporate simplification, witness this Commission's statement in regard to a unification of a number of separate trucking firms into a consolidated company,

"Many duplications exist in the operations of the carriers involved. Maintenance of separate corporations under common control, rendering substantially the same service, frequently has been condemned by us as wasteful. Indeed, we would be unwilling to authorize acquisition of control of the carriers involved, if each were to continue its separate existence and duplicating operations under common control."[101]

In closing this section, it should be noted that the ICC has consistently favored and encouraged corporate simplification in Section 5 trucking unification proceedings.[102]

6

The Competitive Issues in Trucking Unification Cases

The Intermodal Competitive Question in Trucking Unifications

The issue regarding the effect of trucking unifications on intermodal competitors, primarily railroads, appears to be less significant today than it was in the earlier days of trucking regulation. However, the ICC still takes cognizance of the effect of trucking mergers on other modes when it considers the broad question of whether the overall transaction is in the "public interest." This section will survey the basic attitude of the Commission on this important facet of trucking unification proceedings.

Early Commission Statements

The earliest ICC trucking merger proceedings did not put too much stress on the fact that the railroads may lose some tonnage as a result of the trucking unification. For example, in a 1938 decision, the ICC summarily denied the railroads' protest that they would be adversely affected by the proposed trucking merger.[1] In another 1938 case the Commission curtly replied to the railroad protestants as follows, "Protesting rail carriers contend existing through rail service is adequate and that applicant may not institute a competitive operation in this manner, except upon proof of public convenience and necessity. We have rejected similar contentions in other cases, and do so here."[2]

This rather unsympathetic attitude toward the effect of trucking unifications on railroads was dramatically reversed in one of the truly landmark trucking unification proceedings—the so-called *P.I.E.-Keeshin* cases of 1950 and 1951.[3]

The P.I.E.-Keeshin Cases

The two *P.I.E.-Keeshin* unification proceedings are of such landmark importance to both this section and future sections that each case will be briefly surveyed before drawing out the features pertinent to the instant discussion.

81

The First ICC Decision

The initial case, formally known as *Pacific Intermountain Exp. Co.–Control and Purchase*,[4] was decided by the ICC on November 6, 1950. In this proceeding, P.I.E. proposed to purchase a bankrupt trucking firm, Keeshin Motor Express.[5] At the time of this case, P.I.E. operated as a motor common carrier, basically transporting general commodities (with exceptions) on a route structure of about 10,500 miles of regular routes from San Francisco and Los Angeles on the west to Chicago and St. Louis on the east, via, in most cases, Salt Lake City, Denver, and Kansas City, Missouri.[6]

As evidence of the relatively large size of P.I.E. prior to its instant unification proceeding, the company at the start of 1950 owned 756 units of equipment, of which 201 were tractors, 433 were semitrailers, 78 were standard trucks, and 44 were service cars and other vehicles. Furthermore, it had 79 units under long-term leases, and it also leased additional equipment as needed on a single-trip basis.[7] Finally, the firm employed 1,491 employees, of which almost 400 were line-haul drivers,[8] and its gross revenue in 1949 was approximately $14,000,000.[9]

The vendor, the Keeshin trucking system, was also a relative giant in 1950. It was a common carrier of general commodities (with exceptions), and it had 15,560 miles of routes in sixteen states. In general, the firm was authorized to serve from Minneapolis-St. Paul, Des Moines, and St. Louis on the west through the central states north of the Ohio River, to cities in the East between Boston and Washington, D.C.[10] The combined Keeshin firms operated 1,412 pieces of equipment that consisted of 114 trucks, 450 tractors, 794 trailers, and 54 service trucks and other vehicles.[11] Finally, Keeshin employed about 1,500 persons and had a gross revenue of about $10,000,000.[12]

If consummated, the P.I.E.-Keeshin system would be able to provide coast-to-coast trucking service under a single management. The previous systems would basically merge at Chicago and St. Louis. It is interesting to note that this unification would have been a classical end-to-end merger, because only 2.35 percent of their combined route system miles were overlapping.[13]

It is not necessary to delve into the financial technicalities or the operating advantages of the proposed merger, because the former is not pertinent to this discussion and the latter has been previously examined (not specifically this case, but in general) in the first part of this paper.

The following discussion will deal exclusively with the topic under examination in the instant section, which is the effect of the unification on intermodal competition, i.e., railroads. This case will also be examined later, when its competitive ramifications on other trucking firms is under discussion.

In general, the rail carriers contended that the P.I.E.-Keeshin merger would have detrimental effects without compensating advantages, upon adequate transportation service to the public; that it would not foster sound economic conditions among the existing transport modes; and that it would set a dangerous precedent in regard to expanded, transcontinental trucking firms.[14] Specifically, a major contention of the railroads was that if the instant trucking merger was authorized, the effect would be a substantial diversion of highly rated traffic from the railways to the truckers. If that took place, the railroads maintained that they would be forced to increase their rates on commodities that, because of their nature, must be transported by rail. Furthermore, the rails contended that this price rise on railbound products would set in motion an undesirable cycle that would critically weaken the railroads' system, seriously damage the nation's economic stability, and weaken its military strength.[15]

One of the primary arguments used by the railroads was that the trucking firms are strictly "specialists" who do not render a complete common-carrier service to all points, but instead serve only a small portion of shippers, mostly manufacturers. On the other hand, the railroads are the only "general practitioners" who can and do transport all types of products to and from all types of transport users. Therefore, the national interests are furthered and preserved by not allowing a trucking consolidation that would weaken the railroads.[16]

The ICC denied the proposed P.I.E.-Keeshin merger, and one major factor was the probable effect of this unification on the railroads' system. A pertinent paragraph from the Commission's conclusion will now be quoted, because it clearly summarizes a basic rationale for this significant decision.

Among other things, we are charged by the national transportation policy set forth in the legislation of September 18, 1940, with the fair and impartial regulation of all modes of transportation subject to the act, so administered as to recognize and preserve the inherent advantages of each, to the end of developing, coordinating, and preserving a national transportation system adequate to meet the needs of the commerce of the United States, of the Postal Service, and of the national defense. It has long been recognized, and this record confirms it, that one important inherent advantage of rail transportation generally is the ability to transport freight in large volume for long distances at low operating costs. Another is the movement of bulk commodities which do not lend themselves readily to motor-truck transportation. The necessity for maintenance of the railroads to meet the needs of the commerce of the Nation is conceded by applicants. The soundness of the argument of the railroads that their financial strength and potential for expansion to meet the needs of national defense must be preserved is beyond question. It is apparent that neither normal needs nor emergency needs can be met by other modes of transportation alone; nor can these needs continue to be met by the railroads, with other modes of transportation, unless the railroads can continue to receive a sufficient traffic volume to maintain their plants and services.[17]

In a later part of the ICC's conclusion, they again stressed the fact that for most commodities moving long distances, the railroad is the low cost mode. Therefore, the ICC was duty bound to protect the mode whose apparent advantage was about to be undermined.[18]

To the above ICC denial, Commissioner Charles D. Mahaffie vigorously dissented. Specifically, he charged, "The majority embark upon what seems to me to be a dubious policy of attempting to afford regulatory protection to the railroad industry generally at the sacrifice of improved motor-carrier service through the unification of these carriers."[19] Furthermore, Mahaffie stated that the Commission's majority obviously believed that the railroads could not effectively compete against a transcontinental trucker. To this conclusion, he took exception. However, he continued, even assuming the rails could not effectively compete, they still had no inherent right to be shielded from the full forces of competition by a regulatory body. Mahaffie noted that the transport statutes currently in effect require each common carrier mode of transport to compete for its respective traffic. Therefore, the mode that is able to generate the most tonnage is the one with the inherent advantage, or in other words, is the mode that is able to furnish the best service in relation to its respective rates.[20] Mahaffie then concluded this argument with the following brilliant analysis of the majority's opinion.

The theory that the growth of one type of carrier must be restricted lest another presently handling the traffic be injured is, as I see it, not only legally unsound but is, from a transportation standpoint, dangerous. If followed over the years such a theory would have greatly retarded the development even of the railroads themselves, in whose behalf it is now invoked. It would have stifled carriage by pipeline as well as by barge. The transportation system of this country has developed to its present adequacy and efficiency principally as a result of the competitive struggle not only between individual units but also between different types of carrier.[21]

In concluding the initial *P.I.E.-Keeshin* merger decision, the author must state that he fully agrees with the closely reasoned logic contained in Commissioner Mahaffie's dissenting statements.

The ICC Reconsideration

The above momentous decision was reconsidered by the ICC and a supplementary finding was issued on April 2, 1951.[22] In this proceeding, the ICC fully upheld its prior finding and used the reconsideration to restate the rationale of its decision.

Initially, the ICC again reaffirmed that under its interpretation of the phrase "public interest," the Commission is duty bound to consider, among other factors, the effect of the proposed merger on the continuance, efficiency, and economy of all existing carriers, including the railroads.[23] In this light, the ICC found that the railroads would lose a large amount of their higher-rated traffic, and that this outcome would be detrimental to the public interest.[24] In addition, the Commission concluded that, "The record is clear that all requirements of the shipping public on traffic moving between points in territories served by the Keeshin companies, on the one hand, and those in territories served by the applicant, on the other, are already being adequately met by existing carriers."[25]

Finally, the ICC stressed the fact that the probable outcome of the merger on the railroads was only one factor considered in reaching their decision. The other major contention involved the merger's ramifications in regard to other trucking firms. This argument will be traced in a later part of this chapter dealing with intramodal competition.[26]

The Trend Since the P.I.E.-Keeshin Reconsideration Case

After the *P.I.E.-Keeshin* reconsideration case, the ICC has generally reversed itself and has tended to discount the effects of trucking unifications on the railroad system. For example, starting with the "key" case (as defined in the research methodology section in Chapter IV) of *Merchants Motor Freight, Inc.—Purchase—Bridgeways*,[27] the Commission took a rather unsympathetic attitude towards the railroad's pleas in this proceeding. This case involved a number of vendees who each wanted to purchase a portion of the operating rights and property of Bridgeways, Inc. Specifically, the eastern railroads opposed these transactions because it would divert, in their opinion, a large percentage of their merchandise or less-than-carload traffic. For example, Roadway Express, after its proposed purchase, would now be allowed to serve directly between Chicago and Grand Rapids. Before the proposed merger, Bridgeways could only serve these points in interline service, while the Pennsylvania Railroad always offered one carrier service between these points.[28] Similar examples of increased one-carrier trucking service were presented by the Baltimore & Ohio Railroad, the Chicago, Burlington & Quincy Railroad, and the Grand Truck Western Railroad.[29]

It is interesting to note that in the ICC's "general discussion and conclusions" section of the instant proceeding, they did not even specifically mention the railroad's arguments against the unification. Instead, the Commission merely observed.

It is probably true that the transaction will cause (and the operations under temporary authority probably has already caused) some readjustments in competitive relations of carriers, and an intensification of competition between many points. This almost always occurs, to a greater or lesser degree, when the purchasing carrier is stronger financially, and from the standpoint of equipment and facilities, than the selling carrier; but we are not convinced that any of the protesting carriers would be unable to meet the readjustments and the added competition without serious impairment of its service and revenue.[30]

Another more recent "key" case that the intermodal competitive issue entered into was the *Consolidated Freightways, Inc.—Control—Silver Fleet* case.[31] In this proceeding, Consolidated Freightways sought to purchase a number of trucking firms. The railroad industry vigorously protested, citing the *P.I.E.-Keeshin* case and the arguments in it, as the reasons for denial of all the instant applications.[32] To this contention, the Commission answered that it must be remembered that the railroads compete against all existing forms of transportation, i.e., pipelines, water carriers, air carriers, private truckers, regulated motor carriers and unregulated truckers. The ICC then continued their forceful statement on intermodal competition as follows:

Their economic difficulties should be attributed to losses of traffic and revenues to all forms of competing transportation and in part only to competition afforded by regulated motor carriers. Consolidated's long-haul service is more vulnerable to competition than its short-haul operations. Denial of these cases would not solve the basic economic problems of the railroads and approval and consummation would not, in our opinion, increase those problems to any appreciable extent. In either event, the basic financial difficulties of the railroads would remain unchanged. *We are of the opinion that the growth of the motor-carrier industry may not properly be frozen within any limited territorial scope to preclude improved and more adequate service on the theoretical ground that the improved service in more extensive territory might possibly cause the railroads to lose traffic, especially since no evidence of record shows that the railroads would actually lose freight.* (Emphasis added)[33]

The ICC then turned its attention to the railroads' argument that their "inherent advantages" must be protected, as required by the National Transportation Policy. To this, the Commission acknowledged that the railroads are the best equipped to render the most efficient long-haul service on heavy and bulky commodities at the least cost. In addition, the ICC noted that in times of national emergency, the railroads' position as the backbone of all transport modes was undebated. Because of the importance of the Commission's basic conclusion, it will be stated verbatim.

However, these arguments are not convincing as a reason for denial of these applications. In our opinion, the preservation of the inherent advantages of the railroad industry does not require that we adopt a policy which would tend to freeze the motor-carrier industry at its present level. Considering the national transportation policy, it is not apparent that Congress intended that the motor-carrier industry, a competing form of transportation, should not be permitted to grow through unifications, or that the size of a unified company should, of itself, warrant denial. The evidence submitted by the railroads, while it justifies a finding that the service provided by them is essential to a sound national transportation economy, does not preclude the conclusion that larger motor-carrier systems should also have a place in the transportation system.[34]

In summary, it is believed that the ICC would consistently follow its new policy in regard to intermodal competition, as expressed in the landmark case of *Consolidated Freightways, Inc.–Control–Silver Fleet*. It should be noted that the author states that he *believes* this to be the current situation, because he did not encounter one case after the above proceeding that involved railroad protestants who argued that the trucking unification involved would produce adverse economic effects on the railway system.

In conclusion, the author finds the attitude of the Commission, after the *Consolidated Freightways* case, as entirely sound and the proper interpretation of the National Transportation Policy in regard to preserving the "inherent advantages" of each mode of transport.

The next section will again examine the competitive issues in trucking, but this time from the intramodal point of view.

The Intramodal Competitive Issue in Trucking Unifications

The intramodal competitive situation is one of the most complex and important issues that the ICC must consider in trucking unifications. The Commission is charged by Section 5 of the Interstate Commerce Act to study each trucking merger application, and if it is found to be just, reasonable, and in the public interest, the ICC is authorized to approve the transaction. The Commission has consistently taken the position that, "the burden of showing that the proposed coordinated operations would meet a public need and would be consistent with the public interest is upon the applicant."[35]

The ICC generally has applied two basic criteria in deciding if a consolidation will be "consistent with the public interest." The first is the anticipated public benefits that will be made available as a result of the unification. This aspect has been previously discussed in detail in the first part of this paper. The second basic consideration is the effect the proposed unification would have on competing carriers.[36] The last section discussed the intermodal aspect of the second criterion and, as was shown, the effect of trucking unifications on other modes of transport appears to be a fairly dead issue at this time. However, the ramifications of each proposed consolidation on the remaining truckers is a very active and controversial aspect of trucking mergers. This section will examine the issue in considerable detail, because of its extreme importance in trucking consolidation cases. As an overview of this topic, the ICC frequently draws the distinction between the outcome of the unification as being either an "improved" service or a "new" service. If the result is an improved service, the protesting carriers have no legitimate reason to contest the merger. However, a new service is usually what is seen by the protesting carriers, and if this is the case, the Commission is required to determine if the benefits to the shipping public outweigh the adverse effects on the protesting truckers involved.[37] Specifically, the dissenting carriers must prove that their operations will be substantially damaged. In a 1967 case, the Commission observed that,

... once applicants have met their burden of showing that the proposed transaction otherwise will be consistent with the public interest, protestants have the burden of demonstrating, with particularity, that an approval thereof is not warranted as it would result in serious harm to their operations. While we should not be unreasonably demanding concerning the evidence adduced by protestant carriers in such cases, we must require that such evidence be reasonably specific in showing adverse effect. A mere apprehension by protestants that they would lose traffic as a result of a unification is not a sufficient reason for denial.[38]

This section will start by briefing the two most significant trucking merger cases that the ICC has decided—the *Assocated Transport* cases and the portion of the *P.I.E.-Keeshin* cases not previously discussed. This will be done for two reasons. First, these landmark cases, one involving an approval and the other a denial, will serve as an excellent introduction and synopsis of the complex regulatory issues involved in regard to intramodal competition. Secondly, these cases are often cited in other proceedings as a precedent for either authorizing or rejecting trucking unifications; and hence, familiarity with them is an excellent working tool for the student of this subject.

After examining these introductory cases, the specific areas and issues of controversy introduced in these cases and others will be expanded upon and clarified, using the 450 regular cases for supplementary information. Specifically, the following topics will be discussed in detail: (a) the ICC's general position towards the effect of trucking unifications on competitors, (b) the effect that prior interlining of freight between vendor and vendee and between vendor and protestants has on unification decisions, (c) the Commission's policy when the vendor was considered an unimportant competitor in his region prior to the merger, (d) the issue of dormancy, (e) the situation of converting irregular-routes authority to regular-routes, (f) the requirement of using specific gateways, (g) the conversion of state common carrier trucking authority to Federal authority, (h) the issue of route split-offs, (i) the question of tacking of route authorities, (j) the problem regarding corporate simplification, and (k) other appropriate miscellaneous situations.

Introductory Case Studies

This sub-section wil discuss the two most famous landmark cases in trucking unifications: the *Associated Transport* cases and the *P.I.E.-Keeshin* proceedings.

The Associated Transport Case

The Associated Transport case, officially known as *Associated Transport, Inc.—Control and Consolidation*,[39] was decided by the ICC on March 16, 1942. This proceeding involved the consolidation of eight formerly separate common carrier trucking firms. Specifically, Associated Transport was organized on March 5, 1941, as a Delaware corporation for the sole purpose of consolidating these eight distinct companies, and therefore at the time of the merger it was not engaged in any sort of business.[40]

Associated's board of directors consisted of nine persons, seven of whom were the chief executives of their respective truck lines.[41] In other words, each of the involved trucking firms wished to unite their operations and form a large consolidated trucking firm.

Without going into detail about the specific route structures of each of the eight involved carriers, suffice it to say that their combined route structures were substantial. Generally, the unified firm would be authorized to transport general commodities on selected regular-routes serving the principal points in Massachusetts, Rhode Island, Connecticut, New York, Eastern Pennsylvania, New Jersey, Delaware, the District of Columbia, Virginia, and North Carolina. In addition, the proposed firm could serve selected points in Ohio, South Carolina, Louisiana, Florida, Georgia, and West Viginia. The above separate route structures involved 37,884 miles of regular-routes,[42] of which 24,338 would be operated by the unified firm. In other words, 13,546 miles of route structure were duplicated by the combined firms; and hence, these duplicate route awards would be cancelled.[43] As a final indication of the size of this proposed merger, the combined firm would operate about 3,300 units of revenue equipment.[44]

The major issue of this case was the intramodal competitive effect on other truckers in the involved area. The Antitrust Division of the Department of Justice strongly opposed the transaction on the ground that Section 5 mergers should only be approved if they would not cause an "unreasonable" restraint of competition as contemplated by the antitrust laws.[45] To this charge the Commission vehemently disagreed and counter-charged as follows:

In our opinion, the Congress intended to place wholly within our judgment the granting or denying of authority for these transactions under Section 5. The specific reference to the antitrust laws only emphasizes the Congressional intent that we should be empowered to approve transactions which otherwise would be violative of the antitrust laws, if we are convinced that the public interest would thus be best served. Stated differently section 5 authorizes us to permit unifications which would, except for such approval, result in restraining competition contrary to the antitrust laws, where the disadvantages of such restraint are overcome by other advantages in the public interest, such as direct betterment in the public service of the carriers or indirect betterment through stabilization of the industry. Determination of the larger question as to whether the proposed unification would be consistent with the public interest involves consideration not only of the competition that would be eliminated, but also of the competition that would remain, and the advantages which would result from the unification.[46]

The ICC then traced in considerable detail the amount of trucking competition that would still exist in each of three basic geographical regions after the instant transaction; the trace proved rather convincingly that the proposed firm would have substantial competition in all major areas.[47]

The Antitrust Division countered the above argument by stating that even though other competitors would exist, they would have a difficult time competing with the largest motor carrier in the United States (based on total revenues). The Commission replied that the past experience has shown that small carriers have always been able to effectively compete against relatively much larger truckers. Furthermore, the ICC observed that:

There is no indication that anything approaching a monopoly has resulted in that territory from the formation and operation of those systems. Considering the great number of motor carriers now operating, the small amount of capital required to enter the motor-transportation field, and the advantages in certain respects which smaller motor carriers have over larger ones through their more intimate relations with shippers and their ability to render a more personalized service, it would seem that monopoly is little to be feared at this stage of the development of the trucking industry.[48]

In addition, the Commission pointed out that one small trucker *favored* the instant transaction because of the common practice of shippers to divide their tonnage among the common carriers who are authorized to serve the required destinations. That is, the small trucker now shared the available tonnage with two competitors who would consolidate into the proposed Associated Transport; and hence he would only have one competitor to share tonnage with after the proposed consolidation.[49]

The ICC concluded by authorizing the proposed unification and stated in no uncertain terms that large size alone in trucking merger cases is not sufficient ground for denial of the application. Furthermore, the Commission noted that if it had ruled otherwise, the logical conclusion would be that the trucking industry would be permanently "frozen" at its present level of firm size. In addition, it was observed by the Federal regulatory body that trucking, compared to both the rail and water carriers, was still in its infancy, and that arbitrary restrictions upon its natural growth and development into larger units would not be in the public interest.[50] The Commission's line of reasoning, which the author believes to be absolutely valid, continued as follows:

There are many thousands of motor carriers of property subject to our jurisdiction. Many of these are very small, and small motor carriers are necessary and have a definite place in the industry. On the other hand, it would seem that larger motor-carrier systems, comparable in size and strength with units of competing forms of transportation, should also have their place in the industry. The legislative history of section 5 indicates a clear Congressional intent to encourage unifications, particularly of railroads. In view of the national transportation policy, as declared in the act, it cannot be supposed that Congress intended that the motor-carrier industry, a coordinate and competing form of transportation, should not also be permitted to grow through consolidations, or that the mere size of the consolidated company should, of itself, be sufficient to warrant denial. Considering the much greater number of motor carriers of property and their size as compared with railroads generally, the need for unification in the trucking field is at least as great as in the case of railroads, which have had many years of development and now comprise comparatively few systems.[51]

Finally, the ICC gave considerable weight to the fact that the executives of the former separate firms advocated this transaction and would still direct its operations at various levels of management. In other words, the Commission was favorably impressed by the fact that the organizers of Associated all conceded to relinquish control of their separate respective companies in order to form the consolidated firm that these executives believed could offer a better service to the shipping public.[52]

The importance of this ICC approval was immense to the trucking industry— so much so that it was appealed by an opposing trucking firm, McLean, to a special three-judge district court and then to the Supreme Court. The next sub-section will examine the latter court's finding.

The McLean Trucking Case

This case, officially known as *McLean Trucking Co. v. U.S.*,[53] was decided by the Supreme Court on January 17, 1944. The principal issue was whether or not the ICC had given due weight to the policies of the antitrust laws.[54] The district court had previously decided in favor of the Commission's interpretation of the antitrust laws.[55]

The high court noted that for the ICC to give prime consideration to the antitrust laws in deciding a trucking merger case would be to ignore and nullify the Congressional policy on this matter. In other words, since Section 5 of the Interstate Commerce Act clearly exempts trucking mergers from the antitrust laws, and if the ICC finds the transaction to be in the public interest, then it is not a valid argument to claim, as McLean did, that the antitrust laws were ignored by the Commission. The Supreme Court then forcefully observed,

It is not for this Court, or any other, to override a policy, or an exemption from one, so clearly and specifically declared by Congress, whatever may be our views of the wisdom of its action. The argument in its full sweep therefore must be rejected.[56]

The high court expanded on its decision by noting that Congress undoubtedly realized, in providing the antitrust exemption, that it was not necessary to make the antitrust laws a controlling factor when the industry was already subjected to strict regulation and supervision.[57] However, the court stated emphatically that,

> ... the fact that the carriers participating in a properly authorized consolidation may obtain immunity from prosecution under the antitrust laws in no sense relieves the Commission of its duty, as an administrative matter, to consider the effect of the merger on competitors and on the general competitive situation in the industry in the light of the objectives of the national transportation policy.[58]

Since the ICC had given appropriate consideration to the effect of the merger on other carriers, the above criterion of the Supreme Court had been fully complied with.

It should be noted that Justices Douglas, Black, and Murphy disagreed with the majority opinion, and Mr. Justice Douglas wrote a dissenting opinion. Specifically, he agreed with the majority that the antitrust laws should not be the controlling factor in a trucking unification proceeding. However, he did state that, in his opinion, the ICC should have given greater weight to the principles of competition than it apparently did.[59] In other words, he stated that Congress did not give the ICC *carte blanche* authority to substitute a system of trucking cartels for the present competitive system.[60] Therefore, Justice Douglas concluded that since, in his opinion, the ICC's interpretation of the importance of competition was erroneous, he would reverse the instant proceeding and remand the case back to the Commission for a new decision.[61]

The P.I.E.-Keeshin Case

The second truly landmark case in trucking unifications was the *P.I.E.-Keeshin* case. Because a general description of this proceeding was traced in the intermodal competitive section,[62] this discussion will deal exclusively with the intramodal competitive issues that were raised.

This proceeding was protested by thirteen motor carriers, primarily on the ground of traffic diversion.[63] Apparently the ICC was receptive to the truckers complaints, because it was one of the main reasons that the instant transaction was denied. The Federal regulatory body took official notice of the fact that the Keeshin companies primarily served cities on their own lines, and hence participated in little interlining, which amounted to only 7 percent of its total revenues. In addition, the amount of freight interlined between Keeshin companies and P.I.E. at Chicago and St. Louis has been negligible.[64]

P.I.E., on the other hand, was a substantial interliner of freight, especially at

Chicago and St. Louis. For the first eleven months of 1949, it had interchanged about 82,000 tons of freight at the latter two points with competitors of the Keeshin system. For the twelve months ending on November 30, 1949, P.I.E. received more than 20 percent of its total tonnage at the St. Louis and Chicago gateways. Furthermore, 15 percent of its gross tonnage was interlined at these gateways for destinations further to the East. Finally, the tonnage that was received from interlining at St. Louis and Chicago amounted to 66.2 percent and 61.1 percent of the total tonnage received at these gateways, respectively.[65] Referring to this situation, the ICC concluded:

Much of this out-bound tonnage would be vulnerable to P.I.E.'s solicitation in eastern territory at the expense of existing carriers, and practically all of the tonnage which it now delivers to interline connections at Chicago and St. Louis would be lost by those carriers. Disruption of existing channels and routes for the movement of this traffic would be inevitable.[66]

The Commission therefore reasoned that because of the lack of prior interchanging between P.I.E. and Keeshin, the effect of the transaction would be a "new competitive service," not indistinguishable from issuing P.I.E. new operating rights to serve the eastern part of the United States. Specifically, it would be a new service in regard to those carriers who had previously interlined freight with the P.I.E. system and now were deprived of this freight. In addition, the Commission believed it would be a new service in both companies' prior territories in that the combined company would be now offering a greatly expanded one-carrier service to many new destinations.[67]

The ICC then observed that it is required in a Section 5 proceeding to find that the transaction is "consistent with the public interest." The Commission noted that while there would be some definite operating economies if the transaction were authorized, they were not significant enough to outweigh the disadvantages to the competing truckers in the involved areas. The Federal regulatory authority then stated,

The words 'public interest' as used in section 5 clearly comprehend the interest of competing carriers. Their interest is no different than that of the general public in preventing the wasteful transportation which results from surplus transportation.[68]

Furthermore, the Commission found that in any case, requirements of the shipping public were being adequately met prior to the proposed merger. The ICC likened the "new service" proposed to a Section 207 application,[69] in which the Commission had consistently found that existing carriers who had made large investments to improve their service to the shipping public should be protected from additional competition, as long as the existing truckers were offering an efficient, economic, and fully adequate service. In other words, the ICC reasoned that in cases of this type, they should use the same rule in

Section 5 proceedings as they had always used in Section 207 cases. Why? Because the effect on the existing carriers is no different if the "new service" results from a Section 207 or a Section 5 proceeding. Finally, since the existing service was found to be fully adequate, the unification proposal was denied.[70]

The P.I.E.-Keeshin Reconsideration Case

The Commission started this case by making it perfectly clear that the only reason it authorized this reconsideration was to clarify and expand on the rationales of its prior decision. In no way was its previous finding either modified or reversed.[71]

This restatement dealt primarily with the intermodal aspect of the case and did not expand too much on the intramodal aspect. Again, the ICC declared that in their opinion a new competitive service would be brought to fruition if the instant transaction was consummated; and therefore, because the benefits to the public were outweighed by the disadvantages to the carriers involved, the transaction was denied.[72]

An interesting concurring opinion was issued by Commissioner Knudson, in which he mentioned that in his opinion the instant decision was in complete consonance with the well developed American concepts of competition. That is, he believed that if the present unification would have been authorized, it would undoubtedly have set off a chain reaction of other giant trucking companies that would be competitive with the P.I.E.-Keeshin system on a transcontinental basis. That result, according to Commissioner Knudson, would undoubtedly have adverse effects on the preservation of small trucking businesses and also would probably clash with the antitrust laws.[73]

General ICC Statements Regarding Intramodal Competition

This sub-section will discuss four general areas of intramodal competition. The following sections will then deal with more specific issues.

Trucking Monopolies

Both of the prior basic cases raised the issue of trucking monopolies in specific areas. In general, it was seen that the Commission favors limited common carrier trucking competition in each region of the country. Thus, in a 1938 proceeding the ICC declared that when authorizing a unification,

Existence of other motor carriers operating over the routes and serving the principal intermediate points negatives [sic] possibility of undue restraint of competition.[74]

In a decision two years later, the Commission observed that:

The competitive situation would not be materially affected as there are numerous motor carriers and railroads affording freight transportation service throughout the considered territory.[75]

In summary, the Commission has constantly favored a limited amount of intramodal trucking competition in each territory that has sufficient traffic to warrant more than one carrier.[76]

The Effect of Increased Competition

The Commission has observed that motor carriers will often incur increased competition from unified truckers because the latter are able to offer a substantially improved service. However, the ICC has consistently found that unless the protesting truckers can prove that their operations will be substantially damaged, the transaction will be authorized. Thus in a 1942 proceeding, the ICC stated:

It is undoubtedly true, as contended by protestants, that vendee, following consummation of the transactions, would be a more formidable competitor than vendors. However, the evidence previously discussed convinces us that the transactions would be consistent with the public interest, notwithstanding the fact that some loss of revenue might result to protestants. The evidence as to such possible effect on protestants does not show such substantial harm as to prejudice their ability to continue to perform their transportation services.[77]

In a 1954 proceeding, a larger trucker, Eastern Freight Ways, Inc., acquired a number of smaller vendors. The result was that the vendee now offered an improved service, because he obtained both additional commodity hauling rights and new destination points. The Commission noted that this increased competition afforded to protesting carriers was a natural result of the unification and was to be expected. Finally, the merger was authorized because the unification would not prevent the protesting carriers' from fulfilling their common carrier obligations.[78]

A very recent case involved a merger in which the vendee was a substantial common carrier trucker and the vendor was a smaller, somewhat unstable carrier. The ICC noted that protestants would undoubtedly face increased competition as a result of the transaction, but this was only to be expected in a merger under these circumstances.[79]

In summary, the ICC has always taken the position that mergers that result in increased trucking competition may be authorized as long as the protestant carriers are not materially damaged. Hence, in a May 1969 case the Federal regulatory body observed, "We have often held that whenever a unification of two operations occurs, some readjustments may be necessary among competing carriers in order to meet the increased competition. This is the situation here."[80]

Alleged Damage to Protestants

This sub-section will examine the Commission's policy towards the effect of trucking unifications on protesting carriers. In general, the ICC takes the position that the protestant must prove, in concrete terms, that he will be materially damaged by the consolidation before the transaction will be denied on these terms. The Commission is often strict in accepting the protestants' claims, as will be seen in this section. Future sections will discuss, in detail, situations in which the ICC has accepted the protestants' position and accordingly denied the proposed unification.

In general, the ICC has taken the stand that often a trucking unification is in the public interest and should be authorized, even though protestants will lose some traffic and revenues, but will not be substantially damaged.[81] For example, in a 1951 case the ICC noted that the interveners in opposition (protestants) were well-established firms in their respective territories and in addition were as well known as the vendee. Therefore, the Commission reasoned that they were in a position to retain much of their present traffic by providing the shipping public an efficient and economical service.[82] In a later case, the Commission stated that in its opinion, the transaction involving a consolidation with Consolidated Freightways, Inc., would not overly damage protestants or cause an oversupply of trucking in the involved territory.[83] A relatively recent case involved Michigan Express, Inc., which was purchasing certain operating rights from McNamara Motor Express, Inc. This transaction was contested by seven common carrier truckers. The Commission approved the application and succinctly noted, "Protestants are large, well-established carriers in the area, and the traffic which they are apprehensive of losing constitutes only a small portion of their total traffic."[84]

To recapitulate, the burden of proof is on the protesting carriers to prove that the unification involved will substantially injure their respective abilities to perform their common carrier trucking obligations.[85]

A basic corollary question in regard to alleged damage to protesting carriers is the *specific* extent of the said injury. It has already been mentioned that an apprehension of lost traffic and revenues by protesting carriers seldom receives much consideration by the ICC. Thus, the Commission has repeatedly stated,

Under the circumstances, we concur in the findings of the examiner that protestants' evidence is too general and provides no proper basis to support a conclusion that operations by vendee under the unified heavy-hauling rights would adversely affect the service now being provided by them. Mere apprehension of loss of traffic has consistently been found by the Commission to be an insufficient reason for denial of a section 5 application.[86]

In closing, the Commission has often admonished protesting carriers to state in specific terms the probable amount of damage they would incur if the proposed merger was consummated. In other words, if only generalities are presented by the protesting truckers, they will undoubtedly receive very little consideration from the ICC.[87]

"New Service" Considerations

The following sections of this chapter will present many situations in which the Commission will decide that the effect of the proposed unification is a "new service"; if the unification can't otherwise be shown to be in the public interest, the application will be denied. This brief discussion will show that all "new service" cases are not automatically rejected.

A 1956 merger involved a proceeding in which the vendee and vendor would establish a new service and not an improved service as a result of the unification. To this situation the Commission authorized the transaction and replied that:

It is possible, therefore, that under the unified rights, some new through service may result. This is not unusual as a result of a proceeding under section 5, just as it is also true that protestants undoubtedly have suffered and will continue to suffer some loss of traffic formerly interlined with each of the carriers whose operations will now be unified.[88]

In another case, the Commission clearly stated that the "new service" precedent of the famous *P.I.E.-Keeshin* cases did not always require a denial in a Section 5 unification proceeding. Furthermore,

Each case can and must be determined on the basis of the evidence of record, and where, as here, the record affirmatively establishes that the proposed plan of operations would meet a public need and that the public interest would best be served by the proposed common control, the application may properly be approved, especially where the competing carriers have failed to establish that their operations or services would be prejudiced to any material degree.[89]

This section has dealt exclusively in generalities. The next topic to be discussed is one of the most pivotal aspects of the intramodal competitive issue, and therefore it will be examined in great detail.

Former Interlining: Its Importance

The importance of former interlining between vendee and vendor became a key factor in unification proceedings after the so-called "new service" theory was enumerated in the landmark *P.I.E.-Keeshin* cases. Specifically, the amount of former interlining between merger applicants has frequently been an element that the Commission gives considerable weight to in determining if a proposed unification will result in a new service. Presumably, the greater the extent of the former interlining, the probability is therefore increased that the proposed transaction will result in an "improved service" and not a "new service."

In addition, the Commission also studies the interlining patterns other than just between vendee and vendor. Hence, the ICC has observed that the interline activities of the vendee must be studied separately in order to see to what extent it interlined freight with carriers other than the vendor. Furthermore, the same procedure is followed on the interlining patterns of the vendor.[90]

Finally, the Commission has repeatedly stated that the overall importance of interlining activity is to be able to accurately evaluate the broader issue of the effect of the unification on competing truckers. Thus, the ICC made the following lucid observation:

The importance in a section 5 proceeding of the factor of the quantum of traffic interlined in the past by applicants pertains entirely to the greater issue of the manner and extent which a transaction will affect the operations of competing carriers. In other words, a substantial interline of traffic between applicants in the past is generally indicative of the fact that existing carriers have already been faced with, and adjusted to, the competition of their joint-line service. Under these circumstances it can be fairly concluded, in most instances, that approval of a transaction would cause little impairment in the existing services of competing carriers. At the opposite extreme, in instances where applicants have not interlined traffic moving between their respective areas of operation with one another or other carriers, it is similarly evident that their unification could readily result in serious disruption of the present competitive balance and the impairment of the operations and services of competing carriers. It should be emphasized, however, that past interchange constitutes only one element in our appraisal of the effects a transaction would likely have upon the operations and services of existing carriers, and, by itself, is not controlling in the determination of the ultimate issue.[91]

This section will begin with two introductory key cases that were significantly influenced by the amount of former interchanging between the applicants. After the above introduction to this topic, three significant typical types of Commission findings in this area will be discussed in some detail.

Introductory Cases

The Merchants-Bridgeways Case. An important "key" case that was strongly influenced by the degree of former interlining between the applicants was officially known as *Merchants Motor Freight, Inc.—Purchase—Bridgeways, Inc.,*[92] and it was decided by the ICC on June 7, 1954. This proceeding involved the sale of the bankrupt trucking giant, Bridgeways, to six separate trucking companies, each of which would acquire part of the operating route structure of the defunct firm.[93]

The applications were opposed by thirty-seven motor carriers,[94] with one of their basic contentions being that totally new services would be developed because applicants and Bridgeways had previously interlined an insignificant amount of freight prior to their temporary authority to use Bridgeways' operating rights.[95] This argument was countered by the applicants, who stated that all the vendees had actively interlined with Bridgeways for many years prior to early 1950, when Bridgeways became so financially unstable that it was considered bad business practice to deal with them. In other words, if Bridgeways had continued to offer a safe and reliable interlining service to the vendees, they would have continuously interlined with Bridgeways up to the time of the unification application.[96]

The ICC accepted the applicants' theory and authorized the transaction. In other words, because of the prior interlining, a new service would not develop. Instead, an existing service would be improved, and this was found to be definitely in the public interest. Finally, the Commission noted that none of the protestants had offered substantial evidence concerning the alleged damage they would suffer as a result of the unification.[97]

The C.F.-Silver Fleet Case. The second "key" proceeding that deeply involved interlining was the *Consolidated Freightway, Inc.—Control—Silver Fleet* case,[98] which was decided in March, 1960. This application basically involved C.F.'s purchase of five separate trucking firms: Silver Fleet, the Motor Cargo companies, Liberty, Bell, and Rutherford.

Basically, the numerous protesting truckers felt that the "new competitive service" theory of the *P.I.E.-Keeshin* case should be applicable here, because the applicants had not previously interlined a substantial amount of freight.[99] The applicants countered by insisting that the amount of interlined traffic between Consolidated and Liberty, Motor Cargo, and Silver Fleet at the Chicago gateway had always been of substantial magnitude.[100]

The ICC agreed that a basic feature of this case was whether or not the "new competitive service" concept should be applicable in the instant proceeding. The Commission stated dogmatically that the "new service" concept had apparently been misinterpreted by the applicants, because even though a new service can develop, this does not automatically mean the unification application must be denied. Instead, the deciding factor is whether or not the protesting carriers are substantially damaged to the point where they can not perform their common carrier obligations.[101]

The ICC concluded that since Liberty and Motor Cargo had always been substantial interline partners with C.F., their unification would result in an improved service.[102] In regard to Silver Fleet, which the ICC found to have had moderate interlining with C.F., and Bell and Rutherford, which had not interlined with C.F., the applications were denied. The rationale of these denials was that if they were authorized, two trucking firms would be substantially damaged. Specifically, one protestant, Central Motor Lines, submitted evidence that it currently interlined traffic with two or more carriers from the Carolinas to Chicago. If C.F. acquired the above three truckers, it could offer single-carrier service from these origin and destination points. The ICC accepted the protestant's testimony that C.F.'s one carrier service would cause Central Motor Lines to lose a substantial amount of traffic and hence jeopardize its very existence as a common carrier.[103] The second protestant, Kansas City Motor Express, had substantially the same argument. That is, if C.F. acquired the rights of Bell and Rutherford and thus offered one carrier service from selected points in Virginia and from Indianapolis to Chicago, Express would be vulnerable to excessive traffic erosion that would threaten its ability to stay in business.[104]

Because of the effects of the merger of C.F. with Silver Fleet, Bell and Rutherford, the Commission concluded,

However, as to the Silver Fleet, Bell, and Rutherford cases, the evidence establishes with reasonable certainty that the transactions would adversely affect the ability of Central and Express to maintain the efficiency and economy of their present services. In view thereof, and of the absence of any showing that those transactions would result in advantage to the public which would more than offset the disadvantages previously set forth, these applications will be denied.[105]

Now that the topic of former interlining has been introduced by means of illustrative cases, the next sections will examine specific aspects of this basic issue in some detail.

Substantial Prior Interlining

The ICC has consistently taken the position that when the vendee and vendor have been substantial interline partners prior to the proposed unification, the result of the transaction is an improved and not a new service.[106] Thus, in a 1963 case in which the applicants had been substantial former interline partners, the Commission observed, "The transaction will not affect competing carriers because they have been confronted with, and adjusted to, applicants' continuous joint-line operations for years."[107]

A case decided in February 1963 involved a situation in which the applicants had interchanged with each other for years. The Commission observed in approving this transaction that they were merely authorizing a single-line service, and that this transaction enabled the prior service level to be improved; it did not inaugurate a totally new service. Furthermore, competitors would not be materially affected because the same basic service had already been in effect for years.[108]

In summary, the Commission's policy toward unifications in which the applicants have been previously interlining together is well spelled out in this February 1966 ICC remark:

It is clear from the evidence that interline of a substantial volume of traffic, consisting primarily of textile products, has been continuously effected between applicants over an extended period of time, and that there would be no significant change from the present service afforded by applicants as a result of the proposed unification of operating rights. Stated differently, existing carriers would be faced with improvement of an existing service rather than a new competitive service, and, having had opportunity to adjust to the present service over a period of years, they should experience little, if any, adverse competitive effect.[109]

Absence of Former Interlining

The ICC's ultimate decision in unification proceedings in which the applicants did not formerly interline freight is not as clearcut as when they had previously interlined. This section will first discuss case situations in which the lack of interlining was a key factor in denying the application. The second topic to be examined will be situations in which the merger application was authorized in spite of the fact that there was little previous interlining between the applicants.

Merger Applications Denied. A 1953 proceeding involved a situation in which the vendee would be able to offer single-carrier service from the North Central United States to the New England area. However, it was shown that the applicant had never interlined with the vendor who owned the New England operating rights. In fact, the vendee had only interlined an extremely small amount of freight with one other carrier into the New England area. The ICC concluded, "In the absence of evidence of joint-line service between applicants or by either with other carriers, the operations proposed by Transamerican under the unified rights would in our opinion, be tantamount to an entirely new service."[110] The application was denied for two basic reasons: first, the applicants failed to show that a public need existed for the new service they proposed to establish; second, the Commission found that the proposed unification would cause substantial damage to the existing truckers in the area.[111]

A second illustrative case involved a situation in which the vendor had previously limited his household moving business to serving the Milford, New Hampshire, area within a radius of 100 miles. Wheaton Van Lines proposed to unify with the vendor and thereby be able to offer one-carrier service from a thirty state area in the central part of the United States to the New England points served by the vendor. The ICC denied the application because the complete lack of former interchange between applicants indicated that a new competitive service in the New England area would be the result. In addition, the Commission found that the new service was not needed in the area and that, if the transaction was consummated, the result would have caused material damage to a number of existing truckers in the New England area.[112]

A final typical case in which the ICC denied an application was decided on December 14, 1964. In this proceeding, the vendee, Great Coastal Express, wished to acquire the vendor in order to secure his operating rights in the Norfolk area. The vendee already possessed rights to serve many other Virginia points to the New England area. The ICC found that the applicants had previously interchanged only a minimal amount of freight and concluded:

Because it [Great Coastal] has not participated in traffic moving between its present authorized points and the Norfolk area, to any appreciable extent, it is held that approval of the proposed transaction would result in a new and additional competitive service (as opposed to mere substitution of service or improvement of an existing service). The result would not be distinguishable in substance from the result of an extension of Great Coastal's service into the Norfolk area through securing new operating authority.[113]

Finally, as in the above cases, this application was denied because there was no apparent need for the proposed new service and because unification would have a detrimental effect on competing carriers.[114]

Merger Applications Approved. An application involving the well-known trucking firm, McLean (especially after their court appeal of the Associated Transport case), was approved even though the applicants had not previously interlined freight. The Commission found that the applicants had proved that the advantages of the transaction would be in the public interest. The ICC then stated:

This transaction merits our approval, unless we find that protestants' ability to discharge their duty to the public as common carriers would be materially impaired by the loss of considerable freight to McLean-Express.[115]

Because the protestants could not meet the test just outlined, the application was authorized.[116]

Another recent case that illustrates that a lack of prior interlining does not necessarily prevent a merger from being authorized involved the Michigan Express trucking company. This firm was the vendee, and although it had not interlined freight with the vendor, it had done so with competitors of the vendor. In this situation, the ICC declared that if the merger was consummated:

... it would represent an improved service rather than a new service. This improved service which vendee offers is the aspect of this proceeding which the protestants fear. However, this record does not show that any protestant has interlined traffic with vendee into vendor's territory.[117]

Again, the Commission found that the overall transaction was in the public interest, and that the protestants had not been able to prove substantial damage, and therefore the transaction was authorized.[118]

We have discussed the importance of former interlining in considerable detail, because it has often proven a pivotal issue in determining the broader question of whether a specific merger would be consistent with the public interest. The next section will examine another important issue in this regard, which is the problem involved when the vendor's competitive activities in his territory were considered minimal prior to the unification proposal.

Vendor's Prior Insignificant Competitive Importance

The importance of the vendor's prior competitive significance is that it can be a basic factor in determining whether a unification proceeding will result in a "new competitive service." If such is the result, the burden of proving that the unification will be in the public interest becomes more difficult for two reasons. First, the applicants must prove to the Commission's satisfaction that a public need exists for the proposed service. Secondly, the vendee and vendor must convince the Federal regulatory authority that any damage incurred by competing carriers will be more than offset by the service and other advantages that the unification will make possible.

It should be noted that this topic is embryonic of, and will serve as an introduction to, the next very significant issue in intramodal competitive considerations—dormancy.

The Commission has consistently found, with one exception to be discussed later, that if the vendor's prior competitive importance has been minimal, the result will be a new competitive service, and therefore the transaction will be denied because the applicants have failed to prove that the unification would be consistent with the public interest. For example, in a 1950 proceeding, the Commission found that the vendor had been relatively inactive in using the operating rights that he proposed to sell to the vendee. Thus the merger application was denied, and the ICC observed that:

Transportation by him [the vendor] of general freight has been sporadic and negligible; and it is clear that he has made no genuine effort to develop such traffic, that he has not been a competitive factor in the territory, and that institution of the services proposed by vendee would be tantamount to a new competitive service.[119]

Specifically, the merger was denied on the grounds that the applicants had not shown a public need for the proposed new service and also that the unification would have had detrimental effects on the existing truckers.[120]

A second typical case involved a situation in which the vendor had hauled only a limited amount of freight under his operating rights. The vendee proposed to purchase these rights and extensively revitalize the operations of the vendor. The ICC, however, denied the application because the service which the vendee proposed to offer bore little resemblance to the former activities of the vendor. The Commission concluded that there was no public need for the additional competitive service because the area was already highly competitive.[121]

A final illustrative case concerned the purchase of the Messinger trucking company. Roy Messinger, president of the company, had died a year prior to the merger application by the vendee, Cedar Rapids Transportation, Inc. The record showed that the operations of Messinger had never been considered significantly competitive when Roy Messinger was living, and that they had become less so after his death. The vendee, however, proposed to significantly upgrade the service level of Messinger and also to increase the sales force in the vendors' territory. To this proposal, the ICC made the following observation in denying the application, "In the light of the evidence, approval of the purchase here proposed, would result in a completely new service, harmful to protestants, and for which no need has been shown."[122]

As previously mentioned, one exception to the above sequence of cases was encountered. In this 1966 proceeding, the ICC accepted the examiner's conclusion that the operations of the vendor, the Cleveland Cartage Company, had been relatively minor and were not considered of competitive significance by the protesting carriers. However, the ICC remarked:

The fact that the operations of Cleveland Cartage may not have been of any competitive significance as found by the examiner, and with which conclusion we agree, does not necessarily mean that they may not be transferred in a proceeding under section 5 if other factors show that the transaction would be consistent with the public interest, giving considerable weight, in this connection, to the traffic needs in the territory and to the possible adverse effect which operations under the unified rights would have on competing carriers.[123]

Specifically, the Commission found that a number of shippers were experiencing difficulties in obtaining sufficient common carrier truck service. That is, a total of eight iron and steel producers in the eastern part of the United States presented evidence that they did not receive adequate truck service for their products moving to the central section of the country. Because there was currently more traffic available than the common carrier truckers in the area could handle, the ICC concluded that the inauguration of the proposed new service would not materially damage any of the existing truckers in the area.[124]

It should be pointed out that this last case is fully consistent with the ICC's previously stated policy in regard to situations in which the vendor was competitively of little significance in his area. That is, the ICC has always referred to a merger of these operating rights as creating a "new competitive service." When there was no public need for the new service, it would have worked a hardship on the existing carriers in the area. But there was a definite public need for new and additional trucking service of steel and iron products. In addition, the proposed new service would not have any detrimental effects on the existing truckers. Therefore, the ICC's conclusion appeared to the author as being fully rational and completely consistent with its prior findings in this area.

The next section will deal with an extremely basic intramodal competitive issue in trucking unifications—the question of dormancy.

The Dormancy Issue

Operating rights are said to be dormant when they are no longer being actively used by the vendor. This researcher can say without doubt that the issue of dormant operating rights is one of the reasons the ICC finds most applicable in denying merger applications. Specifically, when a vendor's operating rights are found to be dormant, the effect of selling these rights to the vendee who would then revitalize them is that of creating a "new competitive service." In other words, the existing carriers have adjusted themselves to the fact that the vendor is competitively "dead." Therefore, if his rights are sold and brought back to life by the vendee, the effect to both the existing carriers and to the shipping public is that a new service is now available which was previously nonexistent. Of course, just because a new service is formed does not mean the unification application is automatically denied. However, the applicant in this case has the burden of proof of establishing a public need for the new service. This is usually done by proving that the existing trucking service is not adequate to meet the shipping needs of the public. In addition, the applicants must prove that the advantages to the public of the unification outweigh any adverse effect on the existing truckers.[125]

This section will start by discussing three "key" cases in which the issue of dormancy was of monumental importance. Then, specific situations in which the question of dormancy have been important will be examined, using the 450 regular cases to supplement the discussion previously contained in the three "key" cases.

Introductory Cases

The Crichton-Lavine Case. The first "key" case to deal with dormancy was the *Crichton—Purchase—C. Lewis Lavine, Inc.* case,[126] decided on August 26, 1940. The vendor had started in business in 1926, but on July 1, 1938 he officially filed bankruptcy proceedings. The trustee ran the firm until March 31, 1939, when the company's activities ceased because of a lack of operating capital.

Sixteen months after the vendor's operations had ceased, the vendee applied to the ICC for permission to purchase the vendor's operating rights under Section 213 (now Section 5). The Commission denied the application because the vendor had abandoned his operations, was no longer a trucker in the eyes of the Interstate Commerce Act, and hence did not come under the unification section of the Act.[127] Specifically, the ICC reasoned as follows:

A motor carrier is one which engages in the physical performance of transportation for compensation in interstate or foreign commerce and discharges its duties in that regard to the shipping public by moving traffic offered; and when such a carrier abandons such performance without present intention of resuming same, it therefore ceases to have the status of a motor carrier.[128]

Because the vendor was not a motor carrier, in the sense of the Act's merger provision, this application had to be dismissed for lack of jurisdiction.[129]

It should be noted that this unique method of handling dormancy questions was abandoned in later proceedings, as will be illustrated in the following sections.

The New Dixie-Jocie Case. The second "key" case is important to the dormancy issue because it introduced a test that helps to determine if, in fact, a vendor's operating rights are dormant. Protestants in the *New Dixie Lines, Inc.–Control–Jocie Motor Lines, Inc.*[130] case took exception to the hearing examiners use of the "test of substantiality" when deciding if the operations of the vendor were dormant. Formerly, the above test had often been used by the ICC in determining "grandfather" application cases. That is, if a carrier could prove that it had served a "substantial" number of cities carrying a "substantial" variety of commodities in a given area, it would qualify for a general commodity certificate of public convenience and necessity that would authorize it to serve all the cities in the area.[131]

In the instant case, the examiner applied the "test of substantiality" to the operations of the vendor. The examiner concluded, and he was upheld by the Commission, that when a vendor has an irregular-route authorization,[132] it is necessary only to have rendered service to a substantial number of points in the authorized territory to prove that the operations are of competitive importance. In addition, the ICC noted that the same rule also applied to regular-route carriers.[133] Because the operations of Jocie met the "test of substantiality," the vendor's operation was not found to be dormant. Finally, the transaction was found to be consistent with the public interest, and it was authorized.[134]

The Glosson-Helderman Case. The final "key" case[135] dealing with dormancy involved a situation in which the protestants claimed that the operations of the vendor, Helderman, were dormant. The ICC used the "test of substantiality" and decided after carefully studying the vendor's records that it had not been a significant carrier of general commodities or household goods. The Commission then stated:

Since the test of substantiality may not be stretched enough to avoid a finding of dormancy, the next step is to determine whether the evidence of shippers and connecting carriers establishes public convenience and necessity for a completely new service by Glosson in the transportation of general commodities and household goods within the North Carolina area. We find it does not.[136]

In this case, however, since the vendor had previously carried a substantial amount of specialized commodities, especially iron and steel products and explosives, the ICC did authorize the transfer of the rights that were not found to be dormant.[137]

Now that the introductory cases have been surveyed, the following sections will analyze specific situations in some detail, because the importance of understanding the dormancy issue cannot be underestimated.

Dormancy Established: Application Denied

The earliest cases in which dormancy was proven and the proposed service found not to be in the public interest followed the precedent of the above *Chrichton-Lavine* case. That is, the unification application was denied because the vendor's dormancy meant that he was no longer a motor carrier in the eyes of the Interstate Commerce Act, and hence not eligible to take advantage of the Section 5 merger provisions.[138]

More recently, the ICC has taken the position that dormancy is a factor to consider in deciding if a proposed unification will result in a "new competitive service." In a 1959 case, the Commission found that the vendor's operations had been so minimal that in effect its entire operations were dormant. In addition, the Federal regulatory authority noted that even though the firm had maintained appropriate tariffs and insurance, and had attempted a limited amount of advertising, the fact that it had actually provided very little transportation service was the ruling consideration. Finally, the ICC found that the applicants had failed to show a public need for the proposed new service, and therefore the application was denied.[139]

This case indicated that the Commission generally does not give much weight to the reason that the vendor's operations have become dormant. This is illustrated by this 1960 ICC remark:

While the accident that befell vendor in February 1956, and which allegedly resulted in the discontinuance of her trucking operations, was unfortunate, we are, nonetheless, constrained to adhere to the view heretofore expressed in numerous reports that the reason for the discontinuance of service is entitled to light weight in determining whether the transaction under section 5, and the reactivation of the service by the purchaser, would be consistent with the public interest.[140]

The Commission concluded that the proposed new service had not been shown to be consistent with the public interest, and therefore it was denied.[141]

In a June 1968 merger case, the ICC found the vendor's operations dormant and issued this observation in regard to the effect of dormancy on competing truckers:

Dormancy is an issue in a section 5 proceeding because, as a rule, any transfer of operating rights under which no service, or only a limited service has been performed would be detrimental to the operations of the existing carriers who have been performing service to the public similar to that authorized by the dormant rights. The possibility also exists that the transfer would create a surplus of transportation in the area involved.[142]

The ICC then stated dogmatically that to overcome the dormancy issue, the applicants must prove a real need for their proposed new service and not a mere preference of shippers to use the applicants. Because the latter test was not met, the instant transaction was not authorized.[143]

In summary, the Commission has found the issue of dormancy of the vendor's operating rights to be the pivotal factor in denying a long series of Section 5 unification proceedings.[144]

Dormancy Established: Application Authorized

Occasionally, even though the vendor's operating rights are shown to be dormant, the merger application is authorized because the applicants have shown that the transaction is in the public interest. Thus, in a 1960 case, the ICC authorized the rights of a dormant United States vendor to be transferred to a Canadian trucking firm. The application was supported by nine motor common carriers, sixteen manufacturers and distributors, three packinghouses, two customs officials, and two managers of bridge traffic at the boundary. The ICC reasoned that such support well established a public need for the proposed new service, so the basic factor was the effect of the transaction on the existing truckers. To this question the ICC observed:

Notwithstanding that vendor has conducted little or no operations under its authority and other carriers serving the territory may suffer some loss of traffic and revenues, we believe that sufficient traffic is available in the area to support the service of vendee as well as that of protestants, and that a resumption of service under vendor's rights to the extent indicated will not prejudice protestants' ability to continue to perform their common-carrier obligations to the shipping public.[145]

In another 1960 case the Commission authorized the sale of dormant rights because it was found that a definite public need did exist for the new service proposed by the vendee. Specifically, the Commission found that there was a lack of adequate trucking service in the applicant's area and therefore authorized the application.[146]

The above section illustrated cases that were authorized *after* dormancy had been proven. The next section will examine case situations in which the condition of dormancy itself is in question.

Alleged Dormancy

It has previously been shown that a considerable number of trucking unifications have been denied because the vendor's operating rights were found to be dormant. Therefore, because of the past success of this plea by protestants in trucking merger cases, it has become a very typical and popular ground for protestants to base their objections on when arguing against a unification application. Because dormancy is so often claimed by protestants, the Commission has, over the years, developed a standard procedure for evaluating the validity of this claim. This section will examine that procedure in some detail.

The Commission had used a *de facto* "test of substantiality" even before it became a *de jure* test in the 1958 *New Dixie-Jocie* case. Thus, in a 1941 proceeding in which the vendor was said by protestants to be dormant, the ICC found that he had conducted operations commensurate with his ability and furthermore that, "It cannot here be found that he refused or would have refused to transport traffic to any point authorized to be served had such traffic been offered and had his truck and driver been available."[147]

In another proceeding in which the vendor was said to be dormant, the ICC took cognizance of the fact that the vendor had:

... operated under the considered rights on a scale commensurate with his financial resources, facilities and traffic tendered.[148]

Hence, this accusation was dismissed by the Commission.[149] The latter reasoning appears to have been the ruling criterion prior to the "test of substantiality."[150]

After the "test of substantiality" was enumerated in the already discussed "key" *New Dixie-Jocie* case of 1958, this rule has been consistently applied to determine if the vendor's operations really are dormant. Thus, in a 1966 case the ICC strongly stated that the operating rights of the vendor are not to be "pulverized" by requiring a specific showing that each and every town on the vendor's route structure had recently been served. All that the "test of substantiality" required was a showing that a representative number of points had been recently served.[151] In a May 1967 proceeding the Federal regulatory body stressed the fact that the "test of substantiality" is a flexible and not a fixed standard. Based on this rule, the operations of Bill's City Transfer, Inc., the vendor, were found to be of substantial and continuous nature, and hence the issue of dormancy in this proceeding was dismissed.[152]

The Commission's current overall attitude toward the issue of determining if dormancy exists is well summed up by this May 1968 observation:

The fact that Coakley [the vendor] has not transported all commodities authorized or handled shipments to and from each and every village and hamlet in the rather extensive territory involved is not a bar to approval of the application in its entirety.[153]

The next section, which is the last one on dormancy, will discuss the restrictions that are occasionally placed on the operating rights that the vendor is allowed to transfer to the vendee in a unification proceeding.

Restrictions on Operating Rights

The ICC has always stated that it prefers not to "atomize" or "pulverize" the operating rights that the vendor is authorized to transfer to the vendee.[154] However, in a number of cases, the Commission has decided that it would be in the public interest to place restrictions on the vendor's transferable rights. This section will examine a number of situations in which such restrictions were put into effect, as they were in the "key" *Glosson-Helderman* case.

In a 1955 case the vendor's rights were found to be inactive in regard to part of his operating authority. The ICC therefore concluded:

... the evidence shows that the operations performed have been so limited and sporadic that they have been of no competitive effect in the area involved. This segment of the operating rights is dormant, and the resumption of services thereunder by Motor Freight without showing that the public needs the service and that existing carriers are not meeting the need, would not be consistent with the public interest.[155]

In another case, the vendor was found to have dormant operating rights in regard to textile products and textile machinery. The ICC found that the current competitive situation on these products was very substantial in the involved territory, and therefore the operating rights to transport the above products was canceled.[156]

In summary, the ICC prefers not to "pulverize" the vendor's operating rights because of dormancy. In fact, the "test of substantiality" was designed to reduce the amount of route pulverization that could take place if a vendor had to prove that he carried every authorized commodity to and from each point in his respective operating territory. However, in some cases,[157] the ICC has felt that because of the significant portion of the vendor's rights that have become completely inactive, it is only fair to competing truckers to cancel these rights if the latter carriers are currently rendering a fully satisfactory service to the shipping public.

We now turn to a situation in which the ICC has occasionally denied trucking merger applications because they involve creating a new competitive service without proving the new service is in the public interest.

Route Authority Conversion

The ICC has always been apprehensive in trucking unification proceedings in which a segment of either of the applicants irregular-route structure would be *de facto* converted into a regular-route, scheduled operation. When such a conversion takes place, a new service is created, without the transaction being authorized by the Commission. This section will start with an introductory "key" case and will then survey situations in which the proposed unifications have been approved and denied. Finally, a specific situation known as gateway restrictions will be surveyed.

Introductory Case Study

An early "key" case that dealt with route authority conversion was the *Thurston–Purchase–Merritt* case[158] decided on December 9, 1938. In this proceeding, the ICC noted that the vendee's regular-route authority did not physically connect with the vendor's regular-routes; in fact, they were separated by approximately fifteen miles. However, the vendee possessed irregular-route authority that physically connected with the vendor.[159] Thus, the ICC authorized the application, but inserted this warning to the applicants:

It is not clear from the application how through service could be rendered without effecting an unlawful conversion of irregular-route operations into regular-route operations. . . . If applicant desires to conduct through (scheduled) regular-route operations over this highway in order to connect the termini of its other regular routes, appropriate application for such authority under section 207 should be filed. However, it must be presumed here that applicant, in operating under the unified rights, will maintain such operations within the scope of the confirmed operating authority.[160]

Applications Approved

The earlier cases on this topic appeared to follow the above precedent of authorizing the transaction while definitely warning the applicants not to illegally convert their irregular-route to regular-route authority. Thus, in a 1941 proceeding concerning applicants who would possess both regular and irregular route authority in about the same territory, the Commission admonished the involved truckers that, "In conducting unified operations thereunder, it will be expected to preserve the separate nature of the regular-route and irregular-route operations as authorized."[161] The same type of warning was frequently enumerated in the earlier trucking unification cases.[162]

Applications Denied

In more recent cases, the ICC has taken a stronger stand against *de facto* route conversion. In a 1961 proceeding, an important factor in denying the application was that the vendee's and vendor's regular-route structure were separated by a sixty-five mile stretch between Birmingham and Memphis. The examiner denied the case because the applicants apparently contemplated offering scheduled regular-route service over these sixty-five miles, which would establish a new competitive service for which no public need had been shown.[163] The ICC concurred, stating:

In the instant case, when considering the importance of both Memphis and Birmingham as traffic and business centers, coupled with the fact that almost without exception Deaton has been handling truckloads only between those points [under prior temporary authority], the conclusion seems almost inescapable that it would convert the irregular-route rights between Birmingham and points within 65 miles thereof. . . .[164]

In a similar 1964 proceeding, the ICC denied the application because of a fifty mile gap between the vendee's and the vendor's regular-route structure. The Commission issued the following rationale, which also serves as an excellent summary of this section:

Consistently, in prior proposed unifications where a conversion of authorized irregular-route operations to regular-route operations seemed inevitable, the transactions have been disapproved. Applicants contend that, upon the unification, vendee can and would maintain the separate nature of the regular- and irregular-route operations but, on the evidence, it is apparent that a conversion of the irregular-route to regular-route operations cannot be avoided. Such a change in the operations would not be lawful.[165]

The next section will examine a corollary situation in which the Commission generally authorizes the transaction, but admonishes the applicants not to create a new competitive service after the merger by ignoring previous relevant gateway restrictions.

Gateway Restrictions[166]

The ICC has always taken the general position in regard to trucking mergers that the service to be performed after the merger consummation should be no greater than each trucker could have previously performed separately by means of interchange agreements. Again, if the overall route authorization is greater than the prior combined route structure, a new competitive service has been created that must therefore be proven to be in the public interest. This section will be introduced by means of summarizing a "key" case on this topic. Then a general discussion of gateway restrictions will be presented.

Introductory Case Study. The landmark case on gateway restrictions is the *B. & E. Transp. Co., Inc.–Purchase–Merchants Transp., Inc.* case,[167] which was decided on March 31, 1941 by the ICC. In this proceeding, B. & E. Transportation, the vendee, purchased the irregular-route authority of Merchants, the vendor. The latter firm was authorized to serve between New York City and all points in six counties in New Jersey. The vendee, however, had regular-route authority through this area of New Jersey to New York City. In addition, it had regular-routes south of the area. However, the number of points served by the vendee was limited compared to the all-inclusive rights of the vendor. Therefore, B. & E. assumed that after the merger it could serve any point previously dealt with by the vendor directly to points on its previous route structure, especially south of the six-county New Jersey area. To this, the ICC stated that B. & E. must preserve the separate nature of its regular-route and irregular-route operations; hence, the traffic must first flow through the New York City gateway. In other words, this gateway had to be used because it was the one common point each applicant could previously serve under their respective regular and irregular-route authorities. The Commission reasoned that, if the applicant was allowed to serve a point previously on the vendor's route structure to another on the vendee's, the effect would be a new competitive service for which no public need had been established.[168]

With this interpretation of the Interstate Commerce Act, Commissioner Porter dissented. This author cannot help but agree with Porter's statement:

The application should be approved. The distinction, however, which the B. & E. is required to observe forever and a day between regular-routes now owned and the irregular-route operations purchased is regulation gone mad. If, as a regular manner of hauling, the purchaser saves time and money and wasteful transportation by avoiding the congested city of New York, that is bad and is here condemned, but if he does so only occasionally so as to preserve the superfine distinction between regular and irregular operations, that is good! I can see no sound reason in the requirement that in the handling of traffic from an origin on the B. & E. to a destination on the Merchants, it will be necessary to move that traffic through New York City as a gateway.[169]

Commissioner Porter then gave an example on the waste that the majority's gateway restriction would precipitate. Assume a shipment moving from Washington, N.J., to Milltown, N.J., a distance of two to three miles. Because of the gateway restriction, the shipment would first have to travel twenty-five miles over congested highways to New York City and then back twenty-five more miles to reach Milltown. Porter then concluded, "Such wasteful transportation is bad enough when voluntarily done by carriers, but it is much more objectionable when required by us."[170]

General Discussion. From time to time after the B. & E. case, the Commission has authorized a transaction and then admonished the applicants to remember that they are expected to preserve the separate nature of regular and irregular-routes, and to use relevant gateways when serving points previously on irregular-routes to other points on the prior regular-route structure.[171]

A relatively recent case involved a situation in which a gateway restriction resulted in a circuitous route for the applicants, who had already obeyed this restriction under temporary authority granted under Section 210 a (b) of the Interstate Commerce Act. The applicants, therefore, in their Section 5 unification proceeding, attempted to have the above gateway restriction nullified. The ICC stated that there are two basic findings that must be proven in order to eliminate the gateway restriction and hence allow a more direct service from city A to city B. First, the applicants must have already transported a substantial amount of tonnage, under their temporary authority, over their present circuitous route. In other words, the applicants must prove that they are at present a competitive factor in transporting goods from city A to city B. Second, they must show that the gateway elimination will not be a new service that will adversely affect the present truckers operating from A to B. In the instant case, the applicants failed to prove the first criterion, and hence their request for the gateway restriction removal was denied.[172]

The Transfer of Intrastate Operating
Rights to Interstate Common Carriers

Almost since the beginning of Federal regulation of trucking in 1935 there have been problems involved in transferring intrastate trucking authority to interstate carriers. This section will introduce the subject by means of two "key" cases and be followed by a general discussion of this topic.

Introductory Cases

The Elliott Case. The first landmark case on this topic was the *C. & D. Motor Delivery Co.—Purchase—Elliott* case[173] decided on September 11, 1942. Elliott's operations were completely within the state of Indiana, but much of its traffic transported was of an interstate nature. Nevertheless, Elliott was allowed to transport this interstate traffic because of an exemption in the Interstate Commerce Act that authorizes this sort of operation.[174]

The ICC took the position that Elliott's state authority could be transferred to an interstate carrier, C. & D. in this case. However, the vendor's operations could only be transferred to the vendee by means of issuing a certificate of public convenience and necessity to cover the former intrastate activities. The Commission decided that the usual burden of proof when applying for a *new* certificate would not be needed in this case:

These operations have been conducted for some time in interstate commerce. Where such is the case and the operations were instituted lawfully, the past continued performance of the transportation is itself evidence of public need for continuance thereof.[175]

The Commission noted that even though a new competitive service did not materialize from the transaction, the effect on competing carriers of authorizing this transaction would receive careful attention. Finally, the ICC concluded that the instant transaction was in the public interest, that it would not materially affect competing truckers; and therefore, the transaction was approved.[176]

The T.I.M.E. Case. Before examining the specifics of this case, a change in the law (since the *Elliott* case) affecting intrastate carriers operating in interstate commerce should be mentioned. Effective October 15, 1962 the second proviso of Section 206 (a) (1) was repealed and each common carrier intrastate trucker that participated in interstate commerce was issued a "certificate of registration."

The vendor in the second "key" case in this area operated exclusively in the state of California. Protesting carriers requested the ICC to reverse the precedent of the *Elliott* case and forbid intrastate carriers' operating rights from merging with interstate carriers. In fact, they argued that under the terms of the amended Section 206 (a), their position had been specifically demanded by Congress. Their argument was based on this portion of Section 206 (a) (7) (A):

Certificates of registration shall be valid only so long as the holder is a carrier engaged in operation solely within a single State, not controlled by, controlling, or under a common control with a carrier engaged in operation outside such State. . . .[177]

The Commission reminded the protestants that the above quote from Section 206 (a) must be interpreted in light of the other pertinent provisions of the act, one of which, of course, is Section 5. The ICC listed numerous prior cases in which second proviso carriers were allowed to transfer their rights to interstate carriers. The Federal regulatory authority then concluded:

Upon comparison of the foregoing principles and conclusions with the provisions embodied in the amendments to section 206 (a), it is evident that the statute, to a substantial degree, effected a codification of the principles and precedents already established by the Commission with respect to single-State interstate operations. It follows, therefore, that, in many respects, there will be little variance between the treatment accorded section 5 proceedings involving section 206 (a), as amended, and that which was accorded proceedings involving the former proviso.[178]

Furthermore, the Commission quoted from a statement by Senator Smathers when he was explaining the provisions of the Section 206 (a) change. The Senator remarked:

. . . all the present rights of intrastate motor carriers engaged in interstate and foreign commerce [under the former proviso] would be preserved by this bill.[179]

In light of the above, the Commission upheld the principles of the *Elliott* case, finding them fully applicable under amended Section 206 (a). Specifically, because the applicants had previously interlined extensively, the ICC concluded that a new competitive service would not be created. The application was authorized because it was found to be in the public interest.[180]

General Discussion

In general, the cases cited primarily established the precedent that allowed intrastate carriers operating in interstate commerce to transfer their operating rights to interstate truckers. Thus, in a 1967 case, the Commission stated that the vendor's certificate of registration commands the same respect as an existing certificate. In fact, the ICC observed that:

. . . it has now been held that the 'test of substantiality' . . . also is applicable to proceedings involving the issuance of certificates of public convenience and necessity which are based on past operations under certificates of registration.[181]

In summary, a long series of cases have now shown that certificates of registration: (a) can be transferred to interstate truckers with appropriate ICC approval (state authorization is not needed, because interstate commerce is involved); and (b) are on a par with certificates of public convenience and necessity in regard to establishing whether a new competitive service will result from a Section 5 trucking unification proceeding.[182]

The Problem of Route Split-Offs

In a substantial number of cases, the problem arises in which the vendor tries to sell one set of operating rights between two cities or territories, and also attempts to preserve another set of rights over the same or similar routes. Another situation involves vendors trying to pulverize their operating rights by splitting-off part of the route authorization that they no longer wish to use. These situations are generally referred to as route "split-offs." In most cases the ICC frowns upon route split-offs, because the net effect is that of creating two competitors over the route involved, where only the vendor existed before. This section will introduce the topic by summarizing a "key" case that set the precedent for future cases dealing with route split-offs. Then cases will be examined in which the ICC has both denied and authorized the merger application, depending on the severity and particular type of route split-off involved.

The Welch-Scannell Case

The landmark proceeding dealing with route split-offs is officially known as the *H.P. Welch Co.–Purchase–E.J. Scannell, Inc.* case,[183] which was decided on September 26, 1939. In this proceeding, the vendor proposed to sell to the vendee part of his route structure. Specifically, the portion between southern New Hampshire and New York City would be sold; but the vendor also proposed to continue to serve these points, because he contended that he had two separate operating rights between these points of which he proposed to sell only one. The vendor based his claim of two separate operating rights between these points on the following rationales. First, because he had offered two separate services over the route in question, two separate operating rights should exist. Secondly, two rights were present because the vendor's certificate lists on two occasions the authority in question, meaning that two operating rights are thus in existence.[184]

The ICC took issue with both of these arguments. Regarding the first, the Commission stated that the internal operating methods of a trucker are always changing so that he can function most efficiently over a given segment of his route structure. Because these methods lack stability, they can not be used to establish the fact of a separate operating right. More important, however, is that the vendor's argument could be extended to any segment of any route structure. Thus, each vendor could sell one operating right over his route structure from A to B and keep one for himself. The Commission concluded that,

Multiple operating rights would thus live on indefinitely in the hands of a single operator, and it would always lie within the power of such operator, without control by us on grounds of public convenience and necessity, to place additional operators on the highways.[185]

In fact, the ICC pointed out that it would be fully feasible for the vendee to dispose of the acquired rights almost immediately, keeping a set of operating rights for himself.[186]

Referring to the vendor's second argument, the Commission noted that the fact that the route segment in question was mentioned twice has no official significance in regard to two separate operating authorities. That is, just because of convenience, or for the sake of clarity, a route segment is repeated more than once surely does not mean that the Commission desires to authorize two separate operating authorities over the same route segment.

The ICC noted in denying the vendor's argument for two route authorities that the problem involved was not unique to the instant case. In other words, many Section 213 (now Section 5) applications were pending in which a vendor proposed to sell one of the operating rights over a segment of his route authority that would be especially valuable and important to the vendee. As to this trend, the Commission stated:

If we should permit such splitting under section 213, and hence without regard to convenience and necessity, we would be thereby failing to properly perform one of our duties under the act and in lieu thereof, would in effect be permitting the creation by the direct parties to the transaction of new rights by contract and without regard to public convenience and necessity.[187]

Therefore, the ICC approved the sale of the vendor's rights to the vendee, *but did not allow the vendor to keep any rights over the transferred route segment.*[188]

Merger Application Denied

Route split-offs have arisen in a number of different situations and each has been condemned by the Commission. This section will examine a number of specific types of illegal route split-offs.

Alternative Route Split-Offs. A common type of route split-off is for the vendor to attempt to sell or lease to the vendee one specific route authorization from A to B, and then for the vendor to also continue to serve between A and B using an alternative authorized route.[189] Thus, in a 1957 case, the vendor claimed that he had two distinct sets of rights between Chicago and Milwaukee because he had previously served these cities by means of two separate highways. The ICC rejected this theory, stating that if the purchase was consummated, the effect would be a new competitive service for which a public need had not been proven.[190]

Commodity Split-Offs. A second type of split-off involves a vendor who sells part of his route structure that transports only certain commodities, and retains the other part of the goods authorized to be transported. Again, the result is that two carriers would be operating where only one had previously. The Commission has often condemned this outcome because the extra carrier in the area complicates the ICC's regulatory task, pulverizes the existing route awards, and in general tends to confuse the shipping public.[191] Thus, in a 1949 case, the lessor would lease to the lessee the former's operating rights to transport new automobiles and trucks from South Bend to points in Virginia. The ICC denied the lease arrangement, stating that:

Lessor proposes to divide and lease the operating rights as proposed, under which it would derive revenues as rental from the operations of lessee, and, in addition the quantum of its own service from and to the same points, for the same shipper, would not be materially affected. The record contains little evidence as to any need for creating two independent and competitive operations out of the single service which lessor has rendered.[192]

In a proceeding decided in June 1968, the vendor proposed to sell a relatively unimportant part of his operating rights that dealt with the transportation of roofing materials. However, as the protestants pointed out, the vendors could probably continue to haul roofing products under their remaining general-commodity authority. The ICC noted the general validity of the protestants' argument, and that the controlling factor in this case would be the intended use of the commodities to be hauled. However, because of the impossible burden of enforcing the commodity split-off proposed, the ICC denied the application. Specifically, the Commission issued the following statement, which will also serve as an excellent summary of this section:

... it is clear that a grant of the instant applicant would result in two carriers operating in the same territory, transporting similar and, perhaps, identical commodities where only one carrier operated in the past. The creation of two independent and competitive operations resulting for the split of a single operating right has consistently been viewed with disfavor by this Commission.[193]

Miscellaneous Split-Offs. One type of split-off occasionally attempted involves the vendor separating his intrastate operating rights from the accompanying interstate rights, and then proposing to sell the latter set of rights. Again, the result is two carriers operating over the same routes, carrying the same commodities, where only one existed previously. In a 1960 case the ICC denied a transaction of this type by stating emphatically:

... we are disposed to deny the application based on one single overriding factor, that of vendor's retention of his intrastate rights in Arkansas which are identical to the interstate rights in that State which he here seeks to transfer.[194]

Another type of split-off involves an irregular-route vendor selling part of his operating rights to the vendee. The Commission has taken the position that this type of transaction is legal only if the portion of the operating rights to be sold can clearly be delineated and segmented from the portion of the rights to be maintained. Thus, in a 1947 proceeding the Commission denied the proposed application because:

The proposed "carving up" of irregular-route authority by the sale of rights between one specified point, out of a number of closely grouped points, and a defined territory, while at the same time retaining rights between all such other points in the same defined territory, has been found to be a division not along clear-cut geographical lines, and approval of such proposals has been withheld by us in a number of prior cases.[195]

Specifically, the ICC denied the application because if the instant case was authorized, the vendor could repeat the process many times in the future, creating many competitors in the area where only the vendor now existed. In addition, because the rights were not clearly segmented, the enforcement of existing operating restrictions would be more difficult. Finally, the ICC stated that, in general, it does not favor the "atomization" of existing route structures because: (a) the additional number of carriers tends to confuse the shipping public; (b) it changes the character of the service contemplated under the original operating rights; and (c) it would tend to increase the level of competition in the area without a public need being shown for it.[196]

A final type of split-off involves a very similar situation in which the vendor would sell his irregular-routes to the vendee, but would retain his regular-route operating rights in the same general territory. In a 1949 case the ICC denied the transaction because, as in the above cases, the vendor's two types of routes could not be clearly segmented. The ICC noted that:

... where the regular- and irregular-route rights authorize service in the same territory, which is the case here, their separation should be permitted only upon a showing that the operations are readily servable or that separate operations thereunder otherwise would be in the public interest. No such showing has been made in this proceeding.[197]

Merger Application Approved

In general, the Commission has taken two basic actions in approving applications where a route split-off situation is encountered. Either the vendor's retained rights are canceled, as in the previous *Welch-Scannell* case, or the transaction is found to be in the public interest in spite of the split-off involved. Each of these situations will now be discussed.

Vendor's Retained Rights Canceled. A very common way that the Commission has handled route split-offs, if they do not involve a major portion of the rights in question, is to merely authorize the transaction but cancel the vendor's proposed retained operating rights.[198] For example, in a December 1965 proceeding the Commission found that the vendor was attempting to sell one set of rights for transporting general commodities from Detroit to Elkhart, Indiana, and also attempting to keep another set of the same operating rights. The Commission decided to approve the transaction, with the understanding that the vendor's duplicate rights would be canceled.[199] As already indicated, this solution to the split-off problem has often been used.[200]

Application Found to be in the Public Interest. The second basic Commission action in approving applications involving split-offs is to find the transaction in the public interest because the split-off involved was legitimately intended to sell one part of the vendor's operating rights while the vendor had no intention of retaining any operating rights over the transferred authority. Thus, in a 1968 case, the ICC noted that often the separation of regular from irregular-routes was denied because the result would be an added competitor in the region without the vendor sacrificing an essential portion of its operating authority. However, in the instant case, the vendor's proposed rights to be sold would clearly be delineated from those that remained. Therefore, since the vendor's right to be transferred would definitely not be retained and used by him, the result would be that no new competitors would be added to the involved territory. In other words, the vendee would completely replace the vendor over the route segments transferred. Finally, because the transaction was found to be in the public interest, it was approved.[201]

The Issue of Tacking

Tacking can be thought of as the process of joining together separate pieces of operating authority. Thus, if the vendee had operating rights to serve from A to B, and he purchased from the vendor rights from B to C, the vendee could then serve from C to A or A to C via B. It should be pointed out that in most cases the vendee is *not* authorized to serve directly to or from A to C without going through B.

In a few unification proceedings, the protestants requested that the ICC not allow or restrict the vendee from "tacking" his newly acquired rights to those he already possessed. The ICC takes the position that to restrict or prohibit the vendee's tacking rights requires a specific showing by the protestants that they would be materially damaged by the vendee's tacking.[202] In addition, if the applicants are not allowed to tack their separate operating rights, the single-carrier service and responsibility argument in favor of trucking unifications would be avoided. In two relatively recent cases the protestants have sought tacking restrictions that have been denied because they failed to prove the severity of the damage claimed.[203] However, in one of the cases the ICC specifically noted that:

This, of course, is not to be construed as implying that a carrier may utilize irregular-route authority for bridging the gap between two sets of regular-route rights as such inevitably would result in conversion of the irregular-route authority to that of regular-route rights, and be unlawful. We see no objection here since the separate nature of the irregular-route rights can be maintained.[204]

Occasionally, the ICC will impose a no-tacking restriction on the vendee. Thus, in a 1968 proceeding, that restriction was imposed because the applicants had interlined very little traffic between certain points. In other words, the Commission believed that if the no-tacking restriction were not imposed on the applicants, a new competitive service would have been established for which no public need had been proven.[205]

Previously in this paper the advantages of corporate simplification has been surveyed.[206] The next section will now examine the issue of corporate simplification from the point of view of its sometimes adverse effect on the intramodal competition.

The Issue of Corporate Simplification

The question of corporate simplification has been a significant factor in denying a number of trucking unification cases. Specifically, the problem is the following. Assume trucking firms A and B both operate between cities X and Y. Companies A and B apply to the Commission to consolidate the *ownership* of the two firms but not the actual trucking firms themselves. The ICC in most cases denies this type of application, because the result would be that firms A and B, which used to compete with each other between X and Y no longer do so because they are both owned by the same corporation. In addition, the possibility of discrimination between customers increases when previously competitive trucking firms come under common control. For example, in a 1940 proceeding, three trucking firms proposed to consolidate the managerial and administrative functions of their respective firms, but not the physical operations. This application was denied, and the Commission remarked that:

Doubtless certain economies might be realized from common control and management of these carriers, but authorization for such common control would give rise to an objectionable situation in permitting and sanctioning preservation of duplicate operating authority in each carrier by means of its separate corporate existence, with attendant duplicate operating expenses, and opportunity for discriminatory rates and other unfair competitive practices.[207]

In a 1960 proceeding, the vendee, Midwest, proposed to purchase the vendor, Chamberland's Express, but did not propose to physically integrate the firms. Again, the Commission denied the application, noting that if it were not for their common control, they would be competitive firms. In addition, the ICC condemned the waste that would result from common control without consolidating the physical operations of the firms.[208]

In summary, the ICC has consistently denied cases that have violated the Commission's policy of achieving corporate simplification by not physically integrating the proposed merger applicants.[200]

Miscellaneous Intramodal Competitive Issues

This section will examine two interesting cases that could not be grouped into the other sections on intramodal completion because of the uniqueness of each proceeding. The first case deals with an unusual situation that the Commission believed culminated in a "new competitive service" for which no public need had been established. The last proceeding is included because the author wishes to finish this very lengthy topic of intramodal competitive issues on a lighter note.

A Unique "New Competitive Service" Situation

A July 1960 case involved the purchase by the vendee, Dallas and Mavis, of the relatively smaller vendor, Billy Baker Co. Both of these firms were common carriers that specialized in transporting heavy and bulky products. This case was vigorously protested by truckers operating in the vendor's territory, but they did not support their contentions by presenting any specific evidence of the extent to which they would be damaged if the merger was consummated. However, the ICC accepted their arguments and denied the application. Why? Because the Commission noted that in this case special circumstances were present. Specifically, it was shown that the vendor had done very little business under the rights he proposed to sell to the vendee prior to when he started interlining with him. The ICC remarked that it is entirely lawful for a carrier to build up a segment of its operating rights in anticipation of selling the involved rights, as long as the augmentation was free from the control of the prospective buyer. In the instant case, the latter proviso was not met by the vendor. That is, the ICC determined that the vendee had solicited all of the traffic that the applicants had formerly interlined. The Commission concluded by stating that, due to these circumstances:

... there can be no question that vendee's operations under the rights here involved would be entirely different from those rendered in the past by vendor and would, in effect, constitute a new service, from which protestants are entitled to protection.[210]

Finally, since the applicants had not established a need for the proposed new service, the application was denied.[211]

A Closing Note

The above pages have recounted many arguments by protesting truckers requesting that mergers be denied by the Commission. However, no discussion of this topic would be complete without the classic argument put forward in a 1942 proceeding. The vendee in this case was Motor Express, Inc. The protesting trucker was Motor City Express, Inc. If the merger was consummated, the vendee would then operate in the vendor's territory, which is where the protestant also operated. Therefore, the protestant carrier argued that because of the similarity of names, which would surely confuse the shipping public, the application should be denied! As would be expected, the ICC did not give much credence to this particular line of reasoning.[212]

7

Additional Significant Considerations in Trucking Unification Proceedings

Leasing Under Section 5

The great majority of Section 5 unification proceedings involves an outright purchase or consolidation by the applicants. However, another method of controlling a trucking firm that falls within the authority of Section 5 is that of leasing. The Commission has stated the theory of Section 5 leasing arrangements in a number of cases, with one of the best being contained in the *Auto Convoy Co.—Lease—Automobile Shippers, Inc.* case[1] of 1949. In that proceeding, the ICC pointed out that Section 5 leases are designed to be of relatively short duration, so that the lessee can determine if the operating rights to be acquired would reasonably well integrate into those he already possesses. In other words, the lease can be thought of as a "trial period" for the lessee to use the acquired rights. Because of the rationale for leasing, the ICC is understandably unreceptive to long lease periods. Thus, in many cases the Commission will specifically limit the maximum period that the lease can run, which is usually five years or less and often only one year.[2] In addition, the ICC vehemently disapproves unreasonably high lease payments. The theory of this position is summarized by this ICC statement:

Because leases at other than nominal rentals exact tolls from the public for use of public highways, and because they involve payments to owners who do not desire to fulfill the carrier obligations which the holding of such rights implies but who nevertheless desire to secure an income from and retain a voice in the selection of operators who shall perform the service in the future, we have, in numerous recent reports, withheld authority for leases of operating rights for longer periods than are required for an appraisal by the lessee of the results of operations with a view to their permanent acquisition or determination by the parties that the service will be rendered by the owner.[3]

This section will begin by examining temporary leasing arrangements under Section 210 a (b), because it is easy to confuse the purpose of that leasing situation to a Section 5 lease. The following two sections will discuss situations that the ICC has looked at with disfavor—permanent leases and very short duration leases—because the lessors in both cases had no real desire to sell the leased operating rights. Leasing arrangements that are of a proper duration and involve a reasonable lease payment will not be examined, because in these cases the ICC uses the same criteria that has been traditionally used in all Section 5 cases, i.e., the transaction must be found to be in the public interest. In other words, except for the situations that will be discussed shortly, all of the previous findings of this book are equally valid in a Section 5 leasing case. It should be clearly noted that in many Section 5 leases the ICC authorizes the lessee to purchase the lessor's operating rights at any time before the expiration of the lease. In other cases, however, the Commission authorizes only the proposed lease and advises the applicants to file another Section 5 application if permanent control of leased rights is desired at a later date.

Section 210 a (b) Leases

The general purpose of Section 210 a (b) leases has been previously indicated.[4] In summary, these leases allow a temporary transfer (not to exceed 180 days) of operating rights to the lessee in an emergency type of situation. As shown, these leases cannot be extended, and if the lessee wishes to continue operation of the lessor's rights, a Section 5 application is in order. Also, leases of less than six months therefore do not come under Section 5, but under Section 210 a (b).[5]

The question of whether prior Section 210 a (b) operations by the lessee (vendee) should be considered in Section 5 unification cases has often come up. In other words, the vendee in many merger cases would like to point to the service improvements and other accomplishments that have taken place since the vendor was acquired under Section 210 a (b). This is done in order to impress the ICC with the public need for the vendee to continue to operate the vendor's rights on a permament basis. The Commission has stated that operations conducted during the temporary authority afforded under Section 210 a (b) are entitled to little consideration.[6] In a 1964 case, the vendee, upon taking over the operations of the vendor under Section 210 a (b), paid off a number of the vendor's outstanding debts and also purchased some new vehicles to use on the vendor's route structure. The vendee undoubtedly wished these factors to be considered by the ICC when deciding if the proposed merger would be in the public interest. To this contention, the ICC replied that:

> ... the extent to which action may reasonably be taken under temporary authority to effect economies and promote efficiencies of operation is largely a discretionary matter since the parties are forewarned that a grant of temporary authority is not to be construed as creating any presumption as to what action may be taken with respect to the related application under section 5.[7]

Permanent Leases

The ICC has always taken a negative view towards long or permanent leases. The reason is that the Commission does not like to see a carrier charging another trucker a fee to use the public highways. For example, witness this lucid remark of the Commission in a 1949 case, "In our opinion, a carrier which no longer desires to render the service required by its certificate or to serve the needs of the communities involved, should dispose of the operations permanently or should request revocation of the rights. It should not be permitted to derive revenue for long periods therefrom as a toll for use by another of the public highways."[8] Because of the ten-year lease involved in the instant case, the application was denied.[9]

A 1960 application was rejected when the applicants requested a five-year extension on their existing leasing arrangement, which had been in effect since 1954. The ICC reasoned that the lessee certainly had had sufficient time to determine if it wished to acquire the lessor's rights on a permanent basis. Therefore, the instant request was denied, but the Commission said it would accept, without prejudice, a new Section 5 application that sought to accomplish a purchase of the formerly leased operating rights.[10]

It should be noted that occasionally the Commission will actually change the Section 5 application before it. This can be done, because as noted previously, the Commission's findings under Section 5 are strictly on a permissive basis, and therefore no carriers are bound to consummate a unification against their will. Therefore, in a 1949 proceeding, the ICC stated that the transaction would be authorized if the proposed ten-year lease was converted to an outright sale of the involved operating rights.[11]

In closing, the Commission has consistently denounced long-term leases for the reasons discussed above.[12]

Temporary Leases

A second situation that the Commission disapproves of involves temporary leases. In this case, the lessor also has no intention of selling his leased operating rights, but he does not have the same motive for leasing them as seen in permanent lease situations. Instead, for some reason, the lessor does not wish to use a portion of his rights at the present time. He knows that if he does not use them, they will become dormant. Hence, he would lose the option of selling these rights at a future date. In addition, if the rights are not used, he obviously will not generate any income from them. Therefore, a solution for the lessor is to lease the involved rights for a period of time, and then at the end of the lease period reclaim the rights and then either use them himself or dispose of them.

An example of this situation occurred in a 1939 proceeding. The president of the leasing firm became very ill and was not able to continue directing the company. He had two sons who were, at the time of his sickness, college students majoring in transportation. Because these young men were not ready to take over their father's firm after his illness, it was decided to lease the father's operating rights for 260 weeks, at which time the sons should have completed their studies and would hence be in a position to take over the formerly leased operating rights of their father. The Commission denied the leasing application, because the purpose of lease arrangements is to give the lessee a "trial period" to determine if he wants to acquire the involved rights on a permanent basis. Since the instant application was not designed to accomplish this end, the proposal was denied.[13]

Another example of this situation was encountered in an October 1952 case. The lessor was losing money on a segment of his operating rights and had therefore leased them to McLean Trucking Company in 1947. In 1951, one year before the 1947 leasing arrangement was to mature, the lessor decided that he would like to resume operations over the leased routes. However, he found out that it would take more time than that available before the original lease agreement terminated to establish an appropriate administrative and operating organization to effectively manage and operate the formerly leased rights. Therefore, the lessor and the lessee applied to the Commission for an extension of the original lease. The Commission denied the application, stating that since the lessor had no intention of selling the involved rights to the lessee, the transaction could not be found to be in the public interest.[14]

Financial Considerations in Section 5 Cases, Not Including Those Situations Dealing with the Vendee's Fitness

This section will examine a number of financial considerations that have been encountered in studying trucking mergers. In general, it can be said that the monetary issues discussed here have not been of particular importance in the great majority of trucking unification proceedings. This section will discuss the major issue under this topic, which is the question of the purchase price involved between the vendee and vendor. Following that, a number of miscellaneous financial considerations in trucking unification proceedings will be examined. Next we shall consider the overall fitness of the vendee and also examine some financial considerations directly involved in determining if the vendee is fit to acquire the vendor.

The Purchase Price

In general, the Commission takes the position that the price arrived at by the applicants should be given considerable weight in determining its reasonableness. Thus, in a July 1968 proceeding the ICC noted that, "In numerous proceedings, we have held that a price arrived at by contracting parties as a result of arms' length bargaining is entitled to great weight."[15] The Commission takes this position so strongly that not one case read by the author was denied because of an excessive purchase price involved for the operating rights. The ICC has mentioned this factor in a number of proceedings.

In a 1939 case, the Commission stated that although the purchase price appeared high, the transaction would not be denied on this account. That is, the public benefits from the merger (in regard to reduced operating costs and significantly improved service level) more than offset the high purchase price involved. Finally, the price was found not to be an important consideration, because it in no way burdened the vendee to pay it.[16]

The Commission has stated that since many vendors have incurred negative profits in the years immediately prior to the merger, obviously the vendor's recent earnings record could not be the sole criterion on which to determine the reasonableness of a purchase price. The Commission noted this in a 1958 case and authorized the purchase price and the overall transaction because the vendee was adding such valuable and needed points to his existing route structure.[17]

Another application was approved even though the purchase price may have been exaggerated and would have burdened the vendee to the point he could not have carried out his common carrier obligations. However, the vendee anticipated this problem and inserted a provision into the agreement to which the ICC commented as follows, "Also meritorious is the provision in the present agreement which would preclude vendee from paying salaries, dividends, or bonuses to its stockholders and officers during the period of the existence of the debt to vendor."[18]

A 1968 case well indicates the Commission's general attitude on the purchase price involved. The ICC stated that ordinarily the purchase price represents the fair commercial value of the properties and operations involved, unless the contrary can be established by definite evidence. Furthermore, the Commission noted emphatically that, "The question of reasonableness of the purchase price is the proper area of investigation rather than the amount of profit or compensation to the seller. . . ."[19] In the instant case, while the purchase price was high, it was deemed reasonable because: (a) the operating rights to be acquired would be a valuable addition to the vendee's route structure by allowing the vendee to offer a substantially improved service to the public while at the same time decreasing his operating costs per unit of service; and (b) the purchase price in no way would burden the vendee's financial condition.[20]

The above cases involving purchase price considerations have all resulted in the transaction being authorized. The final case to be examined was also approved by the majority of the ICC, with Commissioner Mahaffie dissenting on the basis of the price consideration. Specifically, Watson Brothers, the vendee, proposed to purchase a portion of the operating rights of the vendor for $150,000. Of this total, $25,000 was paid upon execution of the agreement, and $20,000 would be payable within ten days after the transaction was authorized by the Commission. The balance of $105,000 would be paid on a monthly basis at the rate of 3 percent of the total revenue received by Watson Brothers on the newly acquired routes, subject to a minimum payment of $500 per month.[21]

The ICC noted that using the minimum payment, it would take 17.5 years to pay off the balance to the vendor. The Commission stated that it preferred a faster debt amortization, and since Watson Brothers could afford to make faster payments, the transaction would only be approved if the entire debt were paid off within six years.[22]

Commissioner Mahaffie disagreed and stated:

In my opinion, these transactions both as proposed and as modified by the division provide for excessive payments for operating rights. If a carrier has on hand the money to pay and is willing to write off immediately the cost of such rights, it is easy to say he can afford to pay for them. When the price paid has to be collected from future shippers a different situation is presented. When, as here, it is proposed to collect for a long period a toll on users of the public highways in order to pay for operating rights over them it seems to me very much the concern of such authorities.[23]

The author disagrees with Mahaffie, because he believes the restriction imposed by the majority sufficiently corrected the purchase price payment problem involved in this proceeding.

Miscellaneous Financial Considerations

Merger Consummation Delay for Tax Advantages. Occasionally, the ICC will allow the merger applicants to delay the consummation of their proposed merger for a short period in order to take advantage of a special tax situation. Thus, in a 1959 case, the Commission authorized a transaction in which the applicants could wait up to two years before consummating their merger in order to gain the advantage of tax loss carryovers of between $250,000 and $260,000.[24] In addition, the applicants were allowed a delay in order to let the shipping public become more familiar with their joint-line service.[25] Finally, the ICC stated that the instant transaction was approved with the above delay because: (a) the tax loss carryover would allow the vendee to significantly improve the service previously offered by the vendor; (b) the protestants could not prove they would be materially damaged; and (c) the transaction was found to be in the public interest.[26]

A Finder's Fee. A finder's fee has been defined as, "A sum of money paid by a banker to one who brings to him a deal out of which he makes money."[27] In unification cases, it generally arises from one of the applicants, usually the vendor, paying a fee to a person who has found a desirable merger partner. The Commission stated in a 1963 case that the payment of a reasonable finder's fee is not objectionable as long as the "finder" does not attempt to be in the business of trafficking[28] in operating rights. Furthermore, the ICC believed that a reasonable finder's fee should not exceed 5 percent of the purchase price involved.[29]

Increased Fixed Costs. As was previously indicated, Section 5 (2) (c) of the Interstate Commerce Act specifically requires the ICC to consider three specific factors, among others, when deciding if a proposed transaction is in the public interest. Two of these factors have already been examined: the effect of the proposed transaction upon adequate transportation service to the public, and the effect of the unification on the employees involved. This section will discuss a third factor, which is that the Commission is not to authorize a merger if the result is an increase in the total fixed costs of the applicants, except upon a specific finding by the ICC that such an increase would not be contrary to the public interest.[30]

This provision relating to increased fixed costs was written with the railroad industry foremost in mind. In other words, as the railways' fixed costs increase, in an industry already known for its excessively high fixed costs, railways become more vulnerable to financial difficulties in any sort of downturn in the economy.[31] Therefore, the importance of the fixed costs provision has been minimal for the trucking industry because of its low percentage of constant costs. In the cases reviewed, the Commission merely stated in a summary manner that the increased fixed costs involved, if any, have been found to be not contrary to the public interest.[32]

Fitness of the Vendee

Section 207 of the Interstate Commerce Act deals with the issuance of certificates of public convenience and necessity. An important finding that must be made before a certificate can be issued is that the applicant is "fit, willing, and able" to perform the service proposed. Likewise, the Commission has consistently stated that before a Section 5 unification application can be authorized, the fitness of the vendee to effectuate the proposed merger and its related service improvements and/or operating economies must be proven. The ICC commented as follows in a 1958 case, "As the fitness of a prospective purchaser under Section 5 is one of the more important questions to be resolved in determining whether a transaction would be consistent with the public interest . . . , we shall consider this matter first."[33]

This section will examine the two major criteria that the ICC has recognized in the question of the vendee's fitness. First, continuing the prior discussion of financial aspects, the issue of the vendee's monetary ability to achieve the objectives of the unification will be surveyed. The second major area of fitness involves an examination of the effect of prior or contemplated illegal activities of the vendee or the vendor.

The Vendee's Financial Condition

The ICC has noted three basic financial situations that could render the vendee unfit to consummate a merger: first, if the vendee does not himself possess the monetary strength to fulfill the objectives of the unification; second, if the vendee is overcapitalized. Third, if the vendee intends to issue securities to pay for intangible assets. Each of these three financial considerations will now be discussed in turn.

Vendee's General Financial Weakness. In a number of cases, the ICC has taken the position that the vendee's financial strength should not be dissipated by attempting to expand its operations by means of the proposed unification. For example, in a 1942 proceeding, the vendee, Century System, Inc., had incurred deficits every year since it was established in 1939. Nevertheless, Century proposed to purchase Mid-West Motor Freight, Inc., for $20,000. The ICC denied the application on the grounds that Century would probably overextend itself and in the process forfeit its ability to perform its current common carrier obligations.[34] In addition, the Commission noted that, "In our opinion, it [Century] is more likely to succeed in this [reducing operating costs] if all its efforts are concentrated upon its present operations, without diversion incidental to organizing and developing operations in additional territory and over new routes."[35]

A more recent application was not authorized because the Commission felt that the vendee would undoubtedly lack working capital after the proposed unification. That is, after the transaction, the vendee's current liabilities would exceed his current assets by $279,999; therefore, additional borrowing would be necessary for meeting the cash flow needs of the firm. The effect of the long-term loans would be to increase its existing small overcapitalization and to worsen its already undesirable debt-equity ratio. Therefore, the application was denied because the ICC believed the vendee was overly risking the solvency of its present company. However, the Commission clearly stated that the transaction could be resubmitted without prejudice if it contained a revised plan designed to improve the ratio of debt to equity and strengthen its working cash position.[36]

A 1959 case was similarly denied because the ICC concluded that the vendee's prior moderately successful operation would not be sufficient to counterbalance the operating losses of the two vendors. In addition, the vendee, Vogel, Inc., had sustained substantial losses when it had operated the vendor's firms under prior temporary authority. Under the circumstances, the Federal regulatory authority remarked that, "Rather than to endanger the entire operation by authorizing the unification, it would be in the public interest to preserve Vogel, Inc., as a separate unit, which it has been demonstrated by past history can be operated on a profitable basis."[37]

To recapitulate, the Commission will occasionally deny a transaction if it appears that the vendee does not have the financial muscle to successfully fulfill his stated merger goals and objectives.[38]

The above discussion basically dealt with the vendee's financial problems in generalities. The next section will examine a specific problem in this area—that of overcapitalization of the vendee.

Vendee's Overcapitalization

General Statements. Capitalization, as defined by the ICC, refers to stock and outstanding long-term debt of the firm. Overcapitalization, therefore, is a situation in which the firm's capitalization, as defined above, exceeds the value of the carrier's tangible assets.[39] The ICC generally denies transactions that result in aggravating a situation where overcapitalization already exists or where it will exist for the first time. The reason, of course, is that if the overcapitalization is in the form of debt that needs to be constantly serviced, the firm becomes burdened with a greater amount of fixed payments than it should have to support. Therefore, the problem is that if a slowdown in the economy should take place, the trucking firm may not be able to meet its fixed payments on its exaggerated debt and may fail. This, of course, is not in the public interest, because it can substantially damage shippers who have always used the vendee's trucking company.

For example, a May 1968 proceeding was denied because the vendee, after the proposed unification, would be overcapitalized by $380,530. Since this overcapitalization would have been in form of a long-term debt, the entire stability of the vendee would be questionable if an economic downturn took place. In addition, the vendee had operated the vendor's firm under temporary authority and had incurred a net loss in the process. Finally, the ICC concluded, "The additional obligation to be incurred by Sites resulting from the acquisition of control as herein proposed may become an unbearable burden if its past history of profit from operations continues."[40]

Although overcapitalization is usually grounds for a merger denial, this is not always the case. Thus, a 1961 proceeding involved a vendee who would be overcapitalized by about $42,000 as a result of the proposed acquisition of the vendor. That is, the firm's capitalizable assets would total about $42,000 less than its present capitalization. The ICC commented that, "Although it would be overcapitalized by $41,872, we have in some instances, approved transactions where overcapitalization would result, upon a showing of an ability to use the acquired rights in the attainment of a net income, after income taxes, sufficient to eliminate the difficulty in a reasonable period of time."[41] Specifically, it was found that based on his past earning record, the vendee could overcome the overcapitalization in less than 2 1/2 years. In addition, the ICC noted with approval that the two controlling stockholders of the vendee were in a strong financial position to come to the aid of the vendee if the need should arise. However, the Commission modified this finding by noting that, "Although the possession of resources by the controlling stockholders of a carrier is no substitute for financial stability of the carrier itself, we have held that, where the stockholders of a vendee have committed themselves to make a sufficient contribution to its capital and have shown that they possess adequate liquid assets to do so, consideration thereof in determining the financial ability of the purchaser is warranted."[42] The vendee was found to be financially fit to consummate the transaction, and it was authorized.[43]

Security Issuance for Intangible Assets. It was previously mentioned that the ICC defines capitalizable assets as those that are tangible. Therefore, intangible assets, such as the purchase price paid for a vendor's operating rights, are not counted as a capitalizable asset. The ICC reasons that there is no dispute that the operating rights are valuable. However, since they originate from a grant by the public, it would be illogical to include their value in the capitalized worth of the firm and then make the public, in effect, pay a rate of return on them. It should be noted, however, that the Commission's position on intangible assets is a direct outgrowth of Section 216 (h) of the Interstate Commerce Act, which specifically states that when the ICC determines the reasonableness and justness of a trucker's rate, it must not consider in the value of the carrier's property the following factors: good will, earning power, or the value of the carrier's operating rights as witnessed by his certificate of public convenience and necessity. For this reason, the Commission has always been very apprehensive about allowing a vendee to issue securities to purchase operating rights that are intangible assets. Why? Because the result is overcapitalization (as defined by the ICC) in the amount of the security issue, assuming that capitalizable assets equaled capitalization before the proposed unification. Thus, a 1953 transaction was denied because the vendee proposed to issue debentures that in effect would be used to purchase the operating rights of the vendor. The Commission, in denying the application, remarked that, "Securities should not be issued to finance the purchase of intangible property."[44]

A 1957 case involved the purchase of the vendor's operating rights and property for $2 million, of which securities would be issued for $1.5 million. The ICC denied this application on the grounds that: (a) securities should not be issued to purchase primarily intangible assets; and (b) after the proposed transaction was brought to fruition, the vendee would be overcapitalized by almost $1 million.[45]

A recent example of the above situation occurred in a November 1965 proceeding. In this case, the vendee proposed to purchase five liquidating truckers. To pay for these operating rights and properties, the vendee intended to issue 8,350 shares of its common capital stock. The Commission stated that since $350,000 of the proceeds from the stock issue would pay for intangible assets, this portion could not be allowed under its accounting rules. Therefore, instead of denying the application, the number of shares authorized to be issued was decreased from 8,350 to 4,850. Furthermore, there would have been an overcapitalization of $350,526. However, the merger was authorized in spite of this, because a large portion of the capitalization was represented by equity (common stock) and therefore the amount of outstanding debt was not unusually great for a trucking firm of its size.[46] Finally, the ICC concluded, "Earnings expected to flow from the merger are considerable and an ability to service long-term debt from earnings and gradually to reduce the overcapitalization is indicated. The economic benefits accruing from a combination of these related companies outweigh the undesirable working capital position and overcapitalization. In our opinion, however, Holmes Transportation should be precluded from declaring and paying cash dividends until the overcapitalization has been eliminated. . . . Our findings will be conditioned accordingly."[47]

Vendee's Illegal Activities

Here we will examine five questionable activities of the vendee, with the most important being discussed first: the illegal consummation of a merger *before* applying to the ICC for authorization.

Unauthorized Merger Consummation

The Commission has both approved and denied trucking unifications when the applicants had consummated their merger without ICC authorization. This section will now examine each type of situation.

Application Approved. In the early days of trucking regulation, most truckers were not familiar with the full extent of the control contemplated and effectuated in the Motor Carrier Act, 1935. Because of this, the ICC often followed, especially in the late 1930s and early 1940s, the precedent of the *Potashnick Truck Serv., Inc.—Control—Bryant Truck Lines* case[48] in regard to truckers who had illegally merged their firms without ICC approval. In that proceeding, the vendee, Potashnick, illegally acquired three trucking firms without ICC authorization and then applied to the Commission on August 2, 1938, for official approval of this transaction. The Federal regulatory body observed that, "We have recognized that in many instances there has been no intent to flaunt [sic] the law, but that the violations have resulted from mistaken interpretations of this section [213, now 5], perhaps normally to be expected in the early days of regulation. . . ."[49] Therefore, because of extenuating circumstances, the law violations were not found to be sufficient grounds to deny the instant transaction, especially in light of the fact that the unifications were otherwise found to be in the public interest.[50]

This precedent was followed in many early cases.[51] That is, the Commission said that because the merger section of the 1935 Act was generally improperly understood at best, or because the applicants were often ignorant of this provision, the ICC would not deny a unification on the grounds of the illegal prior merger consummation.

Illegal merger consummations have also resulted when applicants were aware of the 1935 Act's merger provisions, but did not believe they applied to acquiring a vendor whose operations were entirely within one state. Again, the ICC usually did not prevent the merger consummation because of this misinterpretation of the law.[52]

A similar case arose when both of the applicants were carriers involved in interstate or foreign commerce. However, each of the applicants operated totally within Alabama, and therefore they believed they could lawfully merge their firms without ICC authorization. The Commission approved the transaction in spite of the law violation and commented that:

It appears, however, that Murray acted in good faith, although upon erroneous legal advice. While this does not excuse the law violation, under the circumstances of record here we are not convinced that we should withhold approval . . . , particularly as the record clearly shows that operating benefits would result and that transaction would be consistent with the public interest.[53]

An interesting situation in which an illegal merger consummation was accomplished out of ignorance took place in a 1958 case. Specifically, both the vendee and the two vendors were Canadian trucking firms. However, the vendors had authority to operate as motor common carriers in the United States. The three Canadian companies merged prior to requesting ICC approval. The Commission authorized the Canadian merger transaction and observed that, "The law violations, however, apparently are not due to disregard for but rather to the lack of familiarity with the law on the part of the applicants."[54]

The above situations all involved cases in which the Commission disregarded the law violations because the applicants did not willfully ignore the unification provision of the 1935 Act. In a few cases, however, the ICC has approved mergers even when the applicants knew they should have had previous ICC authorization to consolidate their respective firms. Thus, in a 1945 proceeding the vendee paid $12,500 to the vendor for the operating rights he wished to possess and started using them on July 1, 1944. It was not until March of the following year that the applicants requested ICC approval of the transaction. The ICC stated that while they surely did not condone this illegal action, they felt that the instant violation was not a sufficient reason to deny an application that was otherwise in the public interest.[55] It should be noted that Commissioner Mahaffie dissented from the majority opinion and would have denied the application on the basis of the illegal merger consummation. Specifically, he stated:

If this is a proper handling of this situation, it would appear that the only risk taken by a person who decides to proceed without conforming to the law is the possibility that he cannot later convince us, on filing an application, that his completed transaction is then shown to be consistent with the public interest. This goes far toward abdicating our authority and our duty under the act. I would deny the application.[56]

In a case ten years later, the vendee bought the vendor for $1 million and then asked the Commission's approval to purchase the only remaining five shares of the vendor's stock, worth $675. The ICC said that they realized that the applicants had in effect consummated the transaction prior to applying to the Commission to purchase the last five shares. However, because the overall transaction was found to have been in the public interest, the ICC overlooked the prior illegal consummation of the merger and authorized the transaction.[57]

The next section will examine cases in which the ICC believed that the illegal prior merger was willfully committed, and therefore the vendee was denied the authorization to continue the existing unification because he was considered unfit.

Application Denied. In the later years after the 1935 Motor Carrier Act, the Commission has generally taken the position that the trucking industry should now be very familiar with Federal trucking regulation, including Section 5 merger procedures. Therefore, when truckers illegally consummate their merger without ICC approval, the Commission has often denied their later Section 5 application because the previous illegal action speaks badly of the overall fitness of the applicants, especially the vendee. For example, in a 1954 proceeding, the vendee in 1951 took over the operations of the vendor, who was in serious financial difficulties. The ICC noted that if an emergency situation existed, a Section 210 a (b) application could have been requested, but had not been. Also, the parties admitted that they knew they were disregarding the Section 5 merger provisions. In addition, after the application for the merger had been initiated, the parties made no attempt to end their illegal relationship.[58] The Commission denied the application and concluded that:

In effect, applicants would have us ignore the unlawful control which has now continued for some years, and authorize the merger on the basis of the evidence presented, which is largely based on the unlawful control and the operations thereunder and directed primarily to the merger. The real issue is whether the common control of these carriers should be sanctioned under the circumstances presented. In our opinion, this record shows such a flagrant disregard for the law that divestiture should be ordered.[59]

An October 1965 case again illustrates the ICC's determination to see that willful violations of Section 5 did not go unanswered. In this proceeding, the vendee wished to acquire the vendor, but did not want to go through the official Section 5 procedure, because in all probability the vendor's operations were dormant. Therefore, the vendee convinced a friend of his, a doctor, to buy the vendor's operations as an investment. Because the doctor was totally unfamiliar with trucking, he consented to let the vendee manage the firm for him. The latter took this opportunity then to effect a *de facto* merger between his firm and that operated for the doctor. To this the ICC commented, "The law violation reflects adversely on the vendee's fitness and warrants denial of the applications . . . , unless the record should demonstrate that the overriding public interest required approval of the proposed transaction."[60] Finally, because this test was not met in the instant case, the transaction was denied.[61]

In closing, the Commission has denied a number of applications because the applicants willfully ignored the Section 5 merger provisions and therefore illegally consummated their unifications without prior ICC authorization.[62]

Vendee's Unfavorable Safety Record

A second aspect of the vendee's fitness is his past safety record. While this factor has been encountered only twice in this study, it is an important enough consideration to warrant a brief discussion. In a 1958 proceeding, a proposed unification was attacked by the protestants on the grounds that the vendee's prior safety violations and deficiencies rendered him unfit to consummate the contemplated unification. The vendee, Transamerican, admitted that his prior safety record was poor, but said that he had started a comprehensive safety program to curtail his past problems. The firm had established vehicle inspection facilities at all its terminals; and its employees were now carefully screened to make sure that no one was hired who had a bad safety record. In addition, a new director of the safety and personnel department had been hired who had achieved an exemplary safety record for Transamerican. The ICC reasoned, therefore, that the vendee's improved overall safety program would void the question of the vendee's unfitness.[63]

A 1965 case also involved the question of the vendee's past safety record. As in the above proceeding, the vendee, Midwest Emery, in realization of its poor past performance, had recently established an elaborate program to combat safety violations. The Commission noted that the vendee's previous safety record had been so deplorable that, "Accordingly, Midwest's certificates could be suspended at this time as requested by the [ICC] Bureau [of Enforcement]. Were it not for the shippers' need for the services of Midwest and the fact that respondent is clearly making progress . . . we would feel so inclined."[64] Although the ICC did not deny the application on the ground of the vendee's former unfitness, it did issue a strict warning to Midwest to prolong its new excellent safety record or face possible revocation or suspension of its operating rights.[65]

Trafficking in Operating Rights

A third thing that has reflected adversely on the vendee's fitness is traffiking in operating rights. Traffiking refers to a person who purchases operating rights with no intention of keeping them, but of selling them as quickly as possible for profit. Obviously, the ICC takes an unfavorable attitude towards this.

To take another example, in 1942 a vendee testified that he had paid more than he had intended for the operating rights in question at the bankruptcy sale and that he had already attempted on two occasions to sell the rights. The Commission's opinion was that the vendee never had the intention of conducting operations over the involved routes, and that at all times he was only interested in securing these rights for resale at a profit.[66] The ICC denied the application and observed that, "The purchase of operating rights of motor carriers merely for speculative purposes, rather than to conduct the business of transportation for the public as authorized, is not consistent with the public interest."[67]

A 1947 application was also denied because the vendee was attempting to traffic in operating rights. In this case, the vendee attempted to acquire the vendor, and then the vendee contemplated selling the combined rights to a third party. Again, the ICC denied the first transaction, because the vendee had no intention of conducting operations over his newly acquired rights.[68]

False Testimony by the Vendee

The fourth factor that can render the vendee unfit to consummate a trucking unification is the supplying of false testimony and/or information to the ICC. Again, this factor was only present in two cases read. The first situation like this was encountered in a 1956 proceeding. In this case, the ICC examiner recommended denial of the Section 5 transaction because it was later learned that the applicants had falsified accounting information to show that the vendor was financially *in extremis*, and hence qualified for a temporary transfer of operating rights under Section 210 a (b). In reality, the owners of the so-called financially weak carrier had a net worth of greater than $380,000. The ICC therefore denied the Section 5 application, primarily because of the flagrant misrepresentation encountered in the previous Section 210 a (b) proceeding.[69]

Undoubtedly one of the most spectacular attempts to falsify information tendered to the ICC took place in a 1963 proceeding. The applicants were aware that the vendor's rights were probably dormant. The applicants had thus perpetrated a fraud by preparing false bills of lading that attempted to show a reactivation of the vendor's operating rights. To lend authenticity to these documents, they were crumpled and trampled in order to appear as having been handled by the vendor's drivers. In addition, shipments supposedly made by the vendor were actually accomplished in the vendee's vehicles. Finally, a number of the applicants perjured themselves during the hearing.[70] Because of the seriousness of such fraud, the Commission's well reasoned reaction will be quoted verbatum.

The deliberate and brazen attempt of the applicant-respondents in these proceedings to mislead this Commission has few parallels in our experience. Moreover, the technique employed here—the submission of false exhibits supported by forged freight bills and false testimony under oath—are not only an affront to this Commission but have subverted the entire regulatory process. Obviously, if this Commission is to exercise informed judgment in discharging its statutory responsibilities, it must be able to rely fully upon the integrity of the basic documents reflecting the business transacted by the transportation companies subject to its regulation. For this reason, we consider the strong measures prescribed in these proceedings necessary to assure that there will not be a recurrence by the applicant-respondents, or others, of the flagrant violations of the law and willful misrepresentations to which this Commission has been subjected here.[71]

The Commission, of course, denied the application, finding the applicants totally unfit to consummate the proposed unification. In addition, the applicants' counsel was severely reprimanded for his actions in the case, with the possibility of disbarment being present. Finally, the Commission notified the Department of Justice to consider criminal proceedings against the applicants' attempt at fraud and to investigate the perjury that apparently took place during the ICC hearing.[72]

Miscellaneous Illegal Activities

The final reason for determining that the vendee or vendor is unfit is constant violation of the provisions of the Interstate Commerce Act. This section will briefly discuss two such cases.

A 1960 proceeding involved a vendor who had arranged with the vendee to lease the latter's equipment on interline movements. Therefore, the vendee's drivers operated the vendee's equipment from origins and destinations in the vendor's territory. However, the vendor never assumed any control over the vendee's equipment and responsibility for its action. The vendee even solicited traffic directly in the vendor's territory. In fact, all the vendor did was to receive $10 for each shipment that was "interlined." The ICC found that the vendee had illegally leased the vendor's rights without prior Section 5 authorization. In addition, the applicants had previously violated two important gateway restrictions. Because of these violations, the unification application was denied.[73]

A February 1968 proceeding was denied because the vendor (Pals) had a long series of past violations of the Interstate Commerce Act. It is not necessary to detail these numerous violations, but it is interesting to note what the Commission stated after denying the proposed unification. In addition, this final ICC statement on the subject of the applicant's fitness will serve as an excellent summary of this topic.

We could perhaps find, in an appropriate case, that Congress did not intend such a harsh result where the applicant was small, unknowing, acting without advice of counsel, or clearly unintentional in its violation. Indeed, this Commission has in the past frequently excused such violations where honest doubt existed, the prior complaint case involving Pals being a case in point. But here we find no extenuating circumstances whatsoever. Pals was a large well-staffed operation. It was at all times represented by counsel quite conversant with the act and our rules and regulations, and who had warned its officers that its chances in a section 5 proceeding before us would be slim because of its unfitness.[74]

Next to be examined will be lack of public benefit resulting from unifications.

Lack of Benefits to the Public

This section will examine a number of cases that were denied because the applicants had not proven that any significant advantages would accrue directly or indirectly to the shipping public. It should be noted that this reason was cited in only a very small percentage of the rejected applications that were read by the author. First to be discussed will be circuitous routes; second will be a lack of an improved service; and last will be insufficient documentary information.

Circuitous Routes

The Commission has occasionally denied a merger when the applicants' primary goal was to obtain a single-line service from city A to city B, but over an extremely circuitous route. The reason for the denial is that the Commission does not want to encourage wasteful transportation. For example, in a 1942 proceeding, the vendee wished to purchase the vendor's operating rights so that the former could offer one carrier service from points in New Jersey to other cities in the southern part of the United States. But because the vendor had an irregular-route structure, the combined firm would have to move all traffic going from one carrier's territory to the other's territory via the New York City gateway. Therefore, the traffic moving through this gateway, between New

Jersey and the southern section of the United States, would necessarily take a very circuitous route.[75] The Commission denied the application and noted that, "During the present emergency, particularly, transportation facilities must be used to maximum capacity, and unification, as here proposed, which would encourage circuitous routing and wasteful transportation should not be approved."[76]

A more recent case was also denied for about the same reason. In this case, the vendee wished to obtain single carrier service from Cedartown, Georgia, to Atlanta. Again, the applicants, if they operated exclusively over their authorized highway between these points, would have a very circuitous route. The Commission rejected the application, remarking that the proposed unification would result in uneconomical and inefficient transport service, which definitely was not in the public interest.[77]

Service Considerations

Only one case was encountered in which the Commission denied the application because of service considerations. This proceeding involved applicants who proposed to unite their operations and offer expedited transportation between their respective territories, but only on truck-load or quantity shipments. In other words, the improved service level would be available only to shippers who tendered goods in large volume. The Commission denied this application, noting that a common carrier has the responsibility to accept all shipment sizes tendered to it, including commodities that the trucker holds himself out to transport.[78] Thus, the ICC observed, "To sanction such a plan of operation, allowing Mid-States to concentrate on the cream of the long-haul traffic, would provide a means whereby Mid-States could justify its refusal to transport small shipments notwithstanding such service would be required under the combined certificates."[79]

Insufficient Testimony

Finally, one case was read in which the application was denied, not necessarily because it did not offer benefits to the public, but because the applicants failed to establish, by means of documentary evidence, the alleged advantages that would accrue to the shipping public. Specifically, in a 1959 proceeding, the applicants did not clearly establish a need for their proposed service, nor did they effectively document the fact that the vendor's operations were not dormant. The Commission turned down the application and issued this statement justifying their action. "In concluding whether the instant transaction should be approved, we are bound by the evidence of record in this proceeding and, in our opinion, applicants have not met their burden of presenting adequate evidence of a competent nature to enable us to determine the basic question of whether approval thereof would be consistent with the public interest."[80]

The next section will survey two important miscellaneous areas unrelated to any subject previously discussed.

Miscellaneous Topics

The two miscellaneous subjects are: (a) the handling of unification proceedings in the early days of regulation, when all "grandfather" claims had not been fully disposed of, and (b) the Commission's attitude on "dual" authority.

"Grandfather" Rights Pending

The ICC generally, with one exception to be noted, has taken the position that the vendee, upon purchasing the vendor's operating rights, also receives the latter's rights to any pending grandfather applications that had not been fully determined. One of the best explanations of the Commission's policy in this area is contained in the *Brooks Transp. Co., Inc.–Purchase–Jacobs Transfer Co.* case.[81] In this proceeding, the protestants claimed that since the extent of the vendor's grandfather rights had not been determined by the Commission, it would be appropriate to defer deciding the unification application until the grandfather rights had been completely determined. The ICC denied this request, noting that currently (1937) there were over 70,000 pending grandfather applications. Therefore, to hold up all merger requests until every grandfather application had been disposed of would mean a virtual cessation of all consolidations. The Commission believed that such would definitely not be in the public interest. Therefore, the policy was followed allowing the vendee to accept the vendor's grandfather rights[82] on a temporary basis until they had been officially decided by the Commission. Of course, if the vendor's claimed grandfather rights were restricted or denied, the assignee of these rights (the vendee) must accept the ICC's ruling.[83]

To recapitulate, the Commission's policy in regard to undecided grandfather rights was to allow the vendee to accept the vendor's future position, whatever it might be, in the pending grandfather application.[84]

One exception and probable contradiction to this procedure was encountered. In a 1941 case, the lessor's grandfather rights were considered by the ICC to be so doubtful because of dormancy and other problems that the Commission denied the proposed lease until it could be determined precisely what rights the lessor did possess. Why? Because the lessor's previous operations had been so irregular, the ICC decided that it could not define them to any practical point, which meant that it was impossible to know what rights could be transferred to the lessee.[85] The author believes that this must have been true in other cases, but applications were not denied on mere speculation of what the pending grandfather application results would have been.

Dual Operating Authority

Section 210 of the Interstate Commerce Act specifically declares that unless the ICC finds dual authority to be in the public interest, it shall be unlawful for a carrier to operate in the same territory as both a common and contract carrier. As previously noted, this provision is intended to prevent a type of discrimination in which the larger shipper demands preferential contract carrier rates or it refuses to use the same trucker's common carrier service. This section will examine situations in which dual authority was both denied and accepted.

Application Denied. The ICC is generally very apprehensive about allowing dual authority unless specific safeguards can be established. Hence, in a 1946 proceeding, the Commission noted that since the applicants wished to combine contract carrier operating rights with those of a common carrier, both of which operated in the same general territory, the application would have to be denied because the vendee would not accept any restrictions on the involved operating rights. In other words, the ICC noted that on some occasions, it was possible to allow dual authority, especially when appropriate restriction would segregate the territories that each type of carrier operates within. However, since the vendee would not consider such restrictions, the application was necessarily denied because of the discrimination that would have developed under the proposed unification.[86]

A 1949 proceeding was similarly denied because the proposed unification of a contract and common carrier would result in both truckers serving the same area and each having authority to transport many of the same commodities. Again, no appropriate restriction could have feasibly separated the two types of operations and prevented the discrimination therefore possible. The application was denied,[87] and the ICC made an interesting observation in regard to the bias that would have been feasible had the merger been authorized. Specifically, it was noted that the special contract rates offered to the larger shippers could be thought of as rebates from the common carrier rates currently in effect.[88]

Applicant Approved. Occasionally, the Commission will approve a transaction involving a dual operation when it is believed that the possibility of discriminatory action is minimal or nonexistent. For example, a 1963 application was authorized because the ICC found that, although the applicant's common and contract operating rights covered the same territory, each type of carrier had previously served and would continue to serve completely different shippers. Therefore, the Commission decided that any opportunity to engage in discriminatory practices, as contemplated by Section 210, would be minimal.[89]

A final similar situation was encountered in a December 1969 proceeding. As in the above case, each of the applicants served totally separate customers within the same territory, and each applicant in this case was an automobile hauler. The vendee was a common carrier, and did nearly all of its work for Chrysler Corporation. The vendor, a contract carrier, operated exclusively for the General Motors Corporation. Occasionally, the vendee had hauled a few automobiles for G.M. The Commission decided that to eliminate any possibility of the discrimination that Section 210 wished to prevent, the certificate of the vendee would be restricted from transporting products for G.M. Finally, as an added precaution, the ICC stated that it reserved the right to impose future restrictions, as needed, in order to prevent any future prejudicial situation, as contemplated by Section 210.[90]

8

General Discussion of the ICC's Administration of Section 5 Trucking Mergers

This chapter will examine a number of issues that have been discussed by other authors on the subject of trucking unifications. It should be noted that this subject has received very sparse attention, especially in scholarly journals. Thus, in April 1957, Senator John Sparkman noted that, "The paucity of data and literature on the subject [trucking mergers] is indicative of the lack of attention that has been given to this aspect of the motor-carrier industry in the past."[1] This observation is still valid in 1973. The author will also add his comments to the following basic topics to be surveyed: (a) the ramifications of increased concentration in the trucking industry; (b) the consistency of the ICC in Section 5 trucking consolidation cases; (c) the ICC's overall merger policy; (d) the question of active or passive ICC regulation of trucking unifications; and (e) the question of whether the ICC protects the status quo in trucking merger cases at the expense of economic efficiency.

The Trend Toward Trucking Mergers: Good or Bad?

It has previously been shown that the trend toward trucking unifications has rapidly accelerated in recent years, especially since the mid-1950s. In 1957, Herbert Burstein observed, "Unless Congress halts or reverses the current trend, interstate motor transportation will be dominated, if not monopolized, by a limited number of relatively large corporate entities."[2]

In light of the brisk movement toward trucking mergers, a relevant question then becomes—is this trend favorable or unfavorable from the point of view of the public interest? Initially, the positions of other writers will be presented, both pro and contra, and then the author will express his opinion on this basic question.

Arguments in Favor of Increased Trucking
Merger Activity

Service Advantages. The ICC has always recognized the service advantages that accrue to a larger consolidated type of trucking firm. For example, in a 1955 Senate hearing, Commissioner Anthony F. Arpaia remarked that, "There is not a

147

shipper in this country who would not prefer to have [a] single-line haul."[3] In a Senate hearing two years later on trucking mergers and concentration, the ICC again reaffirmed that a primary advantage of a larger consolidated trucking firm was the service improvement that accrued to the shipping public.[4] Specifically, Dr. Walter Adams, Professor of Economics at Michigan State University and co-author with Dr. James B. Hendry of a Senate Select Committee on Small Business study entitled *Trucking Mergers, Concentration, and Small Business: An Analysis of Interstate Commerce Commission Policy, 1950-56,* was having a heated debate with the then current (1957) chairman of the ICC, Owen Clarke. Professor Adams had asserted that it was not apparent to him that trucking mergers would automatically increase the overall efficiency of a firm. To this assertion Commissioner Clarke replied:

Dr. Adams apparently assumes that increased efficiency and improved service are synonymous. They certainly are not. In the case of Associated Transport, while the year 1955 may have resulted in a deficit for that company, nevertheless Associated Transport today and in 1955 was capable of rendering much better service than the seven separate companies that went to make up Associated could render prior to their consolidation, because it enabled the shippers to have single-line service from one point to another. Obviously that means a reduction in time in transit; it means other savings for the shipper, and that is a factor which apparently Dr. Adams ignores when he merely looks at the financial table to judge efficiency, and doesn't consider what benefits have gone to the shipper as a result.[5]

It should not be assumed that only the ICC recognizes the service advantages of larger trucking firms. This point was illustrated by the testimony of Mr. A.W. Hawkins at the Senate's Select Committee on Small Business hearings entitled *ICC Administration of the Motor Carrier Act.* Mr. Hawkins noted that his father had started a small trucking firm prior to the 1935 Motor Carrier Act. The grandfather rights obtained were quite limited, and the result was that the firm had a difficult time in soliciting traffic. Hawkins stated that, "I would take my pitiful little point list into shippers showing the points I could serve and they would say: 'Son, this is all right, but you just don't cover enough ground for us. We appreciate your interest in stopping in but you are not big enough.' "[6] Therefore, Mr. Hawkins stated that his firm was currently trying to purchase additional operating rights, in order to be able to offer the shipping public a more complete service covering a wider geographical territory.[7]

Another trucking industry spokesman who favored continued consolidation in his industry was J.H. Fles, executive vice-president of Associated Truck Lines, Inc., of Grand Rapids, Michigan. In July, 1957, he wrote a letter to Senator John Sparkman, explaining his view on the trend towards trucking mergers. He stated:

My fourth observation is that concentration in the motor-carrier field has been of tremendous help to the shipping public. As long as a competitive situation still exists between lines, a trucking company serving a large territory is of real attraction to the shipping public. A shipper does not like to dibble-dabble by giving a few pounds of freight to 50 different carriers and thus disturb his outbound and inbound shipping operations. As long as he has a proper election he would much rather give 50 shipments to 5 carriers to alleviate his own shipping problems. Thus a carrier offering a multiplicity of shipping points to a shipper in turn saves cost to that shipper on his own shipping facilities. The main objective of transportation is not to create an artificial number of carriers, but to create a nationwide transportation system that meets the needs of the shippers. We feel that the service on the part of the trucking industry to the shipping public is much better today than it ever has been in the history of our country. Nothing like it has ever been achieved anywhere in the world. There must be further merger and consolidation in the trucking industry in the future to better this service to the shipping public, always keeping in mind that no one carrier should achieve monopoly which will diminish that service.[8]

Finally, it should be noted that even some academicians have noticed that in general larger trucking firms can offer the shipping public a superior service. Dr. James C. Nelson, professor of Economics and Transportation at Washington State College has cautiously commented that, "Perhaps the service is adjudged superior when rendered by fewer and larger firms. There is some evidence that shippers prefer, other things being equal, to deal with fewer firms with larger geographical ranges of service and perhaps with greater financial responsibility."[9]

Greater Financial Stability. A second advantage of larger trucking firms is the greater financial stability that generally results from a larger operation. This argument was used by ICC Commissioner Owen Clarke when he stated that the Congressional intent favored increased trucking unifications. Clarke observed that:

This intent was and is that the Commission shall administer the act, and particularly section 5, so as to foster the growth of motor carriers, for the purpose, among other things, of alleviating some of the evils with which the motor-carrier industry was afflicted prior to 1935, especially unrestrained competition. That this was the intent of Congress is abundantly clear from a reading of the opinion of the Supreme Court in the *McLean Trucking Co., Inc.*, case, supra. The Court quoted with approval from the studies published as House and Senate documents, and which provided the basis for the legislation. These reports stated one of the purposes of the then proposed legislation was to encourage the "organization of stronger units," thus enabling the industry to put itself on a sounder basis.[10]

On another occasion Commissioner Clarke reiterated that, "The legislative history of the Motor Carrier Act and the Transportation Act of 1940 clearly show that it was the intent of the Congress that we should encourage the growth of the motor-carrier industry by taking such action as might be necessary to make it more stable and dependable, by consolidation or by other means."[11]

Along this same line of reasoning, the American Trucking Associations stress the fact that the number of Class I truckers, those who are the most financially stable, is increasing every year.[12] In 1966 there were 1,298[13] Class I truckers, and by 1972 this number had increased to 1,771.[14] Of course, not all of this increase was due to consolidations, but a substantial portion resulted from trucking unifications. The advantages of larger trucking firms with greater financial stability are the following, according to the American Trucking Associations:

The growth trend by individual large carriers has resulted in gains for the carrier, the shipper, and the public. The greater financial resources available are permitting these carriers to mechanize their terminals, invest in more efficient vehicles, and to computerize their operations. Also, the resultant stability of the individual firms has improved the image of the industry as a whole, as shown by increased public interest and confidence. These efficiencies reflect themselves to the shipper in the form of faster and more reliable service, greater rate stability, and, most importantly, the assurance of sufficient capacity by the carriers to handle the constantly growing freight volume generated by our burgeoning economy.[15]

No Significant Decrease in Competition. Another factor in favor of trucking unifications is that because a large percentage of them are of the end-to-end variety, the number of competitors between any two cities does not decrease. In fact, the viability of the competition often increases. From Figure 8-1 it can be seen that three mergers could take place without any decrease in competition. In other words, each city would have the same number of competitors running to

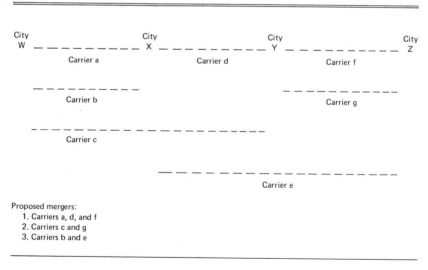

Figure 8-1. End-to-End Trucking Mergers

each other city as it had before the merger. In addition, the shippers in each city now have, with no loss in competition, a considerably increased number of points from which they can ship via one-carrier service.[16]

Of course, some trucking mergers are partially or totally of a side-by-side nature, and therefore the number of competitors between any two cities in question necessarily decreases. In this case, the ICC has concluded that the operating advantages and/or service improvements of the merger more than offset the decrease in trucking competition.[17]

*Arguments Against Increased
Trucking Merger Activity*

Decreased Competition. Professors Walter Adams and James B. Hendry have charged the ICC with allowing an excessive decrease in trucking competition via the consolidation route. "Whether by design or as the result of a policy vacuum—the intent is really irrelevant—the day approaches when the vigorously competitive motor carrier industry may become effectively monopolized by administrative action."[18] This concern about decreased competition and all the inefficiencies that result as monopolization replaces competition is also expressed by Professor Dudley F. Pegrum.[19]

No Apparent Economies of Scale. The issue of trucking economies has been previously discussed at some length. On the assumption that scale economies in the trucking industry are very limited at best, Professors Adams and Hendry have asserted that the ICC approves trucking mergers " . . . without any clear showing by the Commission that its policies reflect a sound economic analysis of the industry."[20] Professor Pegrum has also submitted that increased average trucking firm size cannot be based on economies of size (scale).[21] Finally, Professor Nelson concurred with the above scholars when he observed, "I am still of that opinion as we are still lacking evidence that strong economies of scale exist in trucking while accumulating evidence in the ICC records themselves suggests that costs in that industry tend to be constant rather than decreasing."[22]

Author's Conclusion

Professor James C. Nelson has outlined the following provocative test in regard to trucking unifications. "If transport policy is to go farther down the road of encouraging oligopoly or duopoly, the evidence should be ample and persuasive that larger firms either bring lower unit and aggregate costs or persuasive service advantages, or both."[23] This rule-of-thumb test will be an excellent starting place to express the author's conclusion on this pivotal issue. To begin with, the author questions whether the trucking industry is really moving so *rapidly* towards an oligopoly situation. Why? Because as previously seen, the number of the largest trucking firms (Class I motor carriers of property), those who would be best able to monopolize the trucking field, are steadily increasing. In 1966 there were 1,298 of these carriers and in 1972 this number had increased to 1,771. In addition, the number of Class III carriers, the relatively smallest truckers, decreased slightly from 11,453 in 1966 to 11,165 in 1972. The number of Class II carriers also decreased in this period, from 2,675 to 2,202.[24] Finally, the total number of Class I, II, and III carriers in 1966 was 15,426, and in 1972 this total was 15,138, for a net decrease of 288 carriers in six years.[25] The answer to why the total number of Class I, II, and III carriers decreased so slightly is twofold. First, a number of interstate truckers merged with strictly intrastate carriers that were never counted as Class I, II, or III interstate carriers. Therefore, this type of merger does not decrease the total number of Class I, II, and III carriers. Secondly, the ICC issues a significant number of totally new certificates each year to applicants who had no previous operating rights. Therefore, each time this takes place, a new carrier is added to the total number of Class I, II, and III interstate common carriers of property.

In any case, the total number of the largest class of interstate carriers is increasing yearly, while the total number of all interstate carriers is dropping very slowly. It is for these reasons that the author finds it difficult to imagine that an oligopoly situation is materializing in the trucking industry.

However, even if one accepts the argument that the trucking industry is moving towards concentration, Professor Nelson suggests that this is not necessarily an unfavorable trend if one or both of these advantages are present: (a) the larger firm is able to achieve lower costs per unit of service, and (b) the unified company can offer the shipping public a superior transportation service.

As to the issue of a larger firm achieving lower costs per unit of service, the evidence is not clearcut. Most writers, including the author, conclude that the scale economies in operating a truck from city A to city B are not impressive. This results from the high variable cost structure of this industry. However, it was previously indicated that the average motor common carrier has a load-factor far less than capacity. Therefore, if combined firms can increase the load-factor of their vehicles, their cost per unit of service rendered would decrease. Apparently there is some evidence to show that because the unified trucker can offer a one-carrier service to an expanded number of points, he is tendered more traffic and hence is able to increase his vehicle load-factor ratio. Another more definite method of increasing load-factors is for firms to consolidate their operations and in the process eliminate prior restrictive grandfather conditions. This factor has been previously examined at some length.

Besides increasing load-factors, the author believes there is no question that larger firms achieve other types of scale economies. Specifically, it was previously shown that the ICC has recognized these operating and administrative advantages: (a) less circuitous routes, (b) less pick-up and delivery expenses, (c) decreased loss and damage claims, (d) reduced maintenance costs, (e) consolidation of terminals and other facilities, (f) better management, (g) overall decreased labor costs, (h) purchasing discounts, (i) decreased paper work, (j) lower insurance costs, and (k) decreased costs of financing.[26]

The author therefore believes that there is conclusive evidence that larger trucking firms have the potential to achieve significantly lower operating costs per unit of service. The first criterion of Professor Nelson has thus been substantially complied with. However, the second condition enumerated by Nelson, that of improved service to the shipping public, is the real "clincher" in favor of unified trucking operations. To the best of the author's knowledge, no writer has disputed the fact that shippers greatly prefer one carrier service and responsibility from city A to city B, as opposed to an interline service. Furthermore, as previously discussed, consolidated truckers offer the shipping public the following additional advantages: (a) faster service, (b) more and better timed schedules, (c) decreased loss and damage, (d) better available equipment, (e) faster tracing, (f) faster payment on loss and damage claims, and (g) decreased shipper and receiver dock congestion.[27]

Another interesting factor in regard to improved trucking service is that if it is not superior to smaller carriers who have to interline their freight, then why do the advocates of reduced merger activity fear larger truckers? Professors Adams and Hendry have asserted that, " . . . the Commission no longer seems alarmed about approving mergers which entail the creation of a single-line service that *dilutes* the traffic of smaller carriers." (Emphasis added)[28] In other words, this dilution of traffic would not take place unless the shipping public preferred a one-carrier service to an interline type of transport.

Finally, it should be noted that shippers generally appear to prefer a larger carrier, especially in terms of its extended route structure and the convenience of one-carrier responsibility to the destination point.[29]

To recapitulate, the author believes that the trend toward trucking mergers substantially complies with the two criteria enumerated by Professor Nelson if this movement towards concentration is to continue.

The opponents of trucking mergers base their opposition basically on the decreased competition issue. The author believes this position does not carry substantial weight. In the first place, most of these authors apparently believe that *every* merger decreases competition, but as previously illustrated, the typical end-to-end merger does not have this result at all. In fact, in many cases the effectiveness of competition is increased when a progressive and modern management absorbs a carrier that had let the managerial and marketing revolutions pass them by. In addition, larger, well managed firms that have an accurate knowledge of their cost structure will encourage an overall increase in the competitiveness of the transport market, but not ruinous competition, which is often the result of an inaccurate knowledge of the direct and indirect costs of producing a unit of transport service.

Finally, even assuming that competition in the trucking market is precipitously on the decline (which it definitely is not), what would be the result of this situation in a *regulated* industry? Professor Clair Wilcox, discussing the evils of a monopoly situation, has asserted that, "The monopolist is likely to increase his profit by raising his price. He will then limit his output to the quantity that the market will take at the price that he has fixed."[30] In a regulated industry, such as trucking, the first phase of such a sequence could not be arbitrarily initiated, because the truckers involved would have to receive prior ICC authorization before a rate increase could legally go into effect. The Supreme Court recognized this basic factor in the landmark *McLean Trucking* case, when they stated that decreased competition could be tolerated in the trucking field because it is a regulated industry. Specifically, the high court upheld the previous approval by the ICC of the gigantic trucking consolidation involved in the instant case and declared that, "In doing so, it [the ICC] presumably took into account the fact that the business affected is subject to strict regulation and supervision, particularly with respect to rates charged the public—an effective safeguard against the evils attending monopoly, at which the Sherman Act is directed."[31]

Therefore, since rates cannot be arbitrarily increased by the remaining carriers, it does not behoove them to restrict their output, because this would not lead to maximum profits.

In addition, the carriers' service cannot decline too significantly under the present regulation. That is, the remaining carriers are not allowed to participate in discriminatory service practices,[32] nor can they offer unreasonably slow or inadequate service.[33] Of course, in the real world there is no significant problem of service deterioration, because the ICC actively encourages a reasonable amount of trucking competition between every pair of cities that will support it. For example, there are approximately fifty motor common carriers of property that are certified to operate between the Twin Cities and Chicago.

In summary, it appears to this author that the decreased competition argument, at this point in the trucking merger picture, does not merit significant concern. That is, thus far the merger movement has not precipitated the usual results of increased economic concentration, i.e., unreasonable rate increases and deteriorating service standards. In fact, excluding the fact that both of the above outcomes are not legal under present regulation, the opposite situation has materialized. Operating efficiencies effectuated by mergers have undoubtedly enabled the trucking industry to seek rate advances less rapidly than the overall recent increases in operating expenses would have indicated.[34] In addition, instead of service levels decreasing because of carrier complacency, the opposite has generally been the result. That is, after the proposed merger has been consummated, the unified carrier is theoretically able to provide and generally offers a significantly improved one-carrier trucking service.[35]

A final argument that the author believes worthy of credence in regard to increased trucking consolidation deals with the theory of countervailing power. This concept assumes sufficient economic power on each side of a market so that neither is able to bully the other side into accepting unreasonable demands.[36] Because this theory mitigates the undesirable use of economic power, Professor Donald S. Watson, in his text on economic policy has observed, "As a matter of policy, countervailing power would be something to rely on and to foster."[37]

The relevance of countervailing power to the discussion of trucking mergers is that at present, in the area of labor relations, the Teamsters Union has a substantial power advantage over the individual trucking firms with whom they negotiate their labor contracts. As previously noted, total labor costs are a very significant portion of the motor common carriers' operating expenses, being equal to approximately 60 percent of that total.[38] At present, the 2 million member[39] Teamster Union (about 30 percent are truck drivers), which had net assets in 1960 of almost $40 million,[40] negotiates a national contract with trucking firms. It would appear that the combined trucking firms would be able to match the power of the Teamsters Union, but this has not proven to be the case. In other words, the collective bargaining arm of the truckers, Trucking Employers, Inc., has not proven to be an effective adversary to the union's demands. This is understandable, because it appears that individual firms have given up trying to fight the powerful Teamsters Union and merely accept the wage demands of the union as an uncontrollable cost factor. Professor Charles A. Taff has observed that:

It is a curious fact that although Class I operators may be negotiating several labor contracts and engaging in the settlement of grievances throughout the year, there are few carriers that employ a full-time labor relations executive. Labor costs constitute approximately one-half of operating expenses, yet motor carrier management sometimes postpones preparations for collective bargaining until the present contract is expiring. Unions, on the other hand, have specialists whose full time is spent preparing for contract negotiations. In order to maintain an even keel in collective bargaining, motor carrier management must devote more attention to the labor-relations problem.

Motor carriers are particularly vulnerable to strikes or interruptions of any type in their service. Motor transportation is an intensely competitive field. A motor carrier faces competition from other motor carriers, from other modes of transportation, and from private carriage, and carriers lack the cash reserves to carry them through any long period of business interruption. Inasmuch as they are engaged in rendering service, they are unable to live off their inventory as production industries can. When they are not able to transport freight, it is just business lost. These factors have undoubtedly had an effect on their collective bargaining with unions.[41]

A recent example of the dominance of the Teamsters Union over the trucking industry took place when the national labor contracts were negotiated in early 1970. The Teamsters proposed a three year contract, starting on April 1, 1970, that called for a 96.4 percent increase in wages and other benefits.[42] By mid-April, despite a few "wildcat" walkouts,[43] the Teamsters and the Truckers Employers, Inc. (TEI), which represents about 12,000 trucking firms, had reached a tentative national agreement calling for a 27.5 percent increase over a 39-month period. The Chicago area teamsters, the only group to bargain separately from the national pact, insisted, however, on a 46.2 percent increase.[44] In fact, this area was struck by the teamsters immediately upon expiration of the old contract. Basically, the rest of the U.S. teamsters stayed on the job and were willing to accept the tentatively agreed on national pact.[45] In response to the Chicago strike, TEI announced that its member had approved a "multi-million dollar revolving assistance fund" to aid the Chicago carriers that had already been subjected to a month-long strike. It should be noted that trucking firms throughout the United States would be affected by the Chicago wage settlement, because the tentatively approved national agreement specifically stated that if the Chicago teamsters won their wage demands, the national contract would subsequently have to be reopened and adjusted upward. Therefore, all trucking firms wished to see the Chicago companies stand pat on demanded wage increases. TEI stated that greater than $1 million per week would be collected nationally and distributed according to need among the Chicago trucking firms.[46] A TEI spokesman declared:

Despite claims that inroads have been made against truck companies of substance in Chicago, the fact is that more than 600 companies of the 700 Chicago truck lines of size remain steadfast—together—against an exhorbitant 46 percent wage demand which would have a disastrously inflationary effect on the Chicago community.

This action by TEI and others (the cooperating Chicago truck employer associations) reinforces the determination of an entire industry that the national 28.7 percent increase already approved by top union and company officials, negotiated in good faith and subject to federally supervised secret ballot, shall not be torn up in a whipsaw effort in one lone city of the nation.[47]

By the end of May, 1970, the Chicago firms were still not accepting the union's wage demands. The national pact had been accepted by the teamsters (subject to reopening if the Chicago laborers won their wage demands). Referring to that contract, a TEI leader noted that, "Industry employers, coast-to-coast, have noted the ratification with mixed feelings. This is a costly settlement, but the best that could be reached. This agreement was defended with courage and unity by the trucking industry in spite of mounting pressures caused by wildcat strikes in many cities."[48] In regard to the fact that the settlement could be higher, according to what happened in Chicago, the TEI spokesman stated: "The trucking industry intends to hold the line in Chicago. We need the support of every informed shipper and civic leader. The Chicago demand, seeking a 46 percent wage increase, would constitute this nation's biggest single engine of inflation."[49]

Finally, on July 3, 1970, the Chicago trucking firms capitulated to the union's full wage demands. The trucking firms involved stated they could not stand the financial drain any longer.[50]

The author has traced the 1970 labor contract in some detail, because he believes it well illustrates the present lack of countervailing power that trucking management currently possesses against the powerful Teamsters Union.[51] The author therefore reasons that as the trucking industry is able to merge together in order to form more Class I firms of substantial financial means, the trucking industry as a whole will be in a significantly improved position to band together under the TEI. At this point, for the first time in this industry, the Teamsters Union will face a sparring partner of equal financial muscle and therefore excessive wage demands will not automatically be tolerated as in the past. Indeed, the following legal maxim would hence forth not be applicable to trucking labor agreement negotiations—*Quod alias bonum et justum est, si per vim vel petatur, malum et injustum efficitur.*[52]

In conclusion, the author believes that the current trend toward trucking mergers has achieved favorable results, especially in terms of increased service standards for the shipping public. He would like to see this trend continue—with one proviso. That is, the ICC should carefully scrutinize future mergers that do not involve end-to-end mergers. The author favors the latter type of unification because it does not decrease the competitiveness of the industry, while it does allow the involved carriers to achieve greater financial stability and to offer the shipping public an improved one-carrier service between an enlarged number of shipping points. On the other hand, all side-by-side unifications should not automatically be denied, but the ICC should require special proof that the proposed merger advantages more than offset the decrease in competition that necessarily results from the transaction.

In addition, the author can not arbitrarily state that when the number of carriers reaches x, all future consolidations should cease and the industry should stabilize at that point. In other words, he can't say that there are approximately 15,200 interstate trucking firms now, and when this number reaches 11,400, 7,900, 5,700, 3,900, 2,800, or 1,300, the trucking merger trend should halt. The answer to this question lies with the body that deals with this issue on a daily basis and also possesses the administrative expertise in this area—the ICC. The author therefore implores the ICC to periodically (probably annually) stop and take specific appraisal of exactly *where* the trucking merger picture currently is and also to determine precisely at *what rate* and *where* the merger trend should be progressing.

Finally, the author would reject the recently proposed "super merger agency," as contemplated by Representative Emanuel Celler, in regard to it having authority over transportation and particularly trucking mergers. The *Wall Street Journal* has reported that the super agency, " . . . would be created out of the conviction that many Federal agencies and laws currently apply a bewildering variety of approaches and standards to merger proposals, with the result that no agency has been truly effective in halting the long-term merger trend or the resulting growth of industrial concentration."[53] While the author is basically sympathetic with the above statement, he believes, for reasons already enumerated, that: (a) the trend towards trucking mergers should continue, primarily because it results in improved service advantages to the shipping public, and (b) the ICC should retain jurisdiction over transportation (and hence trucking) mergers, because only the Commission commands the technical expertise to fully comprehend and evaluate in what direction the transportation unification movement should be progressing.

Trucking Consolidations: A Natural Occurrence or Artificially Prompted by ICC Actions?

The author basically believes that the trend towards trucking mergers has been a natural phenomenon that would have taken place with or without Federal economic regulation. Both sides of this issue will now be examined.

An Artificially Stimulated Trend

The strongest proponents of the argument that the ICC has artificially stimulated the trucking unification trend are Professors Adams and Hendry. "If giantism and oligopoly come to the trucking industry, this will not be the result of natural economic forces but of a benign tolerance, if not active promotion by the Interstate Commerce Commission."[54] These authors believe that since there are no scale economies or other significant advantages of larger, consolidated firms, the trend toward unifications would not take place as a natural occurrence. Therefore, the current trend to unifications must be artificially prompted by the Commission.

The same position is also advocated by Professor Pegrum. He has stated that since trucking does not display any marked scale economies, the current trend of mergers, which the ICC has authorized, is causing trucking firms to expand to a larger size than economies would warrant.[55]

A Natural Trend

The author believes that the trucking merger movement is basically a natural phenomenon. He feels that all of the aforementioned authors have failed to realize that the primary advantage of unified firms is *not* scale economies, but an increased route structure so that more points can be served by the same carrier.[56]

Transport lawyer Herbert Burstein has validly commented, in the author's opinion, that: "The same forces which account for mergers and consolidation in industry, as a whole, promote 'bigness' in motor transportation. Mergers and consolidations are more than a response to the imperatives of a complex economic system; frequently, they mark out the only route to survival."[57]

There can be no question that industry in general has been pursuing a policy of increased concentration in the decade of the 1960s. The Federal Trade Commission issued a resolution on July 2, 1968, which declared that, " ... the merger movement appears to have reached the highest levels in American industrial history. ... "[58] An FTC study based on the resolution found that, "The American economy is experiencing a major change in industrial organizations as the result of a merger movement of unprecedented dimensions. For nearly two decades mergers have been increasing. During the years 1967 and 1968 and early in 1969 they have reached all-time peaks."[59] Such statements indicate that industry in general has been consolidating for various tax, financial, administrative, managerial, and other advantages.[60] The author maintains that most of these factors would also apply to the trucking industry. Therefore, this industrial segment, with or without economic regulation, has tended towards the same unification policy that American industry in general has been following. In fact, the author believes that a strong argument could be made for the theory that trucking would have experienced considerably greater economic concentration than at present if it were not for the ICC. If we assume that the only impediment to trucking mergers was the antitrust laws, it is hard to imagine that too many—if any—mergers would be hampered, considering that there are more than 15,000 interstate regulated for-hire truckers and that the largest, Consolidated Freightways, Inc., had only 1.84 percent of the total industry gross revenues in 1967.[61] On the other hand, the ICC has blocked a substantial number of trucking mergers, as shown in the previous chapters. One of the most significant denials was the *Transport Co.–Control–Arrow Carrier Corp.* case,[62] in which the Transport Co. was formed especially to unite forty-nine separate motor carriers. After the denial, seven of the forty-nine companies proposed a unification, and this consolidation has been previously examined in detail. A second key rejection was the famous *P.I.E.-Keeshin* case,[63] which has also been surveyed in a previous chapter.

In summary, the author believes that the current trend of trucking mergers is basically a natural occurrence that is merely paralleling the same trend in other American industries.[64] Again, the main goal is to increase the size of the route structure, so that a greater number of cities can be served by one carrier.

The Issue of the ICC's Consistency in Section 5 Trucking Merger Cases

This section will examine two basic charges against the ICC in the area of the Commission's case decision consistency. Both of these accusations were issued by Professors Adams and Hendry.

Overall Commission Consistency:
Is the ICC Vague and Vacillating?

Professors Admas and Hendry have bluntly asserted that, "The Commission seems to follow a vague and vacillating policy toward the carriers it regulates—a policy that shows little underlying consistency in approach or decision. What is embraced in one opinion as a natural and inevitable result of the economic facts of life is rejected in a second as not shown to be in the public interest. Where the fears of competitors are waved aside in one instance, the probable plight of competitors is of great importance in another."[65]

The author must immediately state that after reading many more cases than have Adams and Hendry, he definitely does not agree with their conclusion in this area. He is not alone in this position. Transport attorney Burstein has in my view validly observed,

The administrative process, by its very nature, produces a multiplicity of results. Cases involving their own unique facts reach different examiners who hold a variety of philosophies. Moreover, the changing composition of the Commission inhibits any tendency to pat formulae. This does not suggest *ad hoc* decision making. *On the contrary, there is a general decisional pattern which serves as a guide to practitioners called upon to process Section 5 cases.* (Emphasis added)[66]

The author completely agrees with Burstein that the ICC has clearly stated, in their case decisions, the facts and procedures that must be established in a Section 5 case to prove that it is in the public interest. In addition, the Commission has also enumerated quite clearly the facts that a protesting carrier must establish in order to prove that a merger is not consistent with the public interest. However, no two cases are exactly the same. As another experienced transport attorney, Kit Clardy, has noted, "Lawyers know that it is a rare thing to find a case on 'all fours' with another."[67] The author believes this is the main point ignored by Adams and Hendry when they charged the Commission with inconsistent Section 5 findings. In other words, the Congress and the courts have clearly stated that the ICC is to decide *each* unification case on the record developed in the proceeding, while considering established precedent when feasible to maintain as much uniformity of decisions as possible.[68] This means that many factors are presented to the Commission in each case. The ICC must carefully weight the relevance of each facet of the proceeding and then come to an ultimate finding. The final decision must necessarily be a value judgment by the Commissioners. That is why it is somewhat precarious to state that the Commission has acted arbitrarily or capriciously, because each decision is based on the evidence of record, and who is to say what factors should have been accorded great weight and which others disregarded. The author can state that, in his opinion, after a careful reading of over 450 cases selected at random, the Commission has generally been very consistent in its findings in cases where approximately the same factual situations were present. Of course, in a few cases, it appeared that the ICC reversed precedent for no apparent reason. But these situations were seldom encountered, and the author strongly believes that the ICC has done an exemplary job in regard to: (a) establishing basic principles to be followed on key issues, such as dormancy, new competitive services, alleged damage to protestants, et cetera, and (b) following these precedents whenever possible in order to allow both shippers and carriers to know under what circumstances a proposed trucking unification will probably be approved or denied.

Discrimination: Large v. Small
Carrier Applications

Professors Adams and Hendry have charged the ICC with following an inconsistent policy in regard to large versus small carriers when each applied for a Section 5 merger. Specifically, they contended that the Commission has exhibited preferential treatment to larger carriers as opposed to smaller ones in approving their respective Section 5 merger applications.[69]

This accusation has been vigorously denied by the ICC.[70] ICC Commissioner Mitchell was asked directly by Senator Thomas H. Kuchel if the ICC showed any preference in merger proceedings towards large versus small carriers. Commissioner Mitchell replied:

Absolutely not. We use the same criteria in small as well as in large cases. Dr. Adams picks out a few small cases. Then he picks out some larger cases. I have been there 10 years and I have never known a time when a question as to whether it was small or whether it was too large was raised or considered. I rather lean toward the small carrier. In fact, Dr. Adams has cited several of my dissents in which I have agreed with the small. But, the other members of the Commission—I have never had any thought whatsoever that they did not use the same criteria. We decide these cases on the record. We care not whether they are large carriers, giants, or small carriers.[71]

The author can state that he read and briefed all the cases in this study with the thesis of Adams and Hendry in mind. After a complete analysis of these cases selected at random, the author can definitely state that he never once got the impression that either relatively large or small carriers were treated unequally or that the criteria used to decide a case were different, based on the relative size of the carriers involved.

Does the ICC Have a Trucking Merger Policy?

The ICC and other independent regulatory commissions have often been charged with failing to develop operating and overall working policies to guide their regulatory actions. Thus, Professor Marver H. Bernstein has observed in regard to all U.S. regulatory commissions that:

The difficulty is that the commissions tend to place so much emphasis in their work on a careful case by case consideration of matters that they tend to be lax in developing general policies which would be applied readily to the cases as they come before them, and thus each application tends to be considered almost as a separate matter without regard necessarily to other cases involving similar factors.

I think with a more careful development of policies which could be applied readily to cases as they come to the desks of the regulatory commissions, the delays that seem to be inherent in the processes could be eliminated.[72]

On the other hand, the question also arises, should any regulatory commission, the ICC in this case, develop policies or should they only administer ones established by Congress? Referring to this issue, contrast the following statement by Attorney Kit Clardy to that of Professor Bernstein above. "I submit the Commission has no business making policy—that is the duty of Congress. Nor has the Commission any business establishing a policy of either granting or denying applications without regard for the facts in each case or to set up a goal to be reached at all costs such as some fixed percentage of grants for small and either the same or another percentage for the so-called large ones."[73]

The author believes that the ICC should develop overall working policies within the general framework that Congress has established for each particular issue. This is undoubtedly what Professor Hugh S. Norton had in mind when he observed, "In the traditional manner of the quasijudicial agency, these commissions [the ICC and CAB] both make and administer policy. In the strict sense, their task is to administer policy made by Congress, but in practice, no clear line can be drawn between policy making and policy implementation."[74] The advantage of the ICC establishing a trucking merger policy within a Congressional framework is that it allows the policy making to be done by the body with the technical expertise in the area of trucking—the ICC.

At present, the ICC does not have a stated, *de jure* type of trucking merger policy. However, it can be argued (and the ICC undoubtedly would) that it would be inappropriate for the Commission to have such a policy. Why? Because it may appear to many observers that the ICC had jumped its jurisdictional fence and invaded the policy-making area of Congress. Therefore, some would say that it behooves the Commission to have an unstated, *de facto* type of consolidation policy if it is to have any at all. The author believes that the ICC does and has established a clear-cut policy in favor of trucking mergers. This policy is readily discernible after a careful examination of their printed cases. In general, the policy is that trucking mergers, especially of an end-to-end type where prior interlining existed, will be approved if certain circumstances[75] are not present. It should be noted that the ICC's basic approval of trucking unification is not something that the Commission attempts to keep secret, except in regard to specific cases in the official casebook series where the actual merger proceedings are printed. Indeed, the opposite has been the case. For example, individual commissioners have spoken out in favor of the trucking merger movement. In a 1957 Senate hearing, then Chairman of the ICC, Owen Clarke, was being questioned by Senator Russel B. Long. The following discourse took place:

SENATOR LONG. How far do you think concentration should go before you begin to consider the monopolistic aspects of the industry?

MR. CLARKE. Well, certainly a lot further than it has gone. While there obviously has been a certain amount of concentration, in my personal opinion, there hasn't been enough concentration. We need more concentration than has occurred if we are going to have a healthy, vigorous motor-carrier industry.[76]

The Commission also clearly enumerates its trucking merger findings in each of its annual reports. In the 1969 annual report, the Commission stated that in fiscal year 1969, 303 Section 5 merger applications were granted in whole or in part, and thirty-one were denied. Also, the ICC briefly discussed its authorization of four major trucking merger approvals. Finally, the Commission also enumerated the basic merger cases that were pending before them.[77] Since each ICC annual report is addressed specifically to the Senate and House of Representatives, it must be assumed that Congress is well aware of the ICC's basic affinity towards approving trucking mergers. Therefore, since Congress has not chosen to enact legislation that would redirect the Commission's trucking merger actions, it can only be assumed that Congress approves of the ICC's current administration of Section 5 trucking unification cases.

The only remaining issue, then, is whether the ICC's present unstated, *de facto* policy should become a written, *de jure* type of policy? The author believes the ICC should adopt the latter position. Interesting enough, so does the Senate's Select Committee on Small Business. In a 1958 statement, it remarked,

It is surprising to learn that the Commission nowhere has indicated formally, either in a written opinion or in a policy statement, its attitude on concentration in the motor-carrier industry. Although the last chairman of the Commission has expressed his own 'personal opinion,' the Commission would do well to consider the issue and indicate publicly its position on a question of such significance to the industry and to the general public.[78]

Of course, the overall policy statement should be relatively broad and general in content, because each case is required by the 1940 Transportation Act to be decided strictly on the record established in each unification proceeding. The primary advantage of a written policy statement by the ICC is that its very creation requires a thoughtful, careful, and comprehensive analysis of the situation in question. In other words, a written policy statement by the ICC would force the elimination of any existing fuzziness and inconsistency from its analysis of the trucking merger situation. It is the internal discipline demanded by a well thought out written policy that makes it the chosen alternative of the author.

ICC Trucking Unification
Regulation: Active or Passive?

An interesting question that has arisen is whether the Commission actively regulates trucking mergers or is it really rather passive in this area?[79] Passive regulation, in the sense meant here, refers to allowing the carriers practically *carte blanche* authority to achieve unifications they desire. The author believes there can be no question that the ICC actively regulates trucking unifications, especially those that are opposed by other carriers, as witnessed by the numerous mergers that were denied in the previous chapters. However, the issue is less clearcut in cases in which there is no opposition to the proceeding. Therefore, the instant discussion will deal exclusively with cases that were unopposed. To attack this active versus passive question, a decision rule had to be developed. Specifically, it was decided to check cases that had no opposition, and if almost all were approved, it could then be concluded that the ICC passively regulated this type of unification proceeding. However, if a substantial number of these unopposed cases were denied, it would have to be assumed that the Commission also actively regulates applications facing no opposition. Of the 450 cases selected at random, 126 contained no protestants. Of these 126 unopposed cases, 28 or 22.2 percent of the total, were denied.[80] A question then arises—how does the approximately 22 percent denial rate of unopposed cases compare with the percentage of cases denied in which there was opposition? Of the remaining 324 opposed transactions, 87 were not authorized, or 26.8 percent of this total. The next question then becomes, is there a statistical difference between the percentages of cases denied when there was no opposition and when there were protestants? Appendix B contains an explanation of the statistical formulas used to prove that there is no statistical difference between the two percentages. In other words, it can be concluded with a reasonable amount of confidence that the two denial rate percentages are about equal, with the differences that have developed being due to chance variation within the sampling plan. Therefore, it can be concluded that the ICC did not act differently when protestants either were or were not participating in the proceeding. This, of course, is understandable, because the Commission has always followed a *de facto* form of *stare decisis*. Hence, the ICC could hardly decide a case in one way when it was not opposed and another way at a later date when a similar proceeding had protestants.

It is interesting to note that the rationales for denying the 28 unopposed cases ran the full gamut of reasons surveyed in the last chapter for not authorizing Section 5 trucking unification proceedings.

To recapitulate, the author's research indicates that the Commission actively regulates trucking unifications. In other words, the Commission attempts to follow consistently the precedents of previous cases, regardless of whether there are or are not protestants in the case.

Does the ICC Protect the Status Quo in Trucking Merger Cases at the Expense of Economic Efficiency?

The area in which the Commission most protects the *status quo* in trucking mergers deals with intramodal competition.[81] The ICC has taken the position that Congress intended the Section 5 phrase ."consistent with the public interest" to also include the interests of the carriers presently serving the involved area. The author basically agrees with this interpretation. Why? Because regulated common carriers are subjected to many restraints that other businesses generally are not required to observe. Thus common carriers must serve without discrimination, their rates are completely regulated, they cannot arbitrarily extend their operations into other territories, they need ICC approval to merge, et cetera. To compensate for these regulatory restrictions on the managerial freedoms of trucking firms, the Congress and the ICC decided that the number of carriers in each area would be restricted by entry control, so that the truckers already in each respective area would be able to generate a reasonable return on their invested capital. The more important reason for entry control, however, was to protect the public against the excessive rate instability that was prevalent prior to the 1935 Motor Carrier Act.

In regard to protecting the intramodal competitors from excessive competition, the Commission has instituted a number of restrictions that have necessarily caused the truckers restricted to operate less efficiently than possible. Three of the worst restrictions in this light, as previously examined in the prior chapter, deal with: (1) gateway restrictions to prevent route authorization conversions, (2) the non-authorization of tacking, and (3) overall commodity and place restrictions based on the vendor's dormancy. The author takes the position that the ICC should make a greater effort to eliminate these types of restriction in future Section 5 cases. Perhaps this could be accomplished by demanding that protesting carriers, those that insist that the restrictions mentioned are necessary to protect their ability to fulfill their common carrier obligations, be placed under a stricter burden of proving their claims.

A second possible solution to help eliminate Section 5 restrictions that result in inefficiencies would be to use indemnity payments, on a need basis, paid by the merger applicants to those carriers that could conclusively prove the extent of their damage as a result of the merger. These payments would be as minimal as needed to keep the protestants solvent and would be of a relatively short duration, probably from six months to a year in length. The theory of the payments would be to allow the protestants a reasonable amount of time to adjust their operations to the new competitive situation in their territory. This type of solution has been previously imposed by the ICC in railroad unification proceedings, with a recent example being the Penn-Central merger case. In that case, the ICC observed:

We recognize that one result of such conditions would be to deny to applicants . . . , for the time being, some of the merger benefits, but they will in no case detract from the present amount and quality of service being provided by applicants either in their operations or merger implementation. In short, they are designed to prevent any loss of revenue over the three railroads as a direct result of immediate consummation of this merger.[82]

In addition, to protect the applications from being taken advantage of by the protestants, the ICC issued this caveat:

In imposing the conditions we anticipate that the petitioners will not relax their own solicitation efforts nor permit the quality of their service to decline upon the expectation that their traffic or revenues are guaranteed by the Transportation Company. Any evidence of such practices brought to our attention may be considered a prima facie reason for reopening these proceedings to consider revision or deletion of the conditions.[83]

To recapitulate, the author believes that in general the protection of existing truckers is a valid part of current trucking economic regulation. Therefore, for example, in cases where a vendor's operations are completely dormant, and no public need has been established for the proposed service, the application should definitely be denied. On the other hand, assume a small segment of the rights are found to be dormant. In this case, the author would prefer to see the vendee, if he so elected, be able to purchase the complete operating rights of the vendor, including the previously dormant segment of the rights. In this way the vendee would not have to purchase a certificate that contained unreasonable place or commodity restrictions. However, to obtain these rights, he would have to assume possible indemnity payments to the protestants if they become unable to fulfill their common-carrier obligations as a result of the transaction.

The same type of reasoning would apply to gateway restrictions. If a transaction is found to be in the public interest, the gateway restrictions could be eliminated and an indemnity payment made available to a carrier that was severely damaged by the applicant's proposed new service. The identical reasoning would also apply to restrictions on tacking.

Finally, the author realizes that he is sailing in uncharted waters when contemplating indemnity payments to protestants in Section 5 trucking merger proceedings. However, he believes this is a worthy mental exercise, because some workable plan must be developed by the ICC to combine the Congressional mandate of entry control with the elimination of certificate commodity and place restrictions which are often the root cause of gross carrier operating inefficiencies.

Appendixes

Appendix A

The "Key" Cases

These cases will be cited chronologically, in order to indicate the relatively even spread of these proceedings over the years. See Chapter IV, supra, for a description of the methodology used to generate the selection of these "key" cases.

Number	Citation	Case Title
1	5 MCC 723 (1938)	Potashnick Truck Serv., Inc.–Control–Bryant Truck Lines
2	15 MCC 358 (1938)	Thurston–Purchase–Merritt
3	25 MCC 558 (1939)	H.P. Welch Co.–Purchase–E.J. Scannell, Inc.
4	35 MCC 661 (1940)	Crichton–Purchase–C. Lewis Lavine, Inc.
5	36 MCC 561 (1941)	B.&E. Transp. Co., Inc.–Purchase–Merchants Transp., Inc.
6	38 MCC 137 (1942)	Associated Transport, Inc.–Control and Consolidation
7	321 US 67 (1944)	McLean Trucking Co. v. U.S.
8	38 MCC 547 (1942)	C.&D. Motor Delivery Co.–Purchase–Elliott
9	57 MCC 341 (1950)	Pacific Intermountain Exp. Co.–Control and Purchase
10	57 MCC 467 (1951)	Pacific Intermountain Exp. Co.–Control and Purchase
11	58 MCC 594 (1952)	Ringsby Truck Lines, Inc.–Control–Northern Transp. Co.
12	60 MCC 229 (1954)	Merchants Motor Freight, Inc.–Purhcase–Bridgeways, Inc.
13	65 MCC 312 (1955)	Mid-Continent Frt. Lines, Inc.–Purchase–Hanson M. Exp.
14	75 MCC 659 (1958)	New Dixie Lines, Inc.–Control–Jocie Motor Lines, Inc.
15	85 MCC 139 (1960)	Consolidated Freightways, Inc.–Control–Silver Fleet
16	97 MCC 310 (1964)	T.I.M.E. Freight, Inc.–Merger
17	101 MCC 151 (1966)	Glosson Motor Line, Inc.–Purchase–Helderman

Appendix B

To test if there was a statistical difference between the two denial rates, the test statistic under the following heading was used: "Test of Hypothesis That Two Population Proportions Are Equal When Each Is Estimated from a Large Number of Observations and When the Estimated Common Proportion Is Not Near 0 or 1," in Helen M. Walker and Joseph Lev, *Statistical Inference* (New York: Holt, Rinehart and Winston, 1953), pp. 77-79.

The following formulas were used:

$$p = \frac{N_1 p_1 + N_2 p_2}{N_1 + N_2} \qquad q = 1 - p \qquad z = \frac{p_1 - p_2}{\sqrt{\dfrac{p\,q\,N}{N_1 N_2}}}$$

$$N = N_1 + N_2$$
$$N = 450$$
$$N_1 = 324$$
$$N_2 = 126$$
$$p_1 = .268$$
$$p_2 = .222$$

By using a level of significance of .05, it can be determined that there is no statistical difference between p_1 and p_2 if the calculated z value falls within the range $-1.96 < z < 1.96$.

The value of p must first be computed.

$$p = \frac{(324)(.268) + (126)(.222)}{324 + 126} = \frac{86.83 + 27.97}{450} = \frac{114.80}{450} = .255$$

Now the value of z can be calculated.

$$z = \frac{.268 - .222}{\sqrt{\dfrac{(.255)(.745)(450)}{(324)(126)}}} = \frac{.046}{\sqrt{\dfrac{85.50}{40,824}}} = \frac{.046}{\sqrt{.0029}} = \frac{.046}{.054} = .85$$

Therefore, since the calculated z is well within the confidence interval of ± 1.96, it can be concluded that the two denial rates are not statistically different.

Notes

Notes

Chapter 1
Introduction

1. Federal Trade Commission, *Economic Report on Corporate Mergers* (Washington, D.C.: U.S. Government Printing Office, 1969), p. 29.

2. Herbert Burstein, "Motor Carrier Acquisitions, Mergers and Consolidation," *ICC Practitioners' Journal* (January 1957), p. 375. Used with permission of the Association of ICC Practitioners.

3. Statement by Senator John Sparkman, in Walter Adams and James B. Hendry, *Trucking Mergers, Concentration, and Small Business: An Analysis of Interstate Commerce Commission Policy, 1950-56*, in U.S. Congress, Senate, Select Committee on Small Business, *Trucking Mergers and Concentration*, 85th Cong., 1st sess. (Washington, D.C.: U.S. Government Printing Office, 1957), p. 213.

4. *Virginia Stage Lines v. United States*, 48 F. Supp. 79, 82 (1942).

5. Donald S. Watson, *Economic Policy: Business and Government* (Boston: Houghton Mifflin Co., 1960), p. 406.

Chapter 2
Characteristics of the Motor
Trucking Industry

1. *New England Motor Carrier Rates* 8 MCC 287, 324 (1938).

2. Interstate Commerce Commission, *54th Annual Report* (Washington, D.C.: U.S. Government Printing Office, 1940), pp. 107-108. The ICC classifies regulated interstate truckers into classes, depending on their annual gross operating revenues. Currently, truckers with gross revenues of $1 million or more are designated Class I carriers, Class II from $300,000 to $1 million, and Class III encompasses carriers with gross revenues of less than $300,000.

3. Interstate Commerce Commission, *69th Annual Report* (Washington, D.C.: U.S. Government Printing Office, 1955), p. 100.

4. Interstate Commerce Commission, *86th Annual Report* (Washington, D.C.: U.S. Government Printing Office, 1972), p. 131.

5. Ibid. Railroads are also classified by the ICC according to their annual gross operating revenues. Class I railroads have revenues of $5 million or more. Class II railroads have revenues of less than $5 million.

6. Interstate Commerce Commission, *81st Annual Report* (Washington, D.C.: U.S. Government Printing Office, 1967), p. 152.

7. Charles A. Taff, *Commercial Motor Transportation* (4th ed.; Homewood, Ill.: R.D. Irwin, Inc., 1969), p. 170.

8. Statement of Edward M. Welliver, American Trucking Associations, Inc., before the House Small Business Committee, June 10, 1948, p. 2, mimeo, in Charles L. Dearing and Wilfred Owen, *National Transportation Policy* (Washington, D.C.: The Brookings Institution, 1949), p. 192.

9. American Trucking Associations, *American Trucking Trends, 1968* (Washington, D.C.: Department of Research and Transport Economics, American Trucking Associations, Inc., 1969), p. 25.

10. Ibid., pp. 16, 23.

11. ICC, *86th Annual Report*, p. 131.

12. Eric Schenker, "Nationalization and Denationalization of Motor Carriers in Great Britain," *Land Economics* (August 1963), p. 222.

13. H. Kolsen, "Structure and Price Determination in the Road Haulage Industry in New South Wales," *The Economic Record* (November 1956), p. 291.

14. John R. Meyer, et al., *The Economics of Competition in the Transportation Industries* (Cambridge, Mass.: Harvard University Press, 1969), p. 216.

15. Richard N. Farmer, "The Motor Trucking Industry," *Business Horizons* (fall 1966), p. 16.

16. "Trucking Rolls Into an Age of Giants," *Business Week* (June 12, 1965), p. 178.

17. Two examples of this fantastic growth of the trucking industry are the following. First, in 1945, all trucking companies (for-hire and private) carried 6.52 percent of all intercity ton-miles. By 1971 this percentage had jumped to 22.26 percent. Alternatively, the total revenues of all regulated freight carriers can be reviewed. In this case, the truckers had 16.39 percent in 1945 and 53.14 percent in 1971. *American Trucking Trends, 1972*, pp. 7 and 16.

18. Interstate Commerce Commission, Bureau of Transport Economics and Statistics, Statement No. 65,200, *Motor Carrier Freight Commodity Statistics* (Washington, D.C.: U.S. Government Printing Office, 1963), p. 3.

19. U.S. Department of Commerce, Bureau of the Census, *1963 Census of Transportation*, Vol. III, Commodity Transportation Survey Parts III and IV, Shipper Groups and Production Areas (Washington, D.C.: U.S. Government Printing Office, 1963), p. 4.

20. U.S. Department of Commerce, Bureau of the Census, Commodity Transportation Survey, *1967 Census of Transportation* (Washington, D.C.: U.S. Government Printing Office), monthly issues: (a) Shipper Group 4, Textile Mill and Leather Products, November 1969, p. 2; (b) Shipper Group 24, Instruments, Photographic Equipment, Watches, and Clocks, December 1969, p. 2; (c) Shipper Group 12, Furniture, Fixtures, and Miscellaneous Manufactured Products, January 1970, p. 2.

21. *American Trucking Trends, 1972*, p. 14. This may appear as an anomaly, because it was just pointed out that truckers specialized in carrying manufactured goods. The answer to this paradox is that these bulk goods are generally transported very short distances, and hence the truck is often the most practical

mode, because rail and water facilities are not available. In addition, these statistics are only *tonnage* figures and not *ton-miles*. (This is a unit measuring the movement of one ton the distance of one mile.) Therefore, if the distance factor was included in the measurement of the movement of these bulk products (i.e., ton-miles), the railroad and water carriers would emerge as the dominant transporters of bulk commodities.

22. Interstate Commerce Commission, Bureau of Economics, Statement No. 67-2, *The Role of Regulated Motor Carriers in the Handling of Small Shipments* (Washington, D.C.: U.S. Government Printing Office, November 1967), p. 7.

23. ICC, *82nd Annual Report, 1968*, p. 16.

24. Earle N. Hoekenga, "A Trucker Looks at the Small Shipment Problem," *Transportation and Distribution Management* (January 1968), p. 26.

25. Dudley F. Pegrum, *Transportation: Economics and Public Policy* (2nd ed.; Homewood, Ill.: Richard D. Irwin, Inc., 1968), p. 33.

26. For a detailed account of the recent history (since 1916) of Federal aid to highways, see: Charles L. Dearing and Wilfred Owen, *National Transportation Policy* (Washington, D.C.: The Brookings Institution, 1949), pp. 105-120.

27. Hudson and Constantin, *Motor Transportation*, p. 81.

28. "More Funds Held Necessary to Finish Construction of the Interstate Highway System," *Traffic World* (April 18, 1970), p. 90.

29. Hugh S. Norton, *National Transportation Policy: Formation and Implementation* (Berkeley, Calif.: McCutchan Publishing Corp., 1966), p. 42.

30. U.S. Department of Commerce, Office of Transportation, "Charges for Private Use of Federally Provided Transportation Services and Facilities" (May 1953), pp. 8-9 in, U.S. Congress, Senate, Committee on Commerce, *National Transportation Policy*, by John P. Doyle and others, Committee Print, Report No. 445, 87th Congress, 1st Session (Washington, D.C.: U.S. Government Printing Office, June 26, 1961), p. 184. This document is generally referred to as *The Doyle Report* in the transportation industry.

31. Ibid., pp. 186-187.

32. The ABC program consists of those state highways that can receive Federal aid. "A" are primary roads, "B" secondary, and "C" urban extensions. The Federal funds available are generally allocated as follows: 45 percent to "A" roads, 30 percent for "B" and 25 percent for "C" roads. See: Taff, *Commercial Motor Transportation*, p. 21.

33. *The Doyle Report*, p. 190.

34. Data for 1940 and 1950 from *Final Report of the Highway Cost Allocation Study*, House Doc. No. 54, 87th Congress, 1st Session, Washington, D.C., 1961, Table III-I. Data for 1963 from U.S. Dept. of Commerce, Bureau of Public Roads, Release, January 30, 1964, Table H F-1. This reference is taken from, Robert H. Harbeson, "Some Allocational Problems in Highway Finance" in *Transportation Economics: A Conference of the Universities–National*

Bureau Committee for Economic Research (New York: National Bureau of Economic Research, 1965), p. 139.

35. *The Doyle Report*, p. 186.

36. Ibid.

37. *American Trucking Trends, 1972*, p. 32.

38. *1963 Census of Transportation*, Vol. III, Parts III and IV, p. 12.

39. *Fifteen Per Cent Rate Case, 1931*, 178 ICC 539, 574 (1931).

40. Taff, *Commercial Motor Transportation*, p. 9. Railroads have traditionally offered slow service on short hauls, because they have felt the need to accumulate a large number of cars before each train departs.

41. J.L. Heskett, Robert M. Ivie, and Nicholas A. Glaskowsky, Jr., *Business Logistics: Management of Physical Supply and Distribution* (New York: The Ronald Press Co., 1964), p. 72. For an interesting article on this subject, see: "Coast-to-Coast Sleeper," *Distribution Manager* (November 1968), p. 37.

42. Paul T. McElhiney and Charles L. Hilton, *Introduction to Logistics and Traffic Management* (Dubuque, Iowa: Wm. C. Brown Co., Publishers, 1968), p. 108.

43. Heskett, Ivie, and Glaskowsky, *Business Logistics*, p. 75.

44. Association of American Railroads, *Yearbook of Railroad Facts–1972* (Washington, D.C.: Association of American Railroads, April 1972), p. 46.

45. Heskett, Ivie, and Glaskowsky, *Business Logistics*, p. 77.

46. Germane, Glaskowsky, and Heskett, *Highway Transportation Management*, p. 125.

47. Germane, Glaskowsky, and Heskett, *Highway Transportation Management*, p. 126.

48. Taff, *Commercial Motor Transportation*, p. 182.

49. John J. Coyle, "Cost-of-Service Pricing in Transportation: Some Reflections," *Quarterly Review of Economics and Business* (spring 1965), p. 73. The arbitrariness of common cost allocation is also concluded by H.E. Stocker, *Motor Traffic Management* (New York: Prentice-Hall, Inc., 1938), p. 64, and Germane, Glaskowsky, and Heskett, *Highway Transportation Mangement*, pp. 125-126.

50. Alfred Marshall, *Principles of Economics* (8th ed.; London: MacMillan & Co., Ltd., 1920), pp. 312-313.

51. Ibid., p. 313.

52. Russell E. Westmeyer, *Economics of Transportation* (Englewood Cliffs, N.J.: Prentice-Hall, Inc., 1952), p. 68.

53. See Germane, Glaskowsky, and Heskett, *Highway Transportation Management*, p. 125, for an example of when "out-of-pocket" costs are less than variable costs.

54. John F. Due and Robert W. Clower, *Intermediate Economic Analysis* (4th ed.; Homewood, Ill.: Richard D. Irwin, Inc., 1961), p. 165.

55. D. Philip Locklin, *Economics of Transportation* (7th ed.; Homewood, Ill.: Richard D. Irwin, Inc., 1972), p. 652.

56. G. Lloyd Wilson, *Motor Traffic Management* (New York: D. Appleton and Co., 1928), p. 47.

57. W.D. Baker, "Motor Carrier Management Strategy," *Transportation Journal* (fall 1968), p. 50. Reproduced with permission from the *Transportation Journal*, a quarterly publication of the American Society of Traffic & Transportation, Inc.

58. Wilson, *Motor Traffic Management*, p. 47.

59. Interstate Commerce Commission, Bureau of Accounts, Cost Finding, and Valuation, Statement No. 1-54, *Explanation of the Development of Motor Carrier Costs with Statement as to Their Meaning and Significance* (Washington, D.C.: U.S. Government Printing Office, April 1954), pp. 71-99. It should be noted that the ICC figure of 90 percent variable costs is an approximation. Specific variable cost percentages were found to be: 95 in the Central Region, 94.7 in the Southern Region, 81.5 in the Northwestern Region, 89.7 in the Midwestern Region, and 93 in the Middle Atlantic Territory.

60. Robert E. Shirley, "Analysis of Motor Carrier Cost Formulae Developed by the Interstate Commerce Commission," *Transportation Journal* (spring 1969), pp. 22-23. Used with permission from the *Transportation Journal*, a quarterly publication of the American Society of Traffic and Transportation, Inc.

61. *American Trucking Trends, 1972*, p. 28.

62. Dudley F. Pegrum, *Transportation: Economics and Public Policy* (2nd ed.; Homewood, Ill.: Richard D. Irwin, Inc., 1968), p. 190.

63. Locklin, *Economics of Transportation*, p. 652. See also George W. Wilson, "The Nature of Competition in the Motor Transport Industry," *Land Economics* (November 1960), p. 389.

64. See: *Coordination of Motor Transportation*, 182 ICC 263 (1932), pp. 308-309, 356-358, 361-362, 376; *New England Motor Carrier Rates*, 8 MCC 287 (1938), pp. 289, 303, 318-319; and Locklin, *Economics of Transportation*, pp. 712-716, which presents an excellent summary of ICC problems with motor trucking rate wars.

65. Gilbert Walker, *Road and Rail* (2nd ed.; London: George Allen and Unwin Limited, 1947), p. 96.

66. Mossman and Morton, *Principles of Transportation*, p. 214.

67. Locklin, *Economics of Transportation*, p. 652.

68. G. Lloyd Wilson, "Effects of Value-of-Service Pricing Upon Motor Common Carriers," *Journal of Political Economy* (August 1955), pp. 337-344.

69. *Motor Carrier Rates in New England*, 47 MCC 657, 600-1 (1948) as summarized in Taff, *Management of Traffic and Physical Distribution* (3rd. ed; 1964), p. 134.

70. Edward A. Starr, *The Interpretation of Freight Tariffs* (Fort Worth, Texas: The Transportation Press, 1961), p. 106.

71. Pegrum, *Transportation: Economics and Public Policy*, p. 238.

72. Interstate Commerce Commission, Bureau of Economics, Statement

No. 67-2, *The Role of Regulated Motor Carriers in the Handling of Small Shipments* (Washington, D.C.: U.S. Government Printing Office, November 1967), pp. 7 and A-3.

73. Taff, *Commercial Motor Transportation*, p. 333.

74. George J. Stigler, *The Theory of Price* (3rd ed.; New York: The Macmillan Co., 1966), p. 153.

75. James C. Nelson, "Coming Organizational Changes in Transportation," in Jack R. Davidson and Howard W. Ottoson, eds., *Transportation Problems and Policies in the Trans-Missouri West* (Lincoln, Nebraska: University of Nebraska Press, 1967), p. 323. Used with permission.

76. Merrill J. Roberts, "Some Aspects of Motor Carrier Costs: Firm Size, Efficiency, and Financial Health," *Land Economics* (August 1956), pp. 228-238.

77. Ibid., p. 231.

78. Robert A. Nelson, "The Economic Structure of the Highway Carrier Industry in New England," in *Motor Freight Transport for New England* (Report No. 5; Boston: New England Governors' Committee on Public Transportation, October 1956).

79. Ibid., p. 35.

80. Edward W. Smykay, "An Appraisal of the Economics [sic] of Scale in the Motor Carrier Industry," *Land Economics* (May 1958), pp. 143-145.

81. Robert A. Nelson, "The Economies of Scale in the Motor Carrier Industry: a Reply," *Land Economics* (May 1959), p. 185. This debate ended with, Edward W. Smykay, "The Economies of Scale in the Motor Carrier Industry: a Rejoiner," *Land Economics* (May 1959), pp. 185-187.

82. Meyer et al., *Competition in the Transportation Industries*, p. 88.

83. Load factor refers to the ratio of capacity in a vehicle actually used compared to the maximum capacity that the vehicle has available. See Oi and Hurter, *Economics of Private Truck Transportation*, p. 131.

84. Meyer et al., *Competition in the Transportation Industries*, p. 216.

85. Robert A. Nelson, "The Economic Structure of the Highway Carrier Industry in New England," *Public Transportation for New England* (Boston: The New England Governor's Conference, November 1957), pp. 31-32, quoted in James C. Nelson, "The Effects of Entry Control in Surface Transport" in *Transportation Economics: A Conference of the Universities: National Bureau Committee for Economic Research* (New York: National Bureau of Economic Research, 1965), p. 408.

86. Highway Research Board Bulletin No. 301, *Line-Haul Trucking Costs in Relation to Vehicle Gross Weights* (Washington, D.C.: Highway Research Board, 1961), p. 114, as quoted by James C. Nelson, "The Effects of Entry Control in Surface Transport" in *Transportation Economics: A Conference*, p. 410.

87. American Trucking Associations, Motor Transport Economics, Current Report No. 21, *Mergers in the Trucking Business Industry* (Washington, D.C.: October 1968), pp. 7-8. There are two general types of trucking (or any other

mode of transport) mergers. One variety is known as end-to-end. In this case, assume one firm ran from cities A to B and another from B to C. If they joined together, this would be an end-to-end merger. The second type of merger would involve two firms coming together which both served from A to B.

88. Roberts, "Some Aspects of Motor Carrier Costs," p. 237. Used with permission.

89. U.S. Congress, Senate, Select Committee on Small Business, *Trucking Mergers, Concentration, and Small Business: An Analysis of Interstate Commerce Commission Policy, 1950-56*, by Walter Adams and James B. Hendry, Committee Print (Washington, D.C.: U.S. Government Printing Office, 1957), p. 315.

90. Paul W. Emery, II, "An Empirical Approach to the Motor Carrier Scale Economies Controversy," *Land Economics* (August 1965), pp. 285-289.

91. Ibid., p. 289.

Chapter 3
The Development of Economic
Regulation in the Trucking Industry

1. Donald V. Harper, *Economic Regulation of the Motor Trucking Industry by the States* (Urbana: University of Illinois Press, 1959), pp. 32-34.

2. Donald S. Watson, *Economic Policy: Business and Government* (Boston: Houghton Mifflin Co., 1960), p. 178.

3. Henry Campbell Black, *Black's Law Dictionary* (St. Paul: West Publishing Co., 1951), p. 1317.

4. 94 U.S. 113. It should be noted that this case was the most significant proceeding in a series of six court cases that tested the validity of the Granger laws, i.e., state legislation (principally in Minnesota, Wisconsin, Illinois, and Iowa) in the early 1870s that attempted to regulate the then current railroad abuses by legislative fiat. These laws were sponsored by the Patrons of Husbandry (commonly called the Grange), an organization of farmers. The Grange believed that the railroads were primarily responsible for the unfavorable economic conditions that farmers were experiencing in the early 1870s. Although the effectiveness of the Granger laws was relatively short-lived, the case of *Munn v. Illinois* clearly established the states' power to regulate industries that affected the public interest. For a complete discussion of the Granger laws, see: Locklin, *Economics of Transportation*, pp. 212-221.

5. Ibid., p. 126.

6. For an excellent review of key cases that attempted to specifically categorize industries affecting the public interest, see: Charles F. Phillips, Jr., *The Economics of Regulation* (Homewood, Ill.: R.D. Irwin, Inc., 1965), pp. 50-76.

7. 291 U.S. 502.

8. Ibid., p. 537.

9. Wilcox, *Public Policies Toward Business*, p. 288.

10. Harper, *Economic Regulation of the Motor Trucking Industry by the States*, p. 32.

11. William J. Hudson and James A. Constantin, *Motor Transportation: Principles and Practices* (New York: Ronald Press Co., 1958), pp. 461-462.

12. Harper, *Economic Regulation of the Motor Trucking Industry by the States*, pp. 26-31.

13. Hudson and Constantin, *Motor Transportation*, p. 462.

14. Roy J. Sampson and Martin T. Farris, *Domestic Transportation: Practice, Theory and Policy* (2nd ed.; Boston: Houghton Mifflin Co., 1971), p. 274.

15. Shan Szto, *Federal and State Regulation of Motor Carrier Rates and Services* (Philadelphia: University of Pennsylvania Ph.D. Dissertation, 1934), p. 13.

16. *Motor Transport Company v. Public Service Commission*, 56 N.W. (2d) 548 (1953) in Harper, *Economic Regulation of the Motor Trucking Industry by the States*, p. 30.

17. Oregon Laws of 1933, Chap. 429, Sec. 4 and New Hampshire Laws of 1933, Chap. 106 as amended by Chap. 169, Sec. 1 in Szto, *Regulation of Motor Carriers*, p. 14.

18. D. Philip Locklin, *Economics of Transportation* (7th ed.; Homewood, Ill.: R.D. Irwin, Inc., 1972), p. 668.

19. For a complete list of for-hire regulatory areas that could be controlled by the states, see Hudson and Constantin, *Motor Transportation*, p. 471.

20. Szto, *Regulation of Motor Carriers*, p. 47.

21. Ibid., p. 50.

22. Ibid., p. 54.

23. John J. George, *Motor Carrier Regulation in the United States* (Band and White, Spartanburg, S.C.: 1929), pp. 85-100, and Szto, *Regulation of Motor Carriers*, pp. 70-88.

24. Szto, *Regulation of Motor Carriers*, p. 70.

25. George, *Motor Carrier Regulation*, p. 100.

26. "He who receives the advantage ought also to suffer the burden."

27. Szto, *Regulation of Motor Carriers*, p. 158.

28. 169 U.S. 466 (1898).

29. The discussion in this subsection leans heavily on Szto, *Regulation of Motor Carriers*, pp. 114-148.

30. A through route has been defined as " . . . an arrangement, express or implied, between connecting carriers, by which they offer through transportation service from a point on the line of one to the destination on the line of another." Kenneth U. Flood, *Traffic Management* (2nd ed.; Dubuque, Iowa: Wm. C. Brown Co., 1965), p. 153. A joint rate is merely a single rate that applies

between the two points, while the division of this rate between the participating carriers is usually a contractual agreement between the involved carriers.

31. Locklin, *Economics of Transportation*, p. 674.

32. *Michigan Public Utilities Commission v. Duke*, 266 U.S. 570 (1925).

33. G. Lloyd Wilson, *Motor Traffic Management* (New York: D. Appleton and Co., 1928), p. 193.

34. 266 U.S. 570, 577.

35. *Frost v. Railroad Commission of California*, 271 U.S. 583 (1926).

36. "The matter has been previously adjudged by a competent court."

37. "We shall follow the previous decision."

38. Edwards, *Principles of Motor Transportation*, p. 330.

39. 287 U.S. 251 (1932).

40. Elwood Murphey, "State Regulation of Motor Transportation and Carriage," *California Law Review* (July 1933), p. 504.

41. *Wabash, St. Louis, and Pacific Railroad Co. v. Illinois*, 118 U.S. 557 (1886). In this case, the state of Illinois attempted to regulate interstate commerce from Gilman and Peoria, Illinois, to New York City. The Supreme Court voided Illinois' position and stated unambiguously that interstate commerce was strictly under the jurisdiction of the Federal government.

42. Murphey, "State Regulation of Motor Transportation and Carriage," p. 498.

43. *Buck v. Kuykendall*, 267 U.S. 307 (1925).

44. Ibid., p. 315.

45. Clayton Yeatter, "Interstate Legal Barriers to Transportation in the Trans-Missouri West," Jack R. Davidson and Howard W. Ottoson, editors, *Transportation Problem and Policies in the Trans-Missouri West* (Lincoln: University of Nebraska Press, 1967), pp. 202-203.

46. *Bush v. Maloy*, 267 U.S. 317 (1925).

47. Ibid., p. 317.

48. Ibid., p. 325.

49. U.S. Congress, House, Document No. 81, *Report of the Federal Coordinator of Transportation*, 1934, 74th Cong., 1st sess. (Washington, D.C.: U.S. Government Printing Office, 1935), p. 113.

50. California Investigation, Dec. No. 25243, October 10, 1932, in Szto, *Regulation of Motor Carriers*, p. 229.

51. Hudson and Constantin, *Motor Transportation*, pp. 475-476.

52. Szto, *Regulation of Motor Carriers*, p. 233.

53. Ibid., p. 234.

54. U.S. Congress, *Report of the Federal Coordinator*, p. 127.

55. George, *Motor Carrier Regulation*, p. 240.

56. U.S. Congress, Senate, *Hearings Before the Committee on Interstate Commerce on S. 1629, S. 1632, and S. 1635*, 74th Cong., 1st sess. (Washington, D.C.: U.S. Government Printing Office, 1935), p. 79.

57. Ibid., pp. 80 and 266.

58. Ibid., p. 266.

59. U.S. Congress, *Report of the Federal Coordinator*, p. 122.

60. U.S. Congress, *Hearings on S. 1629*, p. 504.

61. Ibid., p. 504.

62. Ibid., p. 505.

63. A disclaimer is necessary at this point. Professor Shan Szto lists thirty-seven motor carrier regulatory bills introduced into Congress from 1925-35. See: Szto, *Regulation of Motor Carriers*, pp. 240-243. This section will discuss only the most important of these regulatory measures.

64. Wilson, *Motor Traffic Management*, pp. 204-205.

65. Hudson and Constantin, *Motor Transportation*, pp. 473-474.

66. Muller, *Federal Regulation of Motor Transport*, p. 4.

67. Ibid., pp. 3-4.

68. Ibid., p. 4.

69. U.S. Congress, *Hearings on S. 1629*, p. 47.

70. Ibid., p. 409.

71. Besides the low rates argument, the farmers also opposed trucking regulation because they believed it would restrict the supply flexibility of trucking service that was essential at harvest time. This argument was responsible for a significant exemption in the Motor Carrier Act of 1935, which will be examined below.

72. U.S. Congress, Senate, Report No. 482, *Motor Carrier Act, 1935*, 74th Cong., 1st sess. (Washington, D.C.: U.S. Government Printing Office, 1935), p. 2.

73. Warren H. Wagner, *A Legislative History of the Motor Carrier Act, 1935* (Denton, Maryland: Rue Publishing Co., 1935), pp. 98-99.

74. The original statutory definition was: Section 203 (a) (14) The term "common carrier by motor vehicle" means any person who or which undertakes, whether directly or by a lease or any other arrangement, to transport passengers or property, or any class or classes of property, for the general public in interstate or foreign commerce by motor vehicle for compensation, whether over regular or irregular routes, including such motor vehicle operations of carriers by rail or water, and of express or forwarding companies, except to the extent that these operations are subject to the provisions of Part I.

Gilman G. Udell, compiler, *Laws Relating to Interstate Commerce and Transportation* (Washington, D.C.: U.S. Government Printing Office, 1966), pp. 229-230.

75. *The Interstate Commerce Act* (Washington, D.C.: U.S. Government Printing Office, 1968), p. 130.

76. *Craig Contract Carrier Application* 28 M.C.C. 629, 637 (1941).

77. Warren H. Wagner, "Common, Contract, and Private Motor Carriers Defined and Distinguished," *ICC Practitioners Journal* (November 1941), p. 128.

78. The ICC has adopted this phrase as a synonym for public convenience and necessity: " . . . a strong or urgent public need." *Utah Railway Terminal Co. Application*, 72 ICC 89, 93 (1922).

79. Hugh S. Norton, *Modern Transportation Economics* (Columbus, Ohio: Charles E. Merrill Books, Inc., 1963), p. 261.

80. "Just" refers to the shippers' point of view. The rate must be fair in regard to what other shippers pay for transporting similar commodities. "Reasonable" implies that the carrier should receive a fair return for his services rendered in the transaction. See: John Guandolo, *Transportation Law* (2nd ed.; Dubuque, Iowa: Wm. C. Brown Co., 1973), p. 360.

81. Westmeyer, *Economics of Transportation*, p. 398.

82. Hudson and Constantin, *Motor Transportation*, pp. 586-587.

83. Taff, *Commercial Motor Transportation*, p. 295. This book, Chapter 13, presents an excellent discussion of the insurance needs in the trucking industry.

84. Guandolo and Fair, *Tedrow's Regulation of Transportation*, pp. 261-262.

85. Pegrum, *Transportation: Economics and Public Policy*, p. 343.

86. The 1935 definition of Section 203 (a) (15) was, The term "contract carrier by motor vehicle" means any person not included under paragraph (14) of this section, who or which, under special and individual contracts or agreements, and whether directly or by a lease or any other arrangement, transports passengers or property in interstate or foreign commerce by motor vehicle for compensation.

Udell, *Laws Relating to Interstate Commerce and Transportation*, p. 230.

87. The 1940 amendment changed Section 203 (a) (15) to: The term "contract carrier by motor vehicle" means any person which, under individual contracts or agreements, engages in the transportation (other than transportation referred to in paragraph (14) and the exception therein) by motor vehicle of passengers or property in interstate of foreign commerce for compensation.

Ibid., p. 229.

88. Fair and Guandolo, *Tedrow's Regulation of Transportation*, p. 223.

89. *Motor Ways Tariff Bureau v. Steel Transportation Co., Inc.* 62 MCC 413, 415 (1954).

90. *United States v. Contract Steel Carriers, Inc.* 350 U.S. 409, 412 (1956).

91. Locklin, *Economics of Transportation*, p. 689.

92. *The Interstate Commerce Act*, p. 130.

93. Taff, *Commercial Motor Transportation*, p. 534. These figures come from the *3rd ed.*, of this text, published in 1961.

94. *Umthun Trucking Co. Extension–Phosphatic Feed Supplements* 91 MCC 691, 697 (1962).

95. Locklin, *Economics of Transportation*, p. 681.

96. For a detailed discussion of the rate regulation of contract carriers, see: Hudson and Constantin, *Motor Transportation*, pp. 609-612.

97. Guandolo, *Transportation Law*, p. 182.

98. Westmeyer, *Economics of Transportation*, p. 403.

99. For an extremely comprehensive discussion of common carrier liability, see: Richard R. Sigmon, *Miller's Law of Freight Loss and Damage Claims* (3rd ed.; Dubuque, Iowa: Wm. C. Brown Co., 1967).

100. *The Interstate Commerce Act*, pp. 130-131.

101. 42 MCC 193 (1943).

102. *Lenoir Chair Contract Carrier Application* 48 MCC 259 (1948).

103. Ibid., p. 264.

104. For an excellent, if somewhat old analysis of the problems involved in defining the private motor carrier, see: John Coggins, "The Private Motor Carrier Definition of the Interstate Commerce Act: An Economic-Legal Battleground," *The George Washington Law Review* (October 1950), pp. 1-22. A concise and very current discussion of the "primary business" test is found in George W. Hilton, *The Transportation Act of 1958: A Decade of Experience* (Bloomington, Indiana: University Press, 1969), pp. 41-42, 167-183.

105. The "gray area" refers to basically illegal actions under the 1935 Motor Carrier Act and its amendments. More specifically, it involves a trucker conducting for-hire operations when he does not possess proper operating authority to do so.

106. See: Hilton, *The Transportation Act of 1958*, pp. 167-174.

107. Ibid., p. 174.

108. Ibid., pp. 174-176.

109. It should be noted that not all private trucking in other countries is so free from governmental edict. Australia and New Zealand are examples of countries where private transportation is restricted in order to help the government owned railway systems increase their tonnage. Locklin, *Economics of Transportation*, (6th ed.) p. 595. In fact, England for at least seven years, from 1947 to 1954, restricted all private trucking to a maximum length of 25 miles. Walker, *Transport Policy Before and After 1953*, p. 104.

110. *The Interstate Commerce Act*, p. 131.

111. Taff, *Commercial Motor Transportation*, pp. 124-125. See also the statement by Charles S. Morgan in U.S. Congress, Senate, Committee on Commerce, *The Motor Carrier Act of 1935: An Evaluation of the Motor Carrier Act of 1935 on the Thirtieth Anniversary of Its Enactment*, Committee Print, 89th Cong., 1st sess. (Washington, D.C.: U.S. Government Printing Office, October 1, 1965), p. 14.

112. Mossman and Morton, *Principles of Transportation*, pp. 91-92.

113. For a complete description of the regulation currently in effect for brokers, see: Taff, *Commercial Motor Transportation*, pp. 394-396.

114. For a complete discussion of any of these exemptions, see the following: Guandolo, *Transportation Law*, Chapter 19, Hudson and Constantin, *Motor Transportation*, pp. 538-539; and Fritz Kahn, *Principles of Motor Carrier Regulation* (Dubuque, Iowa: Wm. C. Brown, 1958), Chapter 2.

115. Taff, *Commercial Motor Transportation*, p. 388.

116. Volotta, *The Impact of Federal Entry Controls on Motor Carrier Operations*, p. 49.

117. Statement of John V. Lawrence, in *The Motor Carrier Act of 1935: An Evaluation of the Motor Carrier Act of 1935 on the Thirtieth Anniversary of Its Enactment*, p. 31.

118. The agricultural exemption applies only to truckers, not the railroads or any other transport mode.

119. *The Doyle Report*, pp. 516-519.

120. Locklin, *Economics of Transportation*, pp. 677-678.

121. *Cache Valley Dairy Association, Investigation of Operations* 96 MCC 616, 622 (1964).

122. *Northwest Agricultural Cooperative Association v. Interstate Commerce Commission* 350 F. 2d 252, 257 (1965).

123. "ICC Head Urges Definition of Co-op Clause by Congress," *Transport Topics* (October 24, 1966), p. 1.

124. *ICC 80th Annual Report, 1966*, pp. 78-79; *ICC 81st Annual Report, 1967*, pp. 66-67; and *ICC 82nd Annual Report, 1968*, pp. 88-89.

125. See, for example: "Defense Department to Use Farm 'Co-op' Trucks to Haul Military Cargo Within U.S.," *Traffic World* (November 12, 1966), p. 38; "Two ICC Members Express Displeasure About DOD's 'Co-op' Transport Policy," *Traffic World* (December 17, 1966), pp. 24-25; and "Carriers Treated Equally in Routing DOD Traffic MTMTS Commander Says," *Traffic World* (January 14, 1967), p. 24.

126. "Truckers, Farm Groups Disagree in Hearings on Bill to Curb Truck Operations of 'Co-ops,' " *Traffic World* (July 29, 1967), p. 18.

127. *ICC 83rd Annual Report, 1969*, p. 91.

128. "ICC Adopts, With Some Changes, Proposed Rules Governing 'Co-op' Transportation," *Traffic World* (May 24, 1969), pp. 62-63.

129. Statement of Senator John Sparkman in, U.S. Congress, Senate, Select Committee on Small Business, *Competition, Regulation, and the Public Interest in the Motor Carrier Industry*, Report No. 1693, 84th Cong., 2nd sess. (Washington, D.C.: U.S. Government Printing Office, March 19, 1956), p. 15.

130. Taff, *Commercial Motor Transportation*, p. 391.

131. *East Texas Motor Freight Lines, Inc. et al. v. Frozen Food Express, et al.*, 351 U.S. 49 (1956).

132. The Bureau of Motor Carriers issued this list on March 19, 1958, in Administrative Ruling No. 107. For this list of both exempt and nonexempt commodities, see: Volotta, *The Impact of Federal Entry Controls on Motor Carrier Operations*, pp. 153-161.

133. For a complete discussion of the issuing of "grandfather" certificates after the 1958 Act, see: Hilton, *The Transportation Act of 1958*, pp. 155-156.

134. "ICC Rules Motor Transport of 'Wild Birdseed Bell' Is Not Subject to Regulation," *Traffic World* (September 20, 1969), p. 45.

135. The "grandfather" provision can be likened to preventing an *ex poste facto* law type of situation.

136. Fair and Guandolo, *Tedrow's Regulation of Transportation*, p. 238.

137. Joseph B. Eastman, as quoted in the statement by Clinton S. Reynolds, in *The Motor Carrier Act of 1935, An Evaluation*, p. 43.

138. John L. Rogers in *The Motor Carrier Act of 1935, An Evaluation*, p. 2.

139. Michael T. Corcoran, in *Motor Carrier Act of 1935, An Evaluation*, p. 21.

140. Borehl, *Trucks: Trouble: And Triumph*, p. 55.

141. Guandolo, *Transportation Law*, p. 65. In addition, any trucker whose operation included three or less states, had his "grandfather" application forwarded to a "joint board" of the states directly involved. See Section 205 (a) of the Interstate Commerce Act.

142. Albert E. Stephan, in the *Motor Carrier Act of 1935, An Evaluation*, p. 25.

143. James C. Nelson, "The Effects of Entry Control in Surface Transport," p. 385.

144. *The Doyle Report*, p. 547.

145. U.S. Congress, Senate, Select Committee on Small Business, *ICC Administration of the Motor Carrier Act*, Committee print (Washington, D.C.: U.S. Government Printing Office, 1955), p. 232.

146. *United States v. Trans-Missouri Freight Association*, 166 U.S. 290 (1897).

147. *United States v. Joint Traffic Association* 171 U.S. 505 (1898).

148. Taff, *Management of Physical Distribution and Transportation*, p. 374.

149. *State of Georgia v. Pennsylvania Railroad Company* 324 U.S. 439 (1945). This case was dismissed by the Supreme Court in 1950.

150. *United States v. Association of American Railroads* U.S. District Court, Lincoln, Nebraska, 4 F.R.D. 510 (filed in 1944).

151. Locklin, *Economics of Transportation*, p. 326.

152. Taff, *Commercial Motor Transportation*, pp. 355,357.

153. Charles F. Phillips, Jr., *The Economics of Regulation: Theory and Practice in the Transportation and Public Utility Industries* (Homewood, Ill.: Richard D. Irwin, Inc., 1965), p. 473.

154. Norton, *National Transportation Policy: Formation and Implementation*, p. 116.

155. Meyer, et al., *Competition in the Transportation Industries*, pp. 210-211. See also: J. Roger Edwards, "Railroad Mergers," *Southwestern Law Journal* (September 1964), pp. 447-448.

156. Public Law 89-170, 89th Congress, H.R. 5401, passed September 6, 1965.

157. W.H. Thompson, "Expected Developments in Transportation Legislation and Implications to Agriculture" in *Transportation Problems and Policies in the Trans-Missouri West*, p. 245.

158. Locklin, *Economics of Transportation*, p. 716.

159. 359 U.S. 464 (1959).

160. U.S. Congress, House, Committee on Interstate and Foreign Commerce, *Regulation of Interstate Motor Buses and Trucks on Public Highways*, H.R. 3836, 73rd Cong., 2nd sess., January 17-February 2, 1934.

161. The Emergency Transportation Act, 1933, created a temporary position, known as the Federal Coordinate of Transportation. This position was filled by J.B. Eastman, former ICC Commissioner, from 1933 to when the post was terminated in 1936. Eastman then returned to the ICC as a commissioner. The Federal Coordinator was charged with two basic duties. First, he was to attempt to get the railroads to work together better, so as to become more efficient, and hence help them to stave off the consequences of the Great Depression. Secondly, he was to make recommendations to Congress when he believed legislation was needed to achieve a stronger and more efficient national transportation system. It was in this latter capacity that Eastman drafted his Federal regulation of motor carriers' act.

162. U.S. Congress, Senate, Committee on Interstate Commerce, *A Bill to Amend the Interstate Commerce Act, as Amended, by Providing for Regulation of the Transportation of Passengers and Property by Motor Carriers Operating in Interstate and Foreign Commerce, and for Other Reasons*, S. 1629, 74th Cong., 1st sess., February 25-March 6, 1935, p. 80.

163. All parts of the Eastman Bill had 300 level designations, because Eastman also proposed to extend regulation to water carriers at this time, and the latter bill carried the 200 level numbers.

164. Hearings on S. 1629 (see: footnote 162, supra), p. 240.

165. U.S. Congress, House, Committee on Interstate and Foreign Commerce, *Regulation of the Transportation of Passengers and Property by Motor Carriers Operating in Interstate and Foreign Commerce*, H.R. 5262, 74th Cong., 1st sess., February 19-March 5, 1935.

166. 79 *Congressional Record* 5665 (April 15, 1935).

167. Ibid., pp. 5654-5655.

168. 79 *Congressional Record* 12,206 (July 31, 1935).

169. Gilman G. Udell, compiler, *Laws Relating to Interstate Commerce and Transportation* (Washington, D.C.: U.S. Government Printing Office, 1966), p. 333.

170. Ibid.

171. U.S. Congress, House, Committee on Interstate and Foreign Commerce, *Amending Section 5(10) of the Interstate Commerce Act Regarding Motor Carrier Mergers*, Report No. 330, 89th Cong., 1st sess. (Washington, D.C.: U.S. Government Printing Office, 1965), p. 2.

172. U.S. Congress, Senate, Committee on Commerce, *Amending Section 5(10) of the Interstate Commerce Act Regarding Motor Carrier Mergers*, Report No. 432, 89th Cong., 1st sess. (Washington, D.C.: U.S. Government Printing Office, 1965), p. 3.

173. Ibid.

174. See: Leslie W. Jacobs, "Regulated Motor Carriers and the Antitrust Laws," *Cornell Law Review* (November 1972), pp. 90-136.

175. For a comprehensive list of the basic Section 212(b) rules and regulations, see: Taff, *Commercial Motor Transportation*, pp. 586-588 (the *3rd ed.*, published in 1961).

Chapter 4
Introduction to Trucking Unifications

1. Hearings on S. 1629 as quoted in the statement by Charles S. Morgan, in U.S. Congress, Senate, *The Motor Carrier Act of 1935: An Evaluation of the Motor Carrier Act of 1935 on the Thirtieth Anniversary of Its Enactment*, p. 12.

2. Ibid.

3. ICC, *54th Annual Report-1940*, pp. 107-108.

4. ICC, *69th Annual Report-1955*, p. 100.

5. ICC, *86th Annual Report-1972*, p. 131.

6. Colin Barrett, "The 'Big-Company' Era in the Trucking Industry," *Traffic World* (February 22, 1969), pp. 81-82.

7. Statement of Owen Clarke, Chairman of the ICC, in U.S. Congress, Senate, Select Committee on Small Business, Committee Print, *Trucking Mergers and Concentration*, 85th Cong., 1st sess. (Washington, D.C.: U.S. Government Printing Office, July 1957), p. 43.

8. U.S. Congress, Senate, *Trucking Mergers and Concentration*, p. 4.

9. Ibid.

10. "Here Come the Trucks," *Forbes* (December 1, 1964), p. 24. Used with permission.

11. American Trucking Associations, Current Report No. 21, *Mergers in the Trucking Industry* (Washington, D.C.: American Trucking Associations, October 1968), pp. 14-15. See also: William O. Craig, "Panelists Discuss Problems, Trends, Prospects of Motor Carrier Industry," *Traffic World* (September 2, 1967), p. 76.

12. Ibid., p. 6.

13. Barrett, "The 'Big-Company' Era in the Trucking Industry," p. 81. Used with permission.

14. Ibid.

15. American Trucking Associations, *Mergers in the Trucking Industry*, p. 11.

16. "Here Come the Trucks," p. 24, and James K. Knudson in U.S. Congress, Senate, Select Committee on Small Business, *ICC Administration of the Motor Carrier Act* (Washington, D.C.: Government Printing Office, 1956), p. 20.

17. "Here Come the Trucks," p. 24.

18. Barrett, "The 'Big-Company' Era in the Trucking Industry," p. 81.

19. Statement by William G. Mahoney, "What is Labor's Stake?," in Nadreen A. Burnie, ed., *Transportation Mergers and Acquisitions: Proceedings of a Two-Day Conference* (Evanston, Ill.: Transportation Center at Northwestern University, 1962), pp. 74-75.

20. Statement by Charles Gregory in ibid., p. 73.

21. "Here Come the Trucks," p. 25. Used with permission.

22. Ibid. Used with permission.

23. "T.I.M.E.-D.C.-L.A.S.M.E. Okay Merger Agreement to Form Major Transcontinental Line," *Traffic World* (July 29, 1967), p. 29.

24. "T.I.M.E.-D.C. International, Los Angeles-Seattle Express Ask ICC to Approve Merger, *Traffic World* (December 2, 1967), p. 55.

25. "Examiner Would Authorize N.C.L. to Control T.I.M.E.-D.C. International, L.A.S.M.E.," *Traffic World* (November 9, 1968), p. 82. Reprinted with permission.

26. Ibid., p. 83.

27. "N.C.L. Control of Trucking Firms Approved by ICC," *Traffic World* (January 4, 1969), p. 31.

28. "Earnings for T.I.M.E.-D.C. Show Large Rise for 1968," *Traffic World* (March 8, 1969), p. 34.

29. *Traffic World* articles of (August 17, 1970), p. 28; (August 31, 1970), p. 29; (December 28, 1970), p. 21; (September 6, 1971), p. 15; (November 15, 1971), p. 26, 40; (December 13, 1971), p. 62; and (July 10, 1972), p. 48. See also, "A Merger That Isn't Quite a Merger," *Business Week* (November 4, 1972), pp. 80-81.

30. Barrett, "The 'Big-Company' Era in the Trucking Industry," p. 82.

31. Statement of Owen Clarke in, U.S. Congress, Senate, *Trucking Mergers and Concentration*, p. 50.

32. Norton, *Modern Transportation Economics*, p. 374.

33. Professor G.W. Wilson points out that in all the controversy about scale economies in trucking, at least no one has ever suggested that larger firms suffer from *diseconomies*. See: Wilson, "The Nature of Competition in the Motor Transport Industry," p. 389.

34. James F. Pinkney, "When Do Mergers Pay?," in Burnie, ed., *Transportation Mergers and Acquisitions*, p. 59.

35. Barrett, "The 'Big-Company' Era in the Trucking Industry," p. 82.

36. Wilson, "The Nature of Competition in the Motor Transport Industry," p. 391. Used with permission.

37. Robert M. Butler, "What Now For Trucking," *Traffic World* (December 14, 1968), p. 35.

38. "Here Come the Trucks," p. 27. Used with permission.

39. Hearings on S. 1629 as quoted in the statement by Charles S. Morgan in U.S. Congress, Senate, *The Motor Carrier Act of 1935: An Evaluation of the Motor Carrier Act of 1935 On the Thirtieth Anniversary of Its Enactment*, p. 12.

40. U.S. Congress, Senate, *Trucking Mergers and Concentration*, pp. 50, 104, and Smykay, "An Appraisal of the Economics [sic] of Scale in the Motor Carrier Industry," p. 148.

41. Anthony F. Arpaia in U.S. Congress, Senate, Select Committee on Small Business, *ICC Administration of the Motor Carrier Act*, p. 176.

42. Locklin, *Economics of Transportation*, p. 649. See also: Walker, *Road and Rail*, p. 173 and *New England Motor Carrier Rates*, 8 MCC 287, 314 (1938).

43. Meyer et al., *Competition in the Transportation Industries*, p. 261.

44. Allan C. Flott, "Merger Trends," in *Transportation Mergers and Acquisitions*, p. 29. See also: American Trucking Associations, *Mergers in the Trucking Industry*, p. 8.

45. Healy, "The Merger Movement in Transportation," p. 443. Used with permission of the American Economic Association.

46. Nelson, "Coming Organizational Changes in Transportation," pp. 322-323.

47. *Motor Carrier Probability Sampling Studies*, 329 ICC 683, 689 (1966).

48. Ibid.

49. Ibid., p. 693.

50. Railroad controlled motor carriers were excluded because the ICC has followed a separate and distinct line of reasoning in these cases, compared to a typical intramodal trucking merger. Specifically, the Commission has generally followed the precedent of the so-called *Kansas City Southern* case, 10 MCC 221 (1938), 28 MCC 5 (1941), in which rail controlled truckers must keep their service supplementary and/or auxiliary to the operations of the parent railroad. For a complete discussion of the special restrictions applied to rail dominated truckers, see: Locklin, *Economics of Transportation*, pp. 864-867.

51. Personal letter from Chairman of the ICC, George M. Stafford to James Craig Johnson, April 6, 1970, p. 1. Used with permission.

52. Ibid., p. 2. Used with permission.

53. John Neter and William Wasserman, *Fundamental Statistics for Business and Economics* (2nd ed.; Boston: Allyn and Bacon, Inc., 1961), p. 437.

54. Cases numbered 0001-0004 are found in volume 1 of the motor carrier case books. All cases numbered past 0004 are printed in the volumes designated as finance reports.

55. Herbert Arkin, *Handbook of Sampling for Auditing and Accounting-Volume I-Methods* (New York: McGraw-Hill Book Co., Inc., 1963), p. 84.

56. Ibid., p. 96.

57. Ibid., p. 370.

58. Specifically, the random numbers used came from, The Rand Corporation, *A Million Random Digits* (New York: The Free Press of Glencoe, 1955).

Chapter 5
The Reasons for ICC Approval of
Trucking Mergers and Consolidations

1. Technically, mergers and consolidations are not synonymous. The former involves one company completely absorbing another, while the acquiring company does not change its name. Consolidations, on the other hand, involve two or more companies coming together, and an entirely new corporation in name is formed. The term unification is more general and refers to either of the above situations. This paper will not make any distinction between any of these three terms, and all will be used interchangeably.

2. *Red Arrow Freight Lines, Inc.–Purchase–Charlton*, 15 MCC 142, 145 (1938).

3. *B. & E. Transp. Co., Inc.–Purchase–Merchants Transp., Inc.*, 36 MCC 561, 563 (1941).

4. *Motor Exp., Inc.–Purchase–Linsley and Thrash*, 37 MCC 503, 505 (1941).

5. *Coordinated Transport, Inc., of Illinois–Purchase–Merillat*, 56 MCC 635, 641 (1950).

6. *Fitterling Transp. Co., Inc.–Control–Shippers Dispatch*, 39 MCC 595, 601 (1944).

7. *Jones Truck Lines, Inc.–Purchase–Capital Freight Lines*, 80 MCC 268, 275 (1959).

8. Section 210a (b) allows the ICC to authorize a trucker to take over the operations of another trucker on a temporary basis (not to exceed 180 days), without a hearing or other proceedings, if one of the following conditions is met. First, if the operations of the carrier to be acquired are failing rapidly, and any delay in the takeover would cause destruction or injury to said carrier, then its operations may be promptly transferred under Section 210a (b). A second valid reason is that if the carrier to be acquired could cease or decrease operations to the harm of the shipping public, then again a Section 210a (b) transfer would be in order. It should be pointed out that Section 210a (b) transfers are strictly of a *temporary* nature, and if the acquiring carrier desires to continue operations of the vendor on a permanent basis, a formal application under Section 5 must be executed.

9. *Mason & Dixon Lines, Inc.–Control–Silver Fleet*, 90 MCC 829, 847 (1963).

10. See, for example: *Service, Inc.–Purchase–Yearly Transfer Co., Inc.*, 59 MCC 517, 522 (1953); *All States Freight, Inc.–Merger*, 90 MCC 51, 56 (1962); and *Interstate Motor Frt. Sys.–Purchase–Eaton Trucks*, 104 MCC 248, 256 (1967).

11. *C. & D. Motor Delivery Co.–Purchase–Wilson*, 65 MCC 733, 750 (1956).

12. *Kerr Motor Lines, Inc.–Consolidation*, 101 MCC 81, 91 (1966).

13. *Lee Way M. Frt., Inc.–Purchase–Superior M. Frt. Lines, Inc.*, 36 MCC 322, 323 (1941).

14. *Matthews Freight Service, Inc.–Purchase–Brodin*, 39 MCC 734, 737 (1944).

15. *Transportation, Inc.–Purchase–Sutton Transfer Co., Inc.*, 15 MCC 665, 666 (1939).

16. *East Texas Motor Freight Lines–Purchase–Dickinson*, 25 MCC 799, 781 (1939).

17. *Novick Transfer Co., Inc.–Purchase–Steinla Transp. Co.*, 85 MCC 543, 547 (1960). See also: *Transcon Lines–Pur.–Kramer–Consolidated Frt., Inc.*, 101 MCC 201, 206 (1966).

18. *Ball Bros. Trucking Co., Inc.–Purchase–Powell*, 60 MCC 449, 451 (1954). See also: *King–Purchase–Ford*, 15 MCC 7, 8 (1938).

19. *Pacific Intermountain Exp. Co.–Control–West Coast*, 60 MCC 301, 315 (1954).

20. See for example: *McLean Trucking Co.–Control–Carolina Motor Exp. Lines*, 70 MCC 279, 287 (1957) and *Transamerican Freight Lines, Inc.–Control and Merger*, 75 MCC 423, 444 (1958).

21. *Johnson–Purchase–Rose*, 5 MCC 70, 72 (1937).

22. *Western Truck Lines–Purchase–Mono Basin Transport*, 36 MCC 347, 349 (1941).

23. *Hennepin Transp. Co., Inc.–Purchase–Oligney Motor Exp. Co.*, 80 MCC 655, 658 (1959) and *Central Wisconsin M. Transport Co.–Purchase–Carlstedt*, 85 MCC 305, 309 (1960).

24. *Frank Cosgrove Transp. Co., Inc.–Purchase–Dawne Transp. Co.*, 80 MCC 191, 197 (1957).

25. *Brooks Transp. Co., Inc.–Purchase–Jacobs Transfer Co.*, 5 MCC 85, 87 (1937) and *Transamerican Freight Lines, Inc.–Control and Merger*, 75 MCC 423, 433 (1958).

26. *Interstate Motor Lines, Inc.–Control and Merger*, 58 MCC 775, 779 (1953) and *Transamerican Freight Lines, Inc.–Purchase–Donaldson*, 59 MCC 351, 357 (1953).

27. *Cantlay & Tanzola, Inc.–Purchase–Lyons*, 25 MCC 756, 758 (1939).

28. *Berman–Control–Birmingham–Columbus Frt. Lines, Inc.*, 35 MCC 449, 451 (1940), *Interstate Motor Lines, Inc.–Control and Merger*, 58 MCC 775, 779 (1953) and *Transamerican Freight Lines, Inc.–Purchase–Donaldson*, 59 MCC 351, 357 (1953).

29. *Northern Transp. Co.–Lease–Terminal Truck Lines, Inc.*, 25 MCC 759, 761 (1939) and *Central Wisconsin M. Transport Co.–Purchase–Carlstedt*, 85 MCC 305, 309 (1960).

30. *Keehsin Transcon. Freight Lines, Inc.–Control–Seaboard*, 5 MCC 25, 31 (1937).

31. *Hancock Truck Lines, Inc.–Purchase–Motor Freight Corp.*, 5 MCC 405, 409 (1938).

32. See, for example: *Transport Corp. of Va.–Purchase–Central Eastern, Inc.*, 15 MCC 681, 684 (1939); *Zabarsky–Purchase–Smith*, 35 MCC 259, 262 (1940); *Miller–Purchase–Wright Line*, 37 MCC 347, 350 (1941); *Rodgers Motor Lines, Inc.–Purchase–Ovens*, 40 MCC 483, 485 (1946); and *Associated Truck Lines, Inc.–Purchase–Adams*, 56 MCC 287, 292 (1950).

33. *Hoover M. Exp. Co., Inc.–Purchase–Cincinnati-S. Motor Exp.*, 15 MCC 627, 628 (1939).

34. *Consolidated Freightways Corp. of Delaware–Control*, 109 MCC 76, 84 (1969). See also: *Red Arrow Frt. Lines, Inc.–Purchase–Galveston*, 104 MCC 820, 824 (1968) and *Western Gillette, Inc.–Control–Desert*, 109 MCC 514, 519 (1970).

35. *Liberty Highway Co.–Purchase–Germann*, 5 MCC 699, 700 (1938).

36. *Gays Exp., Inc.–Purchase–Beattie*, 5 MCC 677, 679 (1938).

37. *Kaplan Trucking Co.–Purchase–D. Wood Trucking Co., Inc.*, 38 MCC 39, 41 (1941).

38. *Denver-Chicago Trucking Co., Inc.–Control–Eck Miller*, 70 MCC 779, 785 (1957).

39. *Cross Transp., Inc.–Purchase–D. & N. Motor Transp. Co.*, 75 MCC 619, 623 (1958).

40. *Associated Transport, Inc.–Control and Consolidation*, 38 MCC 137, 146 (1942).

41. This point is well summarized by a statement by Professor James C. Nelson in Chapter 3, supra.

42. See Chapter 2, supra.

43. For early cases where this was an important factor, see: *McCarthy Freight System, Inc.–Merger*, 5 MCC 684, 686 (1938). *Blue Arrow Transport Lines, Inc.–Purchase–Mammina*, 35 MCC 37, 39 (1940); and *Heller–Control–Conyes Freight Lines*, 35 MCC 721, 727 (1940).

44. *Zabarsky–Purchase–Smith*, 35 MCC 259, 262 (1940).

45. *Pomprowitz–Purchase–Noble*, 39 MCC 415, 418 (1943). See also: *Lang Transp. Corp.–Purchase–Bray Truck Lines, Inc.*, 36 MCC 133, 138 (1940); and *Pacific Intermountain Exp. Co.–Control and Purchase*, 57 MCC 467, 468 (1952).

46 *New Dixie Lines, Inc.–Purchase–Jocie Motor Lines, Inc.*, 57 MCC 707, 713 (1951).

47. See, for example: *Contract Cartage Co.–Lease–Automobile Convoy Co.*, 45 MCC 518, 522 (1947); *Beard-Laney, Inc.–Purchase–Hagler*, 55 MCC 465, 469 (1949); *Campbell Sixty-Six Exp., Inc.–Control and Merger*, 57 MCC 767, 773 (1951); *Black–Purchase–Buzby*, 60 MCC 519, 523 (1954); *Mid-Continent Frt. Lines, Inc.–Purchase–Hanson M. Exp.*, 65 MCC 312, 319 (1955); *A. Duie Pyle, Inc.–Purchase–New Way Transport Co.*, 70 MCC 93, 94-95 (1956); *Cross*

Transp., Inc.–Purchase–D & N Motor Transp. Co., 75 MCC 619, 623 (1958); *Johnson M. Lines, Inc.–Control–Atlantic States Motor*, 80 MCC 459, 464 (1959); and *Hennepin Transp. Co., Inc.–Purchase–Oligney Motor Exp. Co.*, 80 MCC 655, 658 (1959).

48. *Dalby Motor Freight Lines, Inc.–Lease–Reynolds*, 39 MCC 204, 206 (1943).

49. *Garton–Purchase–National Hauling Contractors Co., Inc.*, 55 MCC 727, 730 (1949).

50. *Murphy Motor Freight Lines, Inc.–Purchase–Hess Motor*, 65 MCC 679, 684 (1956).

51. *Arkansas-Best Freight System, Inc.–Purchase–Bradsher*, 87 MCC 67, 70 (1960). See also: *W.T. Byrans Motor Exp., Inc.–Purchase–Fred S. George & Son, Inc.*, 85 MCC 503, 507 (1960); *Deaton Truck Line, Inc.–Purchase–Magnolia Truck Line*, 87 MCC 674, 678 (1961); and *U.S. Van Lines, Inc.–Purchase–Holien*, 90 MCC 657, 659-60 (1962).

52. *Black Motor Lines, Inc.–Purchase–Shamburger*, 37 MCC 787, 789 (1941).

53. *Sheridan & Duncan, Inc.–Purchase–F.J. Martin, Inc.*, 39 MCC 156, 158 (1943).

54. *Holdcroft Transp. Co.–Purchase–Jaffa*, 39 MCC 551, 554-5 (1944).

55. *Novick Transfer Co., Inc.–Purchase–Steinla Transp. Co.*, 85 MCC 543, 545 (1960).

56. *Dougherty Storage & Van Co.–Purchase–Bell Transfer*, 5 MCC 366, 367 (1938).

57. *Powell Bros. Truck Lines, Inc.–Purchase–Bryan*, 38 MCC 104, 107 (1941).

58. See: *A. Duie Pyle, Inc.–Purchase–New Way Transport Co.*, 70 MCC 93, 94 (1956); *Johnson M. Lines, Inc.–Control–Atlantic States Motor*, 80 MCC 459, 463 (1959); and *Novick Transfer Co., Inc.–Purchase–Steinla Transp. Co.*, 85 MCC 543, 545 (1960).

59. *Keeshin Transcon. Freight Lines, Inc.–Control–Seaboard*, 5 MCC 25, 31 (1937). See also: *Davis–Purchase–Caverly Transfer Lines, Inc.*, 35 MCC 499, 502 (1940).

60. 38 MCC 137, 143 (1942).

61. *Pacific Intermountain Exp. Co.–Control–West Coast*, 60 MCC 301, 311 (1954).

62. See, for example: *B. & E. Transp. Co., Inc.–Purchase–Merchants Transp., Inc.*, 36 MCC 561, 563 (1941); *Lecrone-Benedict Ways, Inc.–Purchase–Le Crone Motor*, 37 MCC 745, 750 (1941); and *Frank Cosgrove Transp. Co., Inc.–Purchase–Dawne Transp. Co.*, 80 MCC 191, 198 (1957).

63. *Hancock Truck Lines, Inc.–Purchase–Motor Freight Corp.*, 5 MCC 405, 409 (1938) and *Pacific Intermountain Exp. Co.–Control–West Coast*, 60 MCC 301, 305 (1954).

64. *Casaroll–Control–Crown Motor Service, Inc.*, 35 MCC 471, 474 (1940); *Consolidated Freightways, Inc.–Purchase–Volck Bros.*, 37 MCC 95, 99 (1941); *Cochrane–Control–Cochrane Transp. Co.*, 80 MCC 691, 694 (1959); and *Associated Transport, Inc.–Control–Keystone Motor*, 87 MCC 409, 413 (1961).

65. *Associated Transport, Inc.–Control and Consolidation*, 38 MCC 137, 144 (1942).

66. See, for example: *Puget Sound-Portland Lines, Inc.–Merger*, 5 MCC 333, 337 (1937), *Hoover Truck Co.–Purchase–Gallatin Truck Co.*, 15 MCC 173, 175 (1938); *McCue–Purchase–Northern Freight Lines, Inc.*, 37 MCC 29, 31 (1941); *Yale Transport Corp.–Control and Merger*, 57 MCC 602, 605 (1951); *Greig Freight Lines, Inc.--Merger*, 58 MCC 271, 275 (1952); *Pacific Intermountain Exp. Co.–Control–West Coast*, 60 MCC 301, 311 (1954); *Associated Transport, Inc.–Control–Keystone Motor*, 87 MCC 409, 413 (1961); *Overnite Transp. Co.–Purchase–Hill City Transfer Inc.*, 90 MCC 749, 754 (1962); and *Midwest Emery Freight System, Inc.–Control and Merger*, 101 MCC 19, 29 (1965).

67. *Associated Transport, Inc.–Control and Consolidation*, 38 MCC 137, 144 (1942).

68. Ibid.

69. See, for example: *Gay's Exp., Inc.–Purchase–Madore*, 15 MCC 177, 178 (1938); *White's Exp. Co., Inc.–Purchase–Freight Forwarders, Inc.*, 15 MCC 492, 494 (1938); and *Blue Arrow Transport Lines, Inc.–Purchase–Mammina*, 35 MCC 37, 39 (1940).

70. *Motor Cargo, Inc.–Merger*, 25 MCC 775, 778 (1939).

71. See, for example: *Puget Sound-Portland Lines, Inc.–Merger*, 5 MCC 333, 336 (1937); *Hancock Truck Lines, Inc.–Purchase–Motor Freight Corp.*, 5 MCC 405, 409 (1938); *Automobile Shippers, Inc.–Purchase–Associated Transports*, 15 MCC 69, 72 (1938); and *Lee Way M. Frt., Inc.–Purchase–Superior M. Frt. Lines, Inc.*, 36 MCC 322, 323 (1941).

72. *B. & R. Freight Lines, Inc.–Purchase–Ranft*, 56 MCC 118, 121 (1949).

73. *Douglas–Purchase–State Trucking Service*, 25 MCC 511, 513 (1939) and *H.P. Welch Co.–Purchase–E.J. Scannell, Inc.*, 25 MCC 558, 562 (1939).

74. *Cortland Fast Freight, Inc.–Purchase–H.J. Korten, Inc.*, 60 MCC 321, 328 (1954).

75. *Bruce Motor Freight, Inc.–Control and Merger*, 87 MCC 436, 440 (1961).

76. Section 5 (2) (c) (4) of the Interstate Commerce Act.

77. See, for example: *Associated Transport, Inc.–Control and Consolidation*, 38 MCC 137, 146 (1942); *Associated Truck Lines, Inc.–Purchase–Adams*, 56 MCC 287, 292 (1950); and *Consolidated Freightways Corp. of Del.–Control*, 104 MCC 658, 660 (1968).

78. See, for example: *Consolidated Forwarding Co., Inc., (Missouri)–Merger*, 25 MCC 583, 585 (1939) and *Cortland Fast Freight, Inc.–Purchase–H.J. Korten, Inc.*, 60 MCC 321, 328 (1954).

79. *Yellow Transit Freight Lines, Inc.–Control and Merger*, 70 MCC 471, 477 (1957).

80. *Bruce Motor Freight, Inc.–Control and Merger*, 87 MCC 436, 441 (1961). See also: *Consolidated Copperstate Lines–Purchase–Sunset M. Lines*, 85 MCC 113, 131-132 (1960).

81. *Baggett Transp. Co.–Purchase–Hunt Freight Lines, Inc.*, 87 MCC 235, 236 (1961).

82. *Helm's Exp., Inc.–Control and Merger*, 93 MCC 142, 150 (1963).

83. Ibid.

84. Ibid.

85. *Consolidated Freightways Corp. of Delaware–Control*, 109 MCC 76, 82 (1969).

86. Ibid., p. 83.

87. The 1936 Robinson-Patman Act was primarily designed to reduce the quantity discounts that large buyers could secure from producers. Briefly, manufacturers are allowed to give quantity discounts only if one of two primary factors can be proven. First, the discount is legal if it can be shown that the costs of dealing with the customer who purchases in large quantities are lower and hence the purchase discounts are justified on a cost basis. Secondly, the discount is authorized if it was given in "good faith" to match the price quoted by a competitor. For the history of the Robinson-Patman Act and a complete discussion of this complex piece of legislation, see: Donald V. Harper, *Price Policy and Procedure* (New York: Harcourt, Brace & World, Inc., 1966), pp. 100-120, and Marshall C. Howard, *Legal Aspects of Marketing* (New York: McGraw-Hill Book Co., 1964), Chapter 3.

88. 5 MCC 25 (1937).

89. Ibid., pp. 31-32.

90. See, for example: *Ramsey–Control–Benedict Lines, Inc.*, 35 MCC 408, 411 (1940); *Consolidated Freightways, Inc.–Purchase–Volck Bros.*, 37 MCC 95, 99 (1941); *Arrowhead Freight Lines–Purchase–Griffin*, 39 MCC 455, 457 (1943); and *Frank Cosgrove Transp. Co., Inc.–Purchase–Dawne Transp. Co.*, 80 MCC 191, 198 (1957).

91. *Jones–Control–Hartman's Transp. Co.*, 58 MCC 614, 622 (1952).

92. *Consolidated Forwarding Co., Inc. (Missouri)–Merger*, 25 MCC 583, 585 (1939).

93. See, for example: *Coordinated Transport, Inc. of Illinois–Purchase–Merillat*, 56 MCC 635, 641 (1950); *Yale Transport Corp.–Control and Merger*, 57 MCC 602, 605 (1951); *Grieg Freight Line, Inc.–Merger*, 58 MCC 271, 275 (1952); *Cortland Fast Freight, Inc.–Purchase–H.J. Korten, Inc.*, 60 MCC 321, 328 (1954); and *Frank Cosgrove Transp. Co., Inc.–Purchase–Dawne Transp. Co.*, 80 MCC 191, 198 (1957).

94. See, for example: *Riss & Co., Inc.–Purchase–Patterson*, 36 MCC 557, 560 (1941) and *Associated Transport, Inc.–Control–Keystone Motor*, 87 MCC 409, 413 (1961).

95. *R.C. Motor Lines, Inc.–Control–Cotton States M. Lines*, 80 MCC 157, 166 (1959).

96. *Keeshin Transcon. Freight Lines, Inc.–Control–Seaboard*, 5 MCC 25, 32 (1937).

97. See, for example: *Ramsey–Control–Benedict Lines, Inc.*, 35 MCC 408, 411 (1940) and *Associated Transport, Inc.–Control and Consolidation*, 38 MCC 137, 145 (1942).

98. *Cole Motor Service, Inc.–Merger*, 15 MCC 218, 219 (1938). See also: *Inland Motor Freight–Merger*, 15 MCC 149, 151 (1938).

99. *Case Driveway, Inc.–Merger*, 25 MCC 15, 17 (1939).

100. *Consolidated Truck Lines, Limited–Consolidation*, 50 MCC 230, 235 (1947).

101. *Associated Transport, Inc.–Control and Consolidation*, 38 MCC 137, 149 (1942).

102. See, for example: *Yale Transport Corp.–Control and Merger*, 57 MCC 602, 605 (1951); *Chemical Tank Lines, Inc.–Control and Merger*, 87 MCC 333, 337 (1961); *Dyer-O'Hare Hauling Co.–Purchase–Merchants Transfer*, 87 MCC 768, 772 (1961); and *All States Freight, Inc.–Merger*, 90 MCC 51, 56 (1962).

Chapter 6
The Intermodal Competitive Question
in Trucking Unifications

1. *Doughtery Storage & Van Co.–Purchase–Bell Transfer*, 5 MCC 366, 366 (1938).

2. *North East Texas Motor Lines, Inc.–Purchase–Perkins*, 5 MCC 459, 460 (1938). See also: *Red Arrow Freight Lines, Inc.–Purchase–Charlton*, 15 MCC 142, 145 (1938).

3. It should be noted that the effect of a giant trucking unification on the railroad industry was not a significant factor in the landmark case of *Associated Transport, Inc.–Control and Consolidation*, 38 MCC 137 (1942) and its appeal to the Supreme Court in *McLean Trucking Co. v. U.S.*, 321 U.S., 67 (1944).

4. 57 MCC 341 (1950).

5. Ibid., p. 342.

6. Ibid., p. 344.

7. Ibid., p. 345.

8. Ibid., p. 346.

9. Ibid., p. 348.

10. Ibid.

11. Ibid., p. 349

12. Ibid., p. 350.

13. Ibid., p. 358.

14. Ibid., p. 362.

15. Ibid.

16. Ibid., p. 367.

17. Ibid., p. 377.

18. Ibid., p. 378.

19. Ibid., p. 381.

20. Ibid., pp. 381-382.

21. Ibid., p. 382.

22. *Pacific Intermountain Exp. Co.–Control and Purchase*, 57 MCC 467 (1951).

23. Ibid., p. 470.

24. Ibid., pp. 471-472.

25. Ibid., p. 472.

26. It should be noted that this case was not appealed to the courts.

27. 60 MCC 229 (1954).

28. Ibid., p. 270.

29. Ibid., pp. 270-271.

30. Ibid., p. 279.

31. 85 MCC 139 (1960).

32. Ibid., pp. 182-183.

33. Ibid., pp. 193-194.

34. Ibid., p. 193.

35. *Ratner–Control–Tompkins Motor Lines, Inc.*, 70 MCC 251, 259 (1956).

36. See, for example: *Transamerican Freight Lines, Inc.–Control and Merger*, 75 MCC 423, 439 (1958) and *O'Connell's Express–Purchase–Bill's City Transfer, Inc.*, 104 MCC 161, 167 (1967).

37. *Mason & Dixon Lines, Inc.–Control–Silver Fleet*, 90 MCC 829, 843 (1963).

38. *O'Donnell's Express–Purchase–Bill's City Transfer, Inc.*, 104 MCC 161, 168-169 (1967).

39. 38 MCC 137 (1942).

40. Ibid., pp. 138-139.

41. Ibid., p. 139.

42. Ibid., pp. 139-140.

43. Ibid., pp. 150, 172.

44. Ibid., p. 140.

45. Ibid., p. 150.

46. Ibid., pp. 150-151.

47. Ibid., pp. 151-159.

48. Ibid., p. 161.

49. Ibid.

50. Ibid., p. 162.

51. Ibid., pp. 162-163.

52. Ibid., p. 172.

53. 321 U.S. 67 (1944).

54. Ibid., pp. 69, 77.

55. Ibid., p. 68.

56. Ibid., p. 79.

57. Ibid., p. 85.

58. Ibid., p. 87.

59. Ibid., p. 92.

60. Ibid., p. 94.

61. Ibid., p. 95.

62. See Chapter 6, supra.

63. *Pacific Intermountain Exp. Co.–Control and Purchase*, 57 MCC 341, 371 (1950).

64. Ibid., p. 379.

65. Ibid.

66. Ibid.

67. Ibid., p. 380.

68. Ibid.

69. Section 207 provides for the issuance of certificates of public convenience and necessity if there is a present or future need for the proposed service covered by the certificate.

70. *Pacific Intermountain Exp. Co.–Control and Purchase*, 57 MCC 341, 380-381 (1950).

71. *Pacific Intermountain Exp. Co.–Control and Purchase*, 57 MCC 467, 468 (1951).

72. Ibid., pp. 471-472.

73. Ibid., p. 474.

74. *Gay's Exp., Inc.–Purchase–Madore*, 15 MCC 177, 180 (1938). See also: *Central M. Freight Co.–Purchase–Michicago M. Exp., Inc.*, 15 MCC 209, 210 (1939).

75. *Zabarsky–Purchase–Smith*, 35 MCC 259, 262 (1940).

76. See, for example: *Consolidated Freightways, Inc.–Control–Silver Fleet*, 85 MCC 139, 190 (1960); *Michigan Exp., Inc.–Purchase–McNamara Motor Exp.*, 101 MCC 314, 322 (1965); and *Consolidated Freightways Corp. of Delaware–Control*, 109 MCC 76, 85 (1969).

77. *National Transp. Co.–Purchase–Basehore*, 38 MCC 611, 615 (1942).

78. *Eastern Freight Ways, Inc.–Merger*, 60 MCC 133, 137-138 (1954).

79. *Wilson Trucking Corp.–Purchase–Compton Lines, Inc.*, 104 MCC 806, 812 (1968).

80. *Consolidated Freightways Corp. of Delaware–Control*, 109 MCC 76, 85 (1969).

81. See, for early cases: *Doughterty Storage & Van Co.–Purchase–Bell Transfer*, 5 MCC 366, 366 (1938); *Hayes Frt. Lines, Inc.–Purchase–Wabash Valley Exp., Inc.*, 25 MCC 199, 202 (1939); and *Blue Arrow Transport Lines, Inc.–Purchase–Mammina*, 35 MCC 37, 40 (1940).

82. *Super Service Motor Freight Co., Inc.–Purchase–Hayes Frt.*, 57 MCC 715, 729 (1951).

83. *Consolidated Freightways, Inc.–Control and Merger*, 70 MCC 715, 721 (1957).

84. *Michigan Exp., Inc.–Purchase–McNamara Motor Exp.*, 101 MCC 314, 322 (1965).

85. See, for example: *Consolidated Freightways, Inc.–Purchase–Volck Bros.*, 37 MCC 95, 102 (1941); *Hubert–Purchase–Service Freight Lines, Inc.*, 45 MCC 717, 731 (1947): *Watson Bros. Transp. Co., Inc.–Lease–Burnett and Freighter*, 55 MCC 277, 285 (1949); and *McLean Trucking Co.–Control–Carolina Motor Exp. Lines*, 70 MCC 279, 295 (1957).

86. *Dallas & Mavis Forwarding Co., Inc.–Purchase–Billy Baker Co.*, 87 MCC 527, 532 (1961).

87. See, for example: *National Transp. Co.–Purchase–North Branford Transp.*, 65 MCC 545, 555 (1955); *Midwest Coast Transport, Inc.–Purchase–Cary*, 70 MCC 213, 215 (1956); *Law & Ingham Transp. Co.–Purchase–Howe Trans., Inc.*, 70 MCC 728, 730 (1957); *Jones Truck Lines, Inc.–Purchase–Capital Freight Lines*, 80 MCC 268, 275 (1959); *Consolidated Copperstate Lines–Purchase–Sunset M Lines*, 85 MCC 113, 130 (1960): and *Miami Transp. Co., Inc. of Ind.–Purchase–Strothman*, 97 MCC 600, 609 (1964).

88. *C.&D. Motor Delivery Co.–Purchase–Wilson*, 65 MCC 733, 749 (1956). See also: *Campbell Sixty-Six Exp., Inc.–Control and Merger*, 57 MCC 767, 778, (1951).

89. *Ringsby Truck Lines, Inc.–Control–Northern Transp. Co.*, 58 MCC 594, 598 (1952).

90. *Hyman Transp. Co.–Purchase–Brelsford*, 70 MCC 481, 485 (1957).

91. *Consolidated Freightways, Inc.–Control–Silver Fleet*, 85 MCC 139, 189-190 (1960).

92. 60 MCC 229 (1954).

93. Ibid., pp. 229-232.

94. Ibid., pp. 230-231.

95. Ibid., pp. 273-274.

96. Ibid., pp. 274-275.

97. Ibid., pp. 279-280.

98. 85 MCC 139 (1960).

99. Ibid., pp. 174-186.

100. Ibid., p. 187.

101. Ibid., p. 189.

102. Ibid., pp. 190, 194.

103. Ibid., p. 195.

104. Ibid.

105. Ibid., pp. 195-196.

106. See, for example: *Interstate Motor Lines, Inc.–Control and Merger*, 58

MCC 775, 786-787 (1953); *Service, Inc.–Purchase–Yearby Transfer Co., Inc.*, 59 MCC 517, 529 (1953); *Mid-Continent Frt. Lines, Inc.–Purchase–Hanson, M. Exp.*, 65 MCC 312, 327 (1955); *Watson Bros. Transp. Co., Inc.–Purchase S.&C. Transport*, 70 MCC 317, 319 (1956); and *Transamerican Freight Lines, Inc.– Control and Merger*, 75 MCC 423, 439 (1958).

107. *Inland Exp., Inc.–Purchase–Frontier Dispatch, Inc.*, 93 MCC 50, 55 (1963).

108. *Jones Motor Co., Inc.–Control–Mundy Motor Lines*, 90 MCC 899, 909 (1963).

109. *Southern Exp., Inc.–Purchase–Gastonia Motor Exp.*, 101 MCC 53, 77 (1966). For similar cases, see: *Mason and Dixon Lines, Inc.–Control–Silver Fleet*, 90 MCC 829, 843 (1963); *Midwest Motor Exp., Inc.–Purchase–Advance-United* 97 MCC 593, 596 (1964); *O'Donnell's Express–Purchase–Bill's City Transfer, Inc.*, 104 MCC 161, 167 (1967); and *Bay Transp. Co., Inc.–Purchase– St. Andrews*, 104 MCC 681, 684 (1968).

110. *Transamerican Frt. Lines, Inc.–Purchase–Allen Motor Lines*, 59 MCC 695, 721 (1953).

111. Ibid., p. 722.

112. *Wheaton Van Lines, Inc.–Purchase–Carleton*, 60 MCC 415, 422-425 (1954).

113. *Great Coastal Exp., Inc.–Purchase–Price Transfer*, 97 MCC 271, 291 (1964).

114. Ibid., pp. 291-292. For additional similar cases, see: *DeCeanne– Purchase–Blumenthal*, 57 MCC 657, 659 (1951); *Herrin Transp. Co.–Control– M.P. & St. L. Exp., Inc.*, 80 MCC 715, 721-722 (1959); *Dealers Transit, Inc.–Control and Merger*, 93 MCC 611, 620 (1964); and *Ryder Truck Lines– Control–Merchants Frt. System*, 109 MCC 654, 665-66 (1971).

115. *McLean Trucking Co.–Control–Carolina Motor Exp. Lines*, 70 MCC 279, 293 (1957).

116. Ibid., pp. 293-295.

117. *Michigan Exp., Inc.–Purchase–McNamara Motor Exp.*, 101 MCC 314, 321 (1965).

118. Ibid., pp. 321, 323. For similar cases, see: *Mercury Motor Exp., Inc.–Consolidation*, 60 MCC 427, 446 (1954), *Central N.Y. Freightways, Inc.–Purchase–Mohawk Exp., Inc.*, 75 MCC 61, 70 (1958), and *Caravan Refrigerated–Purchase–Bilyeu Refrigerated*, 109 MCC 843, 854 (1972).

119. *Auclair Transp., Inc.–Purchase–Moore*, 57 MCC 262, 265 (1950).

120. Ibid., pp. 265-266. For similar cases before 1953, see: *Bowman– Purchase–Brown*, 38 MCC 783, 788 (1943); *Vollmer Transp. Inc.–Purchase–B. Clayman & Sons*, 55 MCC 599, 607 (1949); *Morgan Drive-Away, Inc.–Pur-chase–Platten*, 56 MCC 23, 32 (1949); *Watson Bros. Transp. Co., Inc.–Pur-chase–West Coast Fast Frt.*, 57 MCC 745, 759 (1951); *Consolidated American Truck Lines, Inc.–Purchase–Vandrwege*, 58 MCC 63, 72 (1951); and *Deaton*

Truck Lines, Inc.–Purchase–Alabama Highway Exp., Inc., 58 MCC 480, 486 (1952).

121. *Motor Cargo, Inc.–Purchase–Ray Williams Frt. Lines, Inc.*, 58 MCC 87, 99-100 (1951).

122. *Cedar Rapids Transp. Inc.–Purchase–Messinger*, 104 MCC 642, 650 (1968). For additional similar cases, see: *Ruan Transport Corp.–Purchase–Hillside Transit Co.*, 65 MCC 203, 210 (1955); and *Ratner–Control–Tompkins Motor Lines, Inc.*, 70 MCC 251, 258 (1956).

123. *B.&P. Motor Exp., Inc.–Purchase–The Cleveland Cartage Co.*, 101 MCC 469, 476 (1966).

124. Ibid., pp. 476-477.

125. *Deaton Truck Line, Inc.–Purchase–Magnolia Truck Line*, 87 MCC 674, 679 (1961).

126. 35 MCC 661 (1940).

127. Ibid., pp. 661-662.

128. Ibid., p. 663.

129. Ibid., pp. 663-664.

130. 75 MCC 659 (1958).

131. Ibid., p. 664.

132. Irregular-route truckers do not operate on fixed schedules nor are they restricted to using only certain specific highways. For additional information, see: Taff, *Commercial Motor Transportation*, p. 110.

133. Regular-route carriers often operate fixed schedules, but others are not required to do so. For additional information, see: Taff, *Commercial Motor Transportation*, pp. 110-111.

134. *New Dixie Lines, Inc.–Control–Jocie Motor Lines, Inc.*, 75 MCC 659, 666-670 (1958).

135. *Glosson Motor Lines, Inc.–Purchase–Helderman*, 101 MCC 151 (1966).

136. Ibid., p. 161.

137. Ibid., pp. 161-164.

138. See, for example: *William C. Barry, Inc.–Purchase–Hunt*, 36 MCC 335, 337 (1941); *Chrispens Truck Lines, Inc.–Purchase–Cuda*, 36 MCC 343, 345-346 (1941); *Robertson–Purchase–City Transfer Co., Inc.*, 36 MCC 569, 570 (1941); and *Hartness–Purchase–Dillon*, 37 MCC 45, 47 (1941).

139. *United States Van Lines, Inc.–Purchase–Davis Transfer*, 80 MCC 135, 143-146 (1959).

140. *Kings Van & Storage–Purchase–Millard*, 85 MCC 110, 112 (1960).

141. Ibid.

142. *Ruffalo's Trucking Service–Purchase–Worster*, 104 MCC 593, 598 (1968).

143. Ibid.

144. See, for example: *Industrial Transport, Inc.–Purchase–Lansing Trans-*

port, 38 MCC 679, 680-681 (1942); *Morgan Drive-Away, Inc.–Purchase–Platten*, 56 MCC 342, 347 (1950); *Ashworth Transfer, Inc.–Purchase–Willcoxon and Fowkes*, 80 MCC 395, 400 (1959); *Cassene Transport Co.–Purchase–Crawford Transport Co., Inc.*, 85 MCC 6, 7-10 (1959); *Exley Exp., Inc.–Purchase–Olsen*, 85 MCC 396, 399 (1960); *Whitfield Transp., Inc.–Purchase–Keller*, 85 MCC 788, 791-792 (1960); *Atlas Truck Line, Inc.–Purchase–Macaulay*, 87 MCC 305, 310 (1961); *Deaton Truck Line, Inc.–Purchase–Magnolia Truck Line*, 87 MCC 674, 678 (1961); *U.S. Van Lines, Inc.–Purchase–Holien*, 90 MCC 657, 660-661 (1962); *Joyce Trucking Co.–Purchase–Selig*, 97 MCC 1, 8-9 (1964); *Refrigerated Transport Co., Inc.–Purchase–Kurtz*, 104 MCC 114, 123 (1967); *Fogarty Bros. Transfer, Inc.–Purchase–Transport Van Lines*, 104 MCC 665, 666 (1968), and *Arkansas-Best–Purchase–Indianhead*, 109 MCC 885,889 (1972).

145. *Lewis Cartage–Purchase–P.J. Garvey Carting & Storage, Inc.*, 85 MCC 96, 101 (1960).

146. *Novick Transfer Co., Inc.–Purchase–Steinla Transp. Co.*, 85 MCC 543, 547-548 (1960). For similar cases, see: *Reinhardt Transfer Co.–Purchase–Lykins*, 38 MCC 665, 667 (1942) and *Mid-Continent Frt. Lines, Inc.–Purchase–Hanson, M. Exp.*, 65 MCC 312, 326 (1955).

147. *Carolina Freight Carriers Corp.–Purchase–Lovette*, 37 MCC 791, 795 (1941).

148. *Midwest Coast Transport, Inc.–Purchase–Cary*, 70 MCC 213, 215 (1956).

149. Ibid., pp. 215-216.

150. See, for example: *Merchants Motor Freight, Inc.–Purchase–Bridgeways, Inc.*, 60 MCC 229, 273 (1954), *Prucka Transp., Inc.–Purchase–Resler Truck Lines*, 65 MCC 219, 237 (1955), and *Weather Bros. Transfer Co., Inc.–Purchase*, 109 MCC 647, 650-51 (1971).

151. *The Adley Corp.–Purchase–New York & Albany Dispatch*, 101 MCC 388, 398 (1966).

152. *O'Donnell's Express–Purchase–Bill's City Transfer, Inc.* 104 MCC 161, 165-167 (1967).

153. *Drake Motor Lines, Inc.–Purchase–Coakley*, 104 MCC 573, 575 (1968). For similar cases, see: *Republic Van & Storage Co., Inc.–Purchase–Eastern Van Lines*, 80 MCC 87, 91-92 (1959); *Michigan Exp., Inc.–Purchase–McNamara Motor Exp.*, 101 MCC 314, 320 (1965); *Dorn's Transp., Inc.–Purchase–Northeastern Transp. Co., Inc.*, 101 MCC 460, 464-465 (1966); and *Red Arrow Frt. Lines, Inc.–Purchase–Galveston*, 104 MCC 820, 823-826 (1968).

154. See, for example: *Gene Adams Refrigerated Trucking Service, Inc.–Control*, 90 MCC 687, 692 (1962) and *Mercury Frt. Lines, Inc.–Purchase–Sam N. Cole*, 109 MCC 123, 135 (1969).

155. *Bruce Motor Freight, Inc.–Purchase–Pittsley*, 65 MCC 563, 568 (1955).

156. *Jones Motor Co., Inc.–Control–Mundy Motor Lines*, 90 MCC 899, 906 (1963).

157. See also: *Helm's Exp., Inc.—Control and Merger*, 93 MCC 142, 150 (1963) *Houff Transfer, Inc.—Purchase—Boward Truck Line, Inc.*, 101 MCC 727, 737 (1967), and *Fischback Trucking Co.—Control—and Merger—Peck*, 109 MCC 739, 745-47 (1971).

158. 15 MCC 358 (1938).

159. Ibid., pp. 359-360.

160. Ibid., p. 359.

161. *Carolina Freight Carriers Corp.—Purchase—Lovette*, 37 MCC 791, 796 (1941).

162. See, for example: *A.A.A. Highway Exp., Inc.—Lease—Augusta Truck Co., Inc.*, 36 MCC 766, 768 (1941) and *Black Motor Lines, Inc.—Purchase—Shamburger*, 37 MCC 787, 789 (1941).

163. *Deaton Truck Line, Inc.—Purchase—Magnolia Truck Line*, 87 MCC 674, 676-677 (1961).

164. Ibid., p. 678.

165. *Schuster's Exp., Inc.—Purchase—Stankovich & Roberts*, 97 MCC 485, 489 (1964).

166. Gateway restrictions can be thought of as "funnels" through which freight must first flow before reaching its final destination. For example, assume a trucker has a gateway restriction of Minneapolis on all outstate traffic flowing into Minnesota. Thus a shipment from Chicago bound for Rochester, Minnesota, must first be transported to the Minneapolis gateway before it can be transported to Rochester. The result of the gateway restriction, in this case, is to cause an inefficient and circuitous route to be used in lieu of the direct route between Chicago and Rochester.

167. 36 MCC 561 (1941).

168. Ibid., pp. 561-563.

169. Ibid., p. 564.

170. Ibid.

171. See, for example: *Black Motor Lines, Inc.—Purchase—Shamburger*, 37 MCC 787, 789 (1941) and *Buffaloe—Purchase—Grieg Freight Lines, Inc.*, 70 MCC 101, 105 (1956).

172. *Sanborn's Motor Exp., Inc.—Purchase—Bemis Exp., Inc.*, 93 MCC 728, 736-737 (1964).

173. 38 MCC 547 (1942).

174. The next introductory case study in this section will specifically set forth the current law on intrastate carriers transporting traffic of an interstate nature.

175. *C.&D. Motor Delivery Co.—Purchase—Elliott*, 38 MCC 547, 553 (1942).

176. Ibid., pp. 554-556.

177. *The Interstate Commerce Act*, p. 157.

178. *T.I.M.E. Freight, Inc.—Merger*, 97 MCC 310, 327 (1964).

179. Ibid. Originally contained in: 106 *Congressional Record* 19, 024 (September 1, 1960).

180. *T.I.M.E. Freight, Inc.–Merger*, 97 MCC 310, 329-331 (1964).

181. *O'Donnell's Express–Purchase–Bill's City Transfer, Inc.*, 104 MCC 161, 166 (1967).

182. For recent cases, see: *Southern Exp., Inc.–Purchase–Gastonia Motor Exp.*, 101 MCC 53, 72 (1966); *Ohio Fast Freight, Inc.–Control and Merger*, 101 MCC 171, 183 (1965); *Dorn's Transp. Inc.–Purchase–Northeastern Transp. Co., Inc.*, 101 MCC 460, 464 (1966); *Consolidated Freightways Corp. of Del.– Control*, 104 MCC 658, 659 (1968); and *Wilson Trucking Corp.–Purchase– Compton Lines, Inc.*, 104 MCC 806, 811 (1968).

183. 25 MCC 558 (1939).

184. Ibid., pp. 562-563.

185. Ibid., p. 565.

186. Ibid.

187. Ibid., p. 564.

188. Ibid., pp. 566-568.

189. See, for example: *Jones–Purchase–M.K. & C. Truck Lines*, 37 MCC 523, 525 (1941); *Chief Freight Lines Co.–Lease–Strickland Transp. Co.*, 55 MCC 739, 760 (1949); *Malone Freight Lines, Inc.–Lease–Safety Transp. Corp.*, 56 MCC 571, 590 (1950: *Watson Bros. Transp. Co., Inc.–Purchase–West Coast Fast Frt.*, 57 MCC 745, 759 (1951); and *Ballard and Skellet Van Lines, Inc.–Consolidations*, 58 MCC 539, 551 (1952).

190. *Pic Freight Co.–Purchase–Steffke Freight Co.*, 70 MCC 761, 767 (1957).

191. See, for example: *Superior Trucking Co., Inc.–Purchase–Moore*, 70 MCC 437, 441-442 (1957); *Atlas Truck Lines, Inc.–Purchase–Macaulay*, 87 MCC 305, 309-310 (1961); *Ringle Exp., Inc.–Purchase–Contract Carriers, Inc.*, 93 MCC 468, 472 (1963); and *Ind-O Transport, Inc.–Purchase–Niman Transfer & Storage*, 97 MCC 587, 591-592 (1965).

192. *Crawford Transport Co., Inc.–Lease–Geo. F. Burnett Co.*, 56 MCC 103, 108 (1949).

193. *Ruffalo's Trucking Service–Purchase–Worster*, 104 MCC 593, 596 (1968).

194. *Arkansas-Best Freight System, Inc.–Purchase–Bradsher*, 87 MCC 67, 71 (1960). See also: *Courier Exp., Inc.–Purchase–Huber Motor Transp. Co.*, 45 MCC 683, 694 (1947); and *Garrett Freight Lines, Inc.–Control and Merger*, 70 MCC 530, 534 (1957).

195. *Hartford Transp. Co.–Purchase–Brown*, 45 MCC 481, 485 (1947).

196. Ibid., p. 486, and *Burlington Truckers, Inc.–Lease–Lipe*, 40 MCC 726, 730 (1946).

197. *Vollmer Transp., Inc.–Purchase–B. Clayman & Sons*, 55 MCC 599, 606 (1949).

198. It should be clearly pointed out that all ICC merger decisions are definitely of a permissive nature. That is, while they may authorize a transaction, the Commission's order in no way forces the applicants to accept the ICC's

amendments. Thus, if the applicants believe that the Commission's changes in the proposed transaction render the merger undesirable, they are under no legal compunction to consummate the unification. That is, they can just cancel the proposed unification at their own desire.

199. *Michigan Exp. Inc.—Purchase—McNamara Motor Exp.*, 101 MCC 314, 322-323 (1965).

200. See, for example: *Malone—Purchase—Crater*, 35 MCC 549, 553 (1940); *Reliable Transfer Co., Inc.—Purchase—Term Transpt. Co.*, 45 MCC 120, 122 (1946); *Navajo Freight Lines Inc.—Lease—Nevada Consolidated*, 50 MCC 252, 257 (1947); and *Sweeney—Purchase—C.A. Conklin Truck Line, Inc.*, 56 MCC 220, 223 (1949). See also: *Control or Consolidation of Motor Carriers*, 109 MCC 448 (1970).

201. *Fredrickson Motor Express Cor.—Purchase—Cope*, 104 MCC 670, 673-674 (1968). For similar cases, see: *Midwest Motor Exp., Inc.—Purchase—Advance-United*, 97 MCC 593, 595-596 (1964), *Michigan Exp., Inc.—Purchase—McNamara*, 101 MCC 314, 323 (1965) and *All American Transport, Inc.—Purchase—Takin Bros.*, 109 MCC 440, 444 (1970).

202. *Daily Express, Inc.—Control and Purchase*, 101 MCC 355, 363-364 (1966).

203. Ibid., p. 364, and *O'Donnell's Express—Purchase—Bill's City Transfer, Inc.*, 104 MCC 161, 168 (1967).

204. *O'Donnell's Express—Purchase—Bill's City Transfer, Inc.*, 104 MCC 101, 168 (1967).

205. *Fogarty Bros. Transfer—Purchase—Grenon & Son*, 104 MCC 444, 447 (1968).

206. See Chapter 5, supra.

207. *Casaroll—Control—Crown Motor Service, Inc.*, 35 MCC 471, 475 (1940). For other similar early cases, see: *Florman—Control—Automobile Convoy Co.*, 35 MCC 521, 523 (1940); *Timmer—Control—Botts*, 38 MCC 60, 64 (1942); and *Brown—Purchase—Brown*, 39 MCC 373, 377 (1943).

208. *Midwest Transfer Co. of Ill.—Control—Chamberlands*, 85 MCC 750, 754 (1960).

209. *DeFenne—Control—Allmen Transfer & Moving Co.*, 65 MCC 211, 215 (1955); *Smith—Control—Cement Transports, Inc.*, 80 MCC 710, 713 (1959); and *Penbrook Hauling Co., Inc.—Purchase—Cooper and Mesharer*, 85 MCC 332, 335 (1960).

210. *Dallas & Mavis Forwarding Co., Inc.—Purchase—Bill Baker Co.*, 85 MCC 521, 532 (1960).

211. Ibid.

212. *Motor Exp., Inc.—Purchase—Erie Freight Lines, Inc.*, 38 MCC 185, 189 (1942).

Chapter 7
Additional Significant Considerations
in Trucking Unification Proceedings

1. 55 MCC 683 (1949).

2. See, for example: *Northern Transp. Co.–Lease–Terminal Truck Lines, Inc.*, 25 MCC 759, 762 (1939); *Point Pleasant Transp. Co., Inc.–Lease–United Trucking*, 58 MCC 198, 202 (1952); and *Shipley Transfer, Inc.–Lease–West Motor Freight, Inc.*, 85 MCC 715, 718 (1960).

3. *Auto Convoy Co.–Lease–Automobile Shippers, Inc.*, 55 MCC 683, 694 (1949).

4. See footnote 8, Chapter 5, supra.

5. *Willett–Lease–Thomas*, 50 MCC 1, 4 (1947).

6. *Law & Ingham Transp. Co.–Purchase–Howe Trans., Inc.*, 70 MCC 728, 730-731 (1957) and *Mason & Dixon Lines, Inc.–Control–Silver Fleet*, 90 MCC 829, 848 (1963).

7. *T.I.M.E. Freight, Inc.–Merger*, 97 MCC 310, 328 (1964).

8. *Chief Freight Lines Co.–Lease–Strickland Transp. Co.*, 55 MCC 739, 761 (1949).

9. Ibid., pp. 761-762.

10. *Shipley Transfer, Inc.–Lease–West Motor Freight, Inc.*, 85 MCC 715, 718-719 (1960).

11. *Watson Bros. Transp. Co., Inc.–Lease–Burnett and Feighner*, 55 MCC 277, 282 (1949).

12. See, for example: *Consolidated Freightways, Inc.–Lease–Mont. Transport*, 25 MCC 428, 432 (1939); *T.S.C. Motor Frt.*, 59 MCC 282, 286 (1953); and *Sullivan Lines, Inc.–Control and Merger*, 90 MCC 229, 232 (1962).

13. *M&R Transp. Co., Inc.–Lease–Malkin Motor Freight Co.*, 25 MCC 798, 799-800 (1939).

14. *McLean Trucking Co.–Lease–Atlantic States Motor Lines*, 58 MCC 567, 570 (1952).

15. *Consolidated Freightways Corp. of Del.–Control*, 104 MCC 658, 660 (1968).

16. *Douglas–Purchase–State Trucking Service*, 25 MCC 511, 513 (1939). See also: *Garrett Freightliners, Inc.–Purchase–Moab Garage Co.*, 59 MCC 615, 619 (1953).

17. *Central N.Y. Freightways, Inc.–Purchase–Mohawk Exp., Inc.*, 75 MCC 61, 68-69 (1958).

18. *Sullivan Lines, Inc.–Purchase–Sullivan*, 80 MCC 453, 457 (1959).

19. *Consolidated Freightways Corp. of Del.–Control*, 104 MCC 658, 660 (1968).

20. Ibid.

21. *Watson Bros. Transp. Co., Inc.–Lease–Burnett and Feighner*, 55 MCC 277, 289 (1949).

22. Ibid.

23. Ibid., pp. 300-301.

24. *E. Brooke Matlack, Inc.–Control–Reader Bros., Inc.*, 80 MCC 349, 352 (1959).

25. Ibid. See also: *Associated Transport, Inc.–Control–Keystone Motor*, 87 MCC 409, 413 (1961).

26. *E. Brooke Matlack, Inc.–Control–Reader Bros., Inc.*, 80 MCC 349, 359-360 (1959).

27. Black, *Black's Law Dictionary*, p. 758.

28. Trafficking in operating rights refers to buying and selling operating rights for the sole purpose of making a profit on each transaction. In other words, a trafficker never intends to keep· the obtained rights, but merely to sell them at his earliest opportunity at a profit.

29. *Lease Plan International Corp.–Control–National*, 93 MCC 203, 207 (1963).

30. Section 5 (2) (e) of the Interstate Commerce Act.

31. Locklin, *Economics of Transportation*, Chapter 7, and *The Doyle Report*, p. 252.

32. See, for example: *Silver Fleet Motor Exp., Inc.–Merger,* 36 MCC 57, 59 (1940); *Plain Motor Exp., Inc.–Purchase–C.&G. Truck Line, Inc.*, 87 MCC 489, 494 (1961); and *Tose, Inc.–Control and Merger–O'Connor's Express*, 104 MCC 869, 893 (1968).

33. *Transamerican Freight Lines, Inc.–Control and Merger*, 75 MCC 423, 428 (1958).

34. *Century System, Inc.,–Purchase–Mid-West M.F. Co., Inc.*, 38 MCC 315, 315-319 (1942).

35. Ibid., p. 318.

36. *Oregon-Nevada California Fast Frt.–Purchase–Coast-Lee*, 90 MCC 5, 9-10 (1962).

37. *John Vogel, Inc.–Control and Merger*, 85 MCC 11, 46 (1959).

38. See for example: *Atlas Truck Lines, Inc.–Purchase–Macaulay,* 87 MCC 305, 310 (1961); *Sullivan Lines, Inc.–Control and Merger*, 90 MCC 229, 232 (1962); *Gene Adams Refrigerated Trucking Service, Inc.–Control*, 90 MCC 687, 690 (1962); and *Mason & Dixon Lines, Inc.–Control–Silver Fleet*, 90 MCC 829, 851 (1963).

39. For an excellent discussion of the ICC's financial regulation of the railroads, which established the precedents for the trucking industry, see: Locklin, *Economics of Transportation*, Chapter 24.

40. *Sites Silver Wheel Frtlines–Control and Merger*, 104 MCC 564, 568 (1968).

41. *Plains Motor Exp., Inc.–Purchase–C.&G. Truck Line, Inc.*, 87 MCC 489, 493 (1961).

42. Ibid., p. 494.

43. Ibid., pp. 494-495. See also: *Universal Transport, Inc.–Purchase–Muck*, 109 MCC 871, 879 (1972).

44. *Garrett Freightliners, Inc.–Purchase–Moab Garage Co.*, 58 MCC 757, 774 (1953).

45. *Central Freight Lines, Inc.–Control–Alamo Exp., Inc.*, 70 MCC 610, 613-614 (1957). See also: *Delta Motor Line, Inc.–Control and Merger*, 70 MCC 615, 622 (1957).

46. *Holmes Transp., Inc.–Merger–Holmes*, 104 MCC 69, 74-75 (1965).

47. Ibid., p. 75.

48. 5 MCC 723 (1938).

49. Ibid., p. 724.

50. Ibid., pp. 732-734. See also: *Von Der Ahe Van Lines, Inc.–Lease and Purchase–Bee-Line*, 90 MCC 888, 896 (1963).

51. See, for example: *United Transports, Inc.–Purchase–Gauntt Transport*, 5 MCC 516, 517 (1938): *Younger Bros., Inc.–Merger*, 5 MCC 781, 782 (1938); *Schultz-Purchase–Hagen*, 15 MCC 13, 14 (1938); *Silver Fleet, Inc.–Purchase–Myerson*, 15 MCC 39, 41 (1938); *Red Arrow Freight Lines, Inc.–Purchase–Chartton*, 15 MCC 142, 143 (1938); *Hoover Truck Co.–Purchase–Gallatain Truck Co.*, 15 MCC 173, 176 (1938); *T.S.C. Motor Freight Lines, Inc.–Purchase–Rush*, 15 MCC 191, 192 (1938); *Cole Motor Service, Inc.–Merger*, 15 MCC 218, 218 (1938); *Merchants' Forwarding Co.–Purchase–Miller*, 15 MCC 354, 355 (1938); *Rocky Mountain Lines, Inc.–Purchase–Phillips*, 15 MCC 441, 442 (1938); *Central Freight Lines, Inc.–Purchase–Tyler*, 15 MCC 515, 518 (1938); *Ramsey–Control–Benedict Lines, Inc.*, 35 MCC 408, 411 (1940); and *Hankison–Control–Mutual Trucking Co.*, 37 MCC 617, 618 (1941).

52. See, for example: *Liberty Highway Co.–Purchase–Germann*, 5 MCC 699, 700 (1938); *Potashnick Local Truck System, Inc.–Purchase–Smith, Griffen*, 37 MCC 565, 567 (1941); and *J.B. Reed Motor Exp. Inc.–Purchase–Overton Motor Exp., Inc.*, 65 MCC 30, 34 (1955).

53. *West Bros., Inc.–Purchase–Murray and Murray Motor*, 70 MCC 143, 149 (1956).

54. *Motorways–Purchase–Mason Cartage*, 75 MCC 306, 310 (1958).

55. *Cochrane–Purchase–Piedmont Mountain Freight Lines*, 40 MCC 233, 235 (1945).

56. Ibid., p. 237.

57. *Baggett–Control–Walker Hauling Co., Inc.*, 65 MCC 522, 525 (1955).

58. *Cortland Fast Freight, Inc.–Purchase–H.J. Korten, Inc.*, 60 MCC 321, 327-329 (1954).

59. Ibid., p. 329.

60. *Ohio Fast Freight, Inc.–Control & Merger*, 101 MCC 171, 186 (1965).

61. Ibid., pp. 184-187.

62. See, for example: *Timmer–Control–Botts*, 38 MCC 60, 64 (1942); *Richards–Purchase–Sunset Transp., Inc.*, 38 MCC 651, 654 (1942); *Manlowe –Control–Interstate Freight Lines, Inc.*, 45 MCC 125, 137 (1946); *Buckingham Transp., Inc.–Control and Merger*, 80 MCC 245, 254 (1959); *Dorn's Transp., Inc.–Purchase–Phillips Exp., Inc.*, 87 MCC 111, 115 (1961); *S & W Motor Lines, Inc.–Control and Merger*, 87 MCC 139, 143 (1961); *Kaplan Trucking Co.–Control–Thomas Boyd, Inc.*, 90 MCC 419, 424 (1962); *Calore Exp. Co., Inc.–Purchase–T.W. Waterman Co., Inc.*, 93 MCC 291, 296 (1963); *Crouse–Control–Nebraska–Iowa Xpress, Inc.*, 109 MCC 159, 163 (1969); and *Reliance Truck Co.–Control and Merger–Millage Trucking, Inc.*, 109 MCC 495, 502 (1970).

63. *Transamerican Freight Lines, Inc.–Control and Merger*, 75 MCC 423, 428-432 (1958).

64. *Midwest Emery Freight System, Inc.–Control and Merger*, 101 MCC 19, 30 (1965).

65. Ibid., pp. 27-30.

66. *Fraps–Purchase–Lindley*, 38 MCC 703, 706 (1942).

67. Ibid., p. 707.

68. *Hubert-Purchase–Service Freight Lines, Inc.*, 45 MCC 717, 726 (1947). See also: *Kaplan Trucking Co.–Control–Thomas Boyd, Inc.*, 90 MCC 419, 424 (1962).

69. *Hughes–Control–M.P.&St. L. Exp., Inc.*, 70 MCC 261, 262-264 (1956).

70. *Calore Exp. Co., Inc.–Purchase–T.W. Waterman Co., Inc.*, 93 MCC 291, 292-297 (1963).

71. Ibid., p. 297.

72. Ibid., p. 298.

73. *Exley Exp., Inc.–Purchase–Olsen*, 85 MCC 396, 399-400 (1960). See also: *Dealers Transit, Inc.–Control and Merger*, 93 MCC 611, 619-620 (1964).

74. *All-American Transport, Inc.–Control and Merger*, 104 MCC 397, 420 (1968).

75. *Novick–Purchase–Fischetto Trucking Co., Inc.*, 38 MCC 477, 478-480 (1942).

76. Ibid., p. 480. For similar cases, see: *Hartford Transp. Co.–Purchase–Brown*, 45 MCC 481, 484 (1947) and *Rocky Mountain Service, Inc.–Lease–Las Vegas Needles*, 60 MCC 361, 371 (1954).

77. *Georgia Highway Exp., Inc.–Purchase–Holloway Motor Exp.*, 80 MCC 779, 782-784 (1960).

78. *Mid-States Freight Lines, Inc.–Purchase–Carlo Transp. Co.*, 57 MCC 581, 594-596 (1951).

79. Ibid., p. 596.

80. *Ashworth Transfer, Inc.–Purchase–Willcoxon and Fowkes*, 80 MCC 395, 400 (1959). See also: *Tri-State Motor Transit Co.–Purchase–Gottula*, 109 MCC 472, 475 (1970).

81. 5 MCC 85 (1937).

82. It must be remembered, as previously pointed out, that the carriers were allowed to operate over the territory claimed by the grandfather rights until the latter operating authority had been officially determined by the Commission.

83. *Brooks Transp. Co., Inc.–Purchase–Jacobs Transfer Co.*, 5 MCC 85, 86 (1937).

84. See, for example: *Johnson–Purchase–Rose*, 5 MCC 70, 72 (1937) and *Albert Transfer & Storage Co.–Purchase–Albertson*, 5 MCC 443, 444 (1938).

85. *Crichton–Lease–Crandon Trucking, Inc.*, 37 MCC 293, 294-296 (1941).

86. *Rodgers Motor Lines, Inc.–Purchase–Ovens*, 40 MCC 483, 485-487 (1946). For similar cases, see: *Colletti–Control–Comet Freight Lines*, 38 MCC 95, 98 (1942); *Norwood Exp. & Drayage, Inc.–Purchase–Norwood Exp.*, 56 MCC 247, 252 (1949); and *Devenne–Control–Allmen Transfer & Moving Co.*, 65 MCC 211, 218 (1955).

87. *Langer–Control–Transport Operators Co., Inc.*, 55 MCC 795, 798-799 (1949).

88. Ibid., p. 799.

89. *Lease Plan International Corp.–Control–National*, 93 MCC 203, 205-208 (1963).

90. *Ryder System, Inc.–Control–Complete Auto Transit*, 109 MCC 275, 286-288 (1969).

Chapter 8
General Discussion of the ICC's Administration
of Section 5 Trucking Mergers

1. John Sparkman, in the forward to the Adams and Hendry study entitled, *Trucking Mergers, Concentration, and Small Business: An Analysis of Interstate Commerce Commission Policy, 1950-1956*, in U.S. Congress, Senate, *Trucking Mergers and Concentration*, p. 213.

2. Herbert Burstein, "Motor Carrier Acquisitions, Mergers, and Consolidations," *I.C.C. Practitioners' Journal* (January 1957), p. 375. Used with permission of the Association of ICC Practitioners.

3. Anthony F. Arpaia in U.S. Congress, Senate, Select Committee on Small Business, *ICC Administration of the Motor Carrier Act*, 84th Cong., 1st sess. (Washington, D.C.: U.S. Government Printing Office, 1956), p. 176.

4. Owen Clarke, chairman of the ICC, in U.S. Congress, Senate, Select Committee on Small Business, *Trucking Mergers and Concentration*, 85th Cong., 1st sess. (Washington, D.C.: U.S. Government Printing Office, 1957), p. 50.

5. Ibid., p. 104.

6. U.S. Congress, Senate, *ICC Administration of the Motor Carrier Act*, p. 8.

7. Ibid.

8. U.S. Congress, Senate, *Trucking Mergers and Concentration*, p. 160.

9. U.S. Congress, Senate, *ICC Administration of the Motor Carrier Act*, p. 236.

10. U.S. Congress, Senate, *Trucking Mergers and Concentration*, p. 42.

11. Ibid., p. 114.

12. American Trucking Associations, *Mergers in the Trucking Industry*, p. 11.

13. *80th Annual Report of the Interstate Commerce Commission–1966*, p. 145.

14. *86th Annual Report of the Interstate Commerce Commission–1972*, p. 131.

15. American Trucking Associations, *Mergers in the Trucking Industry*, pp. 11-12. Used with permission, Dept. of Research and Economics, A.T.A.

16. Statement by ICC Commissioner Richard F. Mitchell in U.S. Congress, Senate, *Trucking Mergers and Concentration*, p. 115.

17. Statement by Commissioner Clarke, in ibid., pp. 101-102.

18. Ibid., p. 221.

19. U.S. Congress, Senate, *ICC Administration of the Motor Carrier Act*, pp. 446-467.

20. U.S. Congress, Senate, *Trucking Mergers and Concentration*, p. 217. See also p. 220.

21. U.S. Congress, Senate, *ICC Administration of the Motor Carrier Act*, p. 466.

22. Ibid., p. 238.

23. Ibid., p. 237.

24. One reason for the increase in Class III carriers and the decrease in Class II carriers was a definitional change. In 1966, a Class II carrier was defined as one having gross transportation revenues from $200,000 up to $1 million. In 1969, this definition of a Class II truckers was increased on the low side to a minimum of $300,000 gross revenues. The result, therefore, was to increase the number of Class III carriers and decrease the number of Class II truckers.

25. *80th Annual Report of the Interstate Commerce Commission–1966*, p. 145 and *86th Annual Report of the Interstate Commerce Commission–1972*, p. 131.

26. See Chapter 5, supra.

27. See Chapter 5, supra.

28. Adams and Hendry, *Trucking Mergers, Concentration, and Small Business: An Analysis of the Interstate Commerce Commission Policy, 1950-56*, in U.S. Congress, Senate, *Trucking Mergers and Concentration*, p. 262.

29. This statement on shipper preference of larger carriers is based on a limited number of personal interviews conducted by the author with traffic personnel of various size firms in the Minneapolis area. The question of shipper preference of "large" v. "small" truckers is an area worthy of additional research.

30. Clair Wilcox, *Public Policies Toward Business* (3rd ed.; Homewood, Ill.: Richard D. Irwin, Inc., 1966), p. 12.

31. *McLean Trucking Co. v. U.S.*, 321 U.S. 67, 85 (1944).

32. This is prohibited by Section 216 (d) of the Interstate Commerce Act.

33. This is prohibited by Section 216 (b) of the Interstate Commerce Act.

34. Transportation revenues per ton-mile for all carriers advanced less than 13 percent from 1950 to 1960, while the cost-of-living index increased 23 percent in the same period. Heskett, Ivie, and Glaskowsky, *Business Logistics*, pp. 15-16.

35. This statement was substantiated by personal interviews conducted by the author with traffic personnel.

36. See: John Kenneth Galbraith, *American Capitalism: The Concept of Countervailing Power* (2nd ed.; Boston: Houghton Mifflin Co., 1956).

37. Donald S. Watson, *Economic Policy: Business and Government* (Boston: Houghton Mifflin Co., 1960), p. 221.

38. American Trucking Associations, *American Trucking Trends: 1972*, p. 28.

39. Ibid., p. 240.

40. Gordon F. Bloom and Herbert R. Northrup, *Economics of Labor Relations* (4th ed.; Homewood, Ill.: Richard D. Irwin, Inc., 1961), p. 142.

41. Taff, *Commercial Motor Transportation*, p. 237.

42. "New Demands of Teamsters Estimated to Cost Truckers $8.9 Billion in Three Years," *Traffic World* (January 10, 1970), p. 17.

43. " 'Wildcat' Walkouts by Teamsters Drivers Hit Truck Industry as Old Pact Expires," *Traffic World* (April 4, 1970), pp. 81-82 and "Strike Spector Hovers Over Truck-Teamster Negotiations," *Traffic World* (April 4, 1970), p. 11.

44. "Trucking Industry Will 'Stand Firm' on Tentative Teamster Agreement—TEI," *Traffic World* (April 18, 1970), p. 36.

45. "Early Settlement Prospect Remains Dim in Teamsters' Dispute With Truckers," *Traffic World* (April 25, 1970), p. 14.

46. "Multi-Million-Dollar Assistance Fund Voted by TEI to Aid Idled Chicago Lines," *Traffic World* (May 9, 1970), p. 34. Used with permission.

47. Ibid.

48. "Teamsters' Union Members Approve New Agreement With Trucking Industry," *Traffic World* (May 23, 1970), pp. 76-77. Used with permission.

49. Ibid., p. 77.

50. "Trucking Industry Expected to Ask About 12% Rate Hike to Offset Higher Labor Cost," *Traffic World* (July 13, 1970), p. 29.

51. For a discussion of the upcoming 1973 labor contracts, see: "Key Bargaining Opens in Trucking Industry, Teamsters Ask 23% Pay Boost Over 3 Years," *The Wall Street Journal* (May 10, 1973), p. 2.

52. "What otherwise is good and just, if sought by force, becomes bad and unjust."

53. Louis M. Kohlmeier, "Celler Seeks Creation of Powerful Agency to Pass Judgment on All Big Merger Plans," *Wall Street Journal* (July 20, 1970), p. 24.

54. Adams and Hendry, *Trucking Mergers, Concentration and Small Business: An Analysis of Interstate Commerce Commission Policy, 1950-56*, in U.S. Congress, Senate, *Trucking Mergers and Concentration*, p. 221.

55. Statement by Professor Dudley F. Pegrum in U.S. Congress, Senate, *ICC Administration of the Motor Carrier Act*, pp. 466-467.

56. The primary point that shippers stressed to the author in a number of personal interviews was that their company almost always preferred one-carrier service and responsibility compared to a trucking firm which had to interline one or more times to serve the destination point.

57. Burstein, "Motor Carrier Acquisitions, Mergers and Consolidations," p. 375. Used with permission of the Association of ICC Practitioners.

58. Federal Trade Commission, *Economic Report on Corporate Mergers* (Washington, D.C.: U.S. Government Printing Office, 1969), p. 1.

59. Ibid., p. 29.

60. Ibid., Chapter 2.

61. Consolidated Freightways, Inc., had gross carrier operating revenues of $105,815,000 in 1967. Source: *Consolidated Freightways, Inc.: 1967 Annual Report*, p. 21. In 1967 Class I, II, and III truckers had combined gross carrier operating revenues of $11,165,000,000. Source: American Trucking Associations, *American Trucking Trends: 1968*, p. 9.

62. 36 MCC 61 (1940).

63. 57 MCC 341 (1950).

64. It should be noted that the word "basically" was used in this sentence. The one exception would be the desire of carriers to effect side-by-side mergers in order to nullify overly restrictive grandfather operating rights that were often issued by the ICC in the early years of Federal economic regulation.

65. Adams and Hendry, *Trucking Mergers, Concentration, and Small Business: An Analysis of Interstate Commerce Commission Policy, 1950-56*, in U.S. Congress, Senate, *Trucking Mergers and Concentration*, p. 218.

66. Burstein, "Motor Carrier Acquisitions, Mergers and Consolidations," pp. 377-378. Used with permission of the Association of ICC Practitioners.

67. Statement by Kit Clardy in U.S. Congress, Senate, *Trucking Mergers and Concentration*, p. 164.

68. Testimony by Owen Clarke, in ibid., p. 43.

69. Adams and Hendry, *Trucking Mergers, Concentration, and Small Business: An Analysis of Interstate Commerce Commission Policy, 1950-56*, in U.S. Congress, Senate, *Trucking Mergers and Concentration*, pp. 217, 218-219, and part ii.

70. See Chairman of ICC, Clarke's letter to Senator John J. Sparkman, in ibid., pp. 88-89. This letter proves rather conclusively by means of statistics that large and small carriers have been treated equally.

71. Ibid., pp. 95-96.

72. U.S. Congress, Senate, *ICC Administration of the Motor Carrier Act*, p. 225.

73. U.S. Congress, Senate, *Trucking Mergers and Concentration*, p. 166.

74. Hugh S. Norton, *National Transportation Policy: Formation and Implementation* (Berkeley, California: McCutchan Publishing Corp., 1966), p. 162.

75. Such as: dormancy, illegal route conversions, route split-offs, unlawful leasing arrangements, vendee lacking appropriate fitness, lack of benefits to the public, and other reasons for unification denials as found in Chapters 7 and 8, supra.

76. U.S. Congress, Senate, *Trucking Mergers and Concentration*, p. 111.

77. *83rd Annual Report of the Interstate Commerce Commission—1969*, pp. 29-32.

78. U.S. Congress, Senate, Select Committee on Small Business, *Mergers and Concentration in the Trucking Industry*, Report No. 1441, 85th Cong., 2d sess. (Washington, D.C.: U.S. Government Printing Office, 1958), p. 7.

79. The author wishes to thank Professor Nicholas A. Glaskowsky, Jr., for suggesting the appropriateness of this topic to the book.

80. A disclaimer is necessary at this point. It should be noted that only approximations can be indicated in this section, because many value judgments had to be made by the author in determining these figures. In other words, the absolute numbers themselves should not be given too much weight, because they are designed to show only the approximate magnitudes of the cases denied and authorized under each situation. As an example of the value judgments involved—when was a case opposed? Obviously, if protestants were present, but what about interveners? In most cases, the author counted the interveners as protestants, because they attended the hearing and helped keep the overall proceeding "honest." Another difficult value judgment involved the situation of when was a case denied or approved? Of course, most cases were all one or the other, but other proceedings, especially ones that combined two or more unification applications, were more difficult. That is, situations were encountered where one application was authorized and another denied, or where one important application was approved and two less significant ones were denied. The author tried to decide the overall importance of each application approved and denied, and then he placed the entire transaction into the authorized or denied category. Again, because of the above value judgments, only the approximate magnitudes are significant, not the exact percentages indicated.

81. The ICC has in general been accused of defending the *status quo* instead of encouraging flexibility of regulation that adjusts to the changing transportation situation. See, for example: The statement of Professor Marver H. Bernstein in U.S. Congress, Senate, *ICC Administration of the Motor Carrier Act*, p. 221, the statement of Professor Dudley F. Pegrum in ibid., pp. 466-467, and Samuel

218

P. Huntington, "The Marasmus of the ICC: The Commission, the Railroads, and the Public Interest," *The Yale Law Journal* (April 1952), p. 470.

82. *Pennsylvania R. Co.—Merger—New York Central R. Co.*, 327 ICC 475, 532 (1966).

83. Ibid., p. 534.

Selected Bibliography

Selected Bibliography

Books

Altazan, John E. *ICC Policy Concerning Consolidation and Acquisition of Control in the Motor Carrier Industry.* New Orleans: College of Business Administration, Loyola University, 1956.

Arkin, Herbert, *Handbook of Sampling for Auditing and Accounting—Volume 1—Methods.* New York: McGraw-Hill Book Co., Inc., 1963.

Broehl, Wayne G., Jr. *Trucks . . . Trouble . . . and Triumph: The Norwalk Truck Line Company.* New York: Prentice-Hall, Inc., 1954.

Burnie, Nadreen A., ed. *Transportation Mergers and Acquisitions: Proceedings of a Two-Day Conference by the Northwestern University Transportation Center.* Evanston, Ill.: Transportation Center at Northwestern University, 1962.

Davidson, Jack R., and Ottoson, Howard W., eds. *Transportation Problems and Policies in the Trans-Missouri West.* Lincoln, Nebraska: University of Nebraska Press, 1967.

Dearing, Charles L., and Owen, Wilfred. *National Transportation Policy.* Washington, D.C.: The Brookings Institution, 1949.

Edwards, Ford K. *Principles of Motor Transportation.* New York: McGraw-Hill Book Co., Inc., 1933.

Fair, Marvin L., and Guandolo, John. *Tedrow's Regulation of Transportation.* 6th ed. Dubuque, Iowa: Wm. C. Brown Co., 1964.

Fitch, Lyle C., and Associates. *Urban Transportation and Public Policy.* San Francisco: Chandler Publishing Co., 1964.

Flood, Kenneth U. *Traffic Management.* 2nd ed. Dubuque, Iowa: Wm. C. Brown Co., 1965.

Friedlaender, Ann F. *The Dilemma of Freight Transport Regulation.* Washington, D.C.: The Brookings Institution, 1969.

Fromm, Gary, ed. *Transport Investment and Economic Development.* Washington, D.C.: The Brookings Institution, 1965.

George, John J. *Motor Carrier Regulation in the United States.* Spartanburg, S.C.: Band and White Co., 1929.

Germane, Gayton E., Glaskowsky, Nicholas A., Jr., and Heskett, J.L. *Highway Transportation Management.* New York: McGraw-Hill Book Co., 1963.

Guandolo, John. *Transportation Law.* 2nd ed. Dubuque, Iowa: Wm. C. Brown Co., 1973.

Harper, Donald V. *Economic Regulation of the Motor Trucking Industry by the States.* Urbana: The University of Illinois Press, 1959.

Harper, Donald V. *Price Policy and Procedure.* New York: Harcourt, Brace, and World, Inc., 1966.

Heskett, J.L., Ivie, Robert M., and Glaskowsky, Nicholas A., Jr. *Business Logistics: Management of Physical Supply and Distribution.* New York: The Ronald Press Co., 1964.

Hilton, George W. *The Transportation Act of 1958: A Decade of Experience.* Bloomington, Ind.: Indiana University Press, 1969.

Hudson, William J., and Constantin, James A. *Motor Transportation: Principles and Practices.* New York: The Ronald Press Co., 1958.

Kahn, Fritz. *Principles of Motor Carrier Regulation.* Dubuque, Iowa: Wm. C. Brown Co., 1958.

Karolevitz, Robert F. *This Was Trucking.* Seattle: Superior Publishing Co., 1966.

Keyes, Lucile S. *Federal Control of Entry Into Air Transportation.* Cambridge: Harvard University Press, 1951.

Locklin, D. Philip. *Economics of Transportation.* 7th ed. Homewood, Ill.: Richard D. Irwin, Inc., 1972.

MacGill, Caroline E., and Staff of Collaborators. *History of Transportation in the United States Before 1860.* Washington, D.C.: Carnegie Institution, 1917.

McElhiney, Paul T., and Hilton, Charles L. *Introduction to Logistics and Traffic Management.* Dubuque, Iowa: Wm. C. Brown Co., 1968.

Meyer, John R., Peck, Merton J., Stenason, John, and Zwick, Charles. *The Economics of Competition in the Transportation Industries.* Cambridge, Mass.: Harvard University Press, 1959.

Mossman, Frank H., and Morton, Newton. *Principles of Transportation.* New York: The Ronald Press Co., 1957.

Muller, Helen M., ed. *Federal Regulation of Motor Transport.* New York: H.W. Wilson Co., 1933.

Nelson, James C. *Railroad Transportation and Public Policy.* Washington, D.C.: The Brookings Institution, 1959.

Norton, Hugh S. *Modern Transportation Economics.* Columbus, Ohio: Charles E. Merrill Books, Inc., 1963.

_____. *National Transportation Policy: Formation and Implementation.* Berkeley, Calif.: McCutchan Publishing Corp., 1966.

Oi, Walter Y., and Hurter, Arthur P., Jr. *Economics of Private Truck Transportation.* Dubuque, Iowa: Wm. C. Brown Co., 1965.

Pegrum, Dudley F. *Transportation: Economics and Public Policy.* 2nd ed. Homewood, Ill.: Richard D. Irwin, Inc., 1968.

Phillips, Charles F., Jr. *The Economics of Regulation.* Homewood, Ill.: Richard D. Irwin, Inc., 1965.

Rohlfing, Charles C. *National Regulation of Aeronautics.* Philadelphia: The University of Pennsylvania Press, 1931.

Ruppenthal, Karl M., ed. *Issues in Transportation Economics.* Columbus, Ohio: Charles E. Merrill Books, Inc., 1965.

Sampson, Roy J., and Farris, Martin T. *Domestic Transportation: Practice, Theory and Policy.* 2nd ed. Boston: Houghton Mifflin Co., 1971.

Sargent, J.R. *British Transport Policy.* London: The Clarendon Press, 1958.

Sharfman, I. Leo. *The American Railroad Problem.* New York: The Century Co., 1921.

Sigmon, Richard R. *Miller's Law of Freight Loss and Damage Claims.* 3rd ed. Dubuque, Iowa: Wm. C. Brown Co., 1967.

Splawn, Walter M.W. *Consolidation of Railroads.* New York: MacMillan Co., 1925.

Starr, Edward A. *The Interpretation of Freight Tariffs.* Fort Worth, Texas: The Transportation Press, 1961.

Stocker, H.E. *Motor Traffic Management.* New York: Prentice-Hall, Inc., 1938.

Szto, Shan. *Federal and State Regulation of Motor Carrier Rates and Services.* Philadelphia: University of Pennsylvania, Ph.D. dissertation, 1934.

Taff, Charles A. *Commercial Motor Transportation.* 4th ed. Homewood, Ill.: Richard D. Irwin, Inc., 1969.

_____. *Management of Physical Distribution and Transportation.* 5th ed. Homewood, Ill.: Richard D. Irwin, Inc., 1972.

Transportation Economics: A Conference of the Universities–National Bureau Committee for Economic Research. New York: National Bureau of Economic Research, 1965.

Volotta, Alexander. *The Impact of Federal Entry Controls on Motor Carrier Operations.* University Park, Pa.: Center for Research of the College of Business Administration, Pennsylvania State University, 1967.

Wagner, Warren H. *A Legislative History of the Motor Carrier Act, 1935.* Denton, Maryland: Rue Publishing Co., 1935.

Walker, Gilbert. *Road and Rail.* 2nd ed. London: George Allen and Unwin Limited, 1947.

Watson, Donald S. *Economic Policy: Business and Government.* Boston: Houghton Mifflin Co., 1960.

Westmeyer, Russell E. *Economics of Transportation.* Englewood Cliffs, N.J.: Prentice-Hall, Inc., 1952.

Wilcox, Clair. *Public Policies Toward Business.* 3rd ed. Homewood, Ill.: Richard D. Irwin, Inc., 1966.

Wilson, G. Lloyd. *Motor Traffic Management.* New York: D. Appleton and Co., 1928.

Articles

Adkins, Leonard D. "Roadblocks to Railroad Mergers." *The Business Lawyer* (April 1962), pp. 519-531.

Barber, Richard J. "Airline Mergers, Monopoly, and the CAB." *Journal of Air Law and Commerce* (Summer 1961-2), pp. 189-237.

Barrett, Colin. "The 'Big-Company' Era in the Trucking Industry." *Traffic World* (February 22, 1969), pp. 81-82, 85.

Barriger, John W. "The Effects of Mergers on Competition." *Transportation Journal* (Spring 1968), pp. 5-17.

_____. "Why Consolidate," in Ruppenthal, Karl M., ed., *Challenge to Transportation.* Stanford, Calif.: Stanford University, 1961, pp. 66-117.

Beverly, Phil C. "Railroad Mergers: The Forces of Intermodal Competition." *American Bar Association Journal* (July 1964), pp. 641-645.

_____. "The Consideration of Antitrust Policy in Determination of Merger and Consolidations of Railroads Under Section 5 of the Interstate Commerce Act." *ICC Practitioners' Journal* (November 1961), pp. 169-178.

Boyle, Lawrence, and Hille, Stanley. "Railroad Mergers—An Alternative." *ICC Practitioners' Journal* (March-April 1967), pp. 405-411.

Brothers, J. David. "The Trucking Industry and 1968." *Traffic World* (December 9, 1967), pp. 37, 40, 186.

Burstein, Hebert. "Motor Carrier Acquisitions, Mergers and Consolidations." *ICC Practitioners' Journal* (January 1957), pp. 375-388.

Butler, Robert M. "What Now for Trucking." *Traffic World* (December 14, 1968), pp. 33, 35.

Cadbury, L.J. "Large and Small Firms: A Note on Costs in the Road Transport Industry." *The Economic Journal* (December 1935), pp. 789-793.

Chisholm, Michael. "Economies of Scale in Road Goods Transport? Off-Farm Milk Collection in England and Wales." *Oxford Economic Papers* (October 1959), pp. 282-290.

Coggins, John. "The Private Motor Carrier Definition of the Interstate Commerce Act: An Economic-Legal Battleground." *The George Washington Law Review* (October 1950), pp. 1-22.

Conant, Michael. "Railroad Consolidations and the Antitrust Laws." *Stanford Law Review* (May 1962), pp. 489-519.

Coyle, John J. "Cost-of-Service Pricing in Transportation: Some Reflections." *Quarterly Review of Economics and Business* (Spring 1965), pp. 63-74.

Edwards, J. Roger. "Railroad Mergers." *Southwestern Law Journal* (September 1964), pp. 439-472.

Emery, Paul W., II. "An Empirical Approach to the Motor Carrier Scale Economies Controversy." *Land Economics* (August 1965), pp. 285-289.

Farmer, Richard N. "The Case for Unregulated Truck Transportation." *Journal of Farm Economics* (May 1964), pp. 398-409.

_____. "The Motor Trucking Industry." *Business Horizons* (Fall 1966), pp. 5-19.

Foley, Henry E., and Fordham, Laurence S. "Mergers In Domestic Aviation: The Role of Competition." *Boston College Industrial and Commercial Law Review* (Winter 1964), pp. 279-297.

Harbeson, Robert W. "Some Allocational Problems in Highway Finance," in *Transportation Economics: A Conference of the Universities—National Bureau Committee for Economic Research.* New York: National Bureau of Economic Research, 1965, pp. 139-160.

Healy, Kent T. "The Merger Movement in Transportation." *American Economic Review* (May 1962), pp. 436-444.

Heflebower, Richard B. "Characteristics of Transport Modes," in Fromm, Gary, ed. *Transport Investment and Economic Development.* Washington, D.C.: The Brookings Institution, 1965, pp. 34-68.

Helmetag, Carl, Jr. "Railroad Mergers: The Accommodation of the Interstate Commerce Act and Antitrust Policies." *Virginia Law Review* (December 1968), pp. 1493-1530.

"Here Comes the Trucks." *Forbes* (December 1, 1964), pp. 24-29.

Hoekenga, Earle N. "A Trucker Looks at the Small Shipment Problem." *Transportation and Distribution Management* (January 1968), pp. 26-31.

Huntington, Samuel P. "The Marasmus of the ICC: The Commission, the Railroads, and the Public Interest." *The Yale Law Journal* (April 1952), pp. 467-509.

"ICC Conditions Merger Approval Upon Retention of Jurisdiction to Allow Inclusion of Additional Railroads in the Future." *Michigan Law Review* (January 1965), pp. 543-549.

Kohlmeier, Louis M. "Celler Seeks Creation of Powerful Agency to Pass Judgment on All Big Merger Plans." *The Wall Street Journal* (July 20, 1970), p. 24.

Kolsen, H. "Structure and Price Determination in the Road Haulage Industry in New South Wales." *The Economic Record* (November 1956), pp. 291-304.

Koontz, Harold D. "Domestic Air Line Self-Sufficiency: A Problem of Route Structure." *American Economic Review* (March 1952), pp. 103-125.

Korbel, Herbert J. "The Interstate Commerce Commission and Monopoly—A Study of the Commission's Power and Duties in the Antitrust Field: The Commission and Railroad Unifications—From Unrestrained Competition to Regulated Monopoly." *ICC Practitioners' Journal* (December 1961), pp. 318-329.

Locklin, D. Philip. "Do We or Don't We Want Railroad Mergers?" *Illinois Business Review* (July 1963).

Liipfert, Eugene T. "Consolidation and Competition in Transportation: The Need for an Effective and Consistent Policy." *The George Washington Law Review* (October 1962), pp. 106-135.

Marion, David H. "The American-Eastern Application: Crucial Test of CAB Merger Policy." *University of Pennsylvania Law Review* (December 1962), pp. 195-219.

McAllister, William. "Trucking Industry Push for Larger Vehicles Meets Wide Opposition." *The Wall Street Journal* (January 28, 1970), pp. 1, 14.

McCormick, J. Byron. "The Regulations of Motor Transportation." *California Law Review* (November 1933), pp. 24-77.

Meck, John F., Jr., and Bogue, Robert W. "Federal Regulation of Motor Carrier Unification." *The Yale Law Journal* (June 1941), pp. 1376-1423.

"Merger and Monopoly in Domestic Aviation." *Columbus Law Review* (May 1962), pp. 851-883.

Miklius, W. "Some Characteristics of Nonregulated For-Hire Truck Transportation of Agricultural Commodities." *Land Economics* (May 1966), pp. 226-230.

Morton, Newton. "Carrier Consolidation." *ICC Practitioners' Journal* (January 1963), pp. 425-448.

Murphy, Elwood. "State Regulation of Motor Transportation and Carriage." *California Law Review* (July 1933), pp. 496-504.

Nelson, James C. "Coming Organizational Changes in Transportation," in Davidson, Jack R., and Ottoson, Howard W., eds. *Transportation Problems and Policies in the Trans-Missouri West.* Lincoln, Nebraska: University of Nebraska Press, 1967, pp. 299-334.

Nelson, James C. "Economies of Large-Scale Operation in the Trucking Industry." *The Journal of Land and Public Utility Economics* (February 1941), pp. 112-115.

_____. "The Effects of Entry Control in Surface Transport." *Transportation Economics: A Conference of the Universities: National Bureau Committee for Economic Research.* New York: National Bureau of Economic Research, 1965, pp. 381-422.

Nelson, Robert A. "The Economies of Scale in the Motor Carrier Industry: a Reply." *Land Economics* (May 1959), pp. 180-185.

Phillips, Charles F., Jr. "Railroad Mergers: Competition, Monopoly, and Antitrust." *Washington and Lee Law Review* (Spring 1962), pp. 1-22.

Roberts, Merrill J. "Some Aspects of Motor Carrier Costs: Firm Size, Efficiency, and Financial Health." *Land Economics* (August 1956), pp. 228-238.

Schenker, Eric. "Nationalization and Denationalization of Motor Carriers in Great Britain." *Land Economics* (August 1963), pp. 219-230.

Shirley, Robert E. "An Analysis of Motor Carrier Cost Formulae Developed by the Interstate Commerce Commission." *Transportation Journal* (Spring 1969), pp. 21-27.

Smykay, Edward W. "An Appraisal of the Economics of Scale in the Motor Carrier Industry." *Land Economics* (May 1958), pp. 143-148.

_____. "The Economies of Scale in the Motor Carrier Industry: A Rejoinder." *Land Economics* (May 1959), pp. 185-187.

Swartz, Thomas R. "Incremental-Cost Analysis—Costs or Benefits." *Transportation Journal* (Spring 1969), pp. 5-10.

Thompson, W.H. "Expected Developments in Transportation Legislation and Implications to Agriculture," in Davidson, Jack R., and Ottoson, Howard W., eds. *Transportation Problems and Policies in the Trans-Missouri West.* Lincoln, Nebraska: University of Nebraska Press, 1967, pp. 243-258.

"Trucking Rolls Into an Age of Giants." *Business Week* (June 12, 1965), pp. 174-176, 178, 180, 184.

Tucker, William H., and O'Brien, John H. "The Public Interest in Railroad Mergers." *Boston University Law Review* (Spring 1962), pp. 160-186.

Tuggle, Kenneth H. "A Perspective for Mergers." Remarks by ICC Commissioner Tuggle at the 38th annual meeting of the Association of ICC Practitioners, San Francisco, California, June 23, 1967, mimeographed.

Wagner, Warren H. "Common, Contract, and Private Motor Carriers Defined and Distinguished." *ICC Practitioners' Journal* (November 1946), pp. 119-163.

Walker, Gilbert. "Transport Policy Before and After 1953." *Oxford Economic Papers* (March 1953), pp. 90-116.

Wilson, George W. "The Nature of Competition in the Motor Transport Industry." *Land Economics* (November 1960), pp. 387-391.

Yeatter, Clayton. "Interstate Legal Barriers to Transportation in the Trans-Missouri West," in Davidson, Jack R., and Ottoson, Howard W., eds. *Transportation Problems and Policies in the Trans-Missouri West.* Lincoln, Nebraska: University of Nebraska Press, 1967, pp. 195-241.

Government Publications

Adams, Walter, and Hendry, James B. *Trucking Mergers, Concentration, and Small Business: An Analysis of Interstate Commerce Commission Policy, 1950-56,* in U.S. Congress, Senate, Select Committee on Small Business, Trucking Mergers and Consolidation, 85th Congress, 1st session. Washington, D.C.: U.S. Government Printing Office, 1957, pp. 211-384.

Civil Aeronautics Board. *Civil Aeronautics Board Reports to Congress—Fiscal Year—1968.* Washington, D.C.: U.S. Government Printing Office, 1968.

Doyle, John P., and others. *National Transportation Policy.* U.S. Congress, Senate, Committee on Commerce, Committee print, Report No. 445, 87th Congress, 1st session. Washington, D.C.: U.S. Government Printing Office, June 26, 1961. This document is generally referred to as *The Doyle Report* in the transportation industry.

Federal Trade Commission. *Economic Report on Corporate Mergers.* Washington, D.C.: U.S. Government Printing Office, 1969.

The Interstate Commerce Act. Washington, D.C.: U.S. Government Printing Office, 1968.

Interstate Commerce Commission. *Annual Reports for 1940, 1955, 1966, 1967, and 1968, 1969, and 1972.* Washington, D.C.: U.S. Government Printing Office, 1940, 1955, 1966, 1967, 1968, 1969, and 1972.

Interstate Commerce Commission, Bureau of Accounts, Cost Finding, and Valuation, Statement No. 1-54. *Explanation of the Development of Motor Carrier Costs with Statement as to their Meaning and Significance.* Washington, D.C.: U.S. Government Printing Office, April 1954.

Interstate Commerce Commission, Bureau of Economics, Statement No. 67-2. *The Role of Regulated Motor Carriers in the Handling of Small Shipments.* Washington, D.C.: U.S. Government Printing Office, November 1967.

Nelson, Robert A. "The Economic Structure of the Highway Carrier Industry in New England," in *Motor Freight Transport for New England*, Report No. 5. Boston: New England Governors' Committee on Public Transportation, October 1956.

Udell, Gilman G., compiler. *Laws Relating to Interstate Commerce and Transportation.* Washington, D.C.: U.S. Government Printing Office, 1966.

U.S. Congress. House. Committee on Interstate and Foreign Commerce. *Amending Section 5(10) of the Interstate Commerce Act Regarding Motor Carrier Mergers*, Report No. 330, 89th Cong., 1st sess. Washington, D.C.: U.S. Government Printing Office, 1965.

U.S. Congress. House. Committee on Interstate and Foreign Commerce. *Regulation of Interstate Motor Busses and Trucks on Public Highways*, H.R. 6836, 73rd Cong., 2nd sess. Washington, D.C.: U.S. Government Printing Office, 1934.

U.S. Congress. House. Committee on Interstate and Foreign Commerce. *Regulation of the Transportation of Passengers and Property by Motor Carriers Operating in Interstate and Foreign Commerce*, H.R. 5262, 74th Cong., 1st sess. Washington, D.C.: U.S. Government Printing Office, 1935.

U.S. Congress. Senate. Committee on Interstate Commerce. *A Bill To Amend the Interstate Commerce Act, As Amended, By Providing For Regulation of the Transportation of Passengers and Property by Motor Carriers Operating In Interstate and Foreign Commerce, And For Other Reasons*, S. 1629, 74th Cong., 1st sess. Washington, D.C.: U.S. Government Printing Office, 1935.

U.S. Congress. Senate. Committee on Commerce. *Amending Section 5(10) of the Interstate Commerce Act Regarding Motor Carrier Mergers*, Report No. 432, 89th Cong., 1st sess. Washington, D.C.: U.S. Government Printing Office, 1965.

U.S. Congress. Senate. Committee on Commerce. *The Motor Carrier Act of 1935: An Evaluation of the Motor Carrier Act of 1935 on the Thirtieth Anniversary of Its Enactment*, Committee print, 89th Cong., 1st sess. Washington, D.C.: U.S. Government Printing Office, 1965.

U.S. Congress. Senate. *Motor Carrier Act, 1935*, Report No. 482, 74th Cong., 1st sess. Washington, D.C.: U.S. Government Printing Office, 1935.

U.S. Congress. Senate. Select Committee on Small Business. *Competition, Regulation, and the Public Interest in the Motor Carrier Industry*, Report No. 1693, 84th Cong., 2nd sess. Washington, D.C.: U.S. Government Printing Office, 1956.

U.S. Congress. Senate. Select Committee on Small Business. *ICC Administration of the Motor Carrier Act*, Committee print, 84th Cong., 1st sess. Washington, D.C.: U.S. Government Printing Office, 1956.

U.S. Congress. Senate. Select Committee on Small Business. *Mergers and Concentration in the Trucking Industry*, Report No. 1441, 85th Cong., 2nd sess. Washington, D.C.: U.S. Government Printing Office, 1958.

U.S. Congress. Senate. Select Committee on Small Business. *Trucking Mergers and Concentration*, 85th Cong., 1st sess. Washington, D.C.: U.S. Government Printing Office, 1957, pp. 1-210.

U.S. Department of Agriculture. Agricultural Marketing Service. *Grain Transportation in the North Central Region*, Marketing Research Report No. 490. Washington, D.C.: U.S. Government Printing Office, July 1961.

U.S. Department of Commerce. Bureau of the Census. *1963 Census of Transportation* and the *1967 Census of Transportation.* Washington, D.C.: Government Printing Office, 1963, 1969-1970.

Other Sources

American Trucking Associations. *American Trucking Trends, 1972.* Washington, D.C.: Department of Research and Transport Economics, American Trucking Associations, Inc., 1972.

American Trucking Associations. Motor Transport Economics, Current Report No. 21. *Mergers in the Trucking Business Industry.* Washington, D.C.: American Trucking Associations, October 1968.

Air Transport Association of America. *1969 Air Transportation Facts and Figures.* Washington, D.C.: Air Transport Association of America, 1969.

Association of American Railroads. *Railroad Merger Scoreboard.* Washington, D.C.: Public Relations Department, Association of American Railroads, March 1968.

Association of American Railroads. *Yearbook of Railroad Facts–1972.* Washington, D.C.: Association of American Railroads, April 1972.

Automobile Manufacturers Association, Inc. *Motor Truck Facts, 1972.* Detroit: Automobile Manufacturers Association, Inc., 1972.

Indexes

Author Index

234

Subject Index

About the Author

James C. Johnson is currently Assistant Professor of Marketing and Transportation at the University of Tulsa. He received the B.S. (Transportation) and M.A. (Economics) from The University of Arizona and the Ph.D. (Marketing and Transportation) from the University of Minnesota. He is an editor of two distribution books and his articles have appeared in the *ICC Practitioner's Journal, The Transportation Journal, Distribution Worldwide*, and *Traffic World.* Professor Johnson has been active in transportation organizations, with membership in the Association of ICC Practitioners, The American Society of Traffic and Transportation (C.M.), Delta Nu Alpha, and the National Council of Physical Distribution Management.

Library of Industrial and Commercial Education and Training

ADVISORY EDITORS:

B. H. Henson, B.Sc.(Econ.) and T. F. West, D.Sc., Ph.D., F.R.I.C., A.M.I.Chem.E.

COMMUNICATIONS
General Editor: M. H. Lovell, C.B.E.

THE LEGAL
LIMITS OF JOURNALISM

THE LEGAL
LIMITS OF JOURNALISM

BY

HERBERT LLOYD

A Solicitor of the Supreme Court
A Fellow of the Institute of Public Relations

THE QUEEN'S AWARD
TO INDUSTRY 1966

PERGAMON PRESS, LTD. 1968

PERGAMON PRESS LTD.

OXFORD · LONDON · EDINBURGH

NEW YORK · TORONTO · SYDNEY

First Edition 1968   Copyright © 1968 Herbert Lloyd

Library of Congress Catalog Card No. 68-22495.

Printed in Great Britain by Dawson & Goodall Ltd. The Mendip Press, Bath.

08 003866 2

Contents

v

3. Libel (*continued*)

4. Slander   23

5. Publication   26

6. What do the Words Mean?—Prove it!   36

7. Defences   40

Publisher's Foreword

THE Industrial Training Act has resulted in an increase in the number of people now being trained or re-trained. LICET books are intended to provide suitable texts which will be easy to read and assimilate for those employed in industry and commerce who are receiving further education and training as a part of their employment. It is hoped that they will be particularly suitable for those attending courses leading to the examinations of the City and Guilds of London Institute, the Regional Examining Unions and other examining bodies.

The books are essentially straightforward, simple and practical in their approach and are designed to provide all the basic knowledge required for a particular trade or occupation. They are structured in such a way that the subject is broken down into convenient and progressive components, and are written by authors specially chosen for their expert knowledge and for their practical and teaching experience of their subjects.

Where appropriate, emphasis has been placed on safety training. In some subjects separate manuals on safety and safety training will be provided; in other texts, authors have been encouraged to emphasise safety precautions at relevant points, or to devote a separate chapter to these matters.

LICET books are published in a number of subject divisions, with each division controlled by a specialist editor responsible for selecting authors and providing guidance and advice to both authors and publishers. It is hoped that the series will make an important contribution to further education and industrial training.

ROBERT MAXWELL
Publisher

Foreword

OTHER peoples' affairs are often of compelling and abiding interest to the public. Newspapers, the radio and television are full of reports and pictures which inform—instruct or entertain. It has been said, "All human life is there". But the publication of these accounts of interest, and often drama and glamour, are subject to legal rules. We must always remember that the law touches and affects each of us in almost all aspects of every-day life and that although ninety-five per cent of the work that lawyers undertake has nothing to do with court cases—the remaining five per cent is of special importance to those who communicate—the journalist, reporter, broadcaster, author—to all who provide facts and opinion for publication. For in gathering and passing on his work the journalist must keep constantly in mind the law of defamation and the risk of being sued. Further he must remember that if guilty of contempt of Court he and his employer may be fined or even imprisoned. There are very definite "Legal Limits to Journalism!" I believe this work has succeeded in its aim of setting out simply and readably just what these legal limits are. It gives warning clearly of the dangers that have to be avoided and contains much useful information and good counsel. It should be of real use to all whose job it is to communicate with the public.

The College of Law,   HERMON J. B. COCKSHUTT
February 1968

Preface

THIS book has been written specially for those starting a career in journalism—for journalists in the widest sense of the word—those using any form of communication—press, radio, television, photography, or art work, etc. It is intended as a guide to the law of libel and slander—written, spoken, camera, caption, or criticism. It gives an introduction to parliamentary and other privilege, and explains some of the techniques developed by communicators to ensure accuracy wherever possible.

The law on the subject of defamation is complex and extensive and it is hoped that this volume will indicate guide lines, point out pitfalls, and explain the legal limits of journalism.

There are a number of leading works in this field and I would like to acknowledge an indebtedness to the following which I found of particular relevance in preparing this volume.

Current Law, Sweet & Maxwell, Stevens & Sons, 1963.
Modern Advertising Law, by PETER LANGDON-DAVIES, Business Publications London, 1963.
Hatred, Ridicule or Contempt, by JOSEPH DEAN, Constable, 1953.
General Principles of the Law of Torts, by PHILIP S. JAMES, Butterworths, 1964.
Discovering the Law, by JAMES DERRIMAN, University of London Press, 1962.
Halsbury's Laws of England, 3rd edn., vol. 24, Butterworths, 1958.
U.K. Press Gazette, Bouverie Publishing Co. Ltd.
The English and Empire Digest, Butterworths.
The Kemsley Manual of Journalism, Thomson Newspapers.
Essential Law for Journalists, edited by L. C. J. McNAE, MacGibbon and Kee, 1964.

Above all stands what is, in my opinion, the leading textbook—*Gatley on Libel and Slander*, by R. L. McEWEN and P. S. C. LEWIS, Sweet & Maxwell.

I am indebted to all authors and publishers for the assistance which I have derived from the above works and for their kind permission to quote from published material in certain cases. All the above works are strongly recommended for further reading.

May I express my gratitude to my old friend Mr. Hermon Cockshutt, of The College of Law, for his wise advice on the treatment of the law stated and for his kindness in writing the Foreword. I am also grateful to Mr. Maurice Lovell for the opportunity to write this book, to Mr. B. G. Tozer for his faith in me; and, finally, I express my appreciation to Mr. Dudley Perkins, Director-General of the Port of London Authority, for his inspiration.

Table of Cases

B

CHAPTER 1

Introduction

Reputation

What kind of person are you? You may think of yourself as kind, considerate, fairly well-tempered, honest, conscientious, hardworking, and so on. You probably realise that you are in fact many people in one. What do people think of you? Those close to you have their own opinions; mother, brother, sister, schoolteacher, employer, neighbours next door—each have views about you. The sum total of all these opinions is your reputation. You may be known to only a small number of people. A lawyer in a town may be known to most. A film star or leading statesman may have worldwide fame.

Have you ever looked up the word *reputation* in a dictionary? Let us do so now. The *Shorter Oxford Dictionary* tells us that it is a late middle English word which comes from the Latin word *reputationem* which means *computation–consideration*. This is interesting because we are back at the sum total of what people consider. The dictionary goes on to give the modern meaning as "The common or general estimate of a person with respect to character or other qualities; the relative estimation or esteem in which a person is held." The second meaning given is the condition, quality, or fact of being highly regarded or esteemed; also respectability, good report. From the year 1553 it has meant one's good name. Of course, reputation may be bad as well as good. People may be poorly, rather than highly regarded; one's name is not necessarily good. Here is an example of the use of the word given: Addison wrote: "This very old woman had the reputation of a Witch all over the country."

You want people to like you—to think well of you, and you probably behave in such a way that they do. You care about the esteem in which you are rightly held—you are jealous of your reputation. Shakespeare summed the matter up supremely well when he made Othello say:

> Good name in man and woman, dear my lord,
> Is the immediate jewel of their soul.
> Who steals my purse, steals trash; 'tis something, nothing
> 'Twas mine, 'tis his and has been slave to thousands.
> But he that filches from me my good name,
> Robs me of that which not enriches him
> And makes me poor indeed.

How can you be robbed of your good name? How can someone change the favourable opinion people hold about you—wrongly and for the worse? Everyone knows about gossip. The usual picture is of two women chatting by the garden fence or over a cup of tea. You have probably heard someone say, "I know I shouldn't tell you this but . . ." or, "You will never believe me but what do you think she did? . . ."

These gossips are talking about people in a way that affects their reputation. Much of what is spoken—and believe me a very great deal is said every day—is harmless. But sometimes something is said which has far-reaching consequences. Someone's reputation is seriously affected. What if someone told a friend that you were a blackmailer or that you were not fit to hold your job because you were dishonest? You would be very angry and want to do something about it—but what could you do?

You would see a solicitor—tell him the facts and he would advise you whether you had a case against the person who had talked about you. He would be dealing with a branch of the law called defamation.

Defamation—What does it Mean?

To defame is to take away the fair fame of a person, to attack his reputation. Such an attack is usually by the spoken or written word. There are many cases on it—and in 1952 Parliament passed the Defamation Act which consolidated the law dealing with it. We will consider this law later on.

As men and women who are going to communicate with others you must realise how very important it is that you should never at any time say or write anything which will involve you or your employers in a law case brought by someone whose reputation you have attacked. This concerns everyone in journalism, whether you are writing for a newspaper, doing something for radio or T.V., printing, publishing, illustrating, or lecturing. If you communicate in any way you must take great care to observe your legal limits.

You are probably saying to yourself—"I would never say or write anything which was untrue." Quite so—but suppose you got your facts wrong? Someone may be badly hurt by what you have done. You must realise the essential need for the greatest possible accuracy in writing or broadcasting. Much of your work will be dealing with people. People have reputations of which they are proud, and it is your duty as a communicator to respect those worthy of respect.

But what if there is some local villain who deserves to be exposed?—and you regard it as your duty to tell an unsuspecting public what a rogue he is. You may stumble on an exclusive story which you think will make your name as a journalist. You will find the editor to whom you present it very cautious indeed. Not because he does not share your indignation—quite the contrary; and he can probably see even more publicity potential in the story than you can. No. His caution is due to experience, solid experience of the limits of journalism.

You may remember the phrase "Publish and be damned" attributed to the Duke of Wellington. But you cannot rely upon the victim of attacking words being so disdainful as to ignore them. Instead, he may actively resent them. Few can afford to publish such words, particularly at the outset of their careers. Few should in any event do so.

3

Learning the Law

How then are you to know what you can or cannot do? You may say I'll read the cases on the subject! This would be an immense task. The leading legal textbook about defamation, *Gatley on Libel and Slander*, has nearly 1000 pages, and reports almost 4000 law cases. Most of them are fascinating and we will deal with some later on, but it is not always easy to reconcile many of the decisions which have been handed down by the judges. Try and master the principles. A journalist in the Press or in radio or T.V. may at any time be confronted by a difficult situation and he must have some knowledge of the guide lines which can tell him what he can and cannot do. If a journalist is to perform his work competently and with confidence he must be familiar with some parts of the law. How can you learn? You should seize every chance of getting your senior colleagues to tell you of the pitfalls and, best of all, get to know your legal advisers or a local solicitor. There are certain general principles which lay down the rights and responsibilities of a journalist and we shall look at these before we go on to deal with defamation in detail. I use the expression journalist to cover all who communicate in any way—by the written or spoken word—in print—photography, film, on radio or T.V.—by art work of any kind—printing, publishing, lecturing.

The Freedom of the Press

The Universal Declaration of Human Rights laid down certain essential freedoms that mankind should have of which freedom of expression is one of the most important. This is what it says: "Everyone has the right to freedom of opinion and expression: the right includes freedom to hold opinions without interference and to seek, receive and impart information and ideas through any media and regardless of frontiers". Although this is not precisely the law of the land, it forms the basis upon which many cases have been decided and Acts of Parliament passed. The Press in this country operates in a democracy. There is freedom of speech, freedom to express opinions, freedom to obtain information—

particularly where it is of interest and importance to the public. These freedoms are enjoyed by the journalist and other citizens alike, but there are certain limitations imposed by law. The State must be protected and so must the individual citizen in certain circumstances. If you are doing a story on the army you cannot expect to be allowed to publish the secrets of the nation's master defence plans in case we are attacked. If you are doing a feature on perfumes you cannot expect a manufacturer to welcome your setting out exact details of his secret formula. The law limits what you can say or do. You must not commit treason by betraying information which affects the national security, nor, as we have seen, must you defame innocent people, and, what is more, you must not interfere with legal administration—particularly in the courts of justice—for if you do you may find that you have committed what is called contempt of court. This does not mean that you hold a low opinion of the court or the judge. One of its meanings is doing something which obstructs or prevents a fair trial. You cannot, for example, while a trial is in progress publish a leading article headed "Tom Jones is Guilty". This is a matter for the jury to decide in due course.

The Journalist is a Citizen

A journalist whether of the Press or of radio or T.V., as we have seen, is in the same position as a private citizen. Just because you are a journalist you have no special legal rights to go further than the man in the street can go—you have only the same legal rights to do things, write articles, give talks, take photographs, print or publish and go places, that anyone else has.

You may say at once, "What about press cards?", which reporters carry and which seem to be a wonderful passport to all sorts of places at most interesting times to see exciting events and meet fascinating people. These cards are proof that the holders are members of a recognised professional journalists' organisation, employed as journalists or freelancing. As a result the holders may enjoy privileges but not rights. Many organisations recognise them and give facilities to the press that they would not give to private individuals.

Courts of Law

When you go to a court of law you will usually see a press box conveniently situated so that reporters can hear what the judge, advocates, and witnesses are saying. The existence of the press box, however, does not give the journalist any better rights to be in court than any other member of the public. If the court decides to sit in camera, that is to hear evidence privately (for the word *camera* comes from the Latin word *camara*, meaning a chamber, and *in camera* means in effect in a judge's private room as opposed to open court), a journalist is in the same position as anyone else—unless his presence at those particular proceedings is especially provided for by an Act of Parliament, e.g. proceedings on the winding up of a public company are one of the matters which must be heard in open court.

Privacy

Privacy too is dealt with in the Universal Declaration of Human Rights. Article 12 reads: "No one shall be subjected to arbitrary interference with his privacy, family, home or correspondence, nor to attacks upon his honour and reputation. Everyone has the right to the protection of the law against such interference or attacks."

Recently a Member of Parliament tried to pass a law which would protect the privacy of the individual.

While you are considering the question of where a journalist may go and what he may or may not do you should at the same time have a very clear idea about this subject. Every now and again there is a great outcry about the invasion of privacy, tempers are lost, cameras wrecked, journalists ejected. Has anyone an absolute right to privacy? Probably not. An Englishman's home may be his castle but this by itself does not prohibit anyone calling upon him to ask him a question. So as a journalist you can go anywhere, you can report anything provided you obey the law. You are not limited in any way just because you happen to be a journalist. There are, however, guide lines, and it is the purpose of this book to tell you what some of them are; the pitfalls which exist and how to avoid them. If you are to do your work properly as a journalist you must have a sound knowledge of the legal limits of journalism.

Cases Referred to and the Defamation Act, 1952

A number of reported cases are referred to in this book with the year in which they were decided. In reading them you should bear in mind that the Defamation Act was passed in 1952. This clarified and simplified the law considerably. As a result the cases should be read in the light of the provisions of the Act. This is set out in full at the end of the book and you would do well to read it through carefully.

CHAPTER 2

Defamation

You have already seen that to defame is to take away the fair fame of a person—to attack his reputation. Such attacks are usually made by people talking or writing, but you may be interested to know that defamation can also take many other forms. Even actions or gestures can be defamatory.

Libel and Slander

Defamation is of two kinds—libel and slander. Broadly speaking the law draws the distinction according to the form the defamation takes. If it is permanent it is libel: slander consists of an attack which is transient. Writing, printing, drawings, paintings, photographs, films, television, radio broadcasts, and even a wax effigy have been considered at law to be permanent forms. How can a wax model be a libel? The Chamber of Horrors in Madame Tussauds Waxworks Exhibition is mostly peopled by effigies of notorious murderers and models of the scenes of their crimes. In 1894, between the Chamber itself and the turnstile, was Napoleon Room No. 2 in which, as well as Napoleon and the Duke of Wellington, Mrs. Maybrick an infamous poisoner, and Pigott who was concerned in the Parnell letters case, were also modelled. Here was placed a wax model of Mr. Alfred John Monson, dressed in a brown knickerbocker suit at "the scene of the tragedy" and beside him was a gun labelled "Monson's Gun". He had been tried in Edinburgh on charges of murder and attempted murder and released on a verdict of not proven which is permitted under Scots but not English law. It was held that the verdict did not entitle the Waxworks to make an attack on Mr. Monson's reputation by placing his effigy so close to the entrance to the Chamber of Horrors. Monson won his case but he was awarded only one farthing damages. Spoken words are the most usual form of slander. Significant sounds, looks, signs, or gestures like the hissing of an actor, the deaf and dumb language or an act of gesticulation, such as holding up an empty purse or the like have all at some time or another been held to be capable of being slanderous.

The Right to Sue

You know that you have a right to your good name. The law protects that right. The way it does this is to give another right—to bring an action for damages against your attacker. Not every statement about you which is unfavourable is defamation—the line must be drawn somewhere. It has been drawn by a definition laid down by the supreme legal tribunal in the country—the House of Lords, when Lord Atkin in the case of *Sim* v. *Stretch* which was decided in 1936, said: "Would the words tend to lower Mr. Sim in the estimation of right thinking members of the public generally?" Other cases have decided that if the attack makes people shun you, or avoid you, or exposes you to hatred, ridicule, or contempt, then you have a right of action. You can bring a case against your attacker in the courts. The judge and jury will hear what you have to say, but even if you prove that the words you complain of were written or said, it does not necessarily follow that you will win the case. The writer may have a good defence. What these defences are you will see a little later on.

CHAPTER 3

Libel

To BE a libel, and equally so for slander, the words complained of must tend to lower you in the estimation of right-thinking members of society *generally*. If the words lower you in the estimation only of a particular section of society they are not libellous. You may consider something said about you to be distasteful or objectionable, and your views may be shared only by members of a society to which you belong; you might not win your case, for it is not enough to prove that the words spoken rendered you obnoxious to a limited class of people. It should be proved that the words are such as would produce a bad impression on the minds of average, reasonable men.

Different Forms of Libel

Now let us look at the different forms of libel. The most usual form is by printed or written words—but remember pictures, photographs, cartoons, television pictures, films, can all be libellous. Broadcasting for general reception, although technically the spoken word, is deemed by the Defamation Act, 1952, to fall into the category of libel. Does a libel have to take a certain form? The answer is no. Your attacker may write explicitly, make direct assertion, or insinuate. Cleverness, ingenuity, and skill in indirect writing will not protect your attacker if it is clear you have been libelled.

Innuendo

A libel may contain what is called an innuendo. This word has been a part of the English language since 1564 and it comes from the same word in Latin which means "by nodding at, pointing to, intimating". It was a medieval Latin formula used to introduce a parenthetical explanation "and that is, meaning, to wit, that is to say". In law it is the injurious meaning alleged to be conveyed by words not in themselves (or *per se*) injurious or actionable. Words which, in an action for libel or slander, are usually introduced into the record and issue by the words "meaning thereby", after the expression alleged to have been used. This may not be easy to understand at first reading. To introduce into the record means that it becomes part of the official court record of the case, which includes the pleadings, the written work, the papers prepared to bring the case to trial. Issue here simply means one of the points in dispute to be decided by the judge or, in certain circumstances, the jury. Let us examine it a little more closely. There has to be an injurious meaning. This we know— for libel is an attack which injures your reputation. It is "alleged" —this seems to be a reporter's favourite word. Why? For example, because it does not say a case has been proved or that an offence has been committed or that Mr. Smith *was* at the scene of the crime at the vital moment (Mr. Smith may have a cast-iron alibi). No. The reporter says that it was alleged that Mr. Smith was there when the alleged burglary took place.

Words may be defamatory in their ordinary sense, but the circumstances surrounding their publication may take away the injurious implications. Conversely words which appear to be quite innocent on the face of it may bear another meaning which is clearly an attack on your reputation. Here are some examples. Someone may write of you that you are a trickster. At first sight it would appear in all the circumstances that the words must be defamatory. But what if you are an amateur conjurer who belongs to a social club of like-minded enthusiasts who call themselves The Tricksters? "He is an angel" sounds pretty good and complimentary. But what if "the angels" referred to is the local nickname for a notorious criminal gang? You see now that the real significance of words can only be evaluated in the light of all surrounding circumstances. Lord Blackburn in 1882 in trying one of the best-known of libel cases—one in which a firm called Henty & Sons sued the Capital and Counties Bank Ltd., said:

> There are no words so plain that they may not be published with reference to such circumstances, and to such persons knowing these circumstances as to convey a very different meaning from that which would be understood from the same words used under very different circumstances.

What happened in this case was that Henty & Sons sent a circular to customers of the bank saying they would not receive in payment cheques drawn on any of the branches of that bank. There was a run on the bank, whose business was injured.

Was there an innuendo? If so, what do you think it was? The answer is that the circular suggested that the bank was insolvent.

The result of the case may surprise you. It was held that the words complained of were not libellous in themselves and the innuendo suggested, namely that the circular imputed insolvency to them, was *not* the inference which reasonable people would draw. The bank lost the case.

Tolley v. *Fry* (1931)

Another famous case on innuendo concerns a well-known amateur golfer named Tolley. One day he saw an advertisement published by the Fry's chocolate firm. It showed a picture of him playing with a packet of chocolate sticking out of his pocket. Below was written:

> The caddie to Tolley said "Oh Sir,
> Good shot, Sir; that ball see it go, sir;
> My word how it flies
> Like a cartet of Fry's
> They're handy, they're good, and priced low sir."

Mr. Tolley had not been asked and received nothing.

What is the innuendo? The key is in the word amateur: Mr. Tolley was not a professional golfer. It was held that the facts supported the innuendo that Mr. Tolley had prostituted his amateur status for advertising purposes and the advertisement was therefore defamatory to a man in his position.

This is a convenient place to review what we have learnt about innuendo so far.

1. The whole circumstances must be taken into account.
2. There are different kinds of words: those, the ordinary meaning of which makes them defamatory; and those which are not defamatory in the ordinary way and which will only become so if there is an innuendo which can be established.
3. Any words, however defamatory they may appear to be, may be explained away in certain circumstances, and conversely the most innocent of words can become very damaging when all the surrounding circumstances are known.

Here are some examples.

Mrs. Morrison who had been married just a month saw a mistaken announcement in the local newspaper that she had given birth to twins. It was held she had a case.

Mr. Hayes said as a joke that Mr. Donoghue had been caught taking dead bodies out of a churchyard and fined. He was sued and lost. The principle is clear—that a person shall not be allowed to murder another's reputation in jest. But if the words be so spoken that it is obvious to every bystander that only jest is meant, no injury is done. It has been held that even words of praise are actionable if you can prove that they were published ironically.

What do the Words Mean Now?

Times change. Words change their meaning. Look at the various interpretations which have been given to the word *nice* down the centuries. In 1560 it meant foolish, stupid. In 1606 wanton, lascivious. In 1720 tender, delicate, over refined. In 1769 agreeable, delightful. In 1830 kind, considerate, pleasant to others. In 1860 refined, in good taste. The attitude of the public is important. When Elizabeth I reigned you could bring an action if someone called you a witch—for practising witchcraft was then a criminal offence. The place where the libel took place is also of significance—words in one country have a different meaning in another.

Caricatures

What about caricatures? Can a leading politician who is constantly being caricatured sue for defamation? Probably not unless his personal reputation was injured by ridicule. But different considerations apply to ordinary people.

Libellous Words

Many words have been held by the judge to be capable of bearing a libellous meaning. Here are some of them: rogue, rascal, dishonest, crook, swindler, coward, liar, immoral, racketeer, intolerant, oppressive.

Insolvency and Credit

There are certain words which have a special significance. For example, it is libellous to write and publish that a man is bankrupt or insolvent or that he is unable to pay his just debts if in fact none of these things is true; but it is not libellous to write that you owe money. For this does not necessarily imply that you cannot or will not pay what you owe. While we are on the subject of money, this seems a convenient moment to examine the position of banks and cheques.

Banks and Cheques

These have given rise to a number of cases dealing with defamation. A bank is very much like a person and stays in business as long as the public has confidence in it. Accordingly, a false accusation that affects its credit—injuring it by causing mistrust—may be libellous. A bank, too, can libel. So far as cheques are concerned it can be defamatory to write that your cheque has been dishonoured—the inference being that you are dishonest or insolvent, or at least are guilty of bad faith. But be careful about "R/D", the notorious "Refer to drawer" which is sometimes written on a cheque by a bank. Mr. Justice Scrutton in a delightful passage said: "I doubt whether the words 'Refer to drawer' written on a cheque returned to the payee is libellous. In my opinion in their ordinary meaning they amount to a statement by the bank 'We are not paying. Go back to the drawer and ask him why,' " But even this is now in doubt by a November 1967 decision.

Other Libels

Statements dealing with decrees and judgments of the courts need to be handled with special care.

Strangely enough it is not libellous to write of a man that he has had a judgment taken against him.

Care must be taken, too, when dealing with reports concerning a man's business, particularly when reports deal with the credit of a firm or its relationships with employees past or present.

The law makes special provisions for allegations of insanity, or that the person attacked suffers from a contagious or repulsive disease. You may think that insanity excites pity not ridicule, and consequently an allegation that a person is of unsound mind does not necessarily expose him to hatred, ridicule, or contempt, but the practical effect of such an allegation usually is to cause the sufferer to be shunned, and the same thing applies to certain diseases.

What happens if you are compared with Ananias or Judas?

15

c

You can be libelled if your character is compared with those of infamous persons. Mr. Justice Erle said as far back as 1848:

> Nothing is easier than to bring persons into contempt by allusion to names well known in history or by mention of animals to which certain ideas are attached. The Court will take judicial notice that such words as Judas have an application very generally known indeed, which application is likely to bring into contempt a person against whom it is directed.

Photographs

You can be libelled by a photograph. One of the most interesting cases on this point was where an advertisement headed "Leg Appeal" showed one girl's head and shoulders and below the bare legs of another lady. The inference was that the owner of the head did not have suitable limbs of her own to complete the picture. She was a model. She sued and she won. [*Griffiths* v. *Bondor* (1935).]

Speeches

Be on your guard when reporting after-dinner speeches. The speaker may make humorous remarks which may also be defamatory. In a case on this it was held that the man attacked had the right to say that it was beside the point that he did not care what the speaker said about him after dinner. He did not choose to be made an object of ridicule, good natured or otherwise, in a newspaper merely to amuse a number of people who knew nothing of him. [*Dolby* v. *Newnes* (1887).]

Immorality—Chastity—Illegitimacy

You may not feel that chastity is as important as it was. Nothing could be more wrong as you will find to your cost if you impute unchastity to those who appear to have led blameless lives. The stigma of illegitimacy has mercifully begun to pass away, but this again presents a danger area to the innocent journalist. It can be libellous to write that a man is illegitimate, and his mother, too, may have a cause of action, for you have imputed unchastity to her.

Death

What if someone writes that you are dead, when you are very much alive? No libel—unless your reputation is affected.

Libels on a Man in his Work

The law has for a long time given special protection to the reputation of people in their office, profession, calling, trade, or business. Its provisions have been codified in the Defamation Act, 1952. We shall deal with this more fully in due course but in the meantime you should note that any written or printed words which disparage a man in the way of his office, profession, or trade may constitute a libel. Not everything which is detrimental is actionable. If someone writes that you have ceased to carry on your business you may be very angry and inconvenienced, and, indeed, your business may suffer injury, but it is not necessarily a libel. Why? Because the bare statement lacks the essential ingredient in that it neither denigrates the way in which you carry on your business nor points to the lack of a necessary factor for its successful running. If the words complained of do not involve any reflection upon your personal character or the manner in which you carry out your official or professional duties or trade, they are not actionable *per se*.

Especial care must be taken in dealing with dismissals from employment and the reasons why.

Office-holders—The Professions

There is a type of case dealing with office-holders which arises when an attack is made alleging corruption, dishonesty, or fraud, or that the office-holder is incapable of carrying out his duties.

It is also actionable to impute unfitness for a profession or office because of lack of the necessary ability. The leading cases on this type of defamation deal with the Church, the law, and doctors. If you write of a clergyman that he has been guilty of immorality or drunkenness you do so at your peril. The Rev. Kelly won a case in 1869 against Mr. Sherlock who wrote that the clergyman had desecrated part of his church by turning it into a cooking department. The Rev. Curtis succeeded against Mr. Argus in 1915, in a New York case, when the complaint was that he had juggled with the collections.

Naturally you would expect lawyers to have the law relating to themselves explicit. It is. Mr. Boydell won his case for defamation against Mr. Jones in 1838, the allegation being that he had been guilty of sharp practice in his profession.

Other matters which have been the subject of court decisions include writing that a lawyer had given his client's case away; that he had been struck off the rolls; or suspended from practice.

What about doctors? To call one a quack may be libellous, for Lord Alverston defined a quack as one who exploits the timid and the credulous for his own advantage. And, of course, to say that the doctor caused the death of the patient by careless treatment may also be actionable, as also are allegations of unprofessional conduct.

As a possible budding journalist, the cases dealing with literary men will probably have a special appeal to you. If you are wrongly accused of a plagiarism, or represented as a literary freak or a writer or publisher of obscene articles, you can probably sue and win.

It has been held libellous to say of an architect of a public building that his appointment can be regarded in no other light than a public calamity.

Sport and entertainment, too, has its share of libel cases— jockeys riding unfairly, vulgar actresses, horizontal boxers, incompetent football coaches, have all featured as allegations in libel cases.

Note that libels on professions must refer to lawful professions.

Trade

We have seen that one of the most important things a trader has is his credit. If this is impeached an action may lie. This can be done by imputing bankruptcy or insolvency. If you are accused of using false weights or selling worthless goods, or that you employ sweated labour, you may have a case. Mr. Justice Chitty summed it up in 1892 when he said:

> If Mr. Marshall states of Mr. Collard who is a trader earning his livelihood by dealing in articles of trade, anything, be what it may, the natural consequences of uttering which would be to injure the trade of Mr. Collard, then Mr. Collard can bring an action. The allegation was that Mr. Collard employed sweated labour—and this was calculated to bring him and his business into hatred and contempt, and to deter respectable persons from dealing with him.

Allegations of incompetence and want of judgment may be libellous. A distinction should, however, be drawn between persons and goods. If your goods alone are attacked and not your personal or trading character, there is no ground for an action for libel. But there is a catch here. Goods can be *slandered*, usually by a malicious falsehood.

Malicious Falsehood—Slander of Title and of Goods

But have you any remedy if your *goods* are attacked? Section 3 of the Defamation Act provides that in an action for slander of goods, slander of title or other malicious falsehood, you need no longer prove special damage if the attack is calculated to cause you pecuniary damage and is in permanent form, or if the attack is calculated to cause pecuniary damage in respect of your office, profession, calling, trade, or business carried on by you at the time of publication.

Consider the following case.

In 1892 Mr. Evans published in his newspaper that a firm of boilermakers and engineers, Ratcliffe & Sons, had ceased to exist. As a result the firm lost a good deal of business and sued. The jury found that the statement was not a libel but that it was an untrue statement not published in good faith and awarded £120 damages.

What do you have to prove to succeed in an action for malicious falsehood?

1. That what was said referred to your goods.
2. The words were untrue.
3. They were published maliciously—and maliciously here means with a dishonest or improper motive.
4. Unless covered by section 3 of the Defamation Act, you suffered special damage.

But remember—mere "puffing"—i.e. commending your own goods, is not actionable.

In 1910 the Advertisers Protection Society published a monthly circular in which they said: "*Observer*. We are informed that it is now selling about 5,000." The circulation was actually 30,000. The paper sued for libel alleging that the statement was false and that they had suffered damage. Mr. Justice Darling said that he did not think that a mere statement that the circulation of a newspaper was 5,000 could amount to libel and held that so far as the action was based on libel there was no case. Dealing with disparaging the plaintiff's property he said they would succeed if the jury agreed that actual damage had been caused by an untrue statement *maliciously made*. The jury found there was no damage and *The Observer* lost the case.

Another point to watch here is "knocking copy". Everyone wants the world to think his product is better than the others—and goes to great lengths in advertising to convince the public this is so. You can only sue if someone imputes some specific defect to your product. If you are associated with consumer protection societies or trade journals this is a branch of the law to which you must give the closest attention.

Supposing someone wrote of the paper you are working for that it has a column for the advertisements of quack doctors, or that it was the lowest now in circulation and this fact was submitted to the consideration of advertisers, then it might be fair to assume that the statements disparaging your paper involves an imputation upon the personal character of your newspaper proprietors and editors.

Proof

What do you have to prove to win?

1. Words are false;
2. they were published maliciously;
3. that the words are defamatory of you in your personal or business or trading character; that they are not merely a disparagement of your goods; and that
4. the words are reasonably capable of bearing the meaning complained of—and it is for a jury to decide what the meaning really is.

We have so far examined the different types of defamation. You can see that there are many kinds and that you can be libelled in all sorts of ways. The examples given should warn you of what can happen and put you on your guard. Above all it should drive home the absolute necessity for scrupulous accuracy in all you do, say, or write and the need for care and caution.

It is not always easy to see the distinction between defaming a person and disparaging his goods. A libel on a thing may be a libel on a person. If you write Lloyd's beer is adulterated, that would be a libel upon him in his trade, not because of the allegation that the beer was bad but because the language would import deceit and malpractice on the part of the brewer. In cases like this the onus is on you to prove that the words are defamatory of you in your personal or business or trading character and not merely an attack on your goods.

These, then, are some of the different forms that libel cases can take. You will probably not find it easy to see a consistent pattern running through the various decisions of the judges. Do not worry. The courts have found themselves in the same difficulty. In *Broadway Approvals* v. *Odhams Press* (1965), in the Court of Appeal Lord Justice Russell said: "To the comparative new-comer, the law of libel seems to have characteristics of such complication and subtlety that I wonder whether a jury on retirement can readily distinguish their heads from their heels" (*Gatley on Libel and Slander*, Preface to 6th edn., 1967). I have set out a large number of examples in this section in order that you may see how easy it is to become involved in libel proceedings and the great need for care both in checking all the available facts and in the actual writing of copy.

CHAPTER 4

Slander

Proof

Although most of your work as journalists may be of a permanent nature and therefore governed by the rules relating to libel, you should also know the essentials of the other type of defamation —slander. Slander is defamation by the spoken word or in some other transitory form. There are four types of case you can bring if you are slandered *without having to prove that you have suffered special damage as a result*. They are:

1. That you have been accused of a crime punishable by imprisonment, e.g. if you are called a thief or a blackmailer. The crime need not be indictable, that is, of the most serious kind, and it is not necessary that the exact offence be specified. The words must impute a criminal offence but slang words are sufficient. The intention of the person attacking you is immaterial and as in the case of libel the whole of the surrounding circumstances have to be considered. If, however, something is said of you which is really vulgar abuse, particularly if it is said in the heat of passion, e.g. that you are a blackguard or a rascal, you are unlikely to win your case.

2. The second category includes words imputing a contagious disease. Leprosy, venereal diseases, the plague, scarlet fever are included. Insanity is not—because it is not catching— and the imputation must be that the individual has the disease now and not merely that he once had it.

3. Words which are calculated to disparage a man in any office he holds, or his profession, calling, trade, or business. The rules here are much the same as for libel. Imputing insolvency to traders, misconduct to clergymen, dishonesty to lawyers, are examples.

4. The fourth class of case where you can sue without proving special damage is if you are a woman or girl and someone imputes unchastity to you. Direct terms are not essential to be a slander. It is enough if the words used would be understood by ordinary people to convey a specific imputation of unchastity. An allegation that a woman is a lesbian has been held to be an imputation of unchastity.

Special Damage

When spoken words complained of do not come under any one of the four types given above, you can only win your case if you can prove that you have suffered special damage. This means the loss of some material advantage which is capable of being estimated in money, such as being sacked from your job or losing a client or customer, or even the loss of free entertainment or the hospitality of your friends. A judge once said bodily illness is not the natural or the ordinary consequence of speaking slanderous words, and consequence of mental suffering does not constitute special damage enabling you to bring an action for slander. Incidentally, the damage you suffer must have been suffered before you bring your action. Haddan was thrown out of Lott's public house by a servant who said he was drunk. Haddan told his father, who threatened to remove his son from the board of a family company unless he could clear his name. Haddan sued Lott for slander and pleaded as special damage the threat of his ceasing to be a board member. He lost. He had not actually suffered the damage.

The special damage must be the natural, reasonable, and direct result of the defendant's words.

A gossip once told a father that his daughter had had a child by her master. The father went to see the master and asked him if it were true. He replied that it was quite false, but sacked the girl from a job as governess to his children because he felt that it might damage both their characters if she remained. The courts held that the gossip should pay; the special damage was proved. Another case concerned a gossip who told a man that his wife was all but seduced by the doctor before her marriage. The man thereupon turned his wife out of the house. The judge held that the man's conduct was not natural or reasonable so could not constitute special damage.

The jury are the people who have to decide what damage has been proved and whether it was a result of what the defendant said. The judge decides whether the damage constitutes special damage and, if so, whether it was the natural and probable result of the words complained of.

CHAPTER 5

Publication

YOU cannot win your case for defamation unless you prove that the words you complain about were published. But what does publication mean? Simply—communication. The law is dealing not just with what was said or written, but passing it on to someone else. Quite a number of people can get involved in this. For example, in the case of a defamatory book the author, publisher, printer, may all be joined in the proceedings. You do not have to tell the public generally. One other person is sufficient. If someone writes you and tells you falsely that Mr. A. is a liar, this is publication. Telegrams and postcards can also constitute publication.

But you must remember that a man's reputation is not the good opinion he has of himself, but the estimation in which others hold him. Accordingly, if someone writes to you privately defaming you, this is not publication. Publication can happen by any act which passes on the defamatory meaning. If you read a defamatory letter out loud to a third party, that is publication. If you hand a defamatory letter to a typist to be copied, that is publication. Likewise if you use a dictating machine and get it transcribed.

But not all communications which affect your reputation, even if publication of the libel takes place, are actionable. Sometimes what is called privilege applies, for there are certain occasions when, in the public interest, freedom of speech must take precedence over the private rights of an individual so far as his reputation is concerned. We will deal with this in detail a little later on.

There can be intentional and unintentional publication.

Letters

So far as letters are concerned, if you write to a particular person you will not be responsible except for publication to that person. Where publication is not intentional, the jury must decide whether the effect of sending a letter is likely to be that someone other than the plaintiff will open it. If you had been a member of the jury in the following 1962 case, what would your verdict have been? Mrs. Theaker and Mrs. Richardson quarrelled. Mrs. Richardson wrote a letter to Mrs. Theaker falsely accusing her amongst other things of being a prostitute and brothel keeper. She typed the name and address on a cheap manilla envelope, sealed the back with Sellotape, and put it in Mrs. Theaker's letterbox. *Mr.* Theaker picked it up off the mat, opened it, and read it. He said he thought it looked like an election address and there was nothing to suggest it was confidential. Well? How would you have decided the case? Libel, or no libel? Publication? The Court held on the facts that taking into account the appearance of the unstamped envelope it was proper to infer that someone other than Mrs. Theaker would open it. She won her case and Mrs. Richardson was liable. If the person to whom you wrote passes the letter on to someone else, that is his own action for which you cannot be held responsible. Some interesting cases have arisen where letters have been sent to addresses where the writer knew they were likely to be opened by clerks; in these cases it has usually been held to be publication. The words must pass on the defamatory meaning for the passing to be publication. If, for example, you write in a foreign language that third parties do not understand there is no publication. But what if you never meant to publish the libel? You may still be held liable unless you can show that there was no want of care on your part. Cases sometimes arise where people raise their voices, not realising they are being overheard. If they should have realised,

27

they can be held liable for the shouted slander. What would you say of the following case of unintentional publication?

Unintentional Publication

In 1875 a Mr. Whitaker, who was the printer of a journal, made a mistake in setting out *London Gazette* announcements. Instead of putting an entry about a Mr. Shepheard under the heading "Dissolution of Partnerships" he put it under "First Meetings in Bankruptcy". There was no malice, and a full apology was published as soon as the mistake was discovered. Nevertheless, Mr. Shepheard won his case and recovered £50 damages.

But you may not win if the libel was unintentional and there is no want of care. What do you have to prove? Not directly that the words were actually communicated. In certain circumstances this may be inferred. For example, if someone libels you on a postcard which is posted, the court will take judicial notice of the document, that it is a postcard, and will presume in the absence of evidence to the contrary that it will be read by people other than the person to whom it is addressed.

Who is Liable?

Who is liable for publication? If the libel is contained in a book, or a periodical, or a newspaper, everyone who took part in publishing it, or procuring its publication, is, on the face of it, liable. This can include the editor, the printer, the journalist, the newsagent, the publisher.

The law, by the way, does in fact protect people who are not printers or authors and who have only taken a subordinate part, the most common examples being those who sell newspapers. A newsvendor will not be liable if he did not know the book or paper contained the libel, or that the book or paper was of such a kind that it was likely to contain a libel, and he was not negligent in not knowing. The newsagent would have to prove these things to escape liability. With a newspaper a good deal depends on its reputation. The law realises that there must be a commonsense approach to the problem of what the newsvendor can reasonably be expected to know. As far back as 1885 this was laid down in a case when Mr. Emmens sued Mr. Pottle for publishing a libel. Mr. Pottle was a newsvendor who sold a newspaper containing a libel. The jury came to the conclusion that Mr. Pottle did not know that the newspaper contained a libel, that he was not negligent in not knowing, and that Mr. Pottle did not know or ought not to have known that the newspaper concerned was of such a kind that it was likely to print libels. The Court of Appeal held that Mr. Pottle was an innocent disseminator and so Mr. Emmens lost his case.

More than one person can be involved in publishing a libel. The B.B.C. could be held liable as joint publishers of a libel on radio or television. In a newspaper, the newsvendor, proprietor, publisher, editor, and printer may all be jointly and severally responsible. If you have been libelled you can sue one or all the people you claim have defamed you.

The law, too, recognises the special relationship of husband and wife. In law for many purposes they are regarded as one person. So if you tell your husband or your wife something defamatory about someone else you cannot be sued. But this does not stop you suing if someone says something defamatory to you about your spouse.

What about publication outside this country? Generally speaking, you can bring an action based on publication abroad if the law of that country recognises it as a wrongful act. The act complained of must be wrongful both by the law of this country and by the law of the country where it was committed. Remember, too, that publications you send abroad should be lawful in the countries to which they are sent.

Identity—Innocent Libel—Reference to the Plaintiff

If you are going to succeed in your action for defamation you must prove several things. Firstly, that the defendant was responsible for publishing the words you complain of; next that those words are defamatory—that is, they tend to lower your reputation in the opinion of right-thinking people; and, most important, that you identify yourself as the person libelled.

Does your name actually have to appear in the statement complained of? No. The test in every case is—would the words be understood by reasonable people to refer to you? The defendant can use blanks, asterisks, initials, or fancy names or descriptions. It does not matter so long as they are such as reasonably in the circumstance would lead people acquainted with you to believe that you were the person referred to. It is not necessary for the reader to know all the facts. You must be understood to be the person defamed. If someone writes that all news broadcasters were dishonest no particular news broadcaster could sue unless there was something to identify the particular individual.

The intention to refer to you is immaterial. It does not matter whether the libeller did not intend to refer to you or did not even know of your existence. Section 4 of the Defamation Act, 1952, has a special provision dealing with this which we shall consider later on.

This is one of the most serious of all legal points concerning journalists. What if you did not know that a man you name even exists—in other words, so that you could not conceivably have intended to refer to him? The law was laid down very clearly in the case of *Hulton* v. *Jones* (1909), when the question was put: "Would the words complained of be understood by reasonable people who knew the plaintiff to refer to him? If so, they are published of and concerning the plaintiff no matter what the intention of the defendant may have been." This case is so important that we shall deal with it in some detail. A very readable account is given in *Hatred, Ridicule or Contempt*—a book of libel cases by Joseph Dean published by Constable, 1953. The following is a précis.

Hulton v. *Jones* and Other Cases

Artemus Jones was at one time a sub-editor of the *Sunday Chronicle* and subsequently joined the *Daily Telegraph*, writing chiefly from the Press Gallery. In 1901 he was called to the Bar.

In 1908 the *Sunday Chronicle* published a feature article headed "Motor Mad Dieppe" by a Mr. Dawbarn.

> Upon the terrace marches the world, attracted by the motor races— a world immensely pleased with itself and minded to draw a wealth of inspiration, and incidentally of golden cocktails, from any scheme to speed the passing hour. Whist! There is Artemus Jones with a woman who is not his wife, who must be, you know—the other thing! whispers a fair neighbour of mine excitedly into her bosom friend's ear. Really is it not surprising how certain of our fellow countrymen behave when they come abroad. Who would suppose by his goings on that he was a church-warden at Peckham? No one, indeed, would assume that Jones in the atmosphere of London would take on so austere a job as the duties of churchwarden. Here in the atmosphere of Dieppe, on the French side of the Channel, he is the life and soul of the gay little band that haunts the casino and turns night into day, beside betraying a most unholy delight in the society of female butterflies.

Artemus Jones was in court at Chester Assizes when he read the article, as did his colleagues. There was comment. Subsequently, wherever he went on the circuit he met the same reaction. He instructed his solicitor to ask for an apology and damages. The *Sunday Chronicle* denied that the article referred to him—said they would put in a disclaim, which they did without first of all showing it to Artemus Jones or his solicitor. This is what the disclaim said:

> It seems hardly necessary for us to state that the imaginary Mr. Artemus Jones referred to in our article was not Mr. Thomas Artemus Jones, barrister, but, as he has complained to us, we gladly publish this paragraph in order to remove any possible misunderstanding and to satisfy Mr. Thomas Artemus Jones we had no intention whatsoever of referring to him.

Mr. Artemus Jones was not satisfied and sued E. Hulton & Co., the printers, proprietors, and publishers of the *Sunday Chronicle*. The trial took place at Manchester Assizes. Artemus Jones gave evidence himself and five witnesses testified that they knew him or knew of him and believed he was the person mentioned in the article. The judge said that if readers of ordinary intelligence understood the article as referring to Artemus Jones, it did not matter if there was one or fifty of them. The editor of the *Sunday Chronicle* and the author of the article swore they had never

31

D

heard of Artemus Jones. The Peckham churchwarden was an imaginary character. In his summing up the judge said that if people chose to publish articles of this kind, they did so at their own risk. The writer's actual intentions were irrelevant. Would the ordinary reader think that the Peckham churchwarden was imaginary or a real person called Artemus Jones? He won his case and was awarded £1750 damages.

Hulton appealed and the fundamental nature of a libel was fully explored. There were two main points of view. Firstly, that a libel was the publication of a malicious untruth by one man about another, and for this the law provided a remedy. But could you defame someone who you believe exists only in your imagination? For you are not writing about someone you know, and how can you have malice for someone you do not know exists?

Secondly, every man is presumed at law to intend the natural consequences of his acts. If you write in such a way that the natural consequence is to lead people to believe you were referring to someone they knew, it does not matter if you have never ever heard of him. He has suffered from an attack by your writing, why should you not pay? Malice was not essential. Hulton went to the Court of Appeal and to the House of Lords. Both courts rejected the appeal. Artemus Jones got his damages and so it was laid down that it was immaterial that the defendant did not know of the plaintiff. The test was—would reasonable people believe the words referred to the man they knew?

The consequences of the case were far-reaching. Lord Chief Justice Goddard said it added a terror to authorship. You will probably have noticed at the beginning of a film or a book an announcement that all the characters are fictitious and that any resemblance to any living person is coincidental. Writers and publishers became very much alive to the dangers of the situation and the disclaim notice was one of the first results of the *Jones* v. *Hulton* case.

The effects on Fleet Street were severe. Year after year cases were brought against newspapers for libelling persons they never knew existed and therefore could not have intended to refer to. A typical example took place in 1928. The *Cassidy Case* cost the

Daily Mirror £500 damages and costs for publishing in a gossip column the photographs of a man and a woman and underneath the words: "Mr. M. Corrigan, the racehorse owner, and Miss X whose engagement has been announced." This was correct. The press photographer had been asked by Corrigan to take the photographs when they were at Hurst Park racecourse. He gave the girl's name and address and permission for the engagement to be reported. Corrigan's real name was Cassidy. He was a married man. The real Mrs. Cassidy sued the *Daily Mirror*.

What do you think was the libel she complained of? The innuendo meant in her view that she was dissolute, an immoral woman, who had imposed on her friends and acquaintances by pretending to be a respectable married woman when in fact she was living in open adultery with her husband. They had separated, but he still came to see her occasionally. She won.

Another case occurred in 1939 when Harold Newstead, a barber from Camberwell, sued the *London Express Newspaper* because they published an article about the trial of Harold Newstead, a Camberwell man, for bigamy.

> Why do people commit Bigamy?
> Harold Newstead, 30 year old Camberwell man, who was jailed for nine months, liked having two wives at once. Married legally for the second time in 1932, his legal wife is pictured above right, he unlawfully married nineteen year old . . . (left above). He said "I kept them both until the police interfered".

The account of the trial was correct, but the fantastic thing here is that the report concerned another Harold Newstead, a barman from Camberwell. Newstead won his case although he only got nominal damages. Sir Wilfred Greene, then Master of the Rolls, said: "If there is a risk of coincidence it ought, I think, to be borne not by the innocent party to whom the words were held to refer but by the party who puts them in circulation."

The rules then laid down were harsh, but their effects have to some extent been mitigated by the Defamation Act, 1952, which is set out in full at the end of this book. Section 4 of the Act deals specifically with unintentional libel and the ways in which amends can be made. These will be dealt with later.

Libel on a Group

Often articles are written about a group of people. If someone wrote all journalists are dishonest no particular writer could sue him unless there was something to point to that particular individual. But have a care. This does not give you the freedom to write what you will about a body of people. If the group is capable of being clearly defined they may be able to sue. Examples are all the directors of a particular company, or the clergy attached to a particular church, or all members of a particular club. And remember that each and every member can issue a writ for defamation against you. In an 1895 case in Scotland a Mr. Macleod said that members of a presbytery should not have taken part in proceedings against their minister for intemperance because of their own excesses. It was held that each member of the presbytery could sue. (*Macphail* v. *Macleod* (1895)).

A young journalist may write an article with the heading "Either Jones or Smith is guilty"—and go on to reveal some scandal. If the attack is libellous he cannot put up the defence that he did not say which one was guilty. If you wrongly attack all members of a jury in a case, all can sue.

Repetition and Republication

The general principle is that if someone knowingly publishes a libel about you he will be held responsible—whether the libel originated with him or not. It will be no defence for him to plead that he got the libel from someone else and, indeed, said so at the time. The fact that one person publishes a libel about you does not entitle someone else to do the same thing. Mr. Justice Best summed it up when he said: "Wrong is not to be justified or even excused by wrong." Here is an example. In 1854 Mr. Ainslie published a pamphlet in which he reprinted extracts from a letter written by someone else libelling Mr. Tidman. Mr. Ainslie honestly believed the statements in the letter to be true, but it was held he had no defence to an action for republication. Journalists must be very careful about this. The fact that a libel has been

34

published in another newspaper is no defence if you republish it. The only thing that indicating the source of the article will do to help you is that it may mitigate any damages awarded against you. The same rules apply to slander.

What if, at the time you repeat the libel, you say you doubt whether it is true? Here you may think you have a good defence. But you would be wrong. It will make no difference to your liability. No one's reputation would be safe if just by saying you did not believe a rumour made you immune from proceedings by the person you defame.

What happens if you libel someone in an article and it is then republished? Are you liable for the repetition? The answer is no. You are not responsible for unauthorised republications for they are not the reasonable consequence of your original publication. Of course, you would be liable if you authorised the repetition, or where republication was a natural result of what you did or where the person to whom you published the original libel was under some special duty to pass the statement on.

A young reporter was told by a man a startling story attacking a prominent local man's reputation, saying it would make good copy for the paper. The story was printed and the man was held liable for he had authorised the republication. The same position arises where a contributor writes an article which turns out to be defamatory. The author is liable for the damage caused by publication. This has been settled law for a long time. As far back as 1890 it was held that Mr. Moiguard, who printed a libel in one edition of his paper, was liable for republication in other editions in other countries, for he knew quite well that the libel would be repeated, and the man libelled—Mr. Whitney—won his case.

Are there any defences to this kind of claim? Yes. If they can prove they were innocent disseminators, i.e. they can prove that they did not know and could not reasonably be expected to know what they were circulating was defamatory, they will have a good defence. It has been said that a person who buys a book is not bound to read it at his peril before he lends it to a friend.

CHAPTER 6

What do the Words Mean?—Prove it!

THE words complained of must be given their ordinary meaning—which is the meaning in which reasonable men of ordinary intelligence with the ordinary man's general knowledge and experience of worldly affairs would be likely to understand them. This was laid down by Chief Justice Lord Mansfield as long ago as 1777.

We have already seen in the case brought by the Capital and Counties Bank against Mr. Henty that where the words are said to have an innuendo or secondary meaning, the manner, occasion, persons concerned, and all the circumstances affecting their meaning in the particular case must be considered. If someone complains that what you have written has another meaning which is defamatory it is up to him to prove it. What you yourself intended to mean is immaterial in deciding whether the words are libellous, and the words must be construed as a whole, in context. For example, if you accuse someone of libelling you in a newspaper, you are entitled to have taken into account not only the offending words but the paragraph, the whole article, and the heading.

When a case comes to court the first question to be decided is whether the words are capable of a defamatory meaning. This is a matter for the judge. Whether the words complained of are defamatory or not is a question of fact for the jury.

Liberace v. Daily Mirror

A case dealing with the construction of words was that brought by Liberace against the *Daily Mirror* in 1959. The *Mirror* published an article in which Liberace was described as "The Summit of Sex—the pinnacle of masculine, feminine and neuter. Everything that He, She, or It can ever want". And, "This deadly, winking, sniggering, snuggling, chromium-plated, scent-impregnated, luminous, quivering, giggling, fruit-flavoured, mincing, ice-covered heap of mother love". The Court was not asked to consider any innuendo as to the meaning of the words complained of. Mr. Justice Salmon asked the jury to decide whether the words (with the exception of fruit-flavoured) connoted homosexuality. The jury said they did and Liberace won. The judge, however, in his judgment said that he had come to the conclusion that the words were just capable of the meaning the jury had found, although he was by no means certain he would have come to the same conclusion of fact.

In *Lewis* v. *Daily Telegraph* (1964), Lord Reid said: "Here there would be nothing libellous in saying that an inquiry into the company's affairs was proceeding: the inquiry might be by a statistician or other expert. The sting is in inferences drawn from the fact that it is the fraud squad which is making the inquiry."

Intended Meaning Immaterial

The intended meaning is immaterial. The question is, not what the writer intended, but what reasonable readers thought was intended. Liability for libel does not depend on the intention of the defamer but on the fact of the defamation. If someone attacks you in ordinary defamatory language, all you have to prove is publication.

If the words complained of on the face of it do not appear to be defamatory, an innuendo or secondary meaning must be pleaded, and in court you must prove not only publication but also that there were facts known to the persons to whom the words or matter were published which might reasonably lead them to understand the words in the attacking way alleged in the innuendo or secondary or hidden meaning. Here is an example of innuendo.

Frank Hough was a popular boxer. The *Daily Express* published an article about him which read: "Frank Hough's curly-headed wife sees every fight. 'I should be more in suspense at home', she says. 'I always get nervous when he gets in the ring, although I know he won't get hurt. Nothing puts him off his food. He always gets a cooked meal at night, however late it is when he gets in.' " The curly-headed lady was not Mr. Hough's wife and the real Mrs. Hough sued. She produced two witnesses. They said they knew Mrs. Hough was the real wife of Frank because they had been at the wedding. There was no suggestion that they had been misled by the article into thinking Mrs. Hough had been living and bearing children in sin. They were very angry about the other so-called Mrs. Hough. In 1940 the Court of Appeal held that it was true that in the eyes of these two witnesses the article cast no imputation on their friend, but others might read it differently. It was no more essential for anyone to have understood the libel for what it was than it was necessary for anyone to have believed in it. The jury awarded Mrs. Hough 50 guineas damages.

Cases on Meanings

Let us now consider a few more cases where the court had to consider whether the words complained of were defamatory.

In 1962 the *Sunday Pictorial* published a report in which they said that a Mr. Bower had been convicted of attempted murder and sentenced to life imprisonment. The paper falsely published that he had been sent to Parkhurst and had had a complete mental breakdown. The jury found that the words complained of were defamatory in their natural meaning and that the statement that he had been sent to Parkhurst was defamatory in the sense that the words meant that he had earlier convictions. Damages of £6500 were awarded for the first libel and £750 for the second. (*The Times*, 7 July; *Current Law* 1743.)

In *Wait* v. *Associated Newspapers Ltd.* the plaintiffs, directors of a football club which was losing money and to which they had all donated generously, put forward a plan for summer football. The defendants, in their newspaper, commented on the plan as being selfish and sounded "a note of caution to the foolish men who want to change our habits to try to grab a bit more money".

In the plaintiff's libel action they claimed that the words meant that they were interested in football primarily for the money and were urging their plan for purely selfish and mercenary reasons. Mr. Justice Paull, on the verdict of a jury, held that there should be a judgment for each of the plaintiffs for £250. (*The Times*, 18 May 1963; *Current Law* 1999.)

Here is a case where the alleged defamatory meaning could only be understood by experts. The defendant, the B.B.C., was the publisher and author of an article which erroneously ascribed to the plaintiff, Mr. Mollo, an expert on contract bridge, the advocacy of a bid at bridge which was said to be insupportable. In the plaintiff's libel action, no innuendo was pleaded. McNair J. dismissing the action, held that the words would not be regarded by ordinary people as disparaging the plaintiff's character, although they might damage his reputation in the minds of those with special knowledge of modern bridge practice. (*The Times*, 2 February 1963; *Current Law* 2003.)

In 1963 Clitherow, the national organiser for the League against Cruel Sports, alleged to representatives of the national press that Arthur had thrashed his horse at Badminton trials with criminal severity. His comments were printed. Clitherow, with certain reservations, admitted publication and apologised to Arthur who was awarded £7500 damages and costs. (*The Times*, 29 June 1963; *Current Law* 2000.)

Television Broadcast

Associated Rediffusion made a television broadcast relating to prostitution in Stepney which included a picture of Mr. Ahmed's club and cafe. Ahmed sued for libel. The jury held that the broadcast did not mean that Ahmed was knowingly providing facilities for indulgence in prostitution, but that the premises were in fact frequented by persons seeking and providing indulgence in prostitution and that neither meaning was defamatory to Ahmed and both were in any event true. The T.V. company won. (*The Times*, 15 May 1963; *Current Law* 2014.)

CHAPTER 7

Defences

You have already seen something of the various types of actions for defamation which can be brought. Now we will consider in some depth the defences which can be pleaded. It is most important that you understand these clearly, for paradoxically, if you know the defences you will probably be a better journalist whether of the Press, radio, or T.V. and do your work in such a way that you will keep out of trouble. Knowledge of the defences are some of the main keys to safe and effective writing.

Seventeen Possible Defences in Actions of Defamation

The following is probably the best and most comprehensive list of defences that are possible in actions of defamation. It is based on *Halsbury's Laws of England*, 3rd edn., vol. 24, p. 10.

1. You never published any of the words complained of.
2. The words complained of did not refer to the plaintiff.
3. The words complained of did not bear any defamatory meaning.
4. The words complained of were true in substance and in fact. (Justification.)
5. The words complained of were published on an occasion of absolute privilege. (Absolute privilege.)

6. The words complained of were published *bona fide* (in good faith) and without malice towards the plaintiff on an occasion of qualified privilege. (Qualified privilege.)

7. The words complained of were fair and *bona fide* comment without malice towards the plaintiff on facts truly stated which were a matter of public interest. (Fair comment.)

8. Offer of amends has been made with a defence of unintentional defamation.

9. In the case of libel in a newspaper or other periodical publication, apology and payment into court.

10. The publication of the words complained of was with the consent and by the authority of the plaintiff.

11. Accord and satisfaction. (Agreement to forego claim.)

12. Written release from liability.

13. Lapse of time—the Statute of Limitation.

14. *Res judicata* (the matter has already been dealt with by the court).

15. The publication was made abroad and is justifiable in the country of publication.

16. In actions of slander (i) the words complained of were mere words of heat or vulgar abuse; (ii) that the words complained of were not actionable without proof of special damage and that no special damage is alleged, or that the special damage alleged is too remote in law; (iii) the words complained of were not calculated to disparage the plaintiff in any office, profession, calling, trade, or business held or carried on by him at any material time.

17. Death of the party concerned.

If you are unfortunate enough to have a libel claim made against you, it is essential that all the facts be most carefully examined to see whether any of the defences set out above are available to you.

We shall now deal with some of the more important ones in detail. They are: justification; fair comment; absolute privilege; and qualified privilege.

Justification

This means that the statement was true in substance and in fact. This can be a risky defence because if you lose you have aggravated the matter. It does not succeed very often. Every relevant fact has to be strictly proved and this is not an easy thing to do when some time has elapsed since publication; hence the necessity of making and keeping for a reasonable time careful notes. Saying a woman is a thief and has stolen £20 cannot be justified by proving that she stole a hen. Nor is stealing a watch the same thing as stealing a clock. The whole slander has to be answered.

If you write of a man that you believe he has committed murder you cannot justify publication by proving that you did believe it. You can only justify it by proving the fact of the murder. In 1940 the English and Scottish Co-operative Properties Mortgage and Investment Society prepared their annual accounts. Their auditor advised them to include an item on the profit side. The official auditor did not agree. In order to resolve the dispute and with no intention of imputing any improper motives to the Society, the Registrar of Friendly Societies issued a summons for wrongly making a false "Return of Profits". Odhams Press reported the matter under the heading "False Profit Return Charge against Society" and subsequently pleaded justification as a defence to libel proceedings. The Court of Appeal held that the word "false" was ambiguous and might mean fraudulent or it might mean incorrect. The jury had come to the right decision and the defence failed. Owing to the difficulties which so often arose in pleading the defence successfully, the matter is specially dealt with by section 5 of the Defamation Act, 1952.

This laid down that if you are sued for a libel in respect of words containing two or more distinct charges against the person you attacked, your defence of justification shall not fail by reason only that you cannot prove the truth of every charge you made. But there is a proviso. What you can not prove must not materially injure the plaintiff's reputation having regard to the remaining charges you made against him. If you write an article which contains statements of fact and of opinion, you must be prepared to prove the facts true and the statements correct. The Commercial

Publishing Company in 1907 published a statement that a Mr. Smith had been arrested on a criminal charge and added a headline and comments which said in effect that the charge was true. They pleaded justification, but the court held it was not enough to prove the arrest on the published charges—the comment which imputed that the charge was true or assumed the guilt of Mr. Smith had to be justified as well. A journalist's reputation is often in the hands of the sub-editor. Headlines are of vital importance and the heading is just as material and important as the text. For an editor to write a heading "How Doctor Smith treats his patients" when the paragraph refers to one case only, even if the case itself was accurately reported—the headline implying that Dr. Smith generally treated his patients badly, cannot be justified.

Substantial justification is sufficient. You do not have to prove the truth of every word of the libel—only as much as meets the sting of the charge. Slight inaccuracies of detail will not prevent the success of the defence, for example in writing that a man had been sentenced to a fine of £1 with the alternative of three weeks imprisonment, whereas in fact the alternative was fourteen days. A material inaccuracy means the defence will fail. If you write that Mr. Weaver has committed various acts of cruelty by beating a horse, including knocking out an eye, proof of all the acts of cruelty except knocking out the eye will not be sufficient. Why? Because your statement that he knocked the horse's eye out imputes a much greater degree of cruelty than the accusation of beating. Here are two more cases dealing with justification.

A man serving a sentence of preventive detention claimed damages for an article in the *People* which, he alleged, meant that he had committed a murder for which he had been tried and acquitted in 1944. The article had been written by prosecuting counsel in the case. The jury found that it had the meaning contended but that it was true. The *People* won the case. [*Loughams* v. *Odhams Press* (1963). *The Times*, 14 February; *Current Law* 2007.]

In a case decided in 1963, £3500 damages were awarded to a man who was a vice-president of a football supporters' club for an attack which alleged that he had been "posing as an official of the club or of the supporters club" and to have been causing some nuisance by seeking admission to matches on this pretext. A plea of justification failed. (*Vaughan* v. *Palmer* (1963); *Current Law* 2008.)

Fair Comment

Fair comment is a very important defence and probably the one most often pleaded in the courts. It is a defence to an action for libel that the words complained of are fair comment on a matter of public interest. This has both scope and limitations, and the implications should be clearly understood. Let us first examine the difference between justification and fair comment. In justification you rely on the truth of what you have written, thus negativing a claim made by the person you have attacked to a reputation he does not deserve. In fair comment you rely upon the honesty of your statement of opinion. It may not matter whether in an objective sense what you have written is true or not but the facts must be true for the comment to be fair. *Remember that fair comment can only be used as a defence where the matter which is commented on is a matter of public interest.*

> A newspaper has the right, and no greater or higher right to make comment upon a public officer or person occupying a public situation than an ordinary citizen would have; [and again] To whatever lengths the subject in general may go, so also may the journalist, but apart from statute law, his privilege is no other and no higher. The range of his assertions, his criticisms, or his comments, is as wide as, and no wider than, that of every other subject. No privilege attaches to his position.

So said Lord Shaw in the case of *Arnold* v. *King-Emperor* (1914). Lord Justice Scott wrote in 1943: "The right of fair comment is one of the fundamental rights of free speech and writing which are so dear to the British nation, and it is of vital importance to the rule of law on which we depend for our personal freedom." (*Lyon* v. *Daily Telegraph* (1943), which is reported more fully later on.)

Fact and Comment

Let us now have a look at the meaning of fair comment and the meaning of public interest. A comment is a statement of opinion on facts. If you write that what John Smith has done is disgraceful, that is a comment. If you write that John Smith did a disgraceful act you are maybe stating a fact, not giving an opinion. It is one thing to comment upon or criticise, even with severity, the acknowledged or proved acts of a public man, and quite another to assert that he has been guilty of particular acts of misconduct. If you make statements of fact and are sued it is up to you to prove the facts to be true.

The same rules apply to the criticism of music, books, plays, films, and television programmes. If an author writes a play or a book, or a composer a musical work, he is submitting that work to the public and so inviting comment. Any words written must be read in their context and any allegation must be recognisable as comment not fact. A comment cannot be fair if it is distorted by malice. In 1906 a malicious reviewer wrote a criticism of a biography by a Mr. Thomas. He headed the paragraph, "Mangled Remains" and cast aspersions on Mr. Thomas's literary ability. He also made allegations of fact which were untrue. It was found that he had personal spite against Mr. Thomas. The Court of Appeal held that it was proper to take malice into account and since the jury had found the review was distorted by malice the defendant could not rely upon fair comment. [*Thomas* v. *Bradbury Agnew* & *Co.* (1904-7).]

Another important case decided that the defence of fair comment may succeed where the facts which form the basis of the comment are not stated by the commentator provided that the nature of the facts can be reasonably inferred from the comment itself. This is the case of *Kemsley* v. *Foot* (1952). What happened?

Mr. Foot published an attack headed "Lower than Kemsley" on a newspaper with which Lord Kemsley was not connected. He sued for libel alleging as innuendo that the effect of Mr. Foot's statement was that the newspapers he owned were of a low character. The defence was fair comment. The Court decided that having regard to all the circumstances, the matter under comment

45

could reasonably be inferred from the heading. It was a newspaper that was attacked and as it was a matter of common knowledge that Lord Kemsley also owned newspapers, it was sufficiently clear that the standard of those newspapers was under attack.

In 1862 Mr. Pickburn published in his newspaper a report of a medical officer of health which asserted that Mr. Popham, a local chemist and druggist, had been issuing false medical certificates and suggested that he should be prosecuted for forgery. It was decided that the report could not be held to be fair comment. Do you agree? If so why?

It was argued that this comment might be justified as being in the public interest. But this is not a comment—it is a statement of fact. *Moral*—never mix up your comments with the facts upon which they are based. One useful tip is always to set out your facts first. Only after you have done this should you go on to comment. The whole should be printed in such a way that the reader can easily see what is fact and what is comment or criticism and so be in a much better position to judge the value of the latter.

There is no complete definition of fair comment. You will probably have realised very quickly that each case has to be considered individually and it is not easy to draw from the many actions which have been fought the fundamental principles which are an essential part of the law if it is to have any certainty.

However, there are three conditions which should be fulfilled. Learn these and you will have your own do it yourself test kit. They are (1) that subject to section 6 of the Defamation Act, 1952, the comment was based on facts set out truthfully; (2) there must be no suggestion that the creator of the work criticised had dishonourable or corrupt motives, unless of course such imputations were warranted by the facts; and, finally, (3) it must be the honest expression of the writer's real opinion.

The Defamation Act, 1952, section 6, provides that if you are sued for libel over something which you have published consisting partly of fact and partly of opinion, your defence of fair comment need not fail simply because you do not prove the truth of every allegation you have made, provided that your expression of opinion is fair comment on what you do prove. Fair comment is a defence to comment only. You will not succeed with your defence unless you prove that the facts upon which the comment was made are *substantially* true. It is a question of relative importance.

You must not invent facts or take lies from others and comment upon them as though they were true. One of the leading cases on this was decided in 1886 when a newspaper editor (Shepstone) published serious allegations about Davis, the Resident Commissioner of Zululand. It said that not only had he himself violently assaulted a Zulu chief, but had ordered his native police officers to attack others. Assuming these statements to be true they strongly commented upon his conduct. The stories were quite untrue. He was awarded £500 damages.

Newspaper Comments

What about newspaper comments? You can comment on the evidence given at a trial and the conduct of a magistrate in dismissing a charge without hearing the whole of the evidence. But you must be fair and give all the relevant facts. In S. Africa in 1926 White Ltd. published that Harris was convicted at assizes of a felony and commented adversely on the fact—but did not go on to say that the conviction was quashed on appeal. Harris won. The defence of fair comment by White failed.

There are certain exceptions to this rule; that the defence of fair comment will fail unless the facts are truly stated, the chief of which are where comment is made on facts stated in a privileged document such as a parliamentary paper or judicial proceedings. We shall deal with privilege in the next chapter.

If you impute corrupt or dishonourable motives you will make your comment unfair unless you can prove that the imputation is warranted by the facts. Spottiswoode attacked Campbell by saying in an article that Campbell was trying to increase the sales of a newspaper he owned by a false pretence that he was seeking to propagate the gospel among the Chinese. It was held in 1863 that this was outside the limits of fair comment. Criticism can cease to be criticism and become a defamatory libel. The true test is now laid down by section 6 of the Act of 1952.

47

E

Lyon v. *Daily Telegraph*

So far as honest comment is concerned lack of motive is essential. Exaggerated comment is not necessarily unfair. The statement must be within the domains of criticism. Consider the case of *Lyon* v. *Daily Telegraph* (1943). The Lyons were radio entertainers. The *Daily Telegraph* published a letter which read:

Flabby Amusement

To the Editor of the Daily Telegraph

SIR,

Early Sunday evening at Church time there was put on the air a costly broadcast which is an insult to British intelligence. The type of humour consists of a vulgar exchange of abuse. One comedian alludes to the other as a "louse" and his chief humorous contribution is to say at intervals, "I'm laughing me blooming 'ead off". The woman artist has a fair voice and sometimes sings a good song, but for the most part she indulges in vulgar wisecracks. We must be a nation of lunatics to permit such a waste of money for such a sordid show.

Yours sincerely,
A. WINSLOW

The Vicarage, Wallington Road, Winchester.

The address was fictitious and there appeared to be no such person as A. Winslow—such was no evidence of malice and the letter itself did not exceed the bounds of fair comment. It was on a matter of public interest. Accordingly the defence of fair comment could be pleaded by the *Daily Telegraph*.

The case raised an interesting point on the duties of editors and correspondents. Lord Justice Scott said that he could not accept that there was a general rule of law making it the duty of every newspaper to verify the signature and address of a writer before publishing a letter. On public grounds it would be desirable to do so, but to hold that the absence of such verification destroys the plea of fair comment would put too great a burden on newspapers. He went on to say that it would be a burden so deterrent in practice as would reduce the valuable contribution to public discussion of correspondence in the Press. If the comment were fair and the editor published it solely in the public interest, he could not see any hardship to the person criticised if the paper succeeded in the plea of fair comment.

He concluded with a forthright defence of the press in the following words:

> To impose such a burden—namely that the onus should be on the newspaper of proving that the writer of the letter honestly held the views expressed—is not desirable from the public point of view and is contrary to the existing law of fair comment. The more freedom in art criticism, music, literature, painting and drama, the better for the aesthetic welfare of the public.

You can see how difficult it is to define fair comment. Everyone has his own standards. We all have our own ideas of good taste and fair play and so in the end it always comes back to the ordinary man. Lord Esher when Master of the Rolls in 1887 summed it up in this way: "Would any fair man, however prejudiced he may be, however exaggerated or obstinate his views, have said what this criticism has said." (*Merivale* v. *Carson* (1887).)

Justice Bray said:

> When you come to a question of fair comment you ought to be extremely liberal, and in a matter of this kind—a matter relating to the administration of the licensing laws—you ought to be extremely liberal, because it is a matter on which men's minds are moved, in which people who do know entertain very, very strong opinions, and if they use strong language every allowance should be made in their favour . . .

Putting it in a nutshell he said: "Could a fair-minded man, holding a strong view, holding perhaps an obstinate view, holding perhaps a prejudiced view—could a fair-minded man have been capable of writing this?" Which you will observe is totally different from the question, "Do you agree with what he has said?"

Public Interest

Now let us turn to public interest. What are matters of public interest? They are many—dealing with anything which may fairly be said to invite comment or challenge public attention. Examples are the prospectus for a new company, advertisements, the conduct of hoteliers, people at public meetings, newspapers. Public figures on stage and screen ask for criticism and get it. If you go on the stage to exhibit yourself to the public or give or organise any kind of performance to which the public is invited, you may be freely criticised—remember the 1967 altercation between the Royal Court Theatre and Milton Shulman. You cannot sue over such criticism, however severe or incorrect it may be so long as it is the honest expression of the critic's real views and not mere abuse or invective under the guise of criticism. Any place to which the public have the right of access may be commented on. Books, films, television programmes, broadcasting, pictures, music, photographs, sculpture, architecture—all works of art—if placed before the public invite fair comment on a matter of public interest. Note—the private life of an author, artist, or journalist, is not necessarily a matter of public interest. But in this type of case there are certain conditions which must be complied with if the defence of fair comment is to succeed. They were laid down in the case of *McQuire* v. *Western Morning News* in 1903. Robert L. McEwen and P. S. C. Lewis, in the sixth edition of *Gatley on Libel and Slander*, the leading textbook on the subject, summarised them as follows:

> However severe, even in a sense unjust, the criticism may be, the critic will not be liable, provided
>
> (1) he does not misrepresent the contents of the book;
> (2) he does not go out of his way to attack the character of the author;
> (3) his criticisms may be fairly termed criticism; and
> (4) his criticism is the honest expression of his real opinion.
>
> The principle underlying the plea of fair comment is that a man who appeals to the public must be content to be judged by the public.

Local authorities and their administration are a fruitful source of topic for criticism as, indeed, is the management of public institutions—such as hospitals, prisons, railways, and the like.

The Administration of Justice

What about the law? The due administration of justice is undoubtedly a matter of public interest and therefore fair matter for public comment. But you must be very careful to wait until a trial is over before commenting upon it. Then the evidence, the conduct of trial, and verdict may be lawfully commented on. There are grave difficulties about commenting pending or during a trial, as it could prejudice a fair trial and result in your being accused of contempt of court.

Contempt of Court

The leading case on this was the one where the editor of the *Daily Mirror* was sent to prison for three months in 1949 while the paper was fined £10,000. The contempt arose over the "acid bath murder" when Haigh was accused of murdering a woman and dissolving her body in acid. While he was remanded in custody the *Daily Mirror* printed a comment which said that so far five murders had been attributed to him and the names of those concerned were given. The case came before the very forthright Lord Chief Justice Goddard who in the course of his judgment on 25 March 1949 pronounced:

> Not only does it describe him as a vampire but in addition to saying he has been charged with a particular murder of which he has been charged, these articles go on to say not merely that he is charged with other murders, but that he has committed others, and gives the names of persons whom they say he has murdered and a photograph of a person whom he is said to have murdered and described the way in which she was murdered.

He went on to say that was a scandalous and wicked case. The fact that Haigh subsequently confessed to nine acid-bath murders did not prevent the *Mirror* from being in contempt of court.

Other Matters of Public Interest

Other matters of public interest are church affairs, sermons— (it was comment on a sermon which was the first step leading to the abdication of Edward VIII), politics, state matters, the proceedings of the House of Commons, royal commissions, government reports, and the public conduct of any man who holds or seeks a public office or position of public trust. It is the judge who decides whether the matter commented on is one of public interest and whether there is any evidence of unfairness, and the jury whether it was fair comment.

Cases on Fair Comment

Here are some more cases on fair comment.

In the case of *Plummer* v. *Charman* (1962)—"To say of a man supporting a bill to make incitement to race hatred unlawful that he had come down on the side of 'coloured spivs and their vice dens' was held defamatory, not a statement of fact, nor fair comment." (*The Times*, 25 October; *Current Law* 1756.)

"Commander Boaks of Streatham whom I usually regard as nutty, sends me a plan for Tower Bridge that I, for once, think brilliant." Defamatory or not? What do you think? A jury decided they were not in the case of *Boaks* v. *South London Press* (1963). (*The Times*, 30 January; *Current Law* 2005.)

In *Saleh* v. *Odhams Press* (1963), Mr. Saleh, a Muslim carrying on business and living in England, complained of an article headed, "Girl Bride Cost Him £800" which appeared in an Odhams newspaper, alleging that it meant he treated his wife as a chattel. Odhams denied this meaning and pleaded justification and fair comment. In the course of the trial the reporter admitted that she did not recognise the published article as her "story". The editor did not give evidence, Saleh was awarded £750 damages. (*Current Law* 2006.)

In *Showerings* v. *Postgate* (1965), the defendant published an article referring to wines which could be obtained in public houses and said: "Beware particularly of a thing called Babycham which looks like champagne. If you read the label carefully you will find it is made of pears. But wines they mostly are, and tricks cannot stop the change." The plaintiffs, the manufacturers of Babycham, claimed damages for libel. The defendant pleaded fair comment and the reply alleged malice. Held on a verdict of the jury there should be judgment for the defendant. (*Current Law* 2259.)

52

CHAPTER 8

Absolute Privilege

SOMETIMES public interest makes it reasonable for the right to freedom of speech to overcome the right to private reputation. When this happens the law treats the circumstances as "privileged". There are two kinds of privilege—"absolute" and "qualified". Absolute privilege means that no action for defamation can be brought in respect of any statement however untrue, false, or wantonly and maliciously made. Qualified privilege can be rebutted by proof of malice in the sense of using the privilege for a purpose for which it was not intended or by proof of excessive publication. We will deal first with the more important matters covered by absolute privilege. No action lies for defamatory statements, however false or maliciously made:

(1) in the course of debates or proceedings in Parliament;

(2) in the course of state communications;

(3) in the course of judicial proceedings and proceedings before tribunals exercising functions similar to those of a court of justice;

(4) in reports published by order of either House of Parliament;

(5) in fair, accurate, and contemporaneous reports in a newspaper or by broadcasting of public proceedings before a court exercising judicial authority within the United Kingdom.

Parliamentary Proceedings

You cannot sue a member of either House of Parliament for defamatory words spoken in the course of any Parliamentary debate or proceeding. Note that the protection here only applies to words spoken *in the House*. If the M.P. causes his speech to be printed in a newspaper he will be liable in the ordinary way. Absolute privilege extends to statements contained in petitions addressed to Parliament and to evidence given before select committees.

State Communications

You cannot sue an army, navy, or air force officer for libelling you in any report he makes to his superior officer. Neither can you sue any officer of State for any defamatory statement he puts into an official report made by him to the head of his department. Why do you think this rule was made? In a famous case brought by Chatterton against the Secretary of State for India in 1895 it was said by the Master of the Rolls, Lord Esher, that the reason was that it would be injurious to the public interest that such an inquiry should be allowed because it would tend to take from an officer of State, his freedom of action in matters concerning the public. If he could be sued, malice could be alleged against him and his independence prejudiced. It is desirable that public servants should be able to write freely on matters affecting the public service without fear of an action. The Civil Service of this country has a very high reputation. In case you are wondering who are the officers of State, look them up in *Whitaker's Almanack*. Some of them are ministers of the Crown, senior officers of the armed forces, and high commissioners. The Lord Great Chamberlain is the sixth officer of State. The documents complained of cannot be produced in evidence, nor can any witness say what they contain, for the obvious reason that they may reveal state secrets. This gives rise to a certain amount of criticism at times. Journalists can be suspicious if, when following a good lead, they find that the head of a department of Government states that the production of a particular document by the department would be injurious to the public interest. The decision may be made by the man who may have the most to cover up and conceal. Absolute privilege is given to official publications such as the *London Gazette*.

Judicial Proceedings

Statements made in judicial proceedings may be privileged. When the Royal Aquarium and Summer and Winter Garden Society Ltd. sued Parkinson in 1892, Lord Justice Lopes said:

> No action of libel or slander lies, whether against judges, counsel, witnesses or parties for words written or spoken in the course of any proceeding before any court recognised by law, and this though the words written or spoken were written or spoken maliciously without any justification or excuse, and from personal ill will and anger against the person defamed. It is immaterial whether the proceedings take place in open court or in private, for if such actions were allowed persons performing their duty would be constantly in fear of actions.

This rule is founded on public policy and should be studied very carefully indeed. The protection incidentally is given not only to what is said at a trial but also to statements such as those made by solicitors preparing the necessary documents to bring the case to court. A judge is not privileged to be malicious but he is privileged from inquiry as to whether he is malicious. The High Court, county courts, quarter sessions, coroners' courts, magistrates' courts, courts martial, are all covered. A witness is protected by a rule established for the benefit of the public—if he were not he would only have to say: "I shall not give you any information at all." Advocates are privileged in what they do and say before the courts; the law allows them that privilege because it is for the advantage of the administration of justice that they should possess an unlimited freedom of speech. Here is an example of the rule applied to a court case.

In 1883 a man was charged before the magistrates with administering drugs to the inmates of Munster's house in order to facilitate the commission of a burglary at it. Munster was the prosecutor

55

and **Lamb** was the defending solicitor. There was some evidence, although of a very slight character, that a narcotic drug had been administered to the people in the house the evening before the burglary, and the accused had been there on that evening. During the proceedings before the court of petty sessions Lamb, acting as advocate for the accused, suggested that Munster might be keeping drugs at his house for immoral or criminal purposes. There was no evidence that he did so. It was held that Munster could not sue Lamb.

Not all bodies which sit to hear evidence are, however, protected by absolute privilege. For example, the following are not covered —the committee of a club, e.g. the Jockey Club. It has never been extended beyond courts of justice and tribunals acting in a manner similar to that in which the courts act.

Parliamentary Reports

By section 1 of the Parliamentary Papers Act, 1840, all reports, papers, votes, and proceedings published by the authority of Parliament are absolutely privileged. The Act protects the publication of *Hansard* but does not include the newspaper coverage of such reports. These may, however, come within the qualified privilege rules.

Newspaper Reports and Broadcasts

In certain cases absolute privilege is given by Act of Parliament. The Law of Libel Amendment Act, 1888, section 3, as amended by the Defamation Act, 1952, sections 8 and 9 (2), provides that:

> A fair and accurate report in any newspaper or by means of wireless telegraphy (as part of any programme or service provided by means of a broadcasting station within the United Kingdom) of proceedings publicly heard before any court exercising judicial authority within the United Kingdom, shall if published contemporaneously with such proceedings, be privileged: provided that nothing in this section shall authorise the publication of blasphemous or indecent matter.

The word newspaper is here defined by reference to the Newspaper Libel Registration Act, 1881, and it means "any newspaper containing public news published in England or Northern Ireland periodically at intervals not exceeding thirty-six days".

There seems to be little doubt that the words "shall be privileged" must be taken to mean absolutely privileged.

Contemporaneously

What does the word "contemporaneously" mean here? It means as nearly at the same time as the proceedings as is reasonably possible having regard to the opportunities for preparation of the report and the time of going to press or of making the broadcast. Sir Richard Webster, the then Attorney-General, said in the House of Commons that the object of inserting this clause was to prevent the raking up of old trials which might be highly disagreeable and injurious to individuals. If your daily newspaper delayed its report for ten or twelve days the report could clearly not be said to have been published contemporaneously with the proceedings.

So far as reports in newspapers or broadcasts are concerned, there are a large number of cases dealing with privilege under the common law. Journalists have a duty to the public. You cannot publish just what you like—it must be fair information on a matter of public interest.

The point to note here is that if you are reporting judicial proceedings your report must be factually accurate—especially as often in newsworthy cases evidence is given which in other circumstances would be highly defamatory. If therefore you file extraneous or incorrect reports you may render yourself virtually defenceless.

Absolute privilege does not cover headlines in a report. The headline must be factual. It must be supported by the facts to which it relates and must be reasonable having regard to the contents of the report. Nor does it cover information which you may have been able to obtain from a charge sheet if the charge sheet was not referred to in the court proceedings. An incorrect address reported may remove the protection and—most important—if you write your report in the form of an article you cannot plead successfully that you were absolutely privileged.

Under certain special circumstances trade unions and solicitors can plead privilege.

CHAPTER 9

Qualified Privilege

I. DUTY AND INTEREST

If you make libellous statements are you always liable? No. For we have seen that in certain circumstances you *are* completely protected; for example if you are a Member of Parliament speaking in the House of Commons. There are, however, a number of other occasions when you may be covered if it conforms to public policy and convenience and you have said what you believe to be the truth, making the statement honestly and without any improper or indirect motive. These occasions are of qualified privilege. How do they arise?

In many ways: such as when you make statements because you are under a duty to do so or because you are protecting your interests. You may also be covered when making reports of certain kinds.

The reason for this protection is for the common convenience and welfare of society and in these cases an absence of improper motive is essential. Chief Justice Coleridge said in 1881:

> It is better for the general good that individuals should occasionally suffer, than that freedom of communication between persons in certain relations should be in any way impeded. But the freedom of communication which it is desirous to protect is honest and kindly freedom. It is not expedient that liberty should be made the cloak of maliciousness.

Duty

What are the principles which are applied to statements made in the course of duty? The occasion is qualified if the statement is fairly made by a person in the discharge of some public or private duty, whether legal or moral, or in the conduct of his own affairs, in matters where his interest is concerned. If fairly warranted by any reasonable occasion or exigency, and honestly made, such communications are protected for the common convenience and welfare of society. An occasion is privileged if you make a statement, having a moral duty to the person you address to do so, and he has an interest in receiving it. Wide publication may sometimes be privileged as the following case shows.

Wide Publication

Mr. Adam was a Member of Parliament. He had been discharged from the army for incompetence. One day in 1917 he made a speech in the House of Commons which falsely charged General Scofell, who commanded the Brigade of which his late regiment of cavalry formed part, with sending confidential reports to headquarters on officers under his command containing wilful and deliberate mis-statements. General Scofell referred the matter to the Army Council. Ward, who was its secretary, wrote a letter to him vindicating him against the charge made by Adam and containing defamatory statements about the former cavalry officer. Ward sent a copy to the Press where it was widely publicised. Adam sued Ward for libel. Ward pleaded that the letter was published on a privileged occasion. The Court held that the occasion was indeed privileged and there was no evidence of malice on the part of either the Army Council or Ward. Having regard to the circumstances under which Adam's charge was made, the publication of the libel was not unreasonably wide. In the special circumstances of the case, the defamatory statements were strictly relevant to the vindication of General Scofell and the whole of the letter was protected. Giving judgment, Lord Atkinson said:

> A privileged occasion is, in reference to qualified privilege, an occasion where the person who makes a communication has an interest or a duty, legal, social or moral to make it to the person to whom it is made. And the person to whom it is made has a corresponding interest or duty to receive it. This reciprocity is essential.

Duty and interest are involved—and interest is used in its broadest sense.

Confidences

What about statements made in answer to confidential inquiries? If your former employer is asked for a reference by your proposed new one, he is not under any legal duty to give one and you can not sue him if he will not. It is, however, his moral and social duty to state all he knows either for or against you, and if he does so honestly and without malice towards you his answer will be privileged.

If your mate is sacked and the boss tells the rest of you why he has done it, such communication may be privileged. The fact that a statement was made voluntarily does not take away privilege and there is a duty to disclose information during criminal investigations. You may be involved in inquiries about credit. It was said that everyone will admit that in carrying on the business of banking confidential inquiries are necessary with regard to the character and credit of customers applying for advances of money. In general the answer to such inquiries will be privileged. But in many instances the paid-for communications of the Mercantile Protection Associations are not. Reports from inquiry agents are usually privileged even if their language may be exaggerated.

There are certain occasions when it is your moral duty to inform Jack of certain facts about Jill, even if he has not asked you anything about it. What if she was about to announce her engagement to him and you know she is already married?

There is a duty to make statements in aid of justice, but the facts should be given in good faith to the proper authorities. Statements made by police officers in the course of their inquiries into a suspected crime are privileged.

Complaints are sometimes made against public officials—but remember that on newspaper publication no privilege will attach if a charge is given out for publication in the newspapers in advance of its delivery to the proper authority for investigation.

In *Standen* v. *S. Essex Recorder* (1934), it was held that the publication of an anonymous letter in a local newspaper commenting on the conduct of a member of a local authority at a meeting of the authority was not privileged occasion. So handle any tip-off you may get of this kind with extreme caution.

Other cases where there is a duty to pass on information arise over candidates for public office, where there is a confidential or close family relationship, clergyman and parishioner, solicitor and client. The modern tendency is to enlarge rather than restrict the scope of moral duty in such cases. It becomes much more difficult to decide when you have a duty to give information to a stranger.

So much for cases where duty is involved. Let us now turn to communications in which you and the person you write to have a common interest.

Common Interest

A communication *bona fide* made on any subject matter in which the party communicating has an interest is privileged if made to a person having a corresponding interest or duty. Here are some examples: communications between intimate friends about their doctors or servants, masters at the same school about a drunken colleague, landlord and tenant about other tenants, part-owners of a ship about the master, the president of a college to the bursar about a student, a medical superintendent to a hospital board about staff, an elector to his fellow electors at a parish meeting about the candidates.

In 1897 the Rev. Garment preached in a way which was long remembered for he was sued as a result by Mr. Goslett. So came the case which laid down that a clergyman may be under a duty to rebuke sin, but it is no part of his duty to refer in the course of his semon to any particular member of his congregation, and if he does so, no privilege will attach to his words, although they were uttered *bona fide* in the honest desire to admonish the person referred to and to warn the rest of the congregation against offending in a like manner.

Qualified Privilege of Newspapers

Section 7 of the Defamation Act, 1952, now confers qualified privilege on fair and accurate reports in newspapers. The Act has two comprehensive schedules. The first deals with statements privileged without explanation or contradiction, such as parliamentary reports, and the second schedule covers statements privileged subject to explanation or contradiction, like reports of public meetings.

Great care has to be exercised in deciding what you can print with impunity. In the case of *Simpson* v. *Downs* (1867) certain members of a town council caused to be published in a local newspaper a letter in which they charged Simpson, who was the contractor for the building of the new gaol, with serious omissions and deviations from the contract. It was held that, although such a charge would have been privileged at a council meeting, it was not in a public newspaper. Why? Because the general public, unlike the members of the town council, had no corresponding interest in the matter.

The Right to Defend

However, it has long been settled in law that where the only possible or effectual mode of discharging your duty or protecting the interest which gives rise to the privilege is to insert a notice in a public newspaper, you and the paper will be privileged.

The publication of defamatory matter in a newspaper will be privileged where the matter published is of general public interest and it is the duty of the newspaper to communicate it to the general public. The *Adam* v. *Ward* case applied here.

However, it has been held that there is no privilege attached to a newspaper which published a letter from a shareholder in a gold-mining company attacking its management and accusing directors of corruption.

To plead qualified privilege successfully, a newspaper has to show that a duty to the public was necessary. The mere fact that it was published as a matter of public news or in the *bona fide* belief that it was in the public interest will not do.

63

F

Chapman in 1932 sued Lord Ellesmere. He had been warned off Newmarket Heath by the Jockey Club because his horse had been drugged. The decision was published in the racing calendar and *The Times*. It was held on appeal that neither publication was privileged and that racing was not a matter of public interest sufficient to create privilege for publication in *The Times!* It should be noted that this type of case now clearly falls within the scope of section 7 of the Defamation Act, 1952.

Statements made to protect your own interests may be privileged if they are fairly made by you in the conduct of your own affairs in matters where your own interest is concerned. Obviously you have a right to reply to demands or attacks being made upon you.

An interesting case arose in 1926 when the Argus Press Ltd. published a book review by Bowen-Rowlands. They quoted a story from the book about a well-known public man who was dead, but it was not very complimentary to his daughter. She wrote a letter to them saying that the story was "pure invention from beginning to end, it is absolutely false both as to matter and manner". The newspaper published her letter without comment. Bowen-Rowlands sued, alleging that he was accused of inventing the story and telling a deliberate lie which was a reflection on him as an author. Was it?

The Court of Appeal decided that the letter, even if it was defamatory of Bowen-Rowlands, was published on a privileged occasion, for the daughter had the right to contradict the story and the newspaper to publish, and there was no evidence of malice. The newspaper won.

Controversy is an important ingredient in the lifeblood of the press. If someone is attacked in a paper, he is entitled to defend himself and retaliate. If he defames in so doing, the occasion is on the face of it privileged. This privilege is not removed by people writing anonymously.

But there are some qualifications to the right of reply in the Press. If your character is attacked you should only reply in the Press if the attack was made on you in the Press or in public. You may not be able to plead qualified privilege if you bring a private quarrel out into the open.

Wright wrote a book which imputed hypocrisy and gross immorality to Gladstone who was dead. Gladstone's son wrote a letter to the secretary of Wright's club calling him a liar, coward, and a foul fellow. Mr. Justice Avory in 1927 ruled that the letter was written on a privileged occasion.

Statements made to obtain redress for a grievance made in good faith can be privileged, as can statements made in reply to questions put by the person libelled. The latter case can happen when someone asks why he got the sack. But irrelevant statements are not privileged. Stick closely to the material facts.

II. REPORTS

There are a number of sources of news which can be affected by the rules governing qualified privilege. Parliamentary proceedings are one of them. Proper reports of debates in either House of Parliament are privileged, but a judge once said that a garbled or partial report, or of detached parts of proceedings published with intent to injure individuals will be disentitled to protection. Also privileged are extracts from parliamentary reports and papers. Under various Acts of Parliament certain registers have to be kept, such as records of court judgments, information under the Companies Act. Fair and accurate copies or extracts from these are privileged. This is a very old right under the common law of the country.

What is the Common Law?

The Norman kings were the first to set up a system of royal law courts covering the whole of England. The methods and rules which these courts used were the same everywhere, and became known as the common law as distinct from the old local laws or customs which varied from place to place. Later on Parliament developed and more and more statutes were passed. The common law remained, although it came to be accepted that if the common law said one thing and an Act of Parliament another, the Act must be followed. To find the common law you must look in law books, especially in the law reports, which are the actual judgments of the courts in past cases. James Derriman has written an excellent book, *Discovering the Law*, 1962. It is well worth reading as a first book on the subject.

But publication in a newspaper or by broadcasting is dealt with now under section 7 of the Defamation Act, 1952. Remember that if you publish an extract from a public document you are responsible if you do not extract or copy it correctly, and it is no answer that you have been misled by a public official. Another group is judicial proceedings. Sir Gorell Barnes, in the case of *Furniss* v. *Cambridge News Ltd.* (1907), said: "The privilege given to reports of proceedings in courts is based upon this; that as everyone cannot be in court it is for the public benefit that they should be informed of what takes place substantially as if they were present". In view of the importance to journalists of the reporting of judicial proceedings we shall consider these in some detail.

Court Proceedings

Discussion often takes place about the value of reporting court proceedings. Some say that the newspaper accounts of criminal trials put ideas into the heads of irresponsible people who may imitate the crime, thus giving rise to "carbon copy" cases. Others hold the view that publicity can be instrumental in bringing forward vital witnesses. Mr. Justice Pearson, in *The Times*, 3 June 1960, said that the main reasons for privilege in the reporting of judicial proceedings were: that the courts were open to the public; the administration of justice was a matter of public concern; the education of the public on such matters; the desirability of fair and accurate reports rather than rumours; and balancing the advantages to the public of the reporting of judicial proceedings against the detriment to individuals of being incidentally defamed.

His comments about educating the public are significant. There is a legal presumption that every man is deemed to know the law and you cannot plead ignorance of the law as a defence. Accordingly, by reporting cases accurately and in a way that the man in the street can understand, the journalist can render a most useful service to the community. Not all proceedings can be reported, nor are all reports privileged; there are exceptions provided for by statute, and, of course, if you write one, no matter how fair and accurate it is, which is immoral or seditious, you will lose the protection of qualified privilege.

Judicial proceedings are those before a properly constituted judicial tribunal exercising its jurisdiction in open court. Nearly all court proceedings are covered, but you should be careful if you are dealing with reports of proceedings in foreign countries as the protection of privilege does not always apply. It did, however, apply in the case of *Webb* v. *Times Publishing Company Ltd.* (1960), which dealt with Hume and Setty.

The Hume and Setty Case

In 1950 an English court found Hume not guilty of murder but guilty of being an accessory after the fact to murder. He went to gaol. At the trial his then wife gave evidence that she had never in her life met Setty, the murdered man. Hume was released from prison in 1958 and the *Sunday Pictorial* published an article by him in which he referred to secret meetings between his wife and Setty. As a result, his wife, by now Mrs. Webb, brought an action against the *Sunday Pictorial* which was settled in May 1959 on the terms of a statement made in open court whereby the *Sunday Pictorial* undertook not to republish passages in the article complained of by Mrs. Webb and agreed to pay her damages. The statement was published in *The Times*. In 1959 Hume was wanted by the English police on charges of attempted murder of a bank clerk and armed robbery of a bank which were alleged to have been committed by him after his release from prison. Later in 1959 he was tried by a Swiss court at Winterthur for attempted murder and armed robbery alleged to have been committed in Switzerland. In the issue of *The Times* of 25 September 1959 the following report of the proceedings before the Swiss court was published:

> Hume admits killing Setty. Body dismembered and thrown from aircraft. Winterthur, Switzerland, September 24. Hume, who is on trial on a charge of murdering a Swiss taxi driver, told the court here today that he robbed the Midland Bank in Brentford, London and shot a clerk. He also admitted killing Setty, a car dealer, out of jealousy, sawing off his limbs and making them into parcels to be dropped from an aircraft. Asked if he was married and had a child Hume replied, "Yes, but it was not mine. The father was Setty."

The report was a contemporaneous report. His former wife sued for libel, alleging that the words of the report meant that she had committed adultery with Setty and had given perjured evidence at the trial of Hume in 1950. *The Times* claimed that qualified privilege attached to the report as a fair and accurate report of foreign judicial proceedings. On a preliminary issue whether (assuming the report to be fair and accurate) the report was protected by qualified privilege it was held: the report was protected by qualified privilege because the subject matter of the report was of legitimate and proper interest to the English public as being matter much connected with the administration of justice in England, and that the reference to the father of the child being Setty, of which Mrs. Webb mainly complained, was a matter germane to Hume's confession of having killed Setty as it explained the alleged motive of jealousy and so was not extraneous matter outside the protection of the qualified privilege. (*The English and Empire Digest*, vol. 32, p. 162.)

The Whole Truth

Usually proceedings take place in open court and you should note that privilege also extends to quasi-judicial tribunals such as the proceedings of the General Medical Council. Reports must, of course, be fair and accurate. In 1936 Mitchell sued Hirst Kidd and Rennie for publishing a report headed, "Stole Motor Car" and "Motor Car Theft". The reporter present at the magistrate's court did not hear the withdrawal of the charge of theft and this was found to have been due to inattention. It was held that the report was not fair and accurate. Mitchell won his case. But you may be excused slight inaccuracies as it has been held that a report in a daily newspaper is not to be judged by the same strict standard of accuracy as a report coming from the hand of a trained lawyer, but as we have seen in the *Mitchell Case* a substantial inaccuracy will deprive the publishers of the defence of privilege.

It is very difficult indeed where proceedings are lengthy for reporters to produce abridged reports which give the essence of the case. The excellent accounts of such proceedings which are printed daily by the press come mostly from skilled and dedicated men of the highest integrity, who go to endless trouble to ensure that their reports, however condensed, do not present a garbled or false version of the case. Indeed, if they were, the possible defence of privilege would be lost. The reports must be impartial. Whatever your own views may be as a reporter, they usually have no place in a factual report of a trial. Again, beware of adding anything, even if it be true, which was not given during the proceedings. A man pleaded guilty in 1925 to assaulting a police officer in the execution of his duty. In mitigation his counsel sought to excuse his violence saying it was due to resentment against another man about whom the lawyer then used very abusive language, but whose name he did not mention. A local reporter found out who the lawyer was talking about and his name was published in a report of the case. The Court held in this Canadian case, *Geary* v. *Alger* (1925), that the report was not fair and accurate.

Great care must, of course, be taken in reporting any judgment given by the court. Where a trial lasts for some time the privilege attaches to the reports of each days' proceedings. You should not, when the case is over, pick on one particular portion of the proceedings and report that if the effect is to make it unfair. Remember that both the heading and the report must be read together. The heading must be a fair index of the matter. Facts and comments should be clearly separated. Often the documents produced in all or part of the proceedings are of special interest to the reporter, but care should be taken in dealing with those which are not brought up in open court. Reports must not be published maliciously. In the case of *Morrison* v. *News of the World*, which is reported in *The Times*, 17 May 1929, an over-enthusiastic journalist wrote an account of a trial, but part of the report was a description not only of what he heard and saw in court but also of the plaintiff's house, the character of his friends, the crowd which gathered to see him, and much more. Mr. Justice Swift held the article could not be defended as a report of judicial proceedings.

Newspaper Defences

Section 7 of the Defamation Act, 1952, says that if you publish in a newspaper a report dealing with a matter set out in the schedule, you shall be privileged unless your publication is proved to be made with malice.

If you are sued for libel in respect of the publication of any such report as is mentioned in Part II of the Schedule to the Defamation Act, 1952, the provisions of section 7 (which I am now quoting) shall *not* be a defence for you if it is proved that you had been requested by the plaintiff to publish in the newspaper, in which the original publication was made, a reasonable letter or statement by way of explanation or contradiction, and you have refused or neglected to do so, or you have done so in a manner not adequate or not reasonable, having regard to all the circumstances [section 7 (11) and (12)]. So qualified privilege can depend on you being asked to make amends and doing so satisfactorily.

You cannot be protected by section 7 (3) for publishing anything prohibited by law or not of public concern or which is not for the public benefit.

Section 7 (4) says that nothing in this Act shall affect subsisting privileges. The Act goes on to define "newspaper" as follows: "any paper containing public news or observations thereon, or consisting wholly or mainly of advertisements, which is printed for sale and is published in the United Kingdom either periodically or in parts or numbers at intervals not exceeding thirty-six days" [section 7 (5)].

Broadcasting

There used to be considerable discussion as to the place of broadcasting in all this, and the question is now firmly resolved by section 9 which says that so far as section 3 of the Parliamentary Papers Act, 1840, is concerned, the reference to printing included a reference to broadcasting by means of wireless telegraphy. There follows a comprehensive section 9 (2) which provides that section 7 of the 1952 Act and section 3 of the 1888 Act as amended shall apply to broadcast reports of any station within the United Kingdom, and it shall have the effect, in relation to any such broadcasting: as if the words "in the newspaper in which" is to be read as "in the manner in which"—which is the lawyer's way of saying that for newspaper reports you can read broadcast reports.

What about the broadcasting stations? These are much in the news these days, particularly over the pirate and local stations. Here it means any station licensed by the Postmaster-General. We have already seen that Part I of the Schedule to the Defamation Act gives a list of seven types of statements which are privileged without explanation or contradiction. Part II deals with statements which are privileged subject to explanation or contradiction, for that is what qualified privilege can mean. I give a synopsis below, but you should read the full Act carefully. It is set out at the end of this book.

Associations

The eight items of the Schedule are concerned with associations. You may be protected if you make a fair and accurate report of the work of any of the following associations, its committees, or governing body thereof:

(a) associations formed in the United Kingdom for art, science, religion, or learning;

(b) associations formed in the United Kingdom for promoting or safeguarding the interests of any trade, business, industry, or profession;

71

(c) associations formed in the United Kingdom for promoting or safeguarding the interests of any game, sport, or past-time.

Meetings

Item 9 of the Schedule covers meetings. You may invoke privilege if you give a fair and accurate report of the proceedings at any *bona fide* and lawfully public meeting held in the United Kingdom for the furtherance or discussion of any matter of public concern, whether the admission to the meeting is general or restricted. The tenth item of the Schedule deals with special kinds of meetings, viz:

(a) local authorities;
(b) Justices of the peace acting otherwise than as a court;
(c) parliamentary, royal, or ministerial commissions, tribunals, committees, or inquiries;
(d) local inquiries;
(e) statutory tribunals, boards, or committees.

Of course, if the meeting is in private, privilege does not arise, for it is a condition that the above, for you to be protected, must not be meetings or sittings, admission to which is denied to representatives of newspapers and other members of the press.

Items 11 and 12 cover company meetings, and fair and accurate reports of matter issued for the information of the public by government departments, offices of state, local authorities, or chief officers of police.

There are many interesting cases on what the Act means. Would you think that a student meeting to commemorate a statesman not confined to the organising body is a public meeting? You would probably say yes, and you would be correct. Watch your step in reporting protest meetings. They can so easily become unlawful by obstructing the highway or be likely to lead to a breach of the peace, and if the meeting is not lawful, your privilege protection vanishes.

In addition to courts of law there are a number of tribunals and bodies exercising discipline and providing good copy for the papers. Local authorities have many meetings which are of considerable interest to the public. Have you as a journalist a right to be present? And if you are allowed in, are there any restrictions on what you can publish? We have seen that you can report a criminal or civil trial with impunity if you give contemporaneously a fair and accurate report of proceedings heard in public in court, for your writing will be privileged. That then is the position regarding the courts. But what of other meetings like those of local authorities? Here only qualified privilege is given. The right of the Press to attend meetings of local authorities is governed by the Public Bodies (Admissions to Meetings) Act, 1960. It enables the Press and other members of the public to be admitted to all meetings of the authority and its committees, but both can be temporarily excluded by resolution if the nature of the business makes it in the public interest to do so. To do so a special resolution must be passed so that exclusion of the Press can only take place whenever publicity would be prejudicial to the public interest by reason of the confidential nature of the business to be transacted, or for other special reason stated in the resolution and arising from the nature of that business or of the proceedings. Public notice must be given of each meeting and copies of the agenda supplied on request and payment of postage to any newspaper or news agency. The agenda need not include matters which are likely to be debated in private. An agenda of and a fair and accurate report of the proceedings of any local authority enjoys qualified privilege, provided that it is not a meeting, admission to which is denied to newspaper representatives and the public. Defamation Act, 1952, section 7 and Schedule, Public Bodies (Admission to Meetings) Act, 1960, sections 1 (5)–2 (1).

Fair and Accurate Reports

As to what is a fair and accurate report, whatever you write, however carefully or ably you write, everyone will have his or her own opinion as to whether what you wrote is fair and accurate. You can only do your honest best. People become so emotionally involved in matters with which they are concerned that it is very difficult for them to look back objectively on what was said or done. Listen to a man telling his friends what he said at a meeting, and if you were present you may be quite surprised at the version he gives. But this is human nature. We all like to think we are pretty good, and that we matter, and consequently what we say matters. This is where the cool detachment of the reporter is of supreme importance.

Anyway, whether your report is fair and accurate is a question of fact to be considered afresh in each individual case. But if you are challenged you will have to prove that it is. We have seen there is no need for the report to be accurate down to the last detail, although it helps if it is. A few slight inaccuracies will not deprive it of protection, but they must be slight. What about the things you left out? This is something which always upsets the man reported. And you must be prepared for this ever-recurring situation. The answer is that you are the reporter and you must make up your own mind as to what is important from a reporting point of view. The speaker cannot do this although he will often try to help you by press handouts, releases with embargoes, and advance texts of speeches. Incidentally, treat the latter with caution. So many speakers give you a splendid release and then go on to say something quite different. You must check the release against the actual speech delivered. What is the legal test on omissions? Where the omission would have made an appreciable difference in favour of the speaker reported, or have counteracted an objectionable statement in the report, you would probably be held at fault with your report and your possible defence of qualified privilege would be of no avail. Much is written piously by journalists of their view that what they do is of public concern and public benefit. And, indeed, so it is. But remember it does not always follow that because the public are interested in a matter it is for their benefit that such a report should be published. It is not enough to prove that the meeting, proceedings, and much of the speeches were all for the public benefit. You must prove that the publication of the actual words complained of was for the public benefit. This often places editors in positions of considerable difficulty. The rule is, however, quite clear and designed to prevent scurrilous attacks made with the object of publicity being given further circulation by newspapers, who would otherwise simply excuse themselves by pleading privilege.

CHAPTER 10

Other Defences

WE SHALL now deal with some of the other defences which may be available to you.

Apology

If you libel someone and then say you are sorry your regret is not a defence. It can, however, materially affect the amount of damages you may be called upon to pay. The person you have libelled is not bound to accept your apology but he cannot stop you bringing the offer forward in mitigation of damages. It is the offer which matters in this situation. You should, however, be careful not to rush in with an apology unless you are quite sure of all the facts. An apology could even result in the matter being aggravated.

Apology and Payment into Court

Before the passing of the Defamation Act, 1952, there was a special defence open to newspapers and periodicals under Lord Campbell's Libel Act of 1843. You could, if you had no better defence, plead an apology and pay a sum of money into court by way of amends. You would still have to prove that there was no malice or negligence in publication. This procedure is not used very often nowadays as it is highly technical and difficult.

Unintentional Defamation

You have learnt that if you libel someone you are liable and that it is no defence for you to plead that you did not intend to libel anyone and that you had been careful. This was very much the position up to 1952 but section 4 of the Defamation Act brought about a very important change.

This section deals with cases where the defamation is unintentional and protects you where the statements complained of were published by you innocently in relation to the plaintiff. First you must make an "offer of amends". This, as we shall see, does not mean an offer of money. If the offer is accepted no proceedings for defamation can be taken against you. The way in which the offer has to be made is clearly laid down. It has, incidentally, to be accompanied by an affidavit specifying the facts you rely on.

If the person attacked does not accept your offer, then if you are sued it can be a defence for you to prove that the words were published innocently and that the offer was made as soon as practicable and that the offer has not been withdrawn.

But what does "publish innocently" mean? It applies if the following conditions are satisfied:

(a) You did not intend to publish [the words] of and concerning the other person and
You did not know of circumstances by virtue of which they might be understood to refer to him; OR

(b) The words were not defamatory on the face of them, and you did not know of circumstances by virtue of which they might be understood to be defamatory of the complainant. [Section 5.]

Offer of Amends

Where the words are deemed to be published innocently you may make an offer of amends. You must make your offer specifically under section 4 of the Act and it must be accompanied by an affidavit setting out the facts you rely on, showing that the words in question were published by you innocently. No further evidence in defence under this section can be given other than

77

evidence of facts specified in the affidavit. The offer of amends means:

(a) In any case, to publish or join in the publication of a suitable correction of the words complained of, and a sufficient apology to the party aggrieved by those words;
(b) where copies of the libel have been distributed by or with your knowledge you will take reasonable steps to notify those concerned that a libel is alleged.

If your offer is accepted and is performed, no proceedings can be taken against you, as the publisher, by the person aggrieved.

Disputes over fulfilment are to be referred to the High Court, whose decision is final. If the offer is not accepted, then you may have a defence under the procedure outlined above if you prove that you published innocently and that the offer was made as soon as practicable after you were notified of the alleged libel and that the offer is still open.

Authorised Publication—Release

There is an old Latin maxim: *volenti non fit injuria*—a volunteer cannot sue if injured. How does this arise in libel? A criminal may agree with you to let you have his memoirs. He supplies all the information and material and in due course you publish them. On reflection he may prefer not to have authorised publication. He cannot sue you even if his reputation has undoubtedly suffered as a result of the articles, for the law will not uphold claims by people who authorised or consented to the acts of which they complain.

Statute of Limitation

Even if someone has got the right to sue you over a libel you have published they cannot let the matter rest indefinitely and then suddenly start proceedings many years after the incident. This rule applies to all kinds of actions as well as to libel, and it is governed chiefly by the Limitation Act, 1939. Actions which are actionable without proof of special damage such as for libel must be brought within six years from the date of publication. Actions where special damage has to be proved must be brought within six years of the date when the damage was sustained.

If, however, the person you have attacked is under a disability, e.g. an infant, or a convict, or of unsound mind, time does not start to run until he is free of the disability.

Res Judicata—Previous Court Action

Another defence you may have and which has to be considered very carefully by your legal adviser is whether the person attacked has already brought an action against you for the publication of the same words. Even although the words complained of are the same, yet if they appear in a different publication the person attacked has a fresh cause of action. The position of news collecting agencies is curious. They may be liable twice—once for passing on the libel, and again jointly with each paper that publishes it.

Death

Finally, if the person about whom you have published a libel dies, that will usually be the end of the matter. The reason for this is because the law regards this type of case as being a personal one to the persons concerned, and reputation in this sense means the esteem in which living people are held. But if you slander goods the right to sue can survive. Your own death may affect the position if you are being sued personally. It may not if your employers are being sued.

These then are the defences to an action for defamation.

Now let us consider who can sue.

CHAPTER 11

Who Can Sue?

Parties to an Action

Special rules govern actions involving ambassadors, foreign statesmen, convicts, foreign subjects, bankrupts, infants, lunatics, drunks, married women, representatives of dead people, corporations at home and abroad, firms, trade unions, organisations, societies, and masters and servants. We will deal here with the last example.

Employers

Your master is liable for defamatory words published by you with his authority or consent or if, in doing what is complained of, you were acting in the scope of your authority, i.e. in the course of an employment which is authorised.

"The proprietor of a newspaper is civilly liable for any libel it publishes, even though published while he was away without his knowledge and contrary to his orders." Why? The editor is his employee and it is within the scope of the editor's authority to send to the printers anything he thinks ought to be published. His liability is not upon the ground of his being the publisher, but because he is responsible for the acts of the actual publisher. Similarly, the printer and publisher are his agents to print and publish whatever matter the editor sends them. (*Gatley on Libel and Slander*, 6th edn., p. 402.)

Lord Tenterden summed it up as far back as 1829 in the case of *R.* v. *Gutch* when he said:

> Surely a person who derives profit from and who furnishes means for carrying on the concern, and entrusts the conduct of the publication to one whom he selects, and in whom he confides, may be said to cause to be published what actually appears, and ought to be answerable although you cannot show that he was individually concerned in the particular publication.

If I write a libellous letter and send it to your editor I shall be liable for the resulting damage. If I give you libellous information, knowing you intend to write an article on it, I shall be liable even though you may have asked me for information and I did not request publication. If I give you a copy of a libellous speech to publish and you do so, you will be my agent and I shall be responsible, possibly alone, provided you have acted in good faith. But I may not be liable if you alter my copy substantially. There are special considerations where you are dealing with translators.

Employees

Malice on the part of a servant or agent may affect the liability of the employer, depending upon whether the occasion was privileged. It is wise to remember that as a general rule every person who publishes a libel is personally liable, for, as Lord Moulton said in the case of *Vacher* v. *London Society of Compositors* in 1913: "It is a fundamental principle of English law that no tortfeasor can excuse himself from the consequences of his acts by setting up that he was acting only as the agent of another." So if you are in employment and you do not know how you stand in your own firm over these matters, the sooner you inquire discreetly the better.

Contempt of Court

All superior courts have the right to punish you if they judge you to be guilty of contempt of court. What is contempt of court?

It is of two kinds, civil and criminal. It can be either (a) words or acts obstructing or calculated to obstruct the administration of justice, or (b) contempt in procedure by disobeying an order of the court or judge. Where any insult or open defiance is offered in the face of the court, the offence is treated as a contempt of court and is punishable at once. In such a case the judge may order a fine or imprisonment or both. A man who threw tomatoes at two appeal judges in 1938 went to gaol for six weeks. There is no trial by jury. It is up to the judge to decide, but nowadays you can appeal. Incidentally, jurors eating in court have been held guilty of contempt. What happens if you are sent to gaol? Generally speaking, you stay there until you have "purged your contempt"—that is, until you have satisfied the court that you are truly repentant. You can be "attached", which means arrested on the order of a judge.

If you publish the photograph of a man charged with a criminal offence when the identity of the accused might be in question, you may commit a contempt. You have probably noticed that the police usually cover up the heads and faces of the accused with sacks or coats. This may keep everyone out of trouble. You must be very careful NOT to take any photographs within the precincts of the court—not even of men with coats over their heads being bundled along near the entrance before or after a trial. The Attorney-General in 1967 issued a special memorandum drawing the attention of editors to this. Note also that a caption of a news film suggesting that an accused man has committed the offence is contempt. [*R.* v. *Hutchinson ex parte McMahon* (1936).]

In 1924 the *Evening Standard* and *Daily Express* were held to be in contempt for allowing its reporters to act as amateur detectives when a man had been arrested on a criminal charge and publishing accounts of their investigations. In the case of a newspaper the order may be made against the proprietor, publisher, editor, author, or printer. What happens if you are in the middle of a crime story and you hear that a suspect has been arrested? The story may have to be stopped at once. This can give rise to some difficulty if the first account has already appeared in earlier editions.

There is no privilege known to the law by which a journalist can refuse to answer a question which is relevant to an inquiry and is one which, in the opinion of the judge, it is proper for him to be asked. So said Lord Justice Donovan in the case brought by the Attorney-General against Mulholland and Foster—two journalists who refused before a tribunal set up under the Tribunals of Inquiry (Evidence) Act, 1921, to name or describe the sources of information in articles written by them which the chairman of the tribunal certified were relevant to the inquiry. One of the journalists was sentenced to six and the other to three months' imprisonment for contempt. (*The Times*, 7 March 1963; *Current Law* 2768.)

Criminal Libel

What you publish may be so provocative that it tends to provoke the person you write about to commit a breach of the peace. This is a public offence. So libel, in addition to being a civil wrong, can also be a crime. It is punishable with a fine or imprisonment. Prosecutions are very rare. At common law truth was never accepted in itself as a defence to proceedings for *criminal* libel, hence the curiously worded maxim "The greater the truth, the greater the libel". No criminal proceedings can be commenced against the proprietor of a newspaper for any libel he may be alleged to have published without the order of a judge. The matter should concern the general interests of the public.

Libel on the Dead

As damage to the plaintiff's reputation is the essence of civil proceedings for defamation, an action claiming damages for libel or slander does not lie in respect of defamation of a dead person.

Naturally, though, the position is different if the defamation of a dead person contains by implication an attack upon the living. If I say "Poor old Mrs. X who died last week was never married at all—she lived in adultery all her life", this implies that the children of Mrs. X are bastards and they certainly can sue me (assuming, of course, that it is untrue) for damages.

A libel on a dead person is not a criminal offence unless it can be clearly shown to have caused injury or annoyance to the living. Criminal proceedings may be taken for a libel on a dead man if the natural consequence is to provoke his family to a breach of the peace, or if it can be proved that it was published with the intention of provoking or injuring his living descendants.

Blasphemy

Blasphemy is profane speaking of God or sacred things— impious reference. If you publish an article ridiculing or vilifying God or Christianity or the Bible in general with intent to insult and shock those who believe, or if your intention was to pervert or mislead the ignorant, you may be guilty of the criminal libel offence of blasphemy. Your intention is the crux of the matter. Times change and much greater freedom of expression is permitted nowadays. Views are freely expressed at present which a few hundred years ago would certainly have resulted in imprisonment. What about religious argument and controversy? These are not blasphemous if they are conducted decently and the views put forward, however extreme, are proferred honestly. Several television and radio programmes demonstrate this in no uncertain way. Much depends on whether the argument was in public or in private. It is the form of expression which is so closely examined, not the content. If you advance your views by way of scurrilous attacks or irreverent language which would shock or outrage the feelings of believers, you may be guilty of blasphemy.

Seditious Libel

A seditious libel is one which tends to degrade or vilify the Constitution, the Sovereign, the Government, Parliament, promote insurrection, create discontent through its members, impugn corruption to judges or the administration of justice, or to excite people otherwise than by lawful means, to raise discontent or disaffection, to promote feelings of ill-will and hostility between different classes of subject.

Blackmailing Actions

There are certain people who regard newspapers as fair game for a lawsuit. They take the slightest opportunity, use the flimsiest pretext of making a claim upon a publisher alleging that they have been libelled. The chances of their succeeding in their action may be remote. That does not prevent them instructing a solicitor to make a claim or subsequently issuing a writ. Often it is quite apparent, even on a superficial examination of the circumstances, that they have not in fact been libelled, that no one could really believe that they were.

The Defamation Act has done a certain amount to put an end to this kind of speculative litigation, but it still persists. You may find a story that you have written accurately and well seized upon by one of these leeches as the basis for a claim. You know it is spurious, your editor knows it, and your lawyer knows it. Why then worry? Fight the case, you are bound to win. True enough, but the snag here is that to fight the case might cost hundreds or, indeed, thousands of pounds, whereas the specious plaintiff might be quite prepared to settle for fifty! This presents a difficult question to the proprietors. The easy way out is, of course, to pay up. This is quite wrong morally, however much better it may be financially. People talk. And if it becomes known that a particular paper is good for a "soft touch"—believe me, they will get plenty of claims. The only way is to be tough and stand firm. This, too, becomes known and the number of blackmailing claims will diminish. It is up to you to see that your copy is so good and so accurate that if this unfortunate situation ever arises with you, your paper will back you with confidence and not settle because there is a slight doubt about the story you have written.

The editors of the sixth edition of *Gatley on Libel and Slander* (1967)—the leading textbook on defamation—wrote in their preface, "All trials are longer than they used to be, and defamation actions have, if anything, a worse record than others." While proceedings are unpredictably expensive (a number of recent long cases have ended in one or more disagreements by the jury), both the pressure that can be exerted by a gold-digging plaintiff and the anxiety that must be felt by a plaintiff with a good case faced by a defendant with a long pocket are increased. So keep your journalism at the highest possible standard of accuracy and integrity.

Keeping Inside the Law

Editing

How does a newspaper keep inside the law? This is a difficult matter and calls for great knowledge and judgment. The problem is all the more complex because of the speed at which papers are published. The first check on legality is with the reporter himself. An experienced reporter should know enough of the elements of the law to avoid the more obvious pitfalls. The next is with the sub-editor or editor who deals with his copy. If the eagle eye of the newsroom has overlooked some doubtful point, the copy taster, or sub-editor, must initiate inquiry by a reporter or one of the experts of the staff. He must also watch for possible libels or contempt of court in copy and, if in doubt, refer these to the editor or the legal adviser. On a national newspaper the full staff of sub-editors numbers twenty or more, headed by the chief sub-editor. The night editor joins them to direct proceedings at crucial moments, and in some offices a legal adviser is present as well to deal with problems which may crop up at a moment's notice. National papers have a night lawyers' roster which ensures that a skilled legal adviser is always at hand if needed. Not all the lawyers are, however, in full-time employment with the paper concerned. Often they are experienced solicitors or barristers who work on a part-time basis.

Proof Reading

Proof readers, too, have a special responsibility in ensuring the accuracy of what is printed. They are chosen for their specialised and expert knowledge and sound judgment. Theirs is primarily the art and practice of finding mistakes in printed matter before publication and of indicating the needed corrections. They may spot a libel or think they have. In either case it is important that the matter shall be queried and passed back to editorial authority.

Clanger Corner

Many offices have their "Clanger Corner" with the howlers stuck up on the wall, and not a few of them are examples of insult, ridicule, or *double entendre*. Read them whenever and wherever you can.

Unlawful Publications

There are many things which it is unlawful to publish—for example, indecent matter or medical or surgical details which, if published, would be calculated to injure public morals, certain divorce case details, matrimonial proceedings, cases involving children, official secrets, replicas of bank notes and stamps, certain advertisements dealing with specified diseases, obscene matter, details of particular medicines and food and drugs, lotteries, financial matters.

There are a great many Acts, rules and regulations, orders, codes of standards and standard conditions, and forms of contract dealing with them. Journalism and advertising are close to each other in these matters. The best book on the subject is *Modern Advertising Law*, by Peter Langdon-Davies.

Checking the Story

Where news has come in from a reputable source such as the Press Association—Reuters, a certain amount of sifting and checking for accuracy will already have been done. The chief sub-editor engaged in "make-up" also has a special responsibility.

No matter how carefully the pages have been planned there is always more news and more type than they will hold, for to be short of type would be disastrous. At this stage and with little time to spare the make-up sub-editor has to act quickly but carefully so that the report is not marred. He must not cut out points mentioned in the headlines or crossheads. What he cuts out can be of vital importance in deciding the question of libel liability. Your story as filed may have been quite correct, but the omission of a paragraph in printing could give the report a totally different aspect and make it much harder to withstand a claim. So make-up is not just a question of style and attractive layout; above all, the fullest report of the truth must still be the guideline.

In a provincial paper the same care is taken to ensure accuracy, although there may not be the same number of people employed; the accent may be on local affairs and varying use will be made of agency copy.

But you will now see that from the moment you start to write your story until the time it is being sold on the streets, quite a number of keen eyes backed with years of experience will have scanned your report to make sure it does not infringe the laws of defamation. You can do a great deal to help them by learning as much as you can about the legal limits of journalism so that you keep within them.

Night Lawyer in the *U.K. Press Gazette* recently wrote:

> Sometimes however people who find themselves on duty at holiday time are juniors. They may be unwilling or unable to seek the guidance of their more experienced colleagues. They may find people with whom they could check details difficult to reach because they are not at work or have gone away from home for the holiday. In provincial offices especially there will be people holding the fort in the familiar way. A young reporter may do the police calls and tour the hospitals with the mayor, and check the fire stations and hospitals all alone for a day or two. He may cover the court where the drunks appear and go to an inquest on some domestic or road tragedy. He may pick up a story with a funny or seasonal or pathetic angle. He will have plenty to do, all alone in the office. Perhaps he would not have appreciated the implication or inaccuracy which might have crept into his copy. When it is left for those who come on duty afterwards he may not be around to answer enquiries. If it gets into print the damage is done.

It is hoped that this book will help you to avoid this kind of situation—one in which we can so easily find ourselves.

New Laws

On 1 January 1968 a new Criminal Justice Act came into force which affects journalists.

Section 1 provides for automatic committal for trial without hearing evidence where it is all in written statements and the defendant is represented. Section 2 imposes the conditions on receiving such statements in evidence.

Section 3 starts on Press provisions. It makes it unlawful to publish in Great Britain a report of committal proceedings except for the details allowed by subsection 4.

But the ban will be lifted on the application of any defendant, and if the magistrates decide not to commit for trial the committal hearing can be reported. The committal hearing can also be reported if anyone wants to after the trial of the last defendant is over.

Where the magistrates turn the preliminary examination into a summary trial for one or more but not all of several defendants, but commit others for trial, it will be lawful to publish the proceedings up to the change as well as after.

Subsection 4 tells you what you can give in a report of committal proceedings.

You may identify the court and give the names of the examining magistrates. About the parties (i.e. the defendant and complainant) and the witnesses you may report their names, addresses, and occupations. Of the defendants and the witnesses you may state their ages. Since the actual complaint is most often going to be laid by a policeman and you can get his age if you want it, the distinction is puzzling. The word "parties" is doubtless used to cover private prosecutions which are uncommon.

You may set out the offences with which the defendants are charged or a summary of them. You may report the names of counsel and solicitors engaged in the case.

The decision of the court is reportable. You can give the committal for trial or the decision to commit some but not others of the defendants, and the decision on the disposal of defendants not committed.

Of those actually committed you may state the charges, or a summary of them, on which they are committed, and the court to which they are committed.

If, as so often happens, the hearing before the examining magistrates is adjourned, you may report the date and place of the next hearing. You may also report any arrangements as to bail on adjournment, or committal, and whether legal aid was granted to the defendants. Under subsection 5, if the limits are exceeded, proprietor, editor, or publisher of the newspaper or periodical which publishes it is guilty of an offence.

If a written report of the proceedings is published otherwise than as part of a newspaper or periodical, the person who publishes it is guilty of an offence. Here is a possible danger for news agency men or freelances sending out reports to customers not for publication in the paper but for background information. That could be a technical publication and make the freelance liable to conviction.

Any member of the public could sit in court and repeat such information *viva voce* and not commit an offence.

The act applies to broadcasts and the maximum penalty for a breach is £500. Prosecution must have the consent of the Attorney-General.

The Clerk of the Court must post up certain notices, and reports published as soon as practicable shall be deemed to be contemporaneous.

The above is a *U.K. Press Gazette* summary.

CHAPTER 12

Scotland

THE legal limits to journalism dealt with in this book refer to the law of England and Wales and not to Scotland. There are a good many differences. In Scotland the police do not act as prosecutors. This is done by Crown officers, chiefly the Procurator Fiscal, who usually carries out preliminary inquiries in private. A verdict of "not proven" can be brought in by the jury (15 people) at a criminal trial, or they can bring in a majority verdict which is now part of English law. Magistrates in Scotland are appointed by the town council and most criminal cases are heard in the sheriff court. Appeals lie to the Appeal Court of the High Court of Justiciary; barristers are known as advocates; solicitors use the initials S.S.C.—Solicitors of the Supreme Court. The Scottish courts have similar powers to the English courts to exclude the Press or the public if they consider it to be in the interests of justice. There are no coroners' courts in Scotland and the sheriff court does the work of the county court. Bankruptcy procedure is quite different. So far as admission of the Press to public meetings is concerned, the position in Scotland is broadly similar to that in England and Wales; the public bodies are listed in the Public Bodies Act, 1960.

There is no provision in Scottish law that a boy under fourteen years of age cannot be guilty of rape. The rules relating to contempt and privilege have general application to Scotland. The Defamation Act, 1952, has a general application to Scotland, but sections 1, 2, 8, and 13 apply only to England. There is no technical distinction in Scottish law between libel and slander. Slander is deemed to be a statement which is false, defamatory, and malicious. The plaintiff in an action is called the pursuer.

The foregoing is set out merely to signpost some of the differences between the two systems of law. If you have an assignment over the border you will find that the general rules of sound reporting apply, but you would be well advised to seek expert advice in Scottish law if in doubt at any time. L. C. J. McNae, former head of the Press Association's Special Reporting Service and one of the leading authorities on Press Law—the editor of *Essential Law for Journalists* (1964)—draws attention in it to a number of distinctions drafted by E. Rosslyn Mitchell and W. L. Taylor, both of Glasgow and both with traditions of legal work for the press in Scotland.

CHAPTER 13

Conclusions

WE HAVE been concerned principally with the legal limits of journalism. Many people like to keep their activities private—but it may be journalists duty to make them public. What about the long-term view? What makes a good journalist? He is the eyes and ears of the paper—with an immense range of interests. He has the highest standards of probity, tact, discretion, wide general knowledge, a love of his fellow men, sympathy, understanding, and a sense of humour. He has the skill to see and record effectively, accurately, and legally. According to the way you do this, so is the reputation of all journalism in your hands.

Appendix
Defamation Act, 1952

15 & 16 Geo. 6 & 1 Eliz. 2   Ch. 66*

Arrangement of Sections

*Reproduced by kind permission of Her Majesty's Stationery Office.

H

CHAPTER 66

**An Act to amend the law relating to libel and slander and
other malicious falsehoods.** **(30th October 1952.)**

BE it enacted by the Queen's most Excellent Majesty, by and with
the advice and consent of the Lords Spiritual and Temporal, and
Commons, in this present Parliament assembled, and by the
authority of the same, as follows:—

Broadcast statements

1. For the purposes of the law of libel and slander, the broadcasting of words by means of wireless telegraphy shall be treated
as publication in permanent form.

Slander affecting official, professional or business reputation

2. In an action for slander in respect of words calculated to
disparage the plaintiff in any office, profession, calling, trade or
business held or carried on by him at the time of the publication,
it shall not be necessary to allege or prove special damage,
whether or not the words are spoken of the plaintiff in the way of
his office, profession, calling, trade or business.

Slander of title, &c.

3.—(1) In an action for slander of title, slander of goods or
other malicious falsehood, it shall not be necessary to allege or
prove special damage—

> (*a*) if the words upon which the action is founded are calcu-
> lated to cause pecuniary damage to the plaintiff and are
> published in writing or other permanent form; or
> (*b*) if the said words are calculated to cause pecuniary damage
> to the plaintiff in respect of any office, profession, calling,
> trade or business held or carried on by him at the time of
> the publication.

(2) Section one of this Act shall apply for the purposes of this section as it applies for the purposes of the law of libel and slander.

Unintentional defamation

4.—(1) A person who has published words alleged to be defamatory of another person may, if he claims that the words were published by him innocently in relation to that other person, make an offer of amends under this section; and in any such case—

(a) if the offer is accepted by the party aggrieved and is duly performed, no proceedings for libel or slander shall be taken or continued by that party against the person making the offer in respect of the publication in question (but without prejudice to any cause of action against any other person jointly responsible for that publication);

(b) if the offer is not accepted by the party aggrieved, then, except as otherwise provided by this section, it shall be a defence, in any proceedings by him for libel or slander against the person making the offer in respect of the publication in question, to prove that the words complained of were published by the defendant innocently in relation to the plaintiff and that the offer was made as soon as practicable after the defendant received notice that they were or might be defamatory of the plaintiff, and has not been withdrawn.

(2) An offer of amends under this section must be expressed to be made for the purposes of this section, and must be accompanied by an affidavit specifying the facts relied upon by the person making it to show that the words in question were published by him innocently in relation to the party aggrieved; and for the purposes of a defence under paragraph (b) of subsection (1) of this section no evidence, other than evidence of facts specified in the affidavit, shall be admissible on behalf of that person to prove that the words were so published.

(3) An offer of amends under this section shall be understood to mean an offer—

(a) in any case, to publish or join in the publication of a suitable correction of the words complained of, and a sufficient apology to the party aggrieved in respect of those words;

(b) where copies of a document or record containing the said words have been distributed by or with the knowledge of the person making the offer, to take such steps as are reasonably practicable on his part for notifying persons to whom copies have been so distributed that the words are alleged to be defamatory of the party aggrieved.

(4) Where an offer of amends under this section is accepted by the party aggrieved—

(a) any question as to the steps to be taken in fulfilment of the offer as so accepted shall in default of agreement between the parties be referred to and determined by the High Court, whose decision thereon shall be final;

(b) the power of the court to make orders as to costs in proceedings by the party aggrieved against the person making the offer in respect of the publication in question, or in proceedings in respect of the offer under paragraph (a) of this subsection, shall include power to order the payment by the person making the offer to the party aggrieved of costs on an indemnity basis and any expenses reasonably incurred or to be incurred by that party in consequence of the publication in question;

and if no such proceedings as aforesaid are taken, the High Court may, upon application made by the party aggrieved, make any such order for the payment of such costs and expenses as aforesaid as could be made in such proceedings.

(5) For the purposes of this section words shall be treated as published by one person (in this subsection referred to as the

publisher) innocently in relation to another person if and only if the following conditions are satisfied, that is to say—

(*a*) that the publisher did not intend to publish them of and concerning that other person, and did not know of circumstances by virtue of which they might be understood to refer to him; or

(*b*) that the words were not defamatory on the face of them, and the publisher did not know of circumstances by virtue of which they might be understood to be defamatory of that other person.

and in either case that the publisher exercised all reasonable care in relation to the publication; and any reference in this subsection to the publisher shall be construed as including a reference to any servant or agent of his who was concerned with the contents of the publication.

(6) Paragraph (*b*) of subsection (1) of this section shall not apply in relation to the publication by any person of words of which he is not the author unless he proves that the words were written by the author without malice.

Justification

5. In an action for libel or slander in respect of words containing two or more distinct charges against the plaintiff, a defence of justification shall not fail by reason only that the truth of every charge is not proved if the words not proved to be true do not materially injure the plaintiff's reputation having regard to the truth of the remaining charges.

Fair comment

6. In an action for libel or slander in respect of words consisting partly of allegations of fact and partly of expression of opinion, a defence of fair comment shall not fail by reason only that the truth of every allegation of fact is not proved if the expression of opinion is fair comment having regard to such of the facts alleged or referred to in the words complained of as are proved.

Qualified privilege of newspapers

7.—(1) Subject to the provisions of this section, the publication in a newspaper of any such report or other matter as is mentioned in the Schedule to this Act shall be privileged unless the publication is proved to be made with malice.

(2) In an action for libel in respect of the publication of any such report or matter as is mentioned in Part II of the Schedule to this Act, the provisions of this section shall not be a defence if it is proved that the defendant has been requested by the plaintiff to publish in the newspaper in which the original publication was made a reasonable letter or statement by way of explanation or contradiction, and has refused or neglected to do so, or has done so in a manner not adequate or not reasonable having regard to all the circumstances.

(3) Nothing in this section shall be construed as protecting the publication of any matter the publication of which is prohibited by law, or of any matter which is not of public concern and the publication of which is not for the public benefit.

(4) Nothing in this section shall be construed as limiting or abridging any privilege subsisting (otherwise than by virtue of section four of the Law of Libel Amendment Act, 1888) immediately before the commencement of this Act.

(5) In this section the expression "newspaper" means any paper containing public news or observations thereon, or consisting wholly or mainly of advertisements, which is printed for sale and is published in the United Kingdom either periodically or in parts or numbers at intervals not exceeding thirty-six days.

Extent of Law of Libel Amendment Act, 1888, s.3

8. Section three of the Law of Libel Amendment Act, 1888 (which relates to contemporary reports of proceedings before courts exercising judicial authority) shall apply and apply only to courts exercising judicial authority within the United Kingdom.

Extension of certain defences to broadcasting

9.—(1) Section three of the Parliamentary Papers Act, 1840 (which confers protection in respect of proceedings for printing extracts from or abstracts of parliamentary papers) shall have effect as if the reference to printing included a reference to broadcasting by means of wireless telegraphy.

(2) Section seven of this Act and section three of the Law of Libel Amendment Act, 1888, as amended by this Act shall apply in relation to reports or matters broadcast by means of wireless telegraphy as part of any programme or service provided by means of a broadcasting station within the United Kingdom, and in relation to any broadcasting by means of wireless telegraphy of any such report or matter, as they apply in relation to reports and matters published in a newspaper and to publication in a newspaper; and subsection (2) of the said section seven shall have effect, in relation to any such broadcasting, as if for the words "in the newspaper in which" there were substituted the words "in the manner in which".

(3) In this section "broadcasting station" means any station in respect of which a licence granted by the Postmaster General under the enactments relating to wireless telegraphy is in force, being a licence which (by whatever form of words) authorises the use of the station for the purpose of providing broadcasting services for general reception.

Limitation on privilege at elections

10. A defamatory statement published by or on behalf of a candidate in any election to a local government authority or to Parliament shall not be deemed to be published on a privileged occasion on the ground that it is material to a question in issue in the election, whether or not the person by whom it is published is qualified to vote at the election.

Agreements for indemnity

11. An agreement for indemnifying any person against civil liability for libel in respect of the publication of any matter shall not be unlawful unless at the time of the publication that person knows that the matter is defamatory, and does not reasonably believe there is a good defence to any action brought upon it.

Evidence of other damages recovered by plaintiff

12. In any action for libel or slander the defendant may give evidence in mitigation of damages that the plaintiff has recovered damages, or has brought actions for damages, for libel or slander in respect of the publication of words to the same effect as the words on which the action is founded, or has received or agreed to receive compensation in respect of any such publication.

Consolidation of actions for slander, &c.

13. Section five of the Law of Libel Amendment Act, 1888 (which provides for the consolidation, on the application of the defendants, of two or more actions for libel by the same plaintiff) shall apply to actions for slander and to actions for slander of title, slander of goods or other malicious falsehood as it applies to actions for libel; and references in that section to the same, or substantially the same, libel shall be construed accordingly.

Application of Act to Scotland

14. This Act shall apply to Scotland subject to the following modifications, that is to say:—

    (*a*) sections one, two, eight and thirteen shall be omitted;
    (*b*) for section three there shall be substituted the following section—

"Actions for verbal injury.

3. In any action for verbal injury it shall not be necessary for the pursuer to aver or prove special damage if the words on which the action is founded are calculated to cause pecuniary damage to the pursuer.";

(*c*) subsection (2) of section four shall have effect as if at the end thereof there were added the words "Nothing in this subsection shall be held to entitle a defender to lead evidence of any fact specified in the declaration unless notice of his intention so to do has been given in the defences."; and

(*d*) for any reference to libel, or to libel or slander, there shall be substituted a reference to defamation; the expression "plaintiff" means pursuer; the expression "defendant" means defender; for any reference to an affidavit made by any person there shall be substituted a reference to a written declaration signed by that person; for any reference to the High Court there shall be substituted a reference to the Court of Session or, if an action of defamation is depending in the sheriff court in respect of the publication in question, the sheriff; the expression "costs" means expenses; and for any reference to a defence of justification there shall be substituted a reference to a defence of *veritas*.

Legislative powers of Parliament of Northern Ireland

15. No limitation on the powers of the Parliament of Northern Ireland imposed by the Government of Ireland Act, 1920, shall preclude that Parliament from making laws for purposes similar to the purposes of this Act.

Interpretation

16.—(1) Any reference in this Act to words shall be construed as including a reference to pictures, visual images, gestures and other methods of signifying meaning.

(2) The provisions of Part III of the Schedule to this Act shall have effect for the purposes of the interpretation of that Schedule.

(3) In this Act "broadcasting by means of wireless telegraphy" means publication for general reception by means of wireless telegraphy within the meaning of the Wireless Telegraphy Act, 1949, and "broadcast by means of wireless telegraphy" shall be construed accordingly.

(4) Where words broadcast by means of wireless telegraphy are simultaneously transmitted by telegraph as defined by the Telegraph Act, 1863, in accordance with a licence granted by the Postmaster General the provisions of this Act shall apply as if the transmission were broadcasting by means of wireless telegraphy.

Proceedings affected and saving

17.—(1) This Act applies for the purposes of any proceedings begun after the commencement of this Act, whenever the cause of action arose, but does not affect any proceedings begun before the commencement of this Act.

(2) Nothing in this Act affects the law relating to criminal libel.

Short title, commencement, extent and repeals

18.—(1) This Act may be cited as the Defamation Act, 1952, and shall come into operation one month after the passing of this Act.

(2) This Act (except section fifteen) shall not extend to Northern Ireland.

(3) Sections four and six of the Law of Libel Amendment Act, 1888, are hereby repealed.

SCHEDULE

Sections 7, 16

NEWSPAPER STATEMENTS HAVING QUALIFIED PRIVILEGE

PART I

Statements Privileged without Explanation or Contradiction

1. A fair and accurate report of any proceedings in public of the legislature of any part of Her Majesty's dominions outside Great Britain.

2. A fair and accurate report of any proceedings in public of an international organisation of which the United Kingdom or Her Majesty's Government in the United Kingdom is a member, or of any international conference to which that government sends a representative.

3. A fair and accurate report of any proceedings in public of an international court.

4. A fair and accurate report of any proceedings before a court exercising jurisdiction throughout any part of Her Majesty's dominions outside the United Kingdom, or of any proceedings before a court-martial held outside the United Kingdom under the Naval Discipline Act, the Army Act or the Air Force Act.

5. A fair and accurate report of any proceedings in public of a body or person appointed to hold a public inquiry by the government or legislature of any part of Her Majesty's dominions outside the United Kingdom.

6. A fair and accurate copy of or extract from any register kept in pursuance of any Act of Parliament which is open to inspection by the public, or of any other document which is required by the law of any part of the United Kingdom to be open to inspection by the public.

7. A notice or advertisement published by or on the authority of any court within the United Kingdom or any judge or officer of such a court.

Statements Privileged Subject to Explanation or Contradiction

8. A fair and accurate report of the findings or decision of any of the following associations, or of any committee or governing body thereof, that is to say—

(*a*) an association formed in the United Kingdom for the purpose of promoting or encouraging the exercise of or interest in any art, science, religion or learning, and empowered by its constitution to exercise control over or adjudicate upon matters of interest or concern to the association, or the actions or conduct of any persons subject to such control or adjudication;

(*b*) an association formed in the United Kingdom for the purpose of promoting or safeguarding the interests of any trade, business, industry or profession, or of the persons carrying on or engaged in any trade, business, industry or profession, and empowered by its constitution to exercise control over or adjudicate upon matters connected with the trade, business, industry or profession, or the actions or conduct of those persons;

(*c*) an association formed in the United Kingdom for the purpose of promoting or safeguarding the interests of any game, sport or pastime to the playing or exercise of which members of the public are invited or admitted, and empowered by its constitution to exercise control over or adjudicate upon persons connected with or taking part in the game, sport or pastime.

being a finding or decision relating to a person who is a member of or is subject by virtue of any contract to the control of the association.

9. A fair and accurate report of the proceedings at any public meeting held in the United Kingdom, that is to say, a meeting bona

fide and lawfully held for a lawful purpose and for the furtherance or discussion of any matter of public concern, whether the admission to the meeting is general or restricted.

10. A fair and accurate report of the proceedings at any meeting or sitting in any part of the United Kingdom of—

(*a*) any local authority or committee of a local authority or local authorities;

(*b*) any justice or justices of the peace acting otherwise than as a court exercising judicial authority;

(*c*) any commission, tribunal, committee or person appointed for the purposes of any inquiry by Act of Parliament, by Her Majesty or by a Minister of the Crown;

(*d*) any person appointed by a local authority to hold a local inquiry in pursuance of any Act of Parliament;

(*e*) any other tribunal, board, committee or body constituted by or under, and exercising functions under, an Act of Parliament,

not being a meeting or sitting admission to which is denied to representatives of newspapers and other members of the public.

11. A fair and accurate report of the proceedings at a general meeting of any company or association constituted, registered or certified by or under any Act of Parliament or incorporated by Royal Charter, not being a private company within the meaning of the Companies Act, 1948.

12. A copy or fair and accurate report or summary of any notice or other matter issued for the information of the public by or on behalf of any government department, officer of state, local authority or chief officer of police.

PART III

Interpretation

13. In this Schedule the following expressions have the meanings hereby respectively assigned to them, that is to say:—

"Act of Parliament" includes an Act of the Parliament of Northern Ireland, and the reference to the Companies Act, 1948, includes a reference to any corresponding enactment of the Parliament of Northern Ireland;

"government department" includes a department of the Government of Northern Ireland;

"international court" means the International Court of Justice and any other judicial or arbitral tribunal deciding matters in dispute between States;

"legislature", in relation to any territory comprised in Her Majesty's dominions which is subject to a central and a local legislature, means either of those legislatures;

"local authority" means any authority or body to which the Local Authorities (Admission of the Press to Meetings) Act, 1908, or the Local Government (Ireland) Act, 1902, as amended by any enactment of the Parliament of Northern Ireland, applies;

"part of Her Majesty's dominions" means the whole of any territory within those dominions which is subject to a separate legislature.

14. In relation to the following countries and territories, that is to say, India, the Republic of Ireland, any protectorate, protected state or trust territory within the meaning of the British Nationality Act, 1948, any territory administered under the authority of a country mentioned in subsection (3) of section one of that Act, the Sudan and the New Hebrides, the provisions of this Schedule shall have effect as they have effect in relation to Her Majesty's dominions, and references therein to Her Majesty's dominions shall be construed accordingly.

TABLE OF STATUTES REFERRED TO IN THIS ACT

Short Title	Session and Chapter
Parliamentary Papers Act, 1840	3 & 4 Vict. c. 9.
Telegraph Act, 1863	26 & 27 Vict. c. 112
Law of Libel Amendment Act, 1888	51 & 52 Vict. c. 64.
Local Government (Ireland) Act, 1902	2 Edw. 7, c. 38.
Local Authorities (Admission of the Press to Meetings) Act, 1908	8 Edw. 7, c. 43.
Government of Ireland Act, 1920	10 & 11 Geo. 5, c. 67.
Companies Act, 1948	11 & 12 Geo. 6, c. 38.
British Nationality Act, 1948	11 & 12 Geo. 6, c. 56.
Wireless Telegraphy Act, 1949	12, 13 & 14 Geo. 6, c. 54.

Bibliography

Current Law, Sweet & Maxwell, Stevens & Sons, 1963, 11 New Fetter Lane, London, E.C. 4.

Modern Advertising Law, by PETER LANGDON-DAVIES, Business Publications Limited, 1963, 180 Fleet Street, London, E.C. 4.

Hatred, Ridicule or Contempt, a book of libel cases by JOSEPH DEAN, Constable, 1953, 10–12 Orange Street, London, W.C. 2.

General Principles of the Law of Torts, by PHILLIP S. JAMES, Butterworths, 1964, 88 Kingsway, London, W.C. 2.

Discovering the Law, by JAMES DERRIMAN, University of London Press, 1962, Warwick Square, London, E.C. 4.

Halsbury's Laws of England, 3rd edn., Simonds edition, in particular vol. 24, *Libel and Slander*, by the HON. SIR GERALD OSBORNE SLADE, one of the Justices of Her Majesty's High Court of Justice, and RICHARD O'SULLIVAN, Esq., Q.C., a Bencher of the Middle Temple, one of Her Majesty's Counsel, Recorder of Derby, Butterworths, 1958, 88 Kingsway, London, W.C. 2.

Gatley on Libel and Slander, 6th edn., by ROBERT L. MCEWEN, Esq., M.A., of the Inner Temple, Barrister at Law and P. S. C. LEWIS, Esq., M.A., of Lincolns Inn, Barrister at Law, Sweet & Maxwell, 1960, 11 New Fetter Lane, London, E.C. 4.

U.K. Press Gazette, Bouverie Publishing Co. Ltd., 2–3 Salisbury Court, Fleet Street, London, E.C. 3 (weekly for Journalists).

The English and Empire Digest, replacement volume No. 32, *Libel and Slander*, by C. A. COLLINGWOOD, Esq., M.A., LL.B., CECIL B. RAMAGE, Esq., B.A., and C. C. CARUS-WILSON, Esq., M.C., B.A., Barristers-at-Law, Butterworths, 1964, 88 Kingsway, London, W.C. 2.

Essential Law for Journalists, 2nd edn., edited by L. C. J. MCNAE, former Head of the Press Association's Special Reporting Service, Staples Press, 1964, 9 Grape Street, London, W.C. 2.

The Kemsley Manual of Journalism, Cassell & Co., 1950, London.

Index